RACE
OF ACES

RACE
OF ACES

WWII'S ELITE AIRMEN
AND THE EPIC BATTLE TO
BECOME THE MASTER OF THE SKY

JOHN R. BRUNING

NEW YORK   BOSTON

Hachette Books
Hachette Book Group
1290 Avenue of the Americas
New York, NY 10104
hachettebookgroup.com
twitter.com/hachettebooks

First Edition: January 2020

Hachette Books is a division of Hachette Book Group, Inc.

The Hachette Books name and logo are trademarks of Hachette Book Group, Inc.

The publisher is not responsible for websites (or their content) that are not owned by the publisher.

The Hachette Speakers Bureau provides a wide range of authors for speaking events. To find out more, go to www.hachettespeakersbureau.com or call (866) 376-6591.

Print book interior design by Six Red Marbles, Inc.

Library of Congress Control Number: 2019951168

ISBNs: 978-0-316-50862-9 (hardcover), 978-0-316-50864-3 (ebook)

Printed in the United States of America

LSC-C

10 9 8 7 6 5 4 3 2 1

*This book is dedicated to my son, Edward Arthur Bruning.
I have watched Ed grow into a gentleman whose empathy and
loyalty to those he loves are rare and noble traits in a world
grown increasingly disconnected. Ten years ago, Ed taught me
an important life lesson: when the worst of the world is thrown
at you, and your heart is broken, fight on for those you love.*

Author's Note

During World War II, less than 5 percent of all fighter pilots succeeded in shooting down five or more enemy planes. Yet, that tiny percentage accounted for almost half the aircraft destroyed in air-to-air combat.

Those few men were known as aces. They were celebrated in the media, worshipped by civilians and, in some cases, by their fellow pilots. They earned generational fame in the sky's killing game.

In the Southwest Pacific Theater of Operations, a highly unusual competition began. At first, it was a race to beat World War I ace Eddie Rickenbacker's record of twenty-six enemy planes. It soon morphed into something greater: a fevered competition to become America's greatest fighter pilot, our ace of aces. For almost three years, this race riveted the nation, made heroes out of ordinary Americans, and changed forever the lives of those who loved them.

This is the story of that race and the fighter pilots who dared to compete for that immortal title.

Contents

Prologue

August 1, 1942
Port Moresby, New Guinea

Five days shy of his fifty-third birthday, Gen. George Kenney lay wet and filthy in a slit trench filled with six inches of brackish water. Flies and mosquitoes buzzed around him as sweat poured off his forehead in the hundred-degree heat. He peered over the lip of the slit trench into what the locals called the Valley of Death. Down there lay the most important piece of real estate in the Southwest Pacific, Seven Mile Drome, and its priceless runway.

A string of Japanese bombs exploded diagonally across the strip like volcanic eruptions. Black smoke and dust billowed skyward as more bombs struck the aircraft dispersal area. Shrapnel ripped into a P-39, setting fire to its fuel tanks. Another one brewed up nearby, and three light bombers, A-24 Dauntlesses, were soon smothered by bombs and flames.

The base's antiaircraft guns thundered a response. Kenney's eyes roamed skyward to see their effect. Far above, set against a cerulean sky, he could see a dozen Japanese Betty bombers in a tight formation. These were the pilots and crews of the legendary 4th Kokutai, Japanese naval aviators who sowed terror from China to Manila and beyond. These crews ranked as among the best in the world, and on this day they gave Kenney an object lesson of their skills by tearing hell out of his new command.

As he watched them parade by, antiaircraft shells burst all over the sky. The gunners shot low and wide, hitting nothing. Accomplishing nothing.

Four minutes warning. That's all they received before the bombs began to fall. Seven Mile Drome, like every other forward base Kenney visited in his new command, lacked everything from vehicles to fuel, mosquito nets, antimalarial drugs, and even a goddamned air raid siren. To compensate for that, General Scanlon, the REMF running this place, conceived a novel idea: use color-coded flags to denote the impending arrival of enemy planes.

White meant all clear. Yellow meant incoming aircraft. Red meant the field was under attack. Black meant grab a rifle and a helmet, paratroops were landing on our heads.

Kenney had arrived earlier that morning to sit in on a bomber briefing. As he walked from his aircraft to the operations tent, a white flag fluttered in the breeze above the field's control tower.

A white goddamned flag.

Yellow seemed infuriatingly fitting, too. When word of the incoming strike reached the field, there was a mad scramble away from it. The engineers working on the strip dropped whatever they were doing and bolted into the jungle, or dove into slit trenches. A few P-39s managed to take off, but they never would be able to catch the bombers in time. Of the forty Airacobras sitting in the dispersal area, less than a dozen took off. The others waited in their protective revetments for bombs to blow them to scrap.

After all the effort, treasure, manpower, and risks to get these birds from Bell's New York factory across the United States, then across the Pacific to Australia, then up to New Guinea, seeing them senselessly destroyed on the ground seemed absurdly comic. The craziness of war.

Except it wasn't funny. The Japanese Army's vanguard just seized a village a couple dozen miles from this airfield. They were coming to take it and capture Port Moresby, the first step in what everyone assumed would be a full-fledged invasion of northern Australia.

Those P-39s needed to be strafing those Japanese troops. They needed to be shooting down bombers. They needed to be sinking barges and shooting up supply dumps. In this crisis, anything would be better than their fate Kenney witnessed that afternoon.

Another string of bombs blasted a fuel depot—just a collection of fifty-five-gallon drums tucked into the nearby jungle without any security on them—and flames shot skyward. Over the roar of the guns and the fall of the bombs, the wounded called for help.

When the bombs stopped falling and the bombers turned for their home base, Kenney and the other generals sharing his slit trench climbed out and tried to clean themselves off as best they could. With water rationed at Port Moresby, they'd have to wait until they returned to Australia to truly get cleaned up. In the meantime, they walked back toward the strip, mud in their shoes, massive mosquitoes still flying in squadrons around them.

"You hear what happened the other night?"

"No," Kenney said to the young pilot who had fallen in with them.

"One of those mosquitoes landed after dark at the end of the strip, and the ground crews put twenty-five gallons of fuel in it before realizing it wasn't a P-39."

Despite what had just happened, Kenney smiled at that.

He was all business a few minutes later, peppering everyone with questions. He listened without comment, gathering information, forming a picture in his head as to what he'd inherited and how he would have to fix it.

This was a beaten, desperate force he now owned. MacArthur shunned his aviators—they'd let him down so often, he'd given up hope that the flyboys would ever be anything but boastful skirt-chasers. When he first met with MacArthur, Kenney listened to his litany of complaints about the 5th. Can't bomb. Can't shoot planes down. Can't fight. No organization. Morale in the tank. Leadership vacuums everywhere.

Now he was seeing firsthand how MacArthur had formed his opinion.

With P-39s all over the field, why had only ten taken off to intercept?

Only ten? Came the response. That was a Herculean effort, something to take pride in here in New Guinea.

The answer left Kenney dumbstruck.

"What? Why?"

Those were the only ones the mechanics could patch together. The others were down with battle damage, missing parts, or some kind of mechanical issue.

Seventy-five percent of the fighters defending the best and biggest air base in New Guinea, it turned out, were out of commission?

It got worse. The planes only flew when it was absolutely crucial that they do so. Every time they went aloft, they consumed fuel, oil, ammunition. Parts wore out and damage was suffered. In summer 1942 New Guinea, they had few spare parts, no real maintenance facilities, and never enough fuel or lubricants. Everything had to come up from Australia to be off-loaded at Port Moresby's single, small dock. The Japanese bombed the town and the ships constantly.

So the planes sat, either broken or waiting for a mission to justify the cost.

The pilots at Moresby looked like castaways, clad in ragged uniforms rotting in the tropical environment. Some wore Aussie shorts and combat boots, shoulder holsters, and little else. The men simply didn't have any other options. It wasn't like there was a place in town at Moresby to go buy uniforms when old ones rotted out. There had been a department store not far from the docks, but an Australian militia unit came through on their way to the front and looted everything. They promptly marched into the steep mountain range beyond Seven Mile Drome known as the Owen Stanley Range, encountered the Japanese, and collapsed. The militia broke and ran, their officers screaming at them to get back in the fight. The Japanese overran some of their units, torturing captives and eating the wounded alive. The reports were clear about that. At times, the Imperial soldiers were seen to grab an Australian and drag him, dead or alive, back to their dugouts to feed.

Other horrors emerged from the mountains as well. Tales of Aussies finding their buddies with their limbs and arms hacked off, bayoneted to trees, their genitals stuffed in their mouths. The men perpetrating such crimes could break through the shaky Aussie defenses and wipe out the airmen at Seven Mile Drome. When Kenney asked for better protection, the Australians answered that they could spare no troops for the airfield's defense.

These men—Kenney's men now—were hanging on a limb. Most looked little better than skeletons—especially the maintenance crews. They'd been living in the jungle for months, eating canned Australian rations, dropping weight as they labored in the scorching heat and humidity. They suffered from stomach parasites, dysentery, malaria, and a dozen other jungle ailments that would confound the VA docs back home for years to come. Yet these men had mettle. They worked day and night to patch together their birds. Without spare parts, they got creative. They stripped wrecks for anything useful. They sent salvage crews into swamps and Japanese-held jungles to find downed planes and carry out whatever they could. One team vanished behind Japanese lines for days, returning to the rendezvous point late because they struck gold out in the bush—crashed bombers and fighters. They enlisted the help of a hundred local natives to carry out everything they could unbolt from the wrecks.

Ten planes getting off the dusty runway at Seven Mile Drome? Kenney understood now what a minor miracle that required. Darkness gave the men no respite. Night after night, the Japanese sent a few aircraft to loiter overhead and drop bombs with surprising accuracy—accuracy aided by Japanese operatives in the jungle around them who fired flares throughout the night to help guide the bombers. These were nuisance attacks designed to keep the men from getting enough sleep. They worked brilliantly. The men dozed fitfully in slit trenches, clouds of mosquitoes feasting on them through these raids. In the morning, the Japanese would hit them again just before lunch from above twenty thousand feet.

When the Imperial Japanese Army started to cross the Owen Stanley Mountains on what was known as the Kokoda Trail, bound for a final assault on Port Moresby, the enemy's vanguard had overrun Moresby's air warning stations. The Allies used to get forty-five minutes warning before an attack. Now, ten minutes was the norm. Sometimes the only warning they received was seeing the red flag hoisted above the control tower as bombs fell around it. Twenty men that summer went "bomb happy" and broke down under the strain. They were evacuated as psychiatric casualties with "more or less permanent dementia."

The Japanese bombed in daylight with near impunity. The P-39 was no high-altitude brawler. Without a supercharger to boost engine power, its speed fell off above fifteen thousand feet so dramatically the plane was easy meat for Japanese Zero fighters. In New Guinea, with worn-out engines and a full combat load of fuel and ammunition, the Airacobra pilots needed at least forty-five minutes to set up a successful intercept.

Kenney listened as the pilots explained they didn't have the time. They went up as the bombers arrived over the field and tried to intercept. They limped toward the enemy formations, their P-39s barely managing one sixty in their climbs at max power.

That's when the Zeroes hit them. They dropped like anvils into their formations, shooting them to pieces while they were slow and sluggish. Sitting ducks. The kill-to-loss ratio said everything about who was winning the air war in New Guinea. One Japanese outfit had more kills over New Guinea than all of the 5th Air Force fighter squadrons combined.

The Fifth included a few aces—pilots who'd shot down five or more planes—but almost all of them had run their scores up in the Philippines, Java, and defending Darwin in northern Australia. Within the six P-39 squadrons—on paper a hundred and fifty fighters—only about fifty Japanese planes had been claimed.

The 'Cobra pilots learned their fighters could not turn with the Zeroes. They could not outclimb them. They could out-dive them and maybe outrun them on the deck. When the executive officer of Port Moresby, Captain Marburg, went to go talk to the P-39 guys earlier in the summer, they seemed to him to be obsessed with the Zero. The Zeroes were always on their tails, or above them, ready to pounce. They never had the tactical advantage, and they hated the planes the Army gave them to fly.

Every day, they climbed into their cockpits, sleep deprived and sickly, knowing that they faced diminishing odds of survival against the Zeroes sure to be waiting for them. They knew if they bailed out, their chances of survival diminished even more. Clambering out of the Airacobra's car door was tough enough, but they soon found that doing so usually resulted in catastrophic injuries as the tail hit them when they free-fell from the cockpit. Those who survived to open their chutes often came down with broken limbs or severe head trauma.

That was assuming they came down over friendly territory. Over the Japanese-held stretches of New Guinea, a bailout meant almost surely ending up dangling helplessly from a tree. Japanese patrols found many Allied aviators in such a state. Their fate? Torture. Execution. Some were eaten by their captors.

In New Guinea, mercy did not exist. The war there was a conflict that brought out the most barbarous elements of the human heart.

Some pilots managed to escape and evade, living in the jungle with the help of friendly natives. They returned weeks after being shot down, usually so sick and starving that they were no longer fit for combat. One reporter who went down with a bomber crew emerged from the jungle after an epic, desperate overland hike. By the time he reached safety, he was delirious, weak, and barely functional. It took him months of hospital rest to finally recover his health and senses and get back on his feet.

Then there were those who tried to escape and evade, only to end up a victim of the jungle. After getting shot down, one pilot began working his way through the Owen Stanleys back to Seven Mile Drome. He came to a creek so deep that he could not wade across it. He started to swim. Halfway across, a crocodile reared out of the creek's depths and sank its teeth into the pilot's midsection. Trapped and flung back and forth by the croc, the pilot somehow managed to draw his survival knife and slam it between the vicious animal's eyes. He staggered to the far bank where some natives found him and carried him to Port Moresby. He lay on a litter, barely conscious, his wounds infected and suppurating, until a transport arrived to fly him to Australia.

The pilots at Moresby watched him go, knowing that they could share such a fate.

Morale was near collapse. Mail hardly ever came. One local Aussie flying boat pilot became a local folk hero for refusing to make the run to Moresby from Townsville without somebody throwing at least a few sacks of mail into his aircraft. But most of the time, the planes and ships arrived with nothing. The mail piled up in Australia, weeks and weeks behind. For men already thinking they were in for a repeat of the Singapore campaign—trapped between the sea and a pitiless Japanese army—the lack of mail pushed some to the breaking point. At least two suicide attempts took place that summer, both traced directly back to the lack of contact with home.

Kenney found his pilots believed they were the forgotten ones of the Army Air Force, thrown into a noose without care, without supplies, parts, proper aircraft, or hope. They were not wrong. When Kenney first arrived in Australia, four days before this inspection trip to Seven Mile Drome, he asked the man he was replacing, General Brett, how many planes the 5th Air Force possessed. Brett had no idea. When he asked questions about everything from command structure to supply chains and aircraft maintenance, the answers were always the same. No clue. I'll get back to you on that, General.

Kenney quickly found out where all the supplies were: Melbourne. The air service command built a massive, $3.5 million facility and was busily filling it with everything from Allison engines to intercoolers for P-40 Warhawks. They took pride in what lay in their warehouses and jealously guarded those parts.

Those parts were needed thousands of miles north, in New Guinea. The supply guys were loath to part with their stash. Before Kenney even went up to Moresby, he knew that to fix this mess he'd have to destroy a lot of careers and send these idiots home. But who would take their place?

Anyone willing to fight, or support the fight, he decided.

General Kenney had inherited the most disorganized and defeated command in Air Force history. To turn it around, he knew he needed two things: an aggressive spirit that pervaded every corner of the 5th Air Force and a plane that could beat the Japanese.

He hoped the Lockheed P-38 Lightning would be that plane. In the meantime, Kenney looked for some way to rally his men, to build their spirit and restore morale. But in New Guinea, there was virtually nothing that could do that. In the weeks that followed, the grind continued, and morale remained a hair's breadth from being broken.

But then, later that fall a plane arrived, carrying America's greatest World War I hero, Capt. Eddie Rickenbacker. Wearer of the Medal of Honor—the highest award for bravery the U.S. government bestows on its warriors—"Captain Eddie" was a legend to every Depression-era kid whose eyes turned skyward and dreamed of flight. He was our best fighter pilot from the Great War—a man who survived the buzz saw over France's Western Front when countless other Americans did not. He not only survived, he became an extraordinary aerial hunter, shooting down twenty-six German planes to become the Army Air Service's ace of aces.

He was the example Kenney's men needed. Tough, resourceful, and built with a bulletproof never-quit attitude that even being lost at sea for weeks could not diminish, he set out to meet Kenney's fighter pilots. This new generation of pilots greeted the old warrior with awe and not a little hero worship. Rickenbacker was touched. He felt for the kids suffering and dying in this primal hellhole.

Kenney seized the moment and challenged his men to beat Eddie's score. The pilots saw what that could mean: hero status, their name in papers across the country, and their faces in the newsreels. Captain Eddie leveraged his fame into running one of the most successful airlines in the country. He'd gone from a simple mechanic to a millionaire, thanks to his prowess in battle over the Great War's trenches.

This was the brass ring dangling in front of Kenney's young pilots that helped spark the renewal of spirit the 5th Air Force's fighter units so desperately needed. The race to twenty-six became the rally point, one led and inspired by a handful of daring fliers who risked everything to unseat Captain Eddie as America's ace of aces. But besting Captain Eddie's score proved to be just the start of what became one of the wildest and most unusual events of World War II: the Race of Aces.

PART ONE

Warm-ups

1

The Country Mouse

May 5, 1942
San Francisco, California

The St. Francis Hotel towered in legendary elegance over one flank of Union Square, the one must-see spot in the city after a visit to the Golden Gate Bridge. It was the Plaza of the West Coast, dominated by ornate columns and high ceilings designed to accentuate its grandeur. The Otis Elevator Company added custom outdoor glass elevators that dazzled riders with thirty-story rides above the city.

Its rooms catered to the finest of the interwar "in" crowd, from Cary Grant to President Roosevelt and boxer Jack Dempsey. In 1939, Salvador Dalí let reporters take his photo in one of the hotel's bathtubs—wearing a lobster on his head, green goggles, and holding a cabbage in one hand.

There were times the in crowd took it too far. Fatty Arbuckle saw his career destroyed there when a young actress died at one of his wild parties.

If the St. Francis was the play place of the elite, the war transformed it into the last hurrah for a generation facing an uncertain fate. Gone were the high-end shops off the first-floor lobby, replaced by temporary rooms for military officers in transit to the Far East. Men from all walks of life and every state came to the St. Francis for a cultural experience they would never forget. They blew their remaining cash to say they had stayed at the hotel fit for world leaders and Hollywood icons. They dined on dollar-fifty brook trout and danced close in the packed confines of the Mural Room, where Harry Owens and his orchestra filled the venue with sensual Hawaiian tunes like "Sweet Leilani" and "Cocoanut Grove." It was their brush with something great, which the hotel's photographers memorialized for a few extra dollars.

In front of the hippest hotel with the hottest entertainment in the most beloved and liberated city in America, five-foot-seven, 150-pound 2nd Lt. Richard Ira Bong, late of Poplar, Wisconsin—population three hundred—stood with barely a penny to his name. The St. Francis was wild and glamorous, Bong the exact opposite. A little stocky, average looking with a decent smile and a quiet demeanor, he appeared entirely ordinary. In the greatest party place on the West Coast, he drank Coke. Though he would never stand out in a crowd, he was a fighter pilot. In wartime America, nothing was more romantic than that.

He watched as his buddy, Danny Robertson, shared a reunion with his girlfriend in epic Hollywood fashion. The young lovers arranged the rendezvous just after Dick and Danny received orders transferring them from Luke Field, Arizona, to the 49th Fighter Squadron at Hamilton Field. Now Dick Bong felt like a third wheel.

Trouble was, he was a third wheel everywhere in this city. A year before, he'd been living on the family farm in his childhood room, a tiny misshapen box at the top of the stairs, defined by a sloping roof so steep that when he slept in his narrow bed, his nose had been inches from the ceiling. Before May 29, 1941, he'd been out of Wisconsin just once in his life, when his family took a road trip to Yellowstone National Park.

He was not worldly, and the glitter of the St. Francis must have made him feel out of place. In the moral ambiguity of a city whose bar scene included a half-naked woman swimming in a goldfish bowl at Bimbo's 365, Bong probably felt out of place everywhere. He was a straight arrow, a young man raised on simple farm principles of hard work and loyalty to God and country. His father imbued him with a rigid sense of right and wrong. In his world, there were no gray areas, though his sense of black and white had never been tested.

San Francisco that spring was a whirlwind of emotions, stoked by wartime romances, tragic partings, and terrible grief. Thanks to the many nocturnal air raid alarms, the city lived with a sword of Damocles over its head, and the people embraced a *live for the day* spirit. The military added to the drama. Throughout the morning, the huge sixteen-inch guns defending the area thundered as the crews trained to hit targets out at sea. Each shot resounded through the city, shaking windows and floors. Overhead, combat aircraft flew back and forth to gunnery ranges off the coast at Big Sur and Point Reyes, adding to the sounds of wartime San Francisco. They lent intensity to the moment.

Richard Bong was even-keeled. He knew how to keep his emotions on lockdown. Depression-era farm kids learned this as a matter of survival, as most faced despairing loss at young ages. You either learned to control it or grief controlled you. The Bong family possessed self-control in even the worst moments. If everyone here was fueled with a higher emotional octane, that was fine with him. He was content to be the rock in the surf.

Union Square hummed around him. Women wore the latest fashions—dirndl skirts made with black rayon crepe, or jersey-print below-the-knee dresses and wide-brimmed hats. Farm women back home had few such luxuries. Dresses and gloves were saved for Sunday church services. Most of the girls he knew back home milked cows and baled hay. These West Coast women were foreigners to a young man whose life was spent hunting and fishing around the family homestead.

The men were different, too. They were dapper and well dressed, while he made do with his Army Air Force "pinks," the khaki uniform pants that turned that color when washed a few times. He wore the olive-brown dress tunic of an aviator, silver wings pinned to his chest. His shoes were brown and worn after a year of use.

The men flowing through Union Square sported the latest in shoe styles: seven-dollar Burma tan and brown Freeman two-tone wing tips, Roblee monk-strap Defenders, or traditional black bluchers, shined and neatly tied. His Air Corps regulation russet oxfords looked tacky in comparison. This was a town that took fashion seriously, and shoes were the mark of a man. He made a mental note to buy a new pair as soon as he got paid.

Those men not in uniform wore a mix of older suits—double-breasted chalk stripes in blues and grays, loosely tailored. The newer suits were less flashy since their designs were rigidly controlled by the federal government to save wool for military use. No pocket flaps on their coats, and pant cuffs were forbidden. Some of the men ignored the latter restriction by simply ordering longer slacks, then having them cuffed. Still, in the mélange of people around him, it was easy to see the extent of the government's wartime reach.

People sat around the square on benches, enjoying the spring weather and reading about that very subject of government control in the local papers. The front page of one listed all the latest civilian items the government outlawed for the duration of the war. Production of purse frames was banned, and perfume atomizers, beer steins, roller coasters, and birdhouses made the list too. Butter knives, attic fans, and BB shot for Red Ryder spring rifles would also not be produced for civilian consumption for the duration of the war.

Bong took all that control in stride. Honoring the responsibilities of citizenship was the bedrock of his small-town education. His eighth-grade graduation ceremony included a speech by two classmates, entitled "I Am an American." Four years later, when he received his high school diploma, the theme of the graduation cere- mony was "Youth Faces the Ideals of Citizenship."

Bong did not see the government's restriction of fashion design to be an intrusion. There was a reason for it. He was a patriot and erred on the side of government. He trusted the country's leaders, even if his folks hadn't voted for FDR.

Bong explored the city that first night in town, taking it all in with his natural even keel. A few months before, he'd seen the Pacific Ocean for the first time and remarked in a letter home that it wasn't all that impressive. It reminded him of Lake Superior. He contextualized the sweeping nature of an ocean with his own small corner of the planet. In a vast world, he existed in a farm-boy bubble, gazing out as an onlooker, not a participant.

So he avoided the prostitutes, and the dive bars, and the pool halls. He was twenty-one, a virgin who didn't drink or gamble. In a city full of vice, he was viceless. His sense of propriety recoiled at the hookers plying their trade through the Tenderloin. He'd had a girl- friend in high school, but that was strictly proper. Bong came from a Christian family. Dating in Poplar meant holding hands.

At length, Bong retreated to his hotel room for the night. He and Danny could not afford the St. Francis, so they picked the Roosevelt on the other side of town. It was a once-majestic Gilded Age hotel that had slipped slowly into disrepair. Five bucks a night for a stained room with two beds, a chair, and a writing desk. This was all he could afford.

Just before nine thirty, the local radio stations went silent. The radar station on Mount Tamalpais detected an unidentified aircraft. Searchlights swept the sky until quarter to ten, seeking to illuminate the mystery craft, which turned out to be a wayward Navy plane. Sometime after midnight, another unidentified aircraft appeared over the bay. Once again, searchlights lanced the darkness over Mare Island and Oakland. Another false alarm, but it kept everyone on edge.

The next morning, Bong awoke early to pen a letter home. He was one of seven children—seven surviving children. Their tiny whitewashed two-story farmhouse managed to keep a roof over everyone's head, but it was cramped and lacking in privacy. In such confines, one might expect the siblings to grow very close. They did, but for Bong, his deepest connection back home was to his mother. He wrote her at least several times a week to describe his experiences since joining the Army Air Force.

This morning, he wrote to his mom about the Bay Bridge. It was an engineering marvel, the longest in the world at that time. Completed six years before, it spanned almost a mile, connecting the East Bay to San Francisco's China Basin district. It was an awesome sight, especially when the fabled California fog shrouded the spans at sunset, a highway into a cloud, standing hundreds of feet above the shimmering bay.

He loved these sorts of engineering achievements. In school, Dick was a hit-or-miss kind of student. He possessed a mechanical mind that took to all types of science, but he limped through art and earned a *D* in U.S. history, unaware that he would become a part of it someday. Chemistry class, where he kept meticulous notes written in the spiky print of an ordered and logical mind, was a different story. After years of working on aging farm machinery, he was a young man comfortable around metal things that moved. Had he not joined the military the previous fall, he might have made a talented mechanical engineer.

Letter written, it was time to report to duty. Danny and Bong drove across the Golden Gate into San Rafael and showed their military identification at the front gate to Hamilton Field. Around the airstrip's perimeter, half-buried light tanks served as stopgap fortifications in case any Japanese troops made it over the Marin Headlands and into the North Bay. Elsewhere, men crewed anti-aircraft guns with binoculars pointed to the sky, rifles nearby and pistols holstered on their hips.

Here, he would learn to be a warrior, not the trainer of warriors-to-be that he was in Arizona. Dick relished the opportunity; everyone, it seemed, wanted a shot at the Japanese after Pearl Harbor. What he did not know was just how unyielding a gaze the media would shed on him when he would find himself at the center of the race to become the deadliest American fighter pilot.

Danny put the sedan in gear after getting their IDs back and drove onto the base to report to their new fighter squadrons, both pilots wondering what kind of pursuit planes they were destined to fly.

2

The Buck Rogers Diving Death Ride

May 7, 1942
Hamilton Field, California

Parked on the ramp at Hamilton Field stood a long row of twenty-five brand-new fighters. The world had never seen anything like these sci-fi wonders resting on tricycle landing gears, slightly raked so their tails drooped. It gave the impression that they were preparing to spring into the air. From the side, they looked pencil-thin and made every other American fighter appear positively bloated. Paradoxically, the narrow profile did not mean small aircraft. In fact, the new fighters dwarfed their more conventional stablemates.

While most every fighter design in the world possessed a single fuselage that encompassed engine, cockpit, and tail, the new fighter didn't have a fuselage at all. Instead, the pilot sat in a cockpit gondola fared directly into the wing, a twelve-cylinder Allison engine on either side of him. Connecting the wing to the tail at the engine nacelles were two long booms, through each of which stretched a top-secret turbo supercharger that gave the fighter remarkable high-altitude performance. Where its stablemates would be limping along just above a stall at twenty-five thousand feet, the new fighter thrived.

This was the Lockheed P-38 Lightning, the most radical fighter plane yet produced by the American aircraft industry. At a time when most American designs lagged behind their European counterparts, the USAAF believed the P-38 would be the great leap forward needed to help win the war. The Lockheed was fast. Straight and level, it could just touch four hundred miles an hour, thanks to the twenty-five hundred horses its engines produced. It possessed good range and could climb at over four thousand feet a minute, making it perfect for intercepting high-altitude bombers.

Though it weighed fourteen thousand pounds and could not outmaneuver single-engine fighters, it possessed heavy firepower with four heavy machine guns and one rapid-fire cannon. It could spew four thousand bullets a minute, with every sixth one an explosive cannon shell. Lockheed packed the guns in the nose, giving the P-38 a cone of concentrated death unlike any other American aircraft.

The three-bladed propellers were driven by purpose-built left and right engines. The left ones rotated left, the right ones rotated right. This was an innovation Lockheed used to ensure the P-38 would be stable and easy to fly, free from strange stall/spin quirks that bedeviled other USAAF fighters.

At the moment, the new Lightnings were especially needed in the Pacific to help stem the Japanese tide of advance. The latest news reports spoke of surrender in the Philippines and a chaotic naval battle in the Coral Sea. The Japanese seemed dominant everywhere, thrashing the Army Air Force at every point of contact. Now, Australia itself seemed threatened with invasion.

The situation in the Pacific was grim. Californians lived in fear that they would soon face Japanese bombs and amphibious armadas offshore. So far, nothing had stopped the enemy. The P-38 became the great hope that finally, American pilots would take to the skies in a plane superior to anything the Japanese possessed.

Needless to say, there was a tremendous sense of urgency to get the Lightning squadrons and their pilots ready for battle.

The P-38 cost a mint—over a hundred thousand dollars—1.7 million in today's dollars. For the price of one P-38, the federal government could buy three P-40 Warhawks. But this was war, and price tag didn't matter. Winning did. The Lightning was the Ferrari of the fighter world. Expensive, technically complex, and very, very hot. By early May 1942, the USAAF had taken delivery of about three hundred P-38s, with perhaps a thousand pilots training on them.

Dick Bong joined that elite cadre of aviators at Hamilton Field, where the 49th Fighter Squadron recently had traded in its P-40 Warhawks for the first combat-ready model of the P-38. The AAF tasked the 49th with two roles: protect San Francisco and produce P-38 pilots. Now, waves of freshly minted flyboys blew into Hamilton Field, straight from advanced training schools, eager to master the new machine.

This looked great on paper, but there was a problem with the P-38 program. The new planes kept killing these new pilots. In April, there were twenty fatal P-38 crashes in California and Washington. Forty more would crash in May. Another thirty in June.

At the air base protecting Seattle, a Lightning pilot lost control on takeoff and careened into the mess hall, killing two enlisted men. Another plunged straight into a home in downtown Olympia, killing both the pilot and a housewife. One fell out of the sky to explode inside a hospital.

Being a P-38 pilot in May 1942 meant having a very short shelf life. Most, like Dick Bong, had no experience with twin-engine aircraft. Though the plane was stable and easy to fly, the cockpit was complex and poorly laid out. Lockheed's engineers placed the fuel system's controls on the cockpit floor to the left of the pilot's seat. They were hard to reach, and the system was so intricate that it required a virtual master's degree to understand. Flip the wrong switch in flight, and the engines could be trying to drink from an empty tank. Take the wrong steps when an engine went out on takeoff or landing, and the pilot was almost sure to die. Dive too steeply, and the P-38's controls locked up in what was later called "compressibility." The nose would tuck under itself, steepening the dive and making it ever harder for the pilot not to end up in a smoking crater. An experienced test pilot was killed that way during the run-up to production. Despite warnings, a lot of young pilots fresh from their cadet classes plunged straight to their deaths.

To make things even more confusing, Lockheed changed the cockpit layout from model to model. In one variant, the placement of the microphone toggle button was moved. Lockheed swapped it with the cannon's trigger. Unwary pilots would sometimes hit that button, launching a burst of high-explosive shells when they intended to simply talk to a flight mate.

There was no two-seat trainer version of the P-38 either. Dick would be on his own the minute he climbed into the '38's cockpit. To prepare him and the other new guys, the 49th put them through a quick ground school, familiarizing them with controls, instruments, and systems.[1]

---

1. Taking a pilot who had flown nothing more advanced than an AT-6 Texan trainer that cruised at 140 miles an hour and putting him in the cockpit of the hottest fighter in the country wasn't the most optimal way to keep him alive. So the P-38 squadrons received access to the same type of plane Amelia Earhart disappeared in back in 1937. This was the twin-engine Lockheed Electra airliner, which the USAAF called the C-40A. It was docile and straightforward, possessed the same twin-tail configuration as the P-38, and could give a young pilot a good feel for what multi-engine flying entailed. The '38 squadrons took to sending five or six new guys aloft with an old hand. The greenhorns would take turns sitting in the copilot seat while the others clustered around behind the flight deck to watch. On his first hop on May 11, Dick sat beside Harold Lewis for thirty minutes before giving his seat up to another new guy. Despite having a more experienced pilot in the cockpit to minimize the chance of a greenhorn screwing up, this type of transition training was still very dangerous. The day after Bong's first twin-engine flight, the P-38 outfit defending Seattle learned that all too tragically when their

Dick's P-38 education began on May 7 when Lt. Harold Lewis gathered all the squadron's greenhorns to teach them the basics of being a Lightning jock. He was the squadron's designated training officer, even though he himself had been flying for less than two years. In 1942, the blind led the blind.

Lewis and Dick Bong had similar life stories. Both grew up in small towns—Lewis was a native of Marseilles, Illinois, and went to Northern Illinois Teachers College, getting a math degree before joining the service. Dick attended Superior State Teachers College before dropping out to join the Air Corps. Both were science minded and devoted to aviation.

That day, as Lewis opened the knowledge fire hose on the new guys, Lt. Jim Butler took one of the squadron's P-38s up for a flight. As he sped down the runway, one engine began to sputter. He limped aloft, but the engine quit and he crashed about a mile from the north end of the field. Miraculously, he survived.

Lewis and the rest of the members of the 49th learned to handle such situations with this dictum: power meant survival. Lose an engine? Push the other one to maximum throttle immediately. It was the only hope of surviving when a fan failed on takeoff.

Except it wasn't. This was the Air Force standard response to a P-38 engine failure, and it produced nothing but casualties. Firewall the throttle with a fan out, and the P-38 would yaw toward the dead engine and start to roll. The more power applied, the faster this would happen and the quicker the pilot lost control and rolled, inverted, into the ground. Lewis didn't have the experience to know

---

C-40 went aloft with four rookies. While practicing touch-and-go landings, one of the new guys lost control after slamming onto the runway too hard, collapsing the left gear. They bounced back into the air, twisted into a spin, crashed, and burned. Everyone aboard was killed. At the same time as this accident, Dick was doing touch-and-go landings at Hamilton in the 49th's C-40. Seven landings later, Lewis deemed him ready for his first P-38 experience.

any better; he was just as much a victim as everyone else struggling to learn this new and complicated aircraft.

Thus, he—a man who had survived the ultimate teachable moment in his crash—taught Dick and the other greenhorns the exact wrong way to survive an engine failure.

It would be months before the AAF bureaucracy unscrewed this one. The proper way to handle such an emergency was for the pilot to throttle back the remaining engine, feather the other one's props, maintain control, then slowly apply power, compensating for the yaw and roll along the way with the yoke and rudders.

Through the next week, word of other crashes in the 49th's sister squadrons filtered to Hamilton. Lots of pilots were losing engines either on takeoff or landing. Depressingly few survived. The new design came with another inherent flaw in such situations. Even if the pilots had the time and altitude to bail out, the only way to do it was to slide off the wing and fall between the booms. Rumors abounded that those who did get out were cut in half by the horizontal stabilizer. Since bailing out was not a great option, many P-38 pilots tried to ride their planes into the ground, hoping to regain control long enough to survive a crash landing.

The reason behind the engine failures remained unsolved for months. For the pilots sentenced to fly the Lightning, every takeoff and landing must have been a gut check moment. They went aloft not knowing when the dice would roll snake eyes and their turn would come. That uncertainty weighed on all of them. Yet it didn't seem to diminish Dick's enthusiasm to try the new beast out. For a small-town farm kid whose early life experience hardened him to death, the chance of getting to be one of the first pilots of America's most advanced plane—and seemingly its most dangerous—put him in a thrilling spot right at bleeding edge. So he studied, learned what he could on the ground, and tried hard not to dwell on the deaths of those around him.

Richard Ira Bong's turn to roll the dice arrived on the morning of May 13. Lucky thirteen. He arrived at the flight line, ducked under the boom of his assigned P-38, and climbed the ladder the ground crew placed at the trailing edge of the wing. He stepped onto the seat, then slid down into it as the plane's crew chief knelt beside him on the wing to help strap him in and close the canopy hatch. He ran through the checklist given to him, fired up the engines, and headed out to the runway.

Now for the gut-check moment. Dick steered the Lightning out onto the runway and opened the throttles. No turning back now. The engines purred. For a huge aircraft, the P-38 proved to be surprisingly quiet. The engines sounded buttery and subdued. The superchargers and their ductwork acted as mufflers, giving the P-38 one of the most distinctive audio signatures of World War II.

Dick held his breath for a moment, focusing on the takeoff checklist. He knew the scale of the power and danger he held at his fingertips. He intended to master it.

He swung onto the runway and opened the throttles. The engines held. As he passed a hundred miles an hour, he felt the P-38 wanting to get airborne. A little more speed. Plenty of runway ahead. The '38's nose rotated just a bit and Dick eased back on the control wheel. The Lightning left the runway and streaked over the bay. This moment changed Dick Bong's life. The aircraft made sense to him. It was an unlikely but perfect match between his ordered mind and a dangerously complex aircraft.

He stayed close to Hamilton that day, making touch-and-go landings and getting the feel of the aircraft. The Bay Area was filled with air traffic, air lanes, no-fly zones, and specified areas for Navy and Army trainers. The map he'd been given of the Bay Area was overlaid with color-coded squares and triangles denoting each aerial training range or off-limits zone. It was confusing at first glance, but each pilot needed to thoroughly understand it, as it was dangerous to wander into certain areas where the antiaircraft gunners might actually open fire on passing planes.[2] He respected that and stayed in his lane, swooping up and down over Hamilton, tires kissing the runway before flitting off into the air again, engines wide open. In those moments, gear retracted, climbing so fast it felt like the world's most epic elevator ride, Dick felt pure elation.

He loved every minute of it, and when the day finally ended, he returned to the Bachelor Officers Quarters uncharacteristically exhilarated. He was born to fly the P-38, as if he had Lockheed coded into his DNA.

He flew almost every day afterward, sometimes several flights. As he gained hours, he made huge leaps forward with what he could do with the aircraft. Of course, it was not enough just to get competent flying the aircraft and landing it. These were weapons of war, and the men of the 49th Fighter Squadron had only a few weeks to learn how to fight with the P-38 as well.

The fact was, the 49th did not have time to learn to do both. Nobody knew how best to employ the P-38, the tactics to use, or even the role it would play once deployed overseas. Instead of working through those questions, the pilots took turns dogfighting each other. In those mock battles, to everyone's surprise, Dick Bong shined.

His fellow pilots found him almost invisible on the ground. Like he was in San Francisco, Dick seemed more an observer than a participant. Never aloof or haughty, he just didn't participate much. When he did join a conversation, the guys discovered Bong possessed a good sense of humor and could be self-effacing. They liked him, but nobody really felt they got to know him. If pressed, they

---

2. This was particularly true around the Mare Island Naval Shipyard, where USN gunners nearly opened fire on USAAF P-40s on several occasions, prompting many outraged messages between the two services.

would have judged him to be the furthest from the "fighter-jock" persona in the squadron—the antithesis of the ego-driven, aggressive, and arrogant type A character whose swagger on the ground matched his skills in the air. Bong had no swagger.

Yet, that farm-boy persona vanished in the cockpit. The straight arrow became the wild man: unpredictable, intuitive, liberated. Bong retracted the landing gear and some switch inside him flipped. No longer the introvert, he became ferociously aggressive, pushing his Lightning just a little further out to the edge of its envelope than others dared to do. The metamorphosis stunned his flight mates, who figured they'd make easy meat of the shy kid. Instead, he feasted on them.

These P-38s had manual controls, just like a car without power steering. It took upper-body strength and steel-belted legs to kite a Lightning around the sky. They'd land after these mock dogfights sweat-soaked and wrung out from the experience. Here again, Dick possessed a secret advantage. His country upbringing gave him endurance and a physicality in the cockpit that others lacked. To him, throwing a Lightning around was nothing compared to bringing in the harvest or baling hay.

That physicality would be useful in combat, but it wasn't much help when the aircraft itself still suffered so many mechanical failures. Death always lingered close. Two days after his first flight, one of his squadron mates, Ed Cahill, rolled snake eyes. Taking off from Hamilton late in the day, his left engine quit. The former University of Alabama student threw max power to the right engine and tried to gain altitude so he could come around for an emergency landing. He did everything as taught, but what he did killed him. The sudden burst of power yawed the nose violently left. The right wing rolled vertically, then the Lightning flipped inverted and spun in from five hundred feet. Cahill's plane hit the ground nose-first. He died instantly, his body incinerated.

His hometown paper back in Jersey, where he'd lived with his widowed mother before joining the Army Air Force, gave his death two paragraphs of ink.

There was no flying for the rest of the day.

In Dick's first month at Hamilton, eight of the twenty-five P-38s available to the 49th Fighter Squadron's parent unit, the 14th Fighter Group, were destroyed in crashes. Given the circumstances, Dick was probably wise not to get too close to anyone. He'd seen fellow cadets die in training, so this was nothing new The frequency of death—that was new. Yet in a grim way, farm life prepared him for the cruel realities of his fighter pilot life.

During a snowstorm in March 1939, Dick's fifteen-year-old sister Betty fell ill. She'd struggled with asthma all her life, but this time, as she burned with fever, seemed different. The roads were impassable due to the snowfall, so Dick's parents set her up in a nest of blankets on the living room couch where they could tend to her more easily. Dick and his brother Carl were trapped by the sudden snowstorm in Poplar and forced to stay with relatives in town. For three days, the snow flurries blanketed the fields around the small village as Dick and Carl chafed, desperate to get home. Finally, they borrowed skis and during a break in the blizzard set off cross-country for their farm. They found Betty weak and racked with fever. No doctors could get to the farm, and they couldn't get Betty out. All day and night, the family grew frantic with worry, caring for Betty as best they could.

On the fourth day, a plow got through Poplar and cleared the main road to Superior. Dick's father attached a blade to one of the farm tractors and cut a path from the house to the main road about a half mile away. Dick scooped Betty up and carried her to the family car, where his mother drove behind the tractor until they got to the main road. From there, Dick's dad drove her to the hospital. She died of pneumonia three days later. Dick's last view of his kid sis was her lying limp in the family's car.

Grief begot grief. Dick's mom was pregnant at the time, and the trauma of losing Betty caused her to go into labor six weeks prematurely. Dick's youngest brother, James, was born at the Superior hospital just after Betty was laid to rest in the Poplar cemetery. He survived, but only after being in an incubator for three weeks.

The death of his sister afflicted the family, but it was a private, suppressed grief. Dick learned to internalize his sense of loss. Perhaps he always felt it, learning to live around it. Perhaps he pushed it deep and tried never to think about it. Either way, he handled the death of friends later with a stoicism that some thought was cold-hearted. But for him it was something else. Farm life taught him to survive such tragedies, he had to keep moving.

After Cahill's death, and another pilot's horrible end a few days later, Dick continued flying. He used every second he could to learn his aircraft and build the skills that could keep him alive in combat. He was not the nostalgic type, nor the type to dwell. He just kept moving. It was easier that way.

3

When Trouble Is Your
Saving Grace

June 11, 1942
Hamilton Field, California

Dick awoke on the morning of Thursday, June 11, dressed, and headed off to chow, eager to get into the air. It was unseasonably cold that spring morning at Hamilton, but the clear skies made for great flying. Dick Bong and the other pilots assigned to fly that day reached the flight line to find the mechanics making last-minute tweaks to the row of olive-drab P-38s. As they worked on their sleek birds, other fighters came and went; transports and bombers rolled down the taxiways to refuel and continue their journeys. Hamilton was one of the busiest airfields on the West Coast that June.

Though Dick had been in the squadron for only a month, the ops officer assigned him command of a flight that morning. This meant he would have three other pilots with him, under his immediate supervision. This was one of Dick's first leadership opportunities.

To be a flight leader at Hamilton required considerable awareness of the airspace around the Bay Area. It was one of the most complex and restricted areas to fly anywhere in the United States. A look at his kneeboard map showed the now familiar dizzying array of color-coded danger areas, no-fly zones and chunks of sky reserved for other types of aviation. To the south, much of the bay down by NAS Alameda was a dedicated Navy preserve. No Army pursuits allowed.

Other areas were off-limits as well, like San Francisco proper, the Golden Gate, and the Bay Bridge. Frankly, there were so many restrictions on flying in the Bay Area that at times it complicated training.

Flying in airspace closely watched by radar and ground observers, defended by antiaircraft gunners and interceptors, made for some serious challenges at a time when there was no electronic way to distinguish friend from foe on an oscilloscope. To make sure friendly planes were not misidentified as incoming bombers, every flight had to be preplanned and approved through channels. Vary from that plan, and chances were good the off-course aircraft would trigger a blackout or an interception.

That morning, Dick led his first command into the morning sky feeling the joy of being in the air again with their sleek new fighters. At nearby Mills Field, the men of the 82nd Fighter Group also took to the sky. Their P-38s joined the 49th's in the air around San Francisco.

Dick was usually a by-the-book sort of kid growing up. His father instilled in him a very strict sense of discipline and respect for authority. Yet at the same time, every now and then he would go off the reservation to have a little fun. As a pilot, that playful rebelliousness occasionally appeared back in Arizona. Once, while on a training flight, he took his AT-6 trainer into the Grand Canyon and looped the loop below the rim. Out in the largely unpopulated Southwest, such stunts attracted no attention. California was a different story. Not only did the military have eyes everywhere; civilians possessed the ability to pick up the nearest phone, say, "Flash" to the operator, and be connected to an air intercept filter center to report an aircraft sighting. He held himself back from trying any tricks, but the temptation seemed irresistible to many around him. Truth was, he was always tempted.

The previous ten days had been rough ones for the P-38 units in the area. The Battle of Midway put the squadrons on high alert. The men had spent nearly two weeks practically living beside their aircraft, waiting for the word to intercept incoming bombers. Their planes were loaded with live ammo, fully fueled. They did no training or noncombat flying. In the end, the tension of waiting on the ground for the "go" order left them eager to get back into the sky again.

This was the first day they'd been released from alert duty, and the pilots were like kids let out late from school. They went off to play—which for fighter jocks meant getting fast and low. Throughout the day, IV Interceptor Command received a barrage of troubling reports. A hysterical housewife called in to report a P-38 blasted over her house at shingle level, scaring her half to death and blowing all her laundry off her backyard clotheslines. At least three P-38s flew under the Golden Gate Bridge, and another reportedly whined down Market Street *between* the skyscrapers. Hell broke loose as IV Interceptor Command tried to figure out who was behind these crazy antics. After all the crashes in the area, the civilians did not appreciate these high-speed buzzings.[1]

Bong later admitted he was the pilot who blew the housewife's laundry around her yard. At some point during that training flight,

---

1. Word of this day later spread throughout New Guinea. Pilots would ask Dick if he flew under the Golden Gate. Reportedly, he stayed mum on the subject, though in a 1944 interview with Lee Van Atta, he copped to buzzing the house in San Anselmo. General Kenney later created a larger legend out of the day in his book, *Ace of Aces: The Story of Fighter Pilot Dick Bong*, which opens with Dick looping the loop around the Golden Gate, then tearing down Market Street between buildings. There is no record in the surviving USN documents, IV Interceptor Command reports, IV Air Force records, judge advocate reports, or the surviving records from Hamilton Field of any of this happening. None of the Bay Area's newspapers reported any of these incidents, and the surviving radio news broadcasts from San Francisco stations make no mention of them either. Clearly, something significant happened that day, but what Dick's exact role was will probably never be fully ascertained.

he peeled off and sped for the trees north of the Golden Gate. A fellow pilot from the 49th lived off post in San Anselmo—about twenty miles north of the bridge. He'd just gotten married, and Dick gave him a belated gift: two thousand eight hundred horses of screaming Allison engines right over his roof. The next-door neighbor was collateral damage.

When Dick returned to Hamilton Field, his crew chief watched as a major and a full colonel came speeding along the flight line in a jeep. They screeched to a stop at Dick's '38, bailed out of the jeep and stood waiting for the farm boy to climb out of the cockpit.

The minute Dick's boots hit the tarmac, the colonel stormed up to him. "As of this moment," he said, "you're grounded."

Dick's first taste of command had ended in complete disaster.

To complete the humiliation, Bong's mother and sister Nelda arrived the next day from Wisconsin. They'd been planning a visit for weeks. Dick had scraped enough money together to pay for half their trip out to California. His sister wanted to get a job at Lockheed in Burbank, working for the same company that made the planes her brother flew, and Dick's mom wanted to see him one more time before he went overseas.

They appeared at the front gate on Friday, only to be told they could not see Dick. His mom complained and gained an audience with the base commander. Eventually, while Nelda waited at the gate, Dick's mom was allowed to see her son. It was a short and tense meeting, one that had to have been heartbreaking for Dick.

Confined to quarters, he and the others faced the end of their flying careers. Anywhere else, such behavior would have usually netted a slap on the wrist. But as IV Interceptor Command searched for the other guilty pilots—two of whom may have been with the 82nd Fighter Group at Mills Field—the Army clearly intended to make examples of them.

The Navy was done with the craziness too. Over in Livermore, one of their instructor pilots buzzed a rodeo. In front of hundreds of spectators, he dove into the arena in a blue and yellow two-seat biplane, chasing bulls and cowboys before pulling up, reversing course and diving straight at the VIP section of the stands. One eye-witness put the plane at thirty feet from the grandstands before the pilot pulled up over the panicked crowd.

The VIP section included the mayor of Livermore and an admiral he invited to the event. The admiral dove for the bottom of the bleachers as the biplane swept overhead, costing him his dignity and whatever check he had on his tempter. He demanded the pilot's scalp. The instructor was thrown out of the Navy at a time when every pilot was needed.

So was the example set. Behave, or go home in disgrace.[2]

Now it was the Army Air Force's turn. IV Interceptor Command launched a full investigation into the events of June 11 with the intent to court-martial the pilots involved. While it unfolded, Dick and three other pilots remained in limbo. Lt. John "Jump" O'Neil, also of the 49th Fighter Squadron, was identified as one of the men who flew under the Golden Gate. Lt. John Mangus, a P-38 pilot from the 82nd, was also grounded for the same reason, though he was not confined to quarters as Dick was.[3] Mangus's

---

2. The surviving 11th Naval District documents located at the San Bruno branch of the National Archives and Records Administration (NARA) include a variety of disciplinary cases that suggest the pilots were not the only ones causing issues. Included in the reports are drunken brawls on trains, an ensign who held up a bar with his service .45, and a decorated and wounded lieutenant commander who kept exposing himself to Stanford coeds. The latter was sent to a psychiatric hospital on the East Coast.
3. Mangus, who hailed from Portland, Oregon, later mentioned to his family that he flew under the Golden Gate, though he was not specific about the date. Information on John's life, including excerpts from his letters home in 1942, came from his nephew, Gary Smith.

wingman, 2nd Lt. James Mitchell, may have also been among those to fly under the bridge, but he escaped punishment and remained on flight status. Four days later, while trying to make an emergency landing at Mills Field, his fighter suffered engine failure. He rolled out of control and plunged straight for a mess hall where scores of men were eating lunch. At the last second, he was able to force the nose over, missing the chow hall but tearing into a nearby hangar. His wing struck a mechanic and killed him instantly. A second later, the plane exploded and spread a fire throughout the hangar. The cause of the engine failure was never determined—the fire pretty much erased the evidence.[4]

Whether or not James flew under the Golden Gate was forgotten. His dying act saved the lives of everyone in that mess hall, and the Army Air Force awarded him a posthumous Distinguished Flying Cross for it.

As the remaining pilots awaited their fate, the 49th Fighter Squadron received its movement orders. The whole 14th Fighter Group would be flying across the continent to the East Coast, where they would refuel and become one of the first American fighter units to fly across the Atlantic to England.

With Dick and Jump O'Neil in the judge advocate general's crosshairs, the 49th transferred them out of the squadron. Dropped from the squadron as it was about to go into combat highlighted the severity of the situation to Dick and Jump O'Neil. Both were outstanding fighter pilots. To leave them behind with the malcontents and malingerers left them near despair. For Dick, knowing that his squadron would prefer to journey on without him must have been

---

4. John Mangus wrote home to his sisters of this terrible accident. He was one of the pilots assigned to escort Mitchell's remains back to Ohio, but he switched with another man in the unit since his sisters were coming down to visit him the following week. It was during that visit he mentioned to them that he'd flown under the Golden Gate with James.

devastating. He later rarely talked about it, and never even discussed this period with his family in any surviving letters. In 1942, there was a vast shortage of trained, capable pilots. To be both trained and capable yet judged untrustworthy to fly in combat must have been akin to an Army Air Force scarlet letter. Dick and Jump O'Neil were the castoffs their own units didn't want.

Yet, remaining behind in California turned out to be a blessing in disguise. The 49th Fighter Squadron went into combat in North Africa in the fall of 1942. Without adequate tactical training, the Luftwaffe's veteran pilots made mincemeat of Dick Bong's former unit. Almost everyone he flew with at Hamilton was either killed in action or captured. Had Dick and Jump O'Neil not been grounded and relieved from the 49th Fighter Squadron, they probably would have shared the same fate.[5]

Sometimes, trouble is your saving grace.

---

5. The situation in North Africa was so bad for the 49th and its parent 14th Fighter Group that eventually morale collapsed and the unit had to be pulled out of combat in early 1943. Veteran leaders from the 1st Fighter Group were brought in to reform it and the outfit quickly went back into combat. However, this was one of the few times during World War II that a USAAF fighter group was withdrawn from battle and reorganized with new leadership as a result of battle casualties and performance.

4

General Summons

July 7, 1942
San Francisco, California

After confining Dick Bong to quarters and dumping him from the 49th Fighter Squadron, the IV Fighter Command needed to find something useful for Bong to do while the inspector general prepared the case against him. In such circumstances, a flying position was out of the question, so the Wisconsin native was sent to work in the intercept center in San Francisco.

He spent his days around the plotting board, scrambling alert fighters against unidentified aircraft, which always proved to be a wayward American plane. He tried to put out of his mind that his flying days might be finished for good. If he were court-martialed and kicked out of the AAF, he could be drafted into the infantry once he got home. A worse fate for a fighter pilot who loved being above the clouds could hardly be imagined.

As he came off shift on Monday, July 6, 1942, he was informed that the commanding general of the 4th Air Force wanted to see him in his office Tuesday morning at ten thirty. The summons made him sick with fear. A second lieutenant should never get on a three-star general's radar. That only happens when a monumental act of bravery is involved, or a monumental screwup. Dick feared he was about to be cashiered from the service.

The next morning, Bong showed up at the southern end of the Financial District, where the 4th Air Force HQ filled a high-rise at 180 Montgomery Street. He took the elevator to the CG's office.

He stepped out and introduced himself to the general's secretary. Jump O'Neil arrived a moment later, looking just about as terrified as Dick felt. The secretary stood up, opened the door to the general's office, and announced, "Your bad boys are outside. You remember— the ones you wanted to see about flying around bridges and down Market Street?"[1]

A gruff and thundering voice replied, "Send them in!"

The secretary nodded, closed the door, and walked over to the two young pilots.

In a formal tone she said, "The general will see you now, Lieutenants."

The two lieutenants marshaled their courage and headed for the door.

Gen. George Kenney stood waiting for them. He looked like a middle-aged bulldog with a buzz cut and the grizzled face of a lifelong aviator who survived not only combat over the Western Front during the Great War but the often-fatal Golden Age when planes and pilots fell out of the sky with distressing frequency.

He was a flying general, a man who loved the cockpit more than anything else in his life, but knew his days of tearing around with his hair afire were over. Now, he rode herd over the men he used to be.

---

1. The accounts of this meeting come from Dick's letters home to his mom (he mentions the incident in early 1943 in one paragraph), the interview with Lee Van Atta in 1944, and from Kenney's own accounts in two of his books, *General Kenney Reports* and *Ace of Aces: The Story of Fighter Pilot Dick Bong.* The latter was essentially a cut-and-paste of the first pages of the former. In his account, Kenney omits mention of Jump O'Neil being there. Some historians have suggested that all of this was fabricated by Kenney after the war, and that he had not actually met Dick in San Francisco. Dick's wartime mentions of it confirm that it happened, if not in exactly the same way as Kenney wrote about later.

The two lieutenants stood at attention at the edge of the general's desk. They introduced themselves.

Kenny tore into them without mercy. They stood rigid, eyes front, trying not to show the crushing fear they must have felt as their general bawled them out not only for the stupid low-level stunts but for getting him in trouble with the civilian authorities as well.

He lectured. He threatened. He growled. Kenney later wrote that after reading the IG case against them, he was inclined to throw Bong to the wolves. That changed when he saw him, a small, scared "cherub" with blue eyes, whose entire life and identity were tied to flying fighters.

In the end, he eased up on them both. In 1917, as Kenney went through flight school in New York during World War I, he used his first solo fight to fly under the East River bridges. He was self-aware enough to admit that he was the kind of pilot Bong and O'Neil were back when he was their age. And what general would not want daring, ballsy pilots like he had once been serving under his command? He knew the USAAF needed such kids, the ones with the moxie to push their planes and their talents to the utmost. Those were the kinds of pilots who either would die very young or would kick the enemy in the teeth.

He ordered them to write a five-thousand-word paper on proper flying safety and deliver it to their assigned unit as an oral report. He also told Dick to go see the housewife in San Anselmo, apologize, and offer to help around the house for a day. "You hang around being useful—mowing a lawn or something—and when the clothes are dry, take them off the line and bring them into the house…I want that woman to think we are good for something besides annoying people."[2]

---

2. Dick mentioned his punishment in his 1944 interview with Lee Van Atta. Kenney also mentioned it in his two accounts.

Dick and Jump O'Neil scrupulously followed through with their punishments. Before dismissing them, Kenney reminded them that if they indulged in any more low-altitude shenanigans, he would see to it that they were court-martialed. They promised to toe the line.

Later in July, after the meeting in Kenney's office, Bong received orders assigning him to the 78th Fighter Group's 84th Fighter Squadron, which had recently arrived at Oakland for its final, pre-deployment training. Dick's grounding and Kenney's lenient punishment came with an unintended consequence: he went through another five weeks of training with a second unit preparing for combat. This gave Dick the opportunity to rack up almost sixty more hours in the P-38, which made him one of the most experienced Stateside second lieutenants on the aircraft. By early September, he counted over a hundred hours in Lightnings and almost six hundred hours total.

Pilots often said that the Lightning was an easy plane to fly but a difficult one to fly well. To fly it well meant spending a lot of time in the cockpit, learning the aircraft's ins and outs thoroughly. The complicated instrument layout, the ergonomic oddities of the fuel control system, the many steps required to prepare to engage an enemy plane tended to overwhelm an inexperienced Lightning pilot.

While Dick's peers were being thrown into battle against the enemy with only a few dozen hours in fighters, his extra summer in the San Francisco Bay Area helped give him the knowledge and nuanced understanding of the P-38 that others lacked.

As Dick flew nearly every day, honing his skills over the Bay and behaving himself, events above his pay grade conspired to alter his future while connecting him for the rest of his life to the general who had just chewed him out. The two had more in common than they realized when they first met and General Kenney saw a bit of himself in Dick's devil-may-care flying

Like Dick, George Kenney felt a little like a castaway, a man who had prepared all his life for a combat command—after proving himself as a pilot in battle during World War I. Through the twenties and thirties, he earned a reputation for being a brilliant engineer who could troubleshoot new aircraft programs and bring them to fruition. He also was considered a renegade, a man who once advised against purchasing the B-17 Flying Fortress—the very weapon that lay at the core of the Army Air Force's self-styled mission: bombing enemy factories. That made him extremely unpopular in the upper echelons of the AAF. Had he not been such a useful engineer, his heresy could have killed his career. Instead, it ensured he would not get a command in Europe, where the Army Air Force was preparing to unleash a full-scale daylight bombing campaign against Germany. So Kenney was sent to the West Coast to troubleshoot the P-38 and figure out why it was killing so many pilots. It looked like he would be stuck Stateside, just as Dick Bong was, helping get the weapons of war ready for a fight he would never be in.

Then one day that summer, the head of the Army Air Forces, Gen. Henry "Hap" Arnold called George Kenney and offered him the worst combat command in the service. He was going to serve under Gen. Douglas MacArthur as the commander of the 5th Air Force, which the Japanese were currently beating the hell out of in New Guinea.

There were a lot of reasons that the Fifth was a terrible command. MacArthur hated his previous Air Force generals and considered the AAF to be all talk and no capability. So Kenney would have to work for a man who inherently disliked aviators and was known to have a cliquish staff that made life impossible for generals who did not fit in.

Worse, the Southwest Pacific Theater was at the tail end of a supply line that stretched across the Pacific. General Arnold made it clear the Fifth was the lowest-priority command outside the United

States. He told Kenney not to expect many reinforcements; he would have to make do with a trickle of new planes and pilots. The real war was going to be fought in the skies over Germany. Kenney wouldn't be at the big show, but at least he would be in combat.

As a sop, he offered a few P-38s—enough for a few squadrons—to Kenney and told him he could pick fifty Lightning pilots from the 4th Air Force to go with him to help bring the new aircraft into battle against the Japanese.

Kenney knew that the 5th Air Force was probably the only combat command he would be offered. Turn it down and he'd be stuck in the States for the duration. That would have been a career dead end. Besides, he wanted to fight. He'd spent his entire adult life preparing for another war; missing out on the fighting would leave him feeling like it had no payoff.

Yet, the downsides were significant. The Fifth was a ragtag, beaten force that the Japanese crushed and ran out of the Philippines, then crushed and ran out of the Dutch East Indies. The same thing was happening in New Guinea now. Morale was low. MacArthur was a notoriously quirky and difficult boss. The head of the AAF stressed he wasn't going to get much support. It seemed like a recipe for failure.

Or a miracle turnaround.

General Kenney accepted the job and started packing. He left the Bay Area just before Bong climbed back into a P-38 that July. Before he departed, he and his staff drafted the list of fifty P-38 pilots from the 4th Air Force who would go with him to the Pacific. Richard Bong, Jump O'Neil, and John Mangus all made that list. The bad boys of the Bay Area would go into battle working for the very general who let them off the hook and saved their careers. Now Kenney was hoping New Guinea would give them all a crack at redemption.

5

The Girl with the Red Umbrella

Friday, June 12, 1942
East of Hamilton Field, California

On the first day of Dick Bong's house arrest in June, an unusual formation of fighters passed just east of his quarters at Hamilton Field. Heading north, the planes touched down outside Sacramento to refuel. The pilots rushed to the supply warehouse, where they drew cold-weather flight suits. A quick lunch and they rushed back to their waiting Bell P-39 Airacobra fighters.

Brand-new like the P-38, the P-39 was supposed to be a hangar mate to the Lockheed that could defeat the German Messerschmitt fighters and the Japanese Zero while taking out incoming enemy bombers. Yet the P-39 was a weird plane, built around a massive 37mm automatic cannon. Bell's designers could not figure out at first how to mount such armament into a single-engine fighter. They finally hit on moving the engine behind the cockpit so they could stick the cannon in the nose. A long driveshaft ran under the pilot's seat from engine to propeller. Instead of a sliding canopy, Bell conceived the car door hatch as the way to get in and out of the cockpit. It made for a very cramped arrangement, which forced the USAAF to select smaller pilots for their new fighter.

The pilots squeezed into those tiny cockpits, took off, and pointed their P-39s northward. The 54th Fighter Group's 57th Squadron was going into action.

As part of the Midway operation, the Japanese invaded the Aleutian Islands, off the Alaskan coast. Now, the American high command feared, the enemy would build bases there that could be a springboard to an invasion of Alaska or even the Pacific Northwest. The defenses in the far north needed immediate reinforcement, which triggered the 57th Squadron's migration north from San Diego

It was a breathless rush north. The need for help was so urgent that the men didn't even have time to pack their belongings. They grabbed overnight kits, stuffed them into their P-39's tiny baggage compartment, and took off for the long journey up the West Coast.

With the 57th that day were two pilots who'd already become close friends despite wildly diverse personalities. Wally Jordan was the squadron's bad-boy party animal who affected a look of casual indifference. He was older than the rest of his lieutenants, with a receding hairline and a Clark Gable mustache that gave him a rakish vibe. Respected as a talented, aggressive pilot, he was gruff, gritty, and devoid of sentimentality. When not partying, he was all business.

Black-haired Gerald Johnson, a five-foot-seven, handsome Oregonian from Eugene, was the squadron wild card. His flying showed great potential. He was a conscientious officer who'd made first lieutenant just six months after graduating from flight training. Yet he was erratic, emotional, and prone to deep depressions.

When he joined the 57th earlier in the year, Johnson was sort of an island, never quite fitting in with most of the other men. He'd joined the squadron straight from flight training with a pilot named Harry Huffman. At first, Harry was his only friend in the outfit. He'd been Harry's best man and hoped Harry could return the favor for him someday.

Among the married pilots, Johnson earned a reputation as a mooch. He'd show up at their off-post houses just in time for dinner and expect a last-second invite. The guys started hassling him about it. In response, Johnson told them to be at Harry's house early with their wives, and he would treat them to a night on the town. He arrived at the appointed time driving a rented limousine, decked out in a chauffeur's uniform. Obsequiously, he ushered them into the limo, holding doors and making deferential comments. Then he climbed behind the wheel and tore off, hell-bent for leather for the restaurant he'd chosen. His guests were flung around in back as Gerald drove over curbs, skidded along sidewalks, and even spun the car in a 180-degree turn that took them bouncing over the center meridian. As the wives screamed in terror and the pilots shouted to Johnson to slow it down, he punched the accelerator, puckish grin on his face, and blew into town like a four-wheeled banshee. He paid for the dinners and drinks, then set off for Harry's house in another wild ride. The night broke the ice, and Gerald was starting to become one of the guys at last.

Then Harry got hurt, and Johnson withdrew. In May 1942, a squadron newbie collided with Harry's fighter during a training mission over Baton Rouge, Louisiana. Harry bailed out but lost part of his leg in the accident. When the squadron moved to San Diego, Harry was left behind in a New Orleans hospital.

This Oregon kid was such a mix of contradictions. After he visited Harry in the hospital, the shock of seeing his best friend in such bad shape caused him to turn inward. It rattled his confidence. At times, Wally Jordan saw a fun-loving, easygoing side to him. Yet, often he came across as high-strung, emotional, equal parts brilliant in the air, and utterly unpredictable. He could be judgmental and morally righteous. He seemed committed to his girl back home, but he would often go out on the town with the other pilots with a date of his own. He had all the trappings of a young man still trying to find out who he really was.

Whatever he was on the ground, in the air Johnson and Wally Jordan shared a similar style. Both men never showed fear and seemed at their best when roaring along on the ragged edge. Johnson was especially tenacious, bordering on reckless at times. Right after the squadron received its P-39s, the young Oregonian was determined to get the highest aerial gunnery score in the outfit. Over Eglin, Florida, each pilot got a chance to shoot at a big fabric sleeve towed by an observation plane. Johnson made such an aggressive attack run that he couldn't pull out in time. He ended up colliding with the tow cable, severing the sleeve from the observation plane, and wrapping a chunk of cable around his propeller and nose. Somehow, he limped back to base and got it on the ground.

Gerald Johnson had the perfect build for an Airacobra jock. He was slender and wiry with muscles born from years of ice climbing, hiking, and hunting in the Cascade Mountains. He'd taken to the aircraft, deciding it was faster than the P-40 and quicker to accelerate. Speed was always his game. As a kid, he pedaled down steep hills on his bike, thrilling at the wind in his hair. As a teen, he raced through Eugene in his dad's car, ignoring speed limits in search of his next adrenaline rush. Now, as a young twenty-something, the P-39 provided that thrill.

Late that afternoon, Johnson's flight passed over the Siskiyou Mountains and reached the Willamette Valley. Below him, Oregon in springtime looked verdant and rich. The valley held some of the most fertile soil on the West Coast, and the May rainstorms transformed the landscape into a rich and colorful sight from above. Orchards dotted the landscape, and broad strawberry fields were just coming into bloom along the Willamette River. On the valley's flanks, tall firs covered the foothills and added to the lushness.

This was home. In this place, Gerald Johnson knew the greatest happiness of his young life. When the family settled in West Eugene in 1936, he made quick friends of the neighborhood kids. They called themselves the Pack Rats and spent their weekends in the Cascade Mountains, exploring old logging trails, finding abandoned cabins as they snowshoed, skied, hiked, or camped their way through the untamed wilderness. As the fighting in Europe drew American involvement, the Pack Rats joined up, one at a time. Now, only a couple were still left in civilian clothes, and they were getting a lot of flak from the community for that.

The flight reached Eugene. Tucked between two buttes, the town looked unremarkable from the air until eyes fell on the University of Oregon and its stately buildings neatly arranged around the city's first cemetery. McArthur Court, a massive gray slab of a building stood out as the tallest structure in this section of the valley. Johnson winged over it, thinking about the many basketball games he'd watched there when he was a Duck.

Then he saw the cemetery. Tall firs and headstones stippled a gentle hill rising across the street from Mac Court. He could see the Civil War memorial at the heart of the graveyard, a statue of a Union soldier standing silent vigil over comrades at peace. The memories came hard and sudden.[1]

The girl walked past that statue, red umbrella open against the light rain. Meticulously dressed yet unafraid to get her shoes and skirt dirty as she followed the muddy trail, an Oregon girl through and through, feminine with that resourceful twist of tomboy.

How many times had he waited for her there, eager to catch sight of her warm eyes and genuine smile?

---

1. Bill Runey, who went to school with Barbara and flew with Gerald in combat, was a pivotal source on both. He remained friends with Barbara until her death, and when he passed in 2015, I helped his sons lay him to rest only a few yards from the Civil War memorial in this cemetery.

That red umbrella had concealed their first kisses as love took hold. Johnson was a freshman in college, Barbara a senior at University High School.

He'd first seen her on a hiking trip up a butte north of town in 1939. The Pack Rats were out rock climbing when the girl with the red umbrella showed up with a group of her Uni High friends to eat lunch among the slabs of stone jutting from the butte. She captivated Gerald from the first moment he saw her. She didn't even notice him.

He asked around to find out who she was. His friends reported her name was Barbara Hall. Determined to meet her, he borrowed his dad's car and staked out her school, waiting each day for a week for her to come out the front door.

No luck. Day after day she never came through the school's front doors. Finally, he got out of the sedan and asked around about her. Somebody told him she always left school from the rear entrance and walked home through the cemetery.

Gerald dashed around the school, plunged into the cemetery grounds and saw her, umbrella in hand, back to him, walking up the slope by the statue of the Civil War soldier.

No matter that his week of waiting by the wrong door must have made him feel a fool. No matter that the venue in which Gerald had chosen to make his move was filled with headstones of pioneers and fallen soldiers. Daring as always, Gerald had called out to her. She stopped, regarded the handsome, black-eyed boy.

They chatted like long-lost old friends, the conversation never running lean. As they sparked and laughed, Gerald felt more at ease than any other time in his life. Then she looked at her watch, mentioned that if she didn't get home, her mother would be angry.[2]

---

2 In letters home to Barbara, Gerald referred several times to their meetings in the cemetery. The details come from many interviews with Barbara conducted 1991–2000.

She hurried off, but not before giving Gerald her number.

The cemetery became their meeting point between college and high school. They shared lunches, picnicking under the trees not far from the Spanish–American War memorial where they could enjoy a view of the U of O campus. They kissed and held each other there as well, hiding from the prying eyes who would report such scandalous behavior to Barbara's iron-willed mother, who clung to the Victorian values under which she'd been raised.

Johnson and his P-39s passed over the cemetery and University High, speeding westward. Ahead, the town's airport came into view. While at the U of O, Johnson learned to fly there, taking a Civilian Pilot Training program class taught by, of all things, the local geography professor.

He led his flight slightly north of the airport to stay out of the pattern, though no aircraft were in sight. Another moment, and his old neighborhood came into view. Stately, middle-class houses nestled under broad-limbed oaks, surrounded by big, fenced yards and wide sidewalks. He spotted his family's two-story, white Edwardian and searched for signs of his family.

Months before, he'd written his dad and mom that if he ever had the chance, he'd give them an epic aerobatics display. "I'll tear the chimney off!" he wrote. It had been a lighter time, his mood not yet thoroughly weighed down by the heft of the world's troubles.

He loved that rush he felt whenever he dared to do something others would never have the courage to do. It electrified him. Always had. In his first days in Eugene, he proved himself to the neighbor kids by racing down the buttes on his bike, going faster than everyone else—with his hands locked behind his head.

He never worried about crashing, never worried about getting hurt. He was confident, and such stunts appeared effortless to everyone who saw them.

Now, since Harry's injury, his head was filled with the memories of the pilots he watched die. Each one was supremely confident that if somebody were to buy it, it wouldn't be him.

Life failed to work that way. Immortality was a lie men believed to keep reality at bay so they could continue to climb into the cockpits of these dangerous machines.

We haven't even seen the enemy yet.

The flight passed over Gerald's old neighborhood. The roar of six Allison engine P-39s sent shock waves through the houses below. People piled through doors to get a look at what was overhead. He could see them, waving and laughing, kids running around excitedly. He hoped his brothers and sister were down there with his folks, looking up and seeing what he'd become.

A fighter pilot.

In 1942 America, there were few more glamorous things to civilians shielded from the dark horrors of such service.

They climbed out over the west-side outskirts of town. Down low, the Airacobra was the fastest thing in the Army Air Force's inventory, faster even than those brand-new P-38s they'd seen in California.

If not for his family, Gerald resolved to fly boldly for Barbara, too, believing it was the wild-eyed man who never showed fear that she'd fallen in love with. She knew only through a few words penned in letters home of the inner struggle he'd endured since Harry's injury, the frightful man he was on track to becoming, and he didn't want to let it get the better of him.

When Gerald saw her next, Barbara would expect the man who volunteered to go join a fighter squadron in the Philippines only three weeks out of flight school. He had been set to depart when Pearl Harbor was attacked, and the planned reinforcements stayed Stateside to defend the West Coast.

How could she love him if he let the threat of injury or death snuff out his spark? All those nights he dared Mrs. Hall's wrath by riding his bike to Barbara's house, climbing up onto her roof as stealthily as a cat just so Barbara could sit beside him in her window box seat and they could whisper together long past midnight. Kid-stuff courage, to be sure. Here, in the air, for the man of twenty-one, Harry's injury became the first real test of that courage and daring. What kind of pilot would emerge from that loss?

Johnson peeled off for a second pass and pushed the throttle forward. The Allison howled, and the crowd below resolved. Lower and lower, until he was practically scraping the trees that shaded his childhood street.

Lower still. Air speed touching three eighty, the 'Cobra rocketing along West Twelfth Street, straight for Gerald's neighbors. A few blocks away now, Johnson rolled on a knife edge, his fighter's wings vertical with the ground. A little less rudder, and he dipped *between* the trees, his wingtip skirting just above car roof level.

In a flash, he passed the crowd, pulling up and executing a victory roll. He flipped inverted, dove back down, and made a final pass before rejoining his formation flight.[3]

Nobody reported their hometown flyboy, and so Johnson escaped Dick Bong's fate.

Even if he'd known what had happened to Bong, it would have been unlikely to stop Gerald. "Safe" just did not exist in his DNA. Better to embrace the fire than live in fear of the death it might inflict.

Energized, Gerald pointed his Airacobra north, his flight gathered like geese on his wing. They sped for Portland, where the girl with the red umbrella waited for him on a hilltop overlooking the city.

---

3. Account of the buzzing comes from interviews with Art Johnson, Gerald's youngest brother.

6

The Price of a Moonlight Moment

June 14, 1942
Portland, Oregon

Johnson left his men in a downtown Portland hotel, cut free for the night to explore the local clubs. The Airacobras sat lined up at the Portland airport, waiting their return in the morning. For now, Johnson could think of only one thing: *Get to Barbara.*

He caught a cab out in front of their hotel, and as he climbed in he asked the driver to take him to the dorms at Oregon Health & Science University. The previous fall, Barbara had moved up to the nursing school on the hill overlooking downtown, living away from home for the first time in her life.

Now, a city away from her mother, Gerald would get to spend one evening with his love before continuing his flight into combat. He relished that thought of Barbara's mom a hundred miles south, cloistered away in the house Mr. Hall had built on Fairmount Avenue a few blocks from McArthur Court.

Ever since that first conversation in the cemetery, Johnson wanted only two things out of life: to be a husband and a father. As young and eager as he was, any talk of waiting fell on deaf ears. Barbara was his one; he didn't need to wait. The impatience of youth driven further by the desire to finally share a bed with the woman he loved merged with a sense of urgency as the Army Air Force tore him away from the Pacific Northwest.

What if he did not return from battle? Well, hopefully he would have left Barbara with a son or daughter who would be the part of him to survive his contact with the enemy.

The thought of that set his mind at ease. A child would ensure his footsteps through life would not be erased. He'd have a legacy. He'd have his love.

His parents never stood in his way of this dream, but Mrs. Hall sabotaged things every chance she got. She considered Gerald "too fun" to be a legitimate husband candidate for her girl. She took shots at him whenever she could and injected herself into the relationship more than once.

Gerald looked out the cab's window as they worked their way through downtown. He and Barbara had spent part of the previous fall and winter exploring the city together, eating dinner at Jantzen Beach, on a little island in the Columbia River, or going to the Oaks Park carnival, where Gerald's marksmanship meant Barbara returned to her dorm room with an armload of stuffed animals.

The 57th had been in Washington through that fall and winter. When it moved to Baton Rouge, the weekend leaves together in the Rose City ended, and their relationship was sustained by long, passionate letters. Long-distance love was an anguish to both of them, but at least with Barbara in Portland, her mother could not throw a wrench in things.

Johnson ground his teeth as he thought about what Mrs. Hall had done the previous year when Gerald was just starting flight school in California. He was living in an abandoned elementary school in the middle of the desert east of Los Angeles, going through primary training at the Cal Aero Academy. Lonely, depressed, surrounded by wild-haired young men, he felt more alone than ever. In a deep blue mood, he wrote home to Barbara, reminiscing about a kiss they'd shared by moonlight early in their relationship.

It was a kiss that had staggered them both. That moment of pure connection, where the energy flowed between them in such a way that it unlocked something deep within them that neither had ever felt before. Being young under a full moon in their quiet little Oregon town, that kiss felt like forever.

Mrs. Hall intercepted the letter. When she read Gerald's gentle and romantic words describing the kiss, she exploded in rage. She ambushed Barbara as she came home from school, waving the letter and yelling at her for allowing a boy to kiss her—especially *that* boy who knew how to have too much fun.

"Now that you've been kissed, I'm *done* with you!" she screamed. Broken and now guilt-racked, Barbara ran upstairs and collapsed on the window seat in her room, wanting only to see Gerald's face appear over the eaves.

Mrs. Hall summarily banned any further communication between the star-crossed lovers. She failed to realize that forbidden fruit is much more sweet, and Gerald was not going to let his would-be mother-in-law wreck his first experience with love.

He organized an underground network to Barbara. His folks, sympathetic to his cause, secretly allowed Gerald's younger brother Art to pass letters between them. This spy ring lasted for many weeks, until finally, Gerald's imposing father, H. V., decided to go to bat for his son. He went over to the house on Fairmount for a frank discussion with the Halls. The kids were in love, ease up, and let them be.

Mrs. Hall relented, but resentment toward Gerald and the Johnson family simmered on through the rest of Gerald's months in training. She not so quietly hoped the separation and distance would torpedo the romance.

The cab started the climb up Marquam Hill. The medical buildings came into sight, tucked between groves of trees. It was a beautiful campus. Had Gerald finished up at the U of O in 1942 as he originally planned, he would have come up here for dental school.

Mrs. Hall intervened one further time. Gerald planned to propose on his way to Baton Rouge when the squadron transferred down from Washington earlier in the year. She saw that coming and headed it off quite ruthlessly. When Gerald left Oregon behind the wheel of his '39 Plymouth, her meddling left him furious and bitter. For a while, he wondered if it was worth the effort to continue the romance when there were so many women drawn to aviators like himself.

He couldn't hold out long, and soon he was back to filling pages for Barbara, expressing his love for her. Day after day, he poured his heart out to her, and she to him. Through those words, they got to know each other on an entirely new level. Instead of deep-sixing the romance, the distance actually proved to each of the lovers how much they needed to be together.

The cab lurched to a stop; Johnson paid the driver and flung himself out of the rig, fairly running for Barbara's dorm. He waited in the lobby until she was called and came down from her room—no boys were allowed upstairs—and he swept her into his arms, smelling her fresh dark hair as the hug lingered and grew intimate.

He proposed on the spot. Barbara knew it was coming, and she accepted without hesitation. They made swift plans for a morning wedding, then called their families. H. V. and Gerald's mom, Hazel, were excited and congratulated them. Then they told their son they'd been at a picnic when he flew over the neighborhood. When they got home, everyone on the block descended on their house to tell stories of Gerald's aerobatics display. Art especially was crestfallen to have missed it.

Hopefully, there'd be other opportunities. Meanwhile, the Johnsons fully engaged in the wild wedding planning.

Then Barbara called her folks. There were no congratulations, just rage and tears. Mrs. Hall announced she was leaving at once for Portland, and Barbara was not to do anything until she arrived.

She got to the campus in two and a half hours, where she hustled Barbara into her dorm room for a private conversation. She forbade her daughter to marry Gerald, demanding that at the very least, she wait until she had finished nursing school.

This may have made sense in normal times. But this was anything but normal. Both Gerald's and Barbara's emotions were pegged at a fever pitch by the war and Gerald's impending departure to it. They'd seen countless Hollywood good-byes and now they had their own. Wedding vows first. A dramatic farewell kiss. And the hero would vanish into the sunset to an unknown fate. It would be perfect.

Mrs. Hall saw the gravity and the consequence. She'd lived through the Great War and knew the depth of loss that could come with such good-byes. Young, eager souls in love would never grasp it. Until it happened to them. To her, they were still kids, playing at life but not understanding the stakes.

Barbara had always been an obedient daughter. She lived in a strict household, where she was raised to respect her elders and God. Her parents' will would always be respected; she did not know how to break free of it. Perhaps that's why Mrs. Hall saw Gerald as such a threat. He was not a man inhibited by convention. If there were rules he didn't like, he found ways around them. That bit of rebel in him always alarmed Mrs. Hall. Rebels have a way of spreading rebellion, after all. Especially to those whom they loved.

The next morning, on what Gerald had hoped would be his wedding day, the couple found themselves instead in the lobby of Barbara's dorm. Tearfully, she described the situation, and Gerald was frustrated by Mrs. Hall's meddling once again.

I could die in Alaska. Without a family of my own, no legacy at all. Without ever knowing Barbara.

They held each other, and Barbara sobbed. At length, she pulled away for a moment. They sat side by side, legs and shoulders touching, as Barbara produced a velvet box. She handed it to Gerald.

Inside was an elegant, ruby ring that once belonged to Barbara's grandmother.

"Take it with you. Know that when the time is right, I will marry you."

It didn't fit his fingers, so Gerald pulled his dog tags off and attached the ring to the chain. It slipped down between the thin metal plates inscribed with his name, serial number, and blood type. When Gerald put them back around his neck, the ring hung right next to his heart.

He promised to never take it off. They kissed, a final, impassioned embrace fueled by the failure of their plans and the uncertain future that awaited them. Then, Gerald was gone.

Barbara, heartsick, climbed the stairs back to her dorm room, where her mother waited. She entered, sat down on her bed, and perhaps for the first time in her life, she found her voice.

"I did what you wanted, Mother. But if Gerald dies before I can marry him, I will never forgive you."

The words sucked the joy out of Mrs. Hall's victory. She realized that maybe this time she might have pushed too hard, and it had cost her some of the power she possessed over her daughter.

A few hours later, as Barbara lay cried out on her bed, her mother gone at last, she heard the distant growl of an Allison engine. She perked up, tilting one ear toward the glass door that opened onto a narrow porch. She and the other nursing students used the porch railings to dry their laundry, and at the moment she had a bath towel draped over hers.

The engine sound grew louder. She sat up, watery blue eyes wide. She went to the door and peered through. An Airacobra was over downtown, following the Columbia River as if it had just taken off from the airport to the east. A moment later, it turned for Marquam Hill.

It was Gerald. It had to be. She watched him bore straight for her building, her anticipation building as the engine screamed closer. Faster and faster, the P-39 resolving until she could see a figure in the cockpit and could almost imagine that puckish grin she loved so much.

At the last second, Gerald flipped the Airacobra on a knife edge barreling toward the building at a football field and a half per second. He flew *between* Barbara's dorm and the building next door. The space was so narrow that in later years, those who saw Gerald's feat had trouble convincing others they'd actually witnessed it.

Barbara watched her fiancé disappear to the east, standing on her porch, the towel fluttering beside her in the June breeze, dreading what the future held for them both.

7

Under an Arctic Rainbow

0300 Hours, September 14, 1942
Adak Island, Aleutians

Gerald Johnson lay in his snivel gear bathed in sweat despite the howling arctic wind lashing his tent. His head throbbed. He felt weak from nausea.

He wasn't sick. He was about to go into battle.

He was captive to his mind that night, unable to stop imagining death scenarios. Around him, his tentmates Maj. Sandy McCorkle and Maj. Wilbur Miller slept soundly. He alternated between hating that and envying their cool.

Our planes are worn out. They've not been properly maintained.

Between the Japanese and Fireplace—the code name for Adak Island—was the unforgiving Bering Sea. Huge swells, forty-degree water, and minimal cold-weather survival gear meant almost certain death if his engine failed.

The water and weather are more an enemy than the Japanese.

He wiped sweat off his brow and listened to the gale outside. At first, he thought McCorkle and Miller had put him in their tent to keep him on a short leash. Then he found out that McCorkle discovered he'd been an Eagle Scout and figured his camping skills would serve them well on this barren hillside above the airfield. Without trees, running water, latrines, or even wood floors in their tents, this was about equal to the most primitive living Johnson did when winter camping in Oregon's Cascade Mountains. The tent's entrance was a couple of flaps held together with bow-tied straps. The wind whistled through the seams and chilled the interior so thoroughly that a few days before, Johnson gathered up a bunch of scrap wood foraged from around the base and planned to replace the flaps with a doorframe.

He rolled on his side and checked his watch. Briefing in an hour. No point in sleeping now. For days, he set his thoughts down in his diary as they waited for the weather to clear so they could strike Kiska Island. How would he react under fire? Would he measure up? Who would be lost? He pinballed from tin bravado ("By golly, it'll be worth a few of us to drive those Japanese from Kiska after what they did to our men and women on Bataan and the East Indies"!) to a bleak assessment of their equipment and the threat of death from exposure while bobbing around in the Bering Sea. At times, he trended toward resignation.

If I die, I've lived a good life.

He thought of his father, H. V. Johnson, the self-made man who'd studied law by candlelight after twelve-hour shifts in a tire factory. If he started to fall asleep, his wife threw cold water on his face. There had been no room for softness in his dad's life. He was rawhide tough, a man who once stopped a rampaging bull chasing his daughter by punching it in the face. He worked twenty-hour days to establish his law practice in Eugene, and in only a few years was considered one of the finest legal minds in the state.

Gerald admired his father tremendously and always sought to make him proud. Part of him, a part he never quite could face, lived in his father's shadow. Subconsciously, he wanted to prove he was even better than his old man.

Well, combat would sort out whether he had any real guts or not. So far, given how badly he wanted to throw up, Gerald was not optimistic. His fever spiked. He hunkered down in his snivel gear, feeling miserable and unsure.

At length, McCorkle and Miller stirred. They crawled out of their cots and hurriedly put on their flight gear and boots. Miller's trademark was a corncob pipe. It sat on a homemade wooden table that functioned as the tent's writing desk. He grabbed it, then said to Gerald, "Hey, Johnson, time to get moving."

Twenty minutes and a freezing-cold jeep ride later, the three men linked up with the rest of the pilots scheduled to fly that day. The briefing began.

The Japanese had landed on Kiska only three months before, but they quickly turned the place into a fortress. Heavy naval guns pulled from decommissioned battleships now guarded the island's main harbor, where transports and a flotilla of submarines had been spotted by air recon flights. Antiaircraft batteries ringed the harbor and the main camp area. On a hill on the island's west side, the Japanese erected one of their first production radar systems. They would be able to detect any inbound raid—unless it came at them from right on the whitecaps.

Four-engine B-24 Liberator heavy bombers composed the heart of the day's strike force. A squadron of P-38 Lightnings would provide escort, as the Japanese were known to have Zero fighters mounted on floats stationed in the harbor. Even with pontoons for water landings, these Zeroes—called Rufes—would be more maneuverable than any American fighter. Plus they carried two cannon in their wings and two machine guns in the nose—heavy firepower that could knock down an Airacobra or even a B-24 with ease.

The P-39s would be the tip of this spear. McCorkle would lead eight of the squadron on the wave tops a few minutes ahead of the main formation. He explained their role: get over Kiska and shoot up the AA batteries, knock down any Rufes trying to get off the water in the harbor, and generally cause as much surprised chaos as possible. As they strafed their way over the island, the B-24s would release their bombs on targets around the harbor while four other P-39s and a squadron of P-38s protected the heavies from those float Zeroes.

The weather was decent. The mission was a go.

The men headed out to their P-39s. When the engineers drained the lagoon and turned it into an airfield, they dropped interlocking metal planks called Marston matting down atop the sandy bottom. The matting made for a Lego-set-like prefab runway that almost anyone with vehicles and a couple of crowbars could assemble. The strip of metal they linked together was bumpy but serviceable. Except after a rainstorm. The lagoon filled with water again after every squall. At the moment a good ten inches of water surged around atop the matting.

A truck carrying the pilots stopped beside each P-39. The assigned flier dropped out the back, waded over to his waiting mount, and climbed onto the wing, boots soaked. When Gerald's turn came, he slung his parachute and splashed into the floodwaters, bound for his plane, *Scrap Iron*.

He climbed onto the wing and strapped his parachute on, looking out over the field. Adak was the most lifeless place he'd ever seen: hills devoid of trees, yellowed grass blown almost flat from the gusts of wind that howled in from the nearby shore. Overhead, a few clouds passed by, but blue skies dominated. That could change in mere minutes. It became a running joke on the island. *Don't like the weather? Count to ten.*

That's what made it so dangerous. One moment, conditions would be fine. The next, a storm would suddenly rage in from the west, and unsuspecting aircrew would be caught in a nightmare of turbulence, hail, and horizontal rain whipped by hurricane-force winds. Many an aircraft took off under an Arctic sun, only to vanish in those sudden dark squalls.

Johnson opened the car door, a mechanic on the wing with him to help him get set. Just before he slipped inside the cockpit, he noticed a rainbow stretching across the end of the runway. Its brilliant colors seemed utterly out of place in this desolate and grim environment.

He settled into the seat and his mechanic strapped him in and closed the car door. He heard it latch with a lonely and distinct *click*.

He stayed focused and out of his head, running through the pre-flight checklist with meticulous precision.

Good to go.

He fired up the bird. The three propeller blades began to turn as the engine sputtered to life. Along the flight line, the other '39s joined him. Soon, a dozen Allisons filled the lagoon with the buttery sound of their power.

Beside him in the next 'Cobra over, McCorkle signaled Gerald. Time to go. Brakes released, he followed his group commander out to the runway. A moment later, they pushed their throttles forward and sped across the flooded strip, each '39 fanning twin rooster tails of water up over their wings until onlookers could only see the noses of each craft. They lumbered through it, their canopies drenched, visibility reduced to almost nothing as they gained speed and hurtled toward the end of the lagoon. Seemingly at the last minute, their noses lifted and they soared skyward, under that Aleutian rainbow.[1]

It took under an hour to get to Kiska. McCorkle kept the squadron right on the waves to sneak in under the Japanese radar coverage. Here is where Johnson shined. He loved this kind of flying, and McCorkle had seen enough of it out of the Oregonian to recognize the kid possessed remarkable skills. That was one of the reasons he

---

1. John Huston's wartime documentary, *Report from the Aleutians*, captured this peculiar aspect of Adak in color. The scenes are harrowing to watch.

wanted Johnson on his wing. The other was to keep an eye on him and make sure he didn't do something crazy again.

Johnson stayed tacked on his leader's wing, singularly focused. Gone were the headache and nausea. The fear drained, crushed by adrenaline and the sheer excitement of finally going into the fight. All the training he'd done since joining the Army Air Force in March 1941 prepared him for this moment.

In the distance, a rocky chunk of land swelled on the horizon. Little Kiska. A flash of light winked from a hillside just off the surf line. A split second later, a flaming red streak arrowed into the water ahead of them, kicking up a plume of water. Gerald regarded this for a moment, not registering what he'd just seen. Then another wink, another red dash, and another splash in the water ahead. With a shock, Gerald realized this was incoming fire from an antiaircraft gun.

They were firing short. A sudden flurry of red streaks tore up the water in front of them, making a pattern on the surface. The Airacobras charged in, all guns blazing. The Americans hit the coast, throttles wide as their bullets swept across the antiaircraft gun and tore the crew to pieces.

McCorkle bounced up to a hundred feet to clear the first low-lying hills. Johnson followed, dropping his nose and hugging the backside slope as they searched for targets. Ahead stood a line of tents arranged on another hill. McCorkle and Gerald opened fire, their bullets shredding the tents. Then they were over and past, leaving their tattered remains to flap in the Arctic wind.

A moment later, the eight Airacobras broke out over the west side of Little Kiska and dove for the main harbor.

Dead ahead, two submarines rode at anchor. Gerald saw McCorkle bank toward the larger of the two and line up for a pass. McCorkle triggered his 37mm cannon. A second later, Johnson joined in as well. They flayed the subs with cannon and machine gun fire, then made for North Head, the spit of land that created Kiska Harbor.

Gerald shot up some shacks and buildings along the water's edge, then zoomed over another row of hills just in time to see the B-24s approaching thousands of feet overhead. Farther north, a bunch of dots swarmed around under a layer of clouds. Gerald angled toward them.

A pair of P-38s streaked down after a Japanese float Zero. The enemy pilot juked to avoid their attack. A split second later, the two American fighters collided in a fiery explosion. Pieces rained down as the wings and booms twisted crazily toward the water off North Head.

A pair of P-39s finished off the Rufe, and got a second one too. Gerald was still too far out to join the fight when it suddenly ended, score tied.

Johnson reversed course to get back over the harbor. He reached North Head again, climbed up into the hills just in time to see a P-39 dive out of a cloud, shooting at something in the harbor on the other side of the next ridgeline.

He passed another set of hills, ducking down low into the draw between them, the Airacobra bare feet over the tundra grass.

A tent lay dead ahead on a flat stretch of ground at the bottom of the draw. Suddenly, a group of Japanese poured out of it. They ran out into the open without any cover in sight. Johnson didn't hesitate. His finger touched the triggers on his control stick. The cannon *whoomp*ed as his machine guns chattered. His bullets ripped into the grass. A 37mm shell exploded. He fed some rudder into the P-39, and the storm of lead and shells walked right through the group of running men.

One took a hit that blew him off his feet. Another ran desperately away from a stream of .50-caliber bullets that kicked up dirt behind him, then finally caught him and ripped his body apart. This was not like the movies where the bad guys died sanitarily. The destructive power of the M2 Browning machine gun was on full display. He later wrote in his diary that his weapons tore the man in half.

In the moment, he didn't dwell. He kept shooting, watching as more men died under the power of his guns. An instant later, his fighter thundered over the shattered men. Overhead, the B-24s released their bombs. Splashes erupted around several transports in the anchorage, while incendiaries exploded inside the Japanese camp at the west edge of the harbor. Boiling clouds of fire mushroomed up over the hills as Johnson banked left over North Head and sped out to sea. He was alone now, McCorkle nowhere in sight.

The squadron met up at the rendezvous point and returned to Adak. The landing proved to be the scariest moment of the mission, as the standing water on the runway threw so much spray over them that they couldn't see out their windscreens. The 'Cobra pilots worked the brakes and prayed they were running straight and true until they slowed down enough that the fans of water spraying over their birds diminished.

Everyone made it. The P-38 squadron would have a sobering night with two empty chairs at dinner. The 42nd Fighter Squadron would be celebrating.

They were veterans now.

8

The Hero's Road

September 14, 1942
Adak Island, Aleutians

At the flight line, the 'Cobra pilots gathered, excitedly relating their own first combat moments. They piled into a truck, still chattering, high on adrenaline and success. At the squadron's operations tent, they sat down and had an informal debrief. Major Miller led it, corncob pipe clamped between his teeth, on his head a ridiculously unmilitary felt fedora with his major's oak leaves pinned on the front.

The squadron shot down two Japanese planes—Gene Arth and Winton Matthews drew first aerial blood for the 54th Fighter Group. The rest of the pilots shot up antiaircraft guns, killed enemy personnel, and strafed three submarines, though nobody knew what kind of damage their bullets and high-explosive shells inflicted on their tough pressure hulls. High command's intel types estimate that the incendiary bombing of the Japanese camp killed five hundred men.

After the briefing, McCorkle took Johnson aside.

"Good job today, Jerry."

"Thank you, sir."

"Remember something, though..."

"Sir?"

"I need you on my wing at all times. Never, ever leave your wing-man position again."

"I lost you in the hills, sir."

McCorkle stared at the young Oregonian. Gerald looked back with his wide, dark eyes, wondering if he'd get in trouble again.

McCorkle didn't want to be too hard on him. He let the moment linger, Gerald standing stock-still, waiting wide-eyed for what McCorkle would do.

Finally, the colonel said, "Next time that happens, you link up with the nearest friendly fighter. Don't go wandering off alone. Understood?"

"Yes, sir."[1]

They hiked back to their tent, Major Miller joining them. The wind picked up, and the temperature dropped. Even in their cold-weather gear, they felt the chill.

As they reached their tent, Johnson suddenly stopped in his tracks. His pile of boards gathered beside the entrance flap was gone.

Perhaps the theft triggered a post-combat parasympathetic back-lash. Perhaps it just made him feel indignant that some rear-area guy had poached his stash while he was off risking his life. Either way, McCorkle saw Johnson's near-euphoric mood evaporate.

He stepped inside his tent, dropped his gear by his cot, and unhol-stered his M1911 Colt .45.

Miller and McCorkle exchanged glances.

What's this kid doing now?

Johnson racked the slide and chambered a round. He checked the safety and stuck it back in his holster. Then he headed for the tent flap.

"Jerry? Where you going?" McCorkle asked.

---

1. The description of Gerald's relationship with McCorkle comes from interviews with General McCorkle and Gerald's diary and letters home from Adak.

"To get my boards back."

Before either field-grade could reply, the young Oregonian disappeared through the entrance. They heard his boots crunching off up the hillside.

"Should we go after him?" Miller asked.

"No. Let's see what he does."

"You don't think he'd kill anyone?"

"No. That was for show. The kid has a flair for drama."

A few hours later, they heard the boot crunching again, followed by the clattering of wood being dropped to the grass.

Johnson slipped into the tent, his face a mask.

Miller was sitting on his cot, writing to his wife and kids. McCorkle was doing paperwork on an ammunition crate turned into a makeshift desk. All of the squadron's clerks were still back in Louisiana, so the squadron largely ignored admin stuff. But for the group commander, there'd always be some of that crap to wade through.

Both officers watched Johnson walk over to his cot, unstrap his holster, and hang it nearby. The Oregonian paused and saw his chain of command regarding him curiously.

"Got my boards back," Gerald reported.

Miller raised an eyebrow. McCorkle stifled a chuckle. Gerald did not elaborate.

Instead, he shucked off his boots, crawled into his snivel gear, and fell into the deepest sleep he'd had in weeks.

The next morning, Miller and McCorkle pulled Gerald aside and made him the acting squadron operations officer, known as the S3. In the Army Air Force's hierarchy, the ops officer ranked third in any squadron. It was a slot given to up-and-coming leaders who would soon make executive officer.

It was a big step for Johnson, but McCorkle felt as long as he continued to mentor and develop him, the kid's rough edges could be smoothed over. Most of all, he needed Johnson to recognize that the air war was never a one-man show. Teamwork kept men alive. Though they trained in flights of six back in Louisiana, the 42nd now flew with four-plane flights. Each flight consisted of a leader, his wingman, the element lead, and his wingman. In combat, the flight may break down or get spread all over the sky, but the watchword McCorkle and Miller tried to instill in every pilot was this: Never, ever leave your wingman. Fight as a pair, you survive. A lone Airacobra is a target waiting to get jumped by a gang of Zeroes.

They tried to hit Kiska again on the twenty-second, hoping to suppress the Japanese there and stifle any further invasions up the Aleutians ladder. If the Adak-based planes could prevent the Japanese from building airfields, or reinforcing the area, they could eventually turn the tables on the Japanese and drive them out of the North Pacific altogether. That September was the shaky, small-time start to that endeavor.

The weather conspired to weaken the aerial counteroffensive. Gerald's squadron made it seventy miles out of Adak before encountering storm clouds just off the whitecaps. They'd already been running at three hundred feet through banks of fog. The sight of this williwaw, as such squalls were called, convinced McCorkle to scrub the mission. The entire raid returned to Adak, dispirited and shaken by the ferocity of the elements.

The break gave Gerald time to build the doorframe. He worked away on it while Major Miller sat on his cot, entertaining everyone with his harmonica. Johnson, Miller, McCorkle, and three other pilots all shared a GP large tent. It made for lots of fart jokes and snoring, as well as lots of bonding, all carried along by the melodies Major Miller fumbled through on his mouth harp.

On the twenty-fifth, the weather cleared just enough to give the Americans a fifteen-hundred-foot ceiling all the way to Kiska. That'd be enough for another below-the-radar attack, so the squadron gathered in Gerald's tent to hear Major Miller detail the mission.

Miller kept these meetings casual. He sat at the end of his cot, wearing his felt fedora and holding a small notebook that he referred to as he talked. The men gathered around their CO, drinking coffee from tin mess cups, their boots flecked with mud.

The strike would launch at 0800. Once again, high command picked the 42nd to be the tip of the spear. Down on the deck, the 'Cobras were to hit Kiska from the southwest this time, instead of the east as on the fourteenth. The Japanese radar system atop a hill just northwest of the main encampment around the harbor would be the priority target. After that, strafe anything that moved.

A squadron of B-24s would be the main effort for the day, escorted by the Aleutian Tigers—Maj. Jack Chennault's P-40 Warhawk squadron. He was the son of the legendary Gen. Claire Chennault, who commanded the famous American Volunteer Group (the Flying Tigers).

Miller paused, then added, "The Canadians are going out with us on this one. Number 111 Squadron's P-40s will be with the bombers."

He looked down at his notebook and read off the names of the pilots assigned for the day's mission. Johnson would be on McCorkle's wing again.

The meeting ended, and most of the pilots hurried off to grab some chow before heading to the flight line. Gerald sat down back at his cot and penned a few words into his diary.

Well, it's 4:30 a.m. Barbie and the sky is fairly clear. Time to go… *wish me luck. If anything happens, I love you even into eternity.*

—x—x—x—xx^2

---

2. Gerald kept a remarkably detailed diary of his time in the Aleutians. He'd been a prolific journal writer ever since leaving Eugene for the Air Corps in 1941. If he kept a diary in New Guinea, it did not survive.

*   *   *

If he died, only Barbara would get that final cryptic remark. Like most lovers, Gerald and Barbara developed their own internal language. From their many writings emerged a code for what they wanted their future to hold. Three kids together someday, plus two more. Twins. They'd have their own basketball team. If the weather and the Japanese on Kiska didn't kill him first.

A few hours later, the 42nd Fighter Squadron followed Colonel McCorkle under the scud layer, once again their props kicking up spray behind them as they raced along the wave tops. They looped around their bat-shaped island target and made landfall from a totally unexpected quarter. The Japanese had no defenses ready.

The Airacobras swarmed over the hills, blasted down canyons, and hammered the surprised Japanese as they fled their tents for ack-ack emplacements or slit trenches. McCorkle and Johnson stayed together, hugging the ground as they sped for the radar site. As they crossed a series of hills, Gerald spotted a Japanese soldier sprinting to an unmanned gun position. He swung his nose toward the man and hit him in full stride with a stream of bullets that ripped him apart. The scene of such gory devastation would stay with him, hardening him to the realities of combat nothing back home prepared him for. This wasn't like hunting elk in the Cascades. It wasn't like Hollywood. It was visceral, terrible, and scarring. He pulled the trigger again. These men he killed were invaders. After all the stories of Japanese savagery in China and the Pacific, he saw them as barbarians. And behind his tail, friends and family lay not too far over the horizon.

He would do anything to protect them.

The P-39s crested another rise. The radar site loomed on a hill before them. McCorkle went in first, raking the hut and the aerials arrayed around it with cannon and machine gun fire. A split second later, Gerald took his turn. He walked his rudder pedals, swinging the nose from side to side to ensure maximum carnage. The aerials collapsed in a tangle of wires and poles. They left the hut shattered and smoking.

Each flight went after different targets, and then the elements broke off to go after others. Now, it was just McCorkle in plane number thirty and Johnson in *Scrap Iron*. The other 'Cobras flicked into sight, then dipped under the hills around them as they worked over antiaircraft guns, huts, and tents while making their way toward the harbor.

McCorkle bolted for Reynard Cove, a small inlet north of the harbor that intelligence thought was being used as a hideout for seaplanes. They ducked around ridges and dove down between hills, shooting up whatever they spotted in front of their long noses.

When Gerald reached the cove, McCorkle was nowhere in sight. Somehow, he'd lost his leader again. He made a quick survey of the area, saw no targets, and wondered what to do next.

Find somebody to join.

Gerald banked right and started for the sea, searching all around him for a friendly P-39. Nothing. Just below the clouds, the B-24s were passing the cove, bound for the harbor, but those were the only planes in sight.

Then he spotted a P-39 a thousand feet above and out over the Bering Sea. He angled toward it and soon recognized the fighter as McCorkle's. A sense of relief flooded through him. Maybe he wouldn't get chewed out for losing him again after all. He began a banking climb to get back on his leader's wing.

A float Zero dropped out of the cloud cover.

The Japanese pilot timed it perfectly. He slid right behind McCorkle. Among the P-39's many flaws, poor visibility to the rear was one of the most serious ones in combat.

McCorkle couldn't see the Japanese fighter as it hurtled toward his undefended tail.

Had Gerald been on his wing, this never could have happened. The pair would have been watching each other's blind spots and seen the enemy plane. Without Johnson up there in position, Sandy McCorkle was in a tight spot.

Puffs of black smoke raked back from the Rufe's wings. Johnson scanned the scene, scrambling for the controls. He realized what that meant: the Japanese pilot was firing his 20mm cannon at his group commander.

McCorkle continued his orbiting turn, unaware of the drama playing out behind him.

Hail Mary time.

Gerald pulled the control stick hard toward his stomach. The P-39 suddenly zoom-climbed straight for the Japanese fighter. He gained a fleeting shot as it sped toward him, the pilot focused on McCorkle. Johnson triggered his machine guns. His tracers speared out of the wings and nose and created a web of bullets that the Rufe flew right through. The Japanese fighter sped over Gerald's canopy, shedding pieces of metal as it passed. Johnson steepened his climb, went over the top, and flipped inverted, trying to keep the enemy fighter in sight.

The Rufe rolled hard right and broke downward for the water. It was a standard tactic the Rufe pilots used against P-39s and P-40s. Somehow, Japanese intelligence learned that American fighters turned tighter to the left than right, due to the direction their propellers spun and the torque that generated.

Gerald saw the fighter diving away while his P-39 remained upside down in a shallow dive speeding away from the fleeing Rufe. He pulled through into a split S—basically, the last half of a loop—but by the time he finished it, the Rufe was nowhere to be seen.

Back at Kiska, Johnson landed right after McCorkle, both planes kicking up massive plumes of water as they rolled along the flooded runway. At the flight line, Gerald cut his switches. The engine died and the props slowly spun to a halt. His crew chief climbed onto the wing and helped him out of the hobbit-sized cockpit.

McCorkle was waiting for him, looking ready to give him hell for leaving formation again.

All was forgiven when the Oregonian told him about the Rufe. Not long after the attack, word came from the B-24 squadron at Cold Bay that they'd seen Gerald's Rufe go straight into the Bering Sea off Reynard Cove.[3]

The 54th celebrated that day. Three kills in two missions without loss. Miller's boys were earning a reputation in the 11th Fighter Command.

A journalist who before the war worked out of the Seattle Associated Press office, happened to be at Adak that day to cover the Kiska raids as a combat correspondent. He interviewed Gerald and some of the other pilots from the 42nd, as well as the Aleutian Tigers, listening as they described shooting up ground targets and strafing another submarine. The skipper of the Canadian P-40 outfit even scored a kill, flaming a Rufe as it tried to intercept the B-24s. In the grand scheme of things, it wasn't much of a raid. But in 1942,

---

3. In interviews with General McCorkle in 1996, he did not recall any of this. He said categorically that Gerald did not shoot down any aircraft during his missions over Kiska. However, Gerald's diary details these first air battles thoroughly, and the contemporary press reports match his personal account closely. He later described and claimed another Japanese floatplane on his final mission over Kiska that had been making passes at a B-24. The squadron and group records are exceptionally thin for this period; there are no Individual Combat Reports or Encounter Reports and no surviving requests for confirmation of victories from the 42nd, as most of the ground echelon was still back in Baton Rouge and the daily duties of running the unit in combat took precedence over paperwork. There are a few mission summaries in the XI Fighter Command documents at NARA, College Park, but nothing that concretely confirms Gerald's two claims. Gerald always assumed he'd been given credit for those two aircraft and added them to his P-38's kill board later in 1943–45.

a fight like this on America's doorstep was front-page news. Worden retreated to his hut and banged away on his portable typewriter.

Four days later, Gerald's kill was national news as Worden's story of the Kiska raid ran in papers across the country, though the initial article credited Johnson with shooting the Rufe off Major Miller's tail. That was corrected in subsequent versions of the story that ran at the end of the month in other papers.

Back in Eugene, on the morning of September 29, Barbara's dad retrieved the morning paper. He went back into the house he had built on a hill overlooking the University of Oregon just before the Depression, and settled down at the breakfast table to read the latest news as Mrs. Hall finished up cooking.

The headline stared out at him. "Eugene Army Lieutenant Bags Jap Fighter Plane in Action Over Kiska Island."

Below it was a portrait photo of his daughter's bad-boy fiancé. He scanned the article. It credited Gerald with scoring one of the first air-to-air kills of the war by one of Eugene's own sons. By now, the news would be all over town. The Johnson boy was taking it to the Japanese as one of the city's first fighting heroes of World War II.

He looked over his shoulder. "Dear, you may want to take a look at this."

9

The Man Without a Place

Friday night, October 2, 1942
The Polar Bar, Nome, Alaska

Sprawled across Alaska's coastal tundra flanking the Bering Sea, 1,051 miles northeast of Kiska, lay the remnants of a boomtown that once was home to Wyatt Earp and his wife Josephine. In its fiery gold-fueled heyday, Nome, Alaska, included seventy-five bars and three churches. It was a place men endured in hopes of striking it rich, but few got off the boat and saw its shanties, tents, and muddy streets as a permanent home. Do what Wyatt Earp did. That was the mantra. Get in fast, make a killing, then bug out to someplace warm and civilized.

The boom turned bust as fast as it started. Where once almost fifty thousand people crowded into Nome, only a tenth of that population remained in 1942. By then, the town was mostly made up of the castaways and dreamers, the hard-luck kind who drank their lives away in the Front Street bars so wild and dangerous that the town earned the nickname Boneyard of the Bering Sea. Every spring, the remaining locals would find a halo of defrosting corpses splayed across the tundra—drunks who wandered outside of town after their red-light benders, only to freeze to death on the tundra. There were so many missing persons in Nome that for years the FBI was convinced a serial killer was responsible. In the end it turned out that the only killer terrorizing the town was cheap booze.

Aside from the locals, the town hummed with airmen. In 1941, the Army Air Force decided Nome would be the last outpost of Alaska's air defenses. The local airport had been expanded, renamed Marks Army Airfield, and became home to a squadron of Canadian Bristol Bolingbroke bombers. After the Japanese invaded the Aleutians, the P-39s of the 56th Fighter Squadron, 54th Fighter Group, arrived to defend Nome from Japanese air attack. The new squadrons lived on the end of a perilous supply line that stretched all the way back to Washington State. This meant they were perpetually short of everything.

In Seattle, the Western Defense Command discovered that sending military supplies to Alaska—and Nome in particular—was anything but an easy task. The ships plying those routes north were filled with booze and cigarettes, and the captains claimed they had no space for military necessities, so the Navy tried to make it illegal to ship hooch to Alaska, which only drove the trade underground, where it continued to thrive.

Down Front Street in the town center sat one of the establishments that specialized in the contraband: the Polar Bar. Established in the depths of the Depression, just after Prohibition ended, the Polar Bar was the classiest dead-end dive bar in western Alaska. On any given night, the area's remaining die-hard miners might stagger in from the cold in their lace-up, knee-high boots and filthy parkas.

Pilots from Marks Field would wander in at dinnertime, still wearing their bulky cold-weather flying gear. After months of dreary patrols over the Bering Sea, their gear was grimy with grease and body oils. They felt filthy, which affected morale. They had nothing else to wear. Like Gerald Johnson and the rest of the 54th down in the Aleutians, the 56th Squadron was sent up from Southern California with nothing but their overnight kits.

More than once, a pilot from the outfit staggered outside so lit he'd get lost and fall off the wooden boardwalk lining Front Street. His buddies would find him hours later, facedown in the mud, bordering on hypothermia. They'd drag him to a car, get him back to the field, and fill him with coffee.

In the mornings, before the next patrol, they fought their hangovers by sitting in their P-39s, sucking oxygen through their masks as their stomachs fluttered. A good ten or twenty minutes of that on the flight line, and the men would be in good enough shape to carry on with the day's mission.

The pilots mingled with an astonishing cast of characters at the Polar Bar. Drunken Inuits came and went. Local schoolteachers got their hangovers on. Toothless miners, shopkeepers, bums, and derelicts would belly up to the bar to sing together or listen to whatever the owner's huge radio set could pick up. Nome was closer to Moscow than Miami, closer to Tokyo than San Francisco. The only Stateside radio station that could be picked up at the Polar at night featured the Mormon Tabernacle Choir. Listening to Radio Moscow or to Tokyo Rose were the only other options.

So, through the hubbub of conversations, clink of drinks, and scraping of cheap wooden chairs across the floor, the bar was often filled with the sounds of Mormon music in tinny mono. Somehow, that seemed appropriate in a place full of every imaginable character.

It was just a few blocks away from this bar, on a Friday night in October 1942, that 2nd Lt. Tommy McGuire, a New Jersey native raised in the Deep South who had never seen the pulsing colors of the aurora borealis, found himself staring at the iridescent night sky. If the rest of the place was a hopeless backwater, the majesty of the phenomenon was an awe-inspiring sight. Those who were blessed to see it would never forget its beauty.

Sunset had come and gone just before seven that evening as the bars and the Glue Pot Café filled with off-duty military bent on making the most of this Friday. In the glow of the northern lights, Tommy could see figures stumbling about down Front Street. A few others were already passed out against the buildings.

He stood beside a road sign that gave directions and distances to points around the globe. Seattle's pointed southeast, and "1,968" was neatly printed under the city's name. The North Pole was 1,739 miles away; Moscow, 4,032. Below that was Miami, 4,475 miles. He glanced at that last one.

Four thousand miles from home.

His nose began to run. He pulled a handkerchief from a pocket and blew it repeatedly. Always a lost cause. His nose always ran. It made him self-conscious and defensive.

What had they called him in school?

Snotty McGuire.

He stepped down to the wooden boardwalk, clad in a meticulously tailored shawl-collared doeskin overcoat. It was a brand-new U.S. Army officer's design, one that he purchased in the States just before coming up here, then took it to a local gentlemen's clothing store, where he had it properly tailored to his unusually slim, five-foot-six frame. The coat made him look taller, and it stood out in Nome since none of his squadron mates brought anything like it up from Harding Field. It gave him a distinctive flair that he relished.

He was a late arrival to the 56th Squadron, a replacement pilot sent to the 54th to cover the Stateside training losses. Being the new guy in a squadron that already had bonded was a tough start. It got worse when he got to Harding Field to report for duty and found the unit had just left for temporary duty in California.

He chased the squadron to California, only to discover it had left for Alaska two days before he arrived. Without a P-39 for him to fly, McGuire climbed aboard one of the transports bringing the squadron's skeleton ground crew to Nome. By that fluke, he became the only pilot in the outfit to reach Marks Field with three large bags of clothing and gear. It made him a prince among paupers, the new guy with the best gear in the combat zone. That made him unpopular right from the start. His bitter tentmates at Marks warned him to watch his stuff; people were so desperate for clothes, his gear stood a good chance of being stolen.

He blew his nose again and walked toward the Polar Bar. His ongoing sinus problems grew worse in the Arctic environment. He was either always blowing his damn nose or snarfing mucus and sounding like a lunger.

He arrived in Nome that June eager to fly and fight. But his first mission set the tone for the deployment. June 21, 1942, was supposed to be a routine familiarization flight for Tommy. Once aloft, he experienced the bitter cold found even in summer at altitude during one of these Bering Sea patrols. Then another recently arrived replacement pilot named Lt. Jimmy Pierce suffered engine failure. His Allison coughed, sputtered, and quit. Too far from Marks Field to make a dead-stick landing, Pierce rode the Airacobra into the whitecaps. He never got out of his plane.

There was a lot of speculation later as to why he went down with the aircraft. Perhaps he was thrown into the instrument panel and smashed his head on the gun sight, knocking himself out as the cockpit filled with water. Or maybe when he hit the water, the doors jammed and he couldn't get out. Maybe he couldn't even get out of his belt and chute. Whatever the case, even if he had been able to get out on the wing, he would have been dead from hypothermia long before a boat could have saved him.

That night, the squadron commander, Capt. Bill Litton, sat down in his tent and wrote Pierce's parents back in San Bernardino, California:

I regret to inform you of the death of your son, James.... The whole squadron had become attached to James, and consider his death a loss to our family also. We will have a hard time filling the gap made by his loss.

Could any epitaph pay proper ceremony to a twenty-six-year-old former Southern Californian clerk who joined the Army Air Force to fulfill his dreams of flight? Then war came, and he died needlessly at the end of the civilized world, thanks to a crappy engine.

For the rest of the summer, Tommy followed his flight leaders into the air on pointless patrols over a cruel and unforgiving sea. Even worse, a pointless mission in these mercurial planes could be as dangerous as any other. Do everything right, and you may just die anyway. A thrown rod, a fouled plug, and the P-39 would end up in the water. That was the lesson of Jimmy Pierce's death. Any flight up here, as boring as they were, could kill you in one of dozens of ways.

McGuire felt a breeze blowing in from the north, and he hunched his shoulders to it. The temperature hovered around forty degrees that evening. Sometimes it howled through the buildings on the waterfront, but tonight it wasn't too harsh.

He thought about how the gentle breeze would make for perfect sailing weather, remembering the Florida sun and the vacations he and his mom would take to the beach. His mom always invited the boys from his class to join them. Some were friends. Some were freeloaders looking to get a weekend away with the rich Yankees. They'd pile aboard a rented sailboat and skim along the surf, the wind cooling them from the tropical sun.

Here such a breeze just added a light touch of suck to the cold. The occasional gusts would send frigid, probing fingers into his overcoat, chilling his neck despite the tightly wrapped silk scarf he wore.

Even modest breezes blew through his living tent back at the airfield. As they got deeper into autumn, he added more layers to the clothing he slept in. His four other tentmates had no choice but to sleep in their heavy cold-weather flight gear, buried under as many wool blankets as they could score from supply.

Winter was on the horizon, and they'd soon be smothered in snowdrifts that surely would keep them from flying. He hoped the rumors were true that they'd be pulled out soon. Nothing had happened since they'd gotten to Nome. Well, nothing besides Pierce's death. No Japanese aircraft appeared, no invasion fleets filled the Bering Sea. It all seemed a colossal waste of time. All the action was down in the Aleutians, where guys like Art Rice and Gerald Johnson were knocking Zeroes out of the sky over Kiska, making headlines that he wanted to make. He should have been with them. Instead, he was rotting in this backwater.

In an alley across the street, a drunken Inuit bent double and projectile vomited into the mud, one arm braced against the backside of a building.

Friday night in Nome. Fucking circus of the damned.

A moment later, he pushed through the Polar Bar's front door. The place was packed, filled with smoke and bad music. At the bar, a collection of locals ignored the stools and stood shoulder to shoulder, belting out "Flat Foot Floogie (with a Floy Floy)" in happy off-key riffs.

Flat foot floogie with a floy, floy
Floy doy, floy doy, floy doy
Yeah, yeah yeah, byah, oh, baby!

Tommy paused at the door, unbuttoning his overcoat as he watched the revelers take shots between lines from that euphemistically dirty Slim Gaillard and Slam Stewart hit.

There's a blast from my senior year.

A couple years after the song cracked the hit parade's top five, Tommy was in a frat at Georgia Tech, when his brothers clued him in on the real meaning of the words. Floogie was a hooker, and "floy floy" was street lingo for the clap.

The singing all but drowned out a Greek miner who sat at a table across the room, playing some sort of stringed instrument called a zither that Tommy had heard only once before. He smiled missing teeth as he played, a bottle of ouzo sitting half drained next to him.

The barkeeper, George, stood behind the bar, slinging drinks and occasionally producing a deck of cards that he used to wow his patrons with magic tricks. When George saw Tommy at the door, he greeted him warmly.

"Evenin', Lieutenant!" he called over the noise. Tommy nodded as he walked past the bar to find a table, shucking off his hat as he went. The Polar Bar did not include a hat- or coat rack, so everyone left their headwear on top of a pile of boxes next to a storeroom door in an alcove at the back of the place.

Tommy found a table in a corner and put his back to the wall after neatly folding his overcoat over the chair beside him. He was wearing a uniform tunic and a tie. He looked ridiculously out of place, like a man wearing a tux in a mosh pit at a death metal concert.

A few other pilots from the 56th sat clustered together around tables nearby. They acknowledged him, but only one got up to talk to him. The aviator stepped over to Tommy's table and pulled his wallet out of his back pocket.

"Here's what I owe you, McGuire."

The pilot handed him a few bills, then returned to the camaraderie of his buddies. Tommy made a mental note to deduct the debt off his books when he got back to his tent. A lot of people owed Tommy McGuire money. To keep it straight, he kept a careful written account of who owed what and how much.

They didn't like him much, but they sure didn't mind borrowing cash from him. He never charged interest—that would have been unfitting for an officer and a gentleman. Besides, thanks to the nightly poker games in the alert shack back on post, McGuire was loaded. He didn't need to charge interest.

A latecomer replacement pilot to the 56th who ran off his mouth and showed up the other fliers after he arrived, Tommy knew he didn't fit in, and, aside from tolerating him on poker nights, the pilots made no pretense of being friendly. A few months back, they were sitting around talking shop and the P-39's crazy spin/stall quirks came up. The other pilots all talked with caution and not a little fear over the plane's nasty habits. Tommy started bragging about what he could do in an Airacobra.

He was cadet class 42B, which meant he'd been an officer and fighter pilot for about five months. A mouthy greenhorn was not welcomed in the ranks of lieutenants who had lived long enough to see some of their friends get killed.

They dared Tommy to put his flying where his mouth was. The next morning, McGuire performed for the rest of the squadron at the end of a patrol. He looped his P-39 over the airfield low enough that his squadron commander confined him to quarters. At the time, Tommy thought the stunt was worth the punishment. But he eventually found that while he may have shown the other pilots what he could do, it did not win him any friends. Neither did buying rounds for the entire bar, which he did with enough frequency to get him noticed by George and the locals. Perhaps he should have known that wouldn't work either, he thought, and resigned himself to his lonely fate. His mother used to throw money around in Florida in hopes of winning over the locals. That didn't work either. They were always considered Yankees in the heart of Dixie.

George's wife came over and took Tommy's order. After she departed, he surveyed the crowd nervously, eyeing an entry into a conversation that wouldn't come. He reminded himself who he was, the *outsider*, and made his peace with it.

He never really had a place. In New Jersey, when he was just a little kid, his father was an outcast among his mom's family there. His own people lived out of state, and his mom's clan rejected him as beneath their class. They bounced around from apartment to apartment as his dad tried to sell cars for a living, his wife's father buying clothes for the family that were far too fine for a working-class household. Instead of looking polished, they came across as aspirational wannabes.

When the marriage failed, Tommy's mom followed her folks to Florida, where she and her children would be even more out of place—a rich Yankee family settling in the heart of a small, blue-collar Southern town. The family offended the strong sense of pride the locals possessed on more than one occasion. Some parents flat-out banned their children from hanging out with Tommy. The few friendships he did develop were fraught with ups and downs. Some only tolerated him because he had a game room, complete with a pool table. Nobody else in town had anything like that. Tommy's mom paid for expensive getaway vacations in high school and went out of her way to dote on those who came over, in hopes of nurturing a social life for Tommy. She also tried donating money to the school and helping kids whose families had limited means. More than once, that triggered a prideful Southern backlash.

In fact, the generosity never worked. Tommy remained an odd duck, a gangly-looking kid whose nose always ran and who spoke without the Deep South accent everyone else had. He wore fashionable clothes in an overalls-and-denim kind of town. Paid for by his grandfather, the clothes came to symbolize his status in town. Never an outcast, but always an outsider.

He came to terms with his station by armoring up. He grew up defensive, prickly, developed a sense of superiority to conceal the insecurities that arose from the bullying he endured. When faced with a choice to fight or run, he almost always ran. Once, after a bully roughed him up, one of his classmates found him crying in the school bathroom.

Thing was, he was smarter than almost every other kid in school. He possessed a near-photographic memory and could think four or five steps ahead of everyone else. He was an accomplished clarinet player, a member of the marching band who possessed real musical talent.

He used his intellect to fight back whenever he could. He developed a razor-sharp tongue and a remarkable knack for intuiting the holes in another person's psychological armor. He exploited that knowledge to twist the knife with snarky comments. Tommy learned to embrace his identity as the outsider who stood out. He would be the smartest, the best at whatever he did. That made him unique. Others were mere followers. Sheep. Like many superintelligent kids, Tommy developed an enduring contempt for mere mortal intellects. He rarely shied away from rubbing their noses in the fact that he was superior to them.

His food arrived. As he ate, the front door swung open and a new group flowed into the place.

Russians.

He watched them find a table and felt vaguely threatened by these guys. They were part of a new group of Red Air Force personnel recently arrived in Alaska to establish an air ferry route from North America across Siberia to the battlefields of the Eastern Front. The Russians needed combat aircraft desperately. Too many Lend-Lease fighters and bombers were being sunk at sea in the convoy battles in the North Atlantic and Barents Sea on the runs to Murmansk. Now the plan was to fly planes straight from America's factories up to Alaska, where Russian pilots would accept them. From Fairbanks, they would fly to Nome, refuel, and start the four-thousand-mile trip to the Eastern Front.

The pilots chosen to initiate this route were rugged veterans who were probably about McGuire's age of twenty-two but looked twice that. Liquor, the stress of combat, and the loss of countless friends at the hands of the Luftwaffe left them hardened, steel-tough, and in no mood to take crap from soft Americans playing at being fighter pilots.

The Russians lived by their own rules and ignored the Army Air Force's. They flew through traffic patterns, ignored the ground controllers trying to direct them, and generally made things very difficult for those trying to establish cooperation. Once, after a Russian pilot was scolded for some aerial infraction over Ladd Field at Fairbanks, the Russian replied, "I have eight Nazis. How many do you have?"

Yet, in small groups or one-on-one, the Russians could warm up to their American hosts. There were transnational friendships forming, tentative as they were. For the most part, they kept to themselves in a clannish sort of way that combat veterans everywhere often do.

Then there was Tommy McGuire, the prickly one who always had to be the best and most distinctive. He loved being the one to let you know that you were second-rate.

He decided to go after the Russians. He stood up, walked over to the table of 56th pilots and announced, "I'm gonna drink those goddamned Commies under the table."

Laughs and scoffs followed. The pilots teased him. There was drinking, then there was Russian aviator drinking. It was a whole new dimension of alcoholism that Americans could only watch with awe.

The Georgia Tech frat boy in uniform sat down with the Soviet aviators and challenged them to a drinking duel. He bought the first round. Vodka shots. The glasses appeared on the table, the bottles soon followed. A crowd gathered. The Russians laughed and pounded down the shots. McGuire struggled to stay with them.

Round after round followed. The Russians looked almost unaffected. Tommy's eyes started watering. His nose ran even more. The world began to tilt. He took another shot and slammed the glass down hard. The Russians laughed and poured another round. Heads tilted with glasses to lips. Down the hatch. The fire spread from throat to belly, and the Russians roared and called for more.

McGuire, barely conscious now, reached for his shot. A Russian poured it for him. He tipped back and sucked it down, trying not to gag. The Georgia Tech frat parties were his metric for hard core. This was out of his league, but he was damned if he was going to give up. He straggled through a few more rounds, keeping upright by sheer force of will. The Russians still looked virtually unaffected. Their veins pulsed with 180-proof plasma.

McGuire would not give up. He drank until he passed out and fell under the table. If his body failed, his will never did. After the morning's sledgehammer hangover passed, he took solace in that fact. Plus, he was the only American in the bar that night to have the balls to take the Russians on in their own game.

Be the best, or die trying. McGuire embodied the sentiment, and that night with the Russians in the Polar Bar was one of many examples of how he lived that creed.

He may never acquire their tolerance to alcohol, but Thomas McGuire Jr. wanted more than anything to be the same steely-eyed combat veteran they were. He longed to be a part of that elite circle. Instead, while his fellow pilots in the 54th battled the Japanese over Kiska, he bitterly climbed into his P-39 for yet another freezing three-and-a-half-hour patrol over the empty Bering Sea.

On October 16, McGuire's time in Nome came to an end. The Army Air Force recalled the 54th Fighter Group. The men fighting the Japanese over Kiska departed first. Not long after, McGuire's squadron received orders sending them back to Anchorage. The weather nearly killed them when they encountered a heavy snowstorm en route. All four P-39s eventually crash-landed not far from McGrath Army Air Base, where they spent a long and frigid night in their cockpits while bears prowled around their damaged P-39s.

A rescue party reached them the next day, and they caught a flight to Anchorage, Tommy more than ready to be done with the forlorn dive bars, predatory animals, and subfreezing temperatures of western Alaska.

They spent the rest of the week at Elmendorf, waiting for the rest of the squadron to make it back from Nome, unsure when the official order sending them Stateside would show up. In the meantime, Litton let his men go check out a couple of P-38 Lightnings sitting down at the flight line.

These new birds were as different as night and day from the P-39s they'd been flying, and the pilots eagerly absorbed all the preflight lessons. Over the course of a few days, they read manuals, got checked out in the cockpits so that they understood the complicated layout, and listened intently as a few men from the Lightning squadron serving in the Aleutians explained to them the ins and outs of their aircraft.

At last, on the twenty-first, McGuire got the keys to the new ride. He scaled the ladder between the booms, walked across the wing, stepped over the side of the canopy, and put his feet on the seat. From there, he sank down, sliding his legs under the instrument panel until his boots reached the rudder pedals. The plane's crew chief helped strap him in, then showed him how to close the hatch. If the P-39 had a strange way of getting in and out of the cockpit, the P-38's was just as unusual. Instead of a sliding canopy like nearly every fighter of the era possessed, Lockheed designed the P-38 with an overhead hatch, almost like a convertible without doors, as the point of entry and exit from the cockpit. Hinged on the right side, spring loaded on the left, where the locking mechanisms were.

McGuire secured the hatch lock, then went through his checklist before heading out to the runway. Both engines fired just fine on takeoff. He retracted the landing gear while climbing out, thrilled with the P-38's power and its ability to rocket skyward. The P-39 seemed like an anemic dog in comparison. This aircraft was in a class of its own.

The revelry ended when the canopy hatch suddenly broke loose. One spring in the lock mechanism failed; the slipstream caught the left front corner of the hatch and wrenched it up and backward. The other lock held firm, which caused the plexiglass to shatter, filling the cockpit with flying shards. A chunk of metal bracing snapped off the hatch and struck Tommy in the head. The blow knocked him senseless.

As he regained his wits, McGuire keyed his radio, declared an emergency, and swung the Lightning back toward the runway. He stayed calm, went through the landing procedure as the slipstream howled a few inches over his head. Gear down, flaps down, a quick, shallow turn onto final, and he painted the aircraft onto the runway twenty minutes after takeoff.

Tommy tried again the following day. This time, he spent thirty minutes aloft, circling the runway and getting a proper feel for the aircraft. The next day, he scored two hours in a '38.

He loved it, even though it almost killed him on his first flight. Fast, surprisingly maneuverable for such a large aircraft, it felt worlds ahead of the P-39s and P-40s he'd flown. He spent his time aloft in it executing touch-and-gos, making six landings through the two hours of stick time he was able to get.

Then it was over. It was such a tease to be given a glimpse of what it was like to be in the cockpit of such a capable aircraft, only to be brought back down to earth again. He fell hard. While waiting for the rest of the 54th Fighter Group to return from the Aleutians and western Alaska, the only flying McGuire got to do was in P-40E Warhawks, which now felt like flying a plane full of lead bricks.

Finally, in mid-November McGuire received leave. He flew back to see his father in New Jersey first, then he headed south to Sebring, Florida, to visit his mother.

When he got to town, things had changed dramatically. Almost everyone he knew from school was gone, scattered to the winds of global military service. His mom never remarried, never even dated after her divorce. She'd settled into a life spent giving to others. She tended to her father through a long illness that eventually claimed him, then did the same a few years after with her mom. When her mom passed, the remaining family disintegrated, torn apart by a battle over the small estate left behind. Tommy's mom won that battle and held onto the house in Sebring as well as the remains of a once-great fortune. It was a pyrrhic victory, since it alienated her from her remaining connections in life. Once Tommy left for college, she became a lonely, almost tragic figure, living in a house far too large for her to care for. She ended up moving into a local hotel, virtually destitute after her inheritance ran out.

Tommy arrived at her room that November and knocked on the door. No answer. He knocked again. Nothing. Her only son was back from his first combat deployment, and she was either not home or not answering the door for some reason.

Tommy went to talk to the hotel staff. They told him she rarely left her room anymore and often would not answer when the staff knocked. He went upstairs and tried again. He called out to her, said he was home from Alaska.

Nothing. He went away puzzled and worried. The town gossip about his mom had always focused on two things: her money and her drinking. Much of the time the gossip about the latter was overblown, but it contained at least a kernel of truth.

The next day, Tommy went back and knocked on her room door a third time. At length, she answered. She looked sickly and worn out. Future generations would have spotted clinical depression.

When her parents died and Tommy started his own life, she was left without a backup plan. She had no family who wanted to see her, and she never succeeded in developing a network of friends in her adopted town. She found no purpose after those she'd devoted her life to either died or left. She simply existed, and for any intelligent human with a big heart, that just wasn't enough.

The reunion was a sad one. Tommy's mom looked so unhealthy that he told her she needed to take better care of herself. She became defensive, talked with increasing self-pity about how nobody came to visit her anymore and how much she regretted the rift the estate battle caused in the family.

It was all too late.

Tommy left Sebring a short time later, never to return.

PART TWO

New Guinea

10

When Everyone Turned a Screw

Late August 1942
Amberley Field, Brisbane, Australia

The first wave of General Kenney's fresh-faced P-38 pilots from California landed at Amberley Field at the end of August, just as Aussie stevedores unloaded the first crates filled with dismantled Lightnings from a cargo ship in Brisbane harbor. They arrived only a few weeks after General Kenney first reached Australia and flew up to New Guinea to see his weary and emaciated combat units. The new planes and men from the Golden State were just what he needed to help defend Port Moresby. Kenney's future would be tied to how they performed.

The replacement pilots were an eager lot, filled with the desire to get into battle that only men who have yet to experience combat can feel.

Kenney wanted these men in New Guinea in the heart of the action as soon as possible. Those fifty '38 jocks would be spread through three squadrons that Kenney planned to reequip with the Lightnings. That way, there would be a mix in every outfit of combat veterans and P-38-trained pilots. It seemed like a great idea, blending knowledge of the new aircraft with the bitterly gained battle experience of the 5th Air Force's best outfits. The new guys would show the old hands how to fly the P-38, while the veterans would teach them how to stay alive in a fight against the Japanese. A quick exchange of knowledge as the mechanics assembled the Lightnings, and the squadrons would race back to New Guinea to jump back into the fight.

It didn't work out that way.

The 39th Fighter Squadron received the first batch of P-38s. Fresh from a grueling tour up at Moresby, the "Cobras in the Clouds" squadron had lost ten planes in six weeks of combat—about 40 percent of their aircraft. Miraculously, all ten pilots survived. Then their squadron commander died during a training mission, leaving the outfit in temporary command of a second lieutenant.

The rush was on to get the 39th back into combat. Mechanics swarmed over those first Lightnings, working day and night to assemble them. The first ones completed were handed off to the newly arrived P-38 pilots, who started checking out the veterans. Everything looked to be going to Kenney's plan.

Then the wheels fell off. The first few test flights at Amberley resulted in near accidents as engines quit on takeoff. Investigating the problem, the mechanics discovered the internal fuel tanks were damaged in transit or improperly manufactured. Most had to be thrown away. Other issues developed. The Fifth had received the newest P-38 model, the F. Between the D, E, and F models, Lockheed undertook over two thousand modifications. They fixed some bugs but created a host of others.

The electrical inverters did not work. The oil intercoolers and superchargers leaked. This was not the savior of the skies Kenney needed. Instead, he received a bird crippled by mechanical gremlins.

As the ground crews tried to solve the problems, the second batch of P-38s arrived. These showed up without the ammunition-feed systems for the guns. Others lacked critical parts.

These could not be manufactured locally; they had to come from the Lockheed factory. Urgent requests for new tanks and parts reached the United States, and top-priority transport planes soon winged across the Pacific to deliver them to Amberley.

As the new fuel tanks arrived, the mechanics and pilots joined forces to get them installed. Each replacement included a thousand screws that needed to be hand-turned. The men grabbed screwdrivers and went to work, sometimes for eighteen hours at a stretch, until their blisters ran crimson with blood.

Gradually, a few birds emerged ready to fly, but it was not the aerial armada Kenney wanted. He had imagined a walloping new force to shock and awe the Japanese. Walking on the field one morning, he took a look at each of the six planes ready for combat, and he could only sigh.

In early September, a new contingent of Stateside '38 pilots arrived at Amberley. Dick Bong was among them, flying across the Pacific and making the best out of the horribly uncomfortable LB-30 used for such journeys. In that long flight, crammed in with his peers, he came across as distinctly un-fighter-pilot-like. He was quiet. Self-contained, nice enough when somebody talked to him, but otherwise he largely kept to himself. Jay Robbins, a second lieutenant from Texas, recalled—in what after the war would seem ludicrous—looking around the plane during the trans-Pacific flight and pegging Dick Bong as the weak link.

Once he arrived at Amberley, he rubbed some of the veterans the wrong way. His confidence in the P-38 and his ability to fly it struck some as cockiness, and it pissed them off. They'd been flying for months while he'd been Stateside, and they were not about to suffer what they saw as a rookie's tinhorn bravado. Especially when that rookie was a fervent believer in a plane that had yet to impress anyone in the 5th Air Force.

Talk developed between old P-40 hands and the new P-38 guys over whose plane was better. Bong somehow ended up in the middle of this growing tension. He was never one to be an advocate or draw

attention to himself, but that is exactly what happened. The jaw-
ing went from good-natured to acrimonious, until finally, challenges
were issued. The new guys received quite a lecture. The P-40 was
the only plane in theater that could fight the Japanese, as long as you
didn't try to dogfight with the Zero. Stay fast, go in, get out. Slashing hit-and-run attacks—that was the name of the game. They all
agreed the '39 was a dog. But over Darwin, the 49th Fighter Group
had shot down almost eighty Japanese planes with their P-40s.

They told the new guys that no fighter as massive as a Lightning
would be able to fight the Zero and its incredible agility. It was a
death sled, a stupid Stateside pipe dream of some Lockheed designer
who knew little about air combat.

The '38 pilots didn't buy it. There may have been some talk about
kicking P-40 ass back in California. Things came to a boiling point. You
think you and your new plane are that good? Prove it in the sky.

Bob McMahon and Frank Adkins represented the P-40 crowd.
They'd seen their war from the cockpit of their Curtiss fighters from
the Philippines to Java. They fought in every lost cause in the Southwest Pacific until finding themselves in P-39s over Port Moresby in
May. Adkins once wrote in an official report that the 39th should be
reequipped with trucks, as they'd climb better and be more maneuverable than their Airacobras. The P-38s' arrival convinced him that
the Air Corps had listened.

They met over Amberley at nine thousand feet. Bong and one of
the other new guys in freshly assembled P-38s, the two old hands in
P-40s borrowed from a nearby depot. Adkins led the P-40 element,
careening straight at the Lightnings in a head-on approach.

At the last second, everyone broke and turned. The fight was
on. Bong and the other P-38 pilot stunted their Lightnings all over
the sky in ways that left the veterans dumbfounded. At one point,
Bong winged over and bored straight for McMahon's P-40. When
Zeroes made this sort of attack, he'd escaped by kicking the rudder,

skidding, and cutting his throttle. In combat, the Zeroes would invariably overshoot, giving him a chance to take a snap shot as they passed by him.

Not so with Bong. The farm boy saw the maneuver and reacted instinctively, yanking the P-38 into a zoom climb the P-40 could not hope to follow. Now he had altitude, and he knew that the pilot who controlled the high ground controlled the fight. He dropped on the P-40s, whose pilots tried to escape with split S dives. Soon, the fight spilled down from nine thousand feet to the deck. Tearing over the trees, the P-40s scissored back and forth, trying to scrape the Lightning off each other's tails.

Nothing worked. Bong and his wingman were relentless. In desperation, the P-40 pilots reverted to a World War I defensive maneuver called a Lufbery Circle. The theory behind it was simple: if two or more planes could circle together on opposite sides of each other, any hostile fighters trying to get on their tail would expose their own tail to the next plane in the circle. Theoretically, it was as solid a defense as the infantry square was to cavalry charges in the Napoleonic wars.

The P-38s countered by keeping the high ground. Staying above the P-40s, Bong and his wingman took turns making slashing, diving attacks into the Lufbery. Before the other P-40 could arrive and help, the Lightnings flitted away, zoom-climbing back up to their perch.

Finally, Adkins surrendered. Point proven. The new plane was a true contender. So were the new pilots.

In mid-September, the crisis in New Guinea reached its peak. Forward Japanese units crested a ridge and looked down upon the Coral Sea and Port Moresby. They were still in the Owen Stanley Mountains, but now they were less than twenty miles from their destination. In desperation, Kenney airlifted American troops into Moresby, with his heavy bombers and transports arriving from the States still crewed by civilian ferry pilots. Meanwhile, the Aussies sent in a veteran infantry division freshly arrived from the Middle East.

Kenney's new energy and expectation for offensive action transformed the culture in the 5th Air Force. The bombers and fighters at Moresby launched attacks against the Japanese supply lines stretching from the north coast into the Owen Stanleys every day. They strafed and bombed troop concentrations and pulled out wounded troops from forward jungle strips whenever practical. New gunships—light A-20 Havoc bombers modified to carry ten forward-firing machine guns by legendary aviator Pappy Gunn—arrived in early September to strike the Japanese with deadly effect from treetop level.

Yet the skies above the battlefield and Port Moresby did not belong to the Allies. When the Japanese bombers attacked, the defenders of Moresby still lacked the ability to intercept them effectively. Those attacks proved incredibly destructive. Japanese bombardiers were highly experienced veterans who scored deadly hits on the airdromes around the port. Men were killed in their slit trenches. Others died trying to get aloft as the bombs fell. Dispersal areas turned into infernos as precious aircraft were blown to burning bits. After each attack, the wounded and dying were carried into the hospital at Moresby, grim, burned, and broken men who bore the brunt of the Allied failures to stop these Japanese raids.

Kenney needed those Lightnings to stop the carnage. He wanted them up high to bounce the Japanese Zero escorts, giving his Airacobras the chance to go after the bombers with their heavy cannon. The pressure was on to get those birds up to New Guinea. Yet, by September 15, only a dozen were deemed combat ready.

A dozen was better than nothing. Kenney ordered the 39th to go with what they could. Meanwhile, the remaining pilots would continue to train on the other '38s as they were completed.

For two months, the advanced element of the 39th operated out of Fourteen Mile Drome, flying local patrols that revealed a dizzying array of issues with their new P-38s. The ground crews, struggling to learn the new planes without manuals or much technical experience, learned as they went. For each problem they solved, two or three more cropped up.

Sixty days passed, and the P-38 accomplished nothing in New Guinea.

Just before Thanksgiving, Capt. Eddie Rickenbacker blew into Port Moresby. Sent by the secretary of war on an inspection trip to the Southwest Pacific, his B-17 crashed at sea en route. America's ace of aces from World War I spent twenty-two days adrift in the Pacific, eating seagulls and drinking rainwater to survive.

He reached General Kenney's headquarters looking like a scarecrow. After a few days of recovery, he met with MacArthur, who briefed him on the situation. Then Kenney took him around to some of the airdromes protecting Port Moresby. He met with the flight crews, talked tactics with them, and generally "flew the hangar" with this new generation of combat aviators to get a sense of what they faced in New Guinea.

While Rickenbacker was visiting a fighter unit, almost certainly not the 39th, the talk turned to air-to-air combat. The young pilots had grown up reading the pulp World War I air combat magazines. Their Depression-era childhoods were spent building models of Captain Eddie's legendary biplane fighter, the SPAD XIII. Here, in the middle of nowhere on a jungle-covered island thousands of miles from home, they met their childhood hero.

He did not disappoint. Eddie Rickenbacker was a brilliant raconteur of tales. He wowed his audience, first with his epic survival story about drifting on a raft in the middle of the Pacific for three weeks, then reached back to his Western Front days, when his squadron battled von Richthofen's Flying Circus in 1918.

The fighter pilots hung on every word. Captain Eddie fought against the best of the best. He'd seen countless comrades go down. Yet, he emerged victorious to become one of the great heroes of his age. His journey stood in stark contrast to what these men endured in New Guinea. The Japanese thrashed them almost every time they met. A plucky few scored kills. The rest were lucky to escape with their lives.

At one point, Kenney stepped into the back-and-forth and mentioned that Captain Eddie scored almost all his twenty-six kills between June and November 1918. Five months of combat.

What was supposed to be a morale-boosting moment suddenly became a stark reminder of their struggles against the Japanese. The men grew quiet. The leading ace in the theater, Buzz Wagner, scored eight kills from the first days of the war in the Philippines through April 1942. He'd left for home a short time later. Since then, nobody had even come close to getting eight.

Let alone twenty-six.

Rickenbacker sensed the mood in the room had changed. The men felt humiliated. He stepped in and said, "Well, you have to remember, the Germans were pretty thick at the front in those days. There were always plenty of targets to shoot at."

That didn't really elevate the mood. They'd seen plenty of Japanese over New Guinea. Somebody sighed and said, almost offhandedly, that it would be a long time before somebody tied Captain Eddie's record of twenty-six.

The comment struck Kenney with inspiration. He announced, "Eddie, I'm going to give a case of scotch to the first one to beat your old record."

Captain Eddie quipped, "Put me down for another case."

The room brightened. The conversation continued, the men unaware that something significant had just been born. The seeds had been planted. Fighter pilots are naturally competitive, hard chargers. The lack of action and success had worn some of that away in New Guinea, but beneath the surface, the best fighter pilots will always be the ones burning to prove they are better than anyone else in the sky.

The challenge stoked that competitive fire and got the wheels turning. Somebody in that group might become the next Captain Eddie, World War II's ace of aces and the next American icon from the new war. The stakes went well beyond a few cases of booze. It meant a path to a better life than what they were born into.

The race to twenty-six had officially begun.[1]

---

1. Kenney placed Bong at this meeting in *Ace of Aces*, but that is likely not the case. Bong didn't see Kenney in New Guinea until late December 1942 and was flying on the day Captain Eddie visited the squadron.

11

Mission Over Maggot Beach

Sunday, December 27, 1942
Fourteen Mile Drome, Port Moresby, New Guinea

The weather ship departed at 0630, rolling down Fourteen Mile Drome's dirt runway with a stripe of dust rising in its wake. The P-38 banked during its climb out, turning for the forbidding Owen Stanley mountain range, which was often shrouded in clouds or fog that concealed its deadly peaks. The first order of the day was to find out what the weather was like over the passes the 39th used to get to the north side of New Guinea.

Over the past two months, the fighting had migrated to the north side of the Owen Stanleys. The Aussies managed to hold the Kokoda Trail. Then, with Kenney's bombers and fighters wreaking havoc on the Japanese supply lines, the Imperial troops ran out of food and ammunition. They fell back, leaving their dead and dying alongside the trail—along with more evidence of how they treated their prisoners of war. Being captured by the Japanese was a sadistic death sentence.

The weather bird continued climbing, turning north to pass over the foothills at the threshold of the Owen Stanleys. Though the 5th Air Force possessed weather planes anweather stations, the 39th's new commander, Major Prentice, did not take any chances. Since Prentice arrived in New Guinea, sending a lone plane off to gather weather intel had become a daily ritual.

The P-38 weaved around packs of cottony cumulus clouds until the pilot reached the pass. The Kokoda Trail lay somewhere below, shrouded by the jungle overgrowth from above.

The pass was clear. The pilot keyed his radio and called back to Moresby, "Wigwam this is Kekini One, over."

"This is Wigwam, go ahead Kekini One."

"Condition okay."

"Roger, Kekini One. Condition okay."

Had the pass been socked in by clouds, the pilot would have called back, "Condition sour."

There would be much flying today.

At Fourteen Mile, the pilots went through their morning routines and gathered at a chalkboard in the operations hut. The ops officer listed every pilot assigned to fly that day, along with his flight and aircraft assignment.

Dick Bong stood shoulder to shoulder with his fellow pilots and studied the board. He found his name under the second flight scheduled to patrol. Beside his name, he saw the number fifteen.

"Bong." The farm kid heard his name called and turned around.

"You're on my wing today."

Tom Lynch regarded him with dark and serious eyes. He was one of the veterans of the 39th, a pilot of rare skill whose intelligence and gentle demeanor on the ground endeared him to the others in the squadron. Though he possessed prototypical movie hero good looks, he was not the prototypical cocky fighter pilot. He was a thoughtful kid who grew up in a small town in Pennsylvania coal country. His dad worked at Bethlehem Steel in Allentown, and before flying became the obsession of his life, Tom Lynch had wanted to join his dad at the plant. He graduated from the University of Pittsburgh with a degree in chemical engineering. Half rugged coal-town kid, half science nerd, he embodied that innate ability to motivate others with just a few soft-spoken words.

It was this combination that helped him survive the 39th Squadron's P-39 deployment. He shot down three Japanese planes in Airacobras over Port Moresby, but returned with a bird full of holes on one occasion. On June 15, 1942, four Zeroes pounced on him. He tried to dive away—the only thing a P-39 could do in its defense—but cannon fire blew holes in his fuselage and knocked out his engine. He ditched in the water off the Moresby beaches, only to have the '39's car-door hatch jam. As the plane sank, he put so much pressure on the door that he broke his arm. He escaped at the last moment and was back flying in August, after his arm healed. Eight days after returning to duty, while flying a freshly assembled P-38 at Amberley, he lost an engine on takeoff and crash-landed. He walked away unscathed. In fact, it didn't even seem to faze him.

Bong, like everyone else, looked up to this quiet veteran. He was about four years older than the other new pilots in the outfit, and when Major Prentice went home, Lynch was sure to get the squadron.

The other two men in Lynch's flight, Ken Sparks and John Mangus, gathered around him. Mangus was one of the Golden Gate '38 pilots, a new kid like Bong who'd already shown tremendous heart and eagerness. He was a consummate team player, willing to do anything to help the outfit.

Lynch sketched the mission for the day. For the past month, a battle had raged on the north coast at a place called Buna. Australian troops and American National Guardsmen from Wisconsin launched repeated assaults against entrenched, desperate Japanese who routinely fought to the last man. They were a mix of starving survivors of the Kokoda Trail and more fit replacements smuggled in at night by the Japanese Navy. Short of everything but courage, the Japanese clung to their shoreside pocket with such fanatical intensity that they stacked their dead around their fighting positions for additional protection. The rotting stench of these corpses proved so overwhelming that some Allied units took to wearing gas masks as they pressed forward in the assault.

On the twenty-seventh, the lead elements of the Wisconsin National Guard captured one of the two Japanese airstrips at Buna. They found the place littered with wrecks and partially intact Zeroes, which Allied intelligence sorely wanted to recover and test-fly.

The 39th would fly two standing patrols along the coast. The first off would cover the area over Cape Hood. Lynch and his flight would patrol directly over Cape Endaiedere, known to the Allied troops as "Maggot Beach." Earlier in the month, a tank-infantry attack took place there in hopes of cracking the Japanese defenses at Buna. The tanks took heavy losses, and the assault failed to gain much ground. Afterward, the surf carried thousands of dead fish to the beach, killed by artillery shells that missed their targets and landed offshore. It was not long before the sand was filled with maggots burrowing in the fish.

When Tom finished the brief, the men headed for a nearby jeep for the drive through the jungle to the flight line and their waiting birds. The patrol seemed routine to Bong. Since arriving in mid-November as part of a contingent of 9th Squadron pilots sent to get some combat experience while the 5th Air Force awaited more P-38s, pretty much all he'd done was patrol over Buna.

They'd seen a whole lot of nothing. In fact, the war seemed more real at Moresby than in the sky over the northern New Guinea coast. At night, the Japanese bombers lingered overhead, keeping everyone awake and driving the men crazy. At one point, an antiaircraft battery moved to a position behind Bong's tent, deep in the jungle off the side of the strip. When one of those obnoxious night intruders passed overhead, the AA guns unloaded, sending Bong flying out of his cot and straight through his mosquito netting, thinking a bomb had just landed nearby. He ran through the night to dive into a nearby slit trench, still entangled in his mosquito net. He lay in there with several other pilots, listening as antiaircraft fallback whistled into the trees around them.

With the Japanese hitting Moresby only at night now, the '38s didn't have any targets. Gen. Ken Walker, the commander of V Bomber Command, wanted the '38s to escort his crews as they pummeled the main Japanese base in the region at Rabaul. The idea was shot down: the P-38 was still untested, there were mechanical failures on every flight, and nobody thought they could fly the eight-hundred-mile round trip to Rabaul without losing half the 39th to gremlins.

So they patrolled over the jungle battlefields and saw nothing but empty sky.

The jeep stopped in front of Tom Lynch's aircraft. He jumped out and walked over to the P-38, his crew chief waiting. The jeep moved down the line to the next Lightning. "Thumper" was painted on its nose behind the number fifteen. Its right-engine nacelle sported a garishly painted shark mouth under a powder-blue-and-white propeller spinner. Between the engine nacelles, two fuel-laden drop tanks hung on the bomb racks.

John "Shady" Lane's ride. He'd beat Bong to the squadron by a month and a half, which made him almost an old hand, and he rated a plane of his own. Bong would be "borrowing" it for the mission, and he knew he'd better damn well bring it back intact. Lane was sort of cool to Bong anyway; if he messed his plane up, it would be bad for the squadron's dynamics.

Dick bailed out of the jeep to go greet *Thumper*'s crew chief. The two chatted about the aircraft.

"We replaced all the Kelsey fifties, Lieutenant," the crew chief told him. "The bird has all Savages now."

Since starting to fly in combat in September, the '38s suffered a series of gun jams. The armorers were going crazy trying to find the problem. Finally, they decided that the guns made by Kelsey-Hayes, a Browning subcontractor, were to blame. The ground crews swarmed over the squadron's birds, pulling out sixty-five of the machine guns and swapping in a fresh batch from the Savage Arms Company's factories. They hoped that would solve the problem.[1]

The first patrol finished warming up their engines and taxied out to the runway. As Bong, Lynch, Sparks, and Mangus fired up their planes, the first flight departed for the north coast, leaving a hazy brown cloud of dust swirling across the airfield.

Ten minutes later, Capt. Thomas Lynch launched with his men. The Pennsylvanian learned back in the spring that altitude determines who holds all the cards in a fight. Practically every time he went into battle, the damned Zeroes dropped on him and his comrades from perches way above their '39s, forcing the Americans on the defensive every time.

Trade altitude for energy. Energy equals speed. Speed equals life.

Now he finally had a plane that could get up high in a hurry and give his men the advantage, and he intended to exploit that. Even laden with their two drop tanks, the '38s climbed out to twenty-three thousand feet in fifteen minutes, higher than the other flight leaders usually chose to go.

Just before noon, they reached their assigned sector. Flying in a finger-four formation with Tom as the middle finger, Dick as the index, Sparks as the ring, and Mangus as the pinkie—tail-end Charlie—they headed out over Maggot Beach to begin a pattern that would take them up and down the coast for the next two hours. The sky as always, it seemed, was empty, but that would not be the case for long.

---

1. The technical bugs plaguing the P-38 are well covered in a series of engineering reports in the V Fighter Command's records for the period. The list of issues the ground crew struggled to fix is daunting, and it is a tribute to them that they were able to get the 39th into combat. Incidentally, the switch to Savage-made guns did not entirely solve the jams.

12

The Veterans of Nomonhan

1150 Hours, December 27, 1942
Buna, New Guinea

As Tom Lynch's flight prepared for the day, a most unusual collection of Japanese aircraft lifted off the coastal strip at Lae. A hundred miles from Buna, Lae remained the most important Japanese air base in Papua, New Guinea, since it served as home to the Imperial Navy's crack 582nd Kokutai. Its pilots were veterans of China, the fighting in the Dutch East Indies, and the Philippines. And, of course, they had been thrashing the 5th Air Force all summer and fall.

Fifteen of their Zeroes and seven Val dive-bombers orbited over Lae that morning, waiting for the veterans of Nomonhan to get aloft and join them.

After the disaster of Kokoda, the Japanese high command wrestled with how to win the air war in New Guinea at the same time the units at Rabaul were supposed to defeat the U.S. Marines and Navy at Guadalcanal in the southern Solomons. The Imperial Navy knew it needed help. They asked the Army to send air units to the Southwest Pacific, and at first, the Army balked—their fighters and bombers were fully engaged against the British, Americans, and Chinese on the mainland. In December, though, they grudgingly agreed to help. An elite brigade of fighters transferred from Sumatra to Truk Atoll in the Central Pacific, then on to Rabaul.

This would be their second mission in New Guinea. On Christmas Day, the 11th Sentai—what the Japanese called their air regiments—staged to Lae and refueled with thirty-one sleek Nakajima Ki-43 Hayabusas, or "Peregrine Falcons." Incredibly agile, they were dangerous opponents in the hands of a capable pilot. The Allies code-named them "Oscars."

The men flying those Falcons ranked as the most experienced veterans in the Japanese Army Air Force. Three years before, the brigade battled the Russian Air Force in a furious border war in Mongolia known as the Nomonhan Incident. The men of this brigade ran up incredible scores—one pilot alone shot down fifty-eight Russian planes during the summer of 1939.

Two of the brigade's fliers went down behind Russian lines. The Army assumed they died at the controls of their fighters. There were ceremonies for their spirits at the Yasukuni Shrine. The press termed them fallen "gods of war."

Then they showed up in the fall of 1939. They'd been taken prisoner by the Russians and released after the border war ended. Rather than being greeted with surprised elation, the Army confined them to quarters and convened a secret court to determine their fate. At the end of the proceedings, coffins were left at their door with pistols nearby. The men accepted their fate. They swallowed the barrels and pulled the triggers.

Message received to the rest of the brigade. Fight to the last breath. Never surrender.

These were the men Dick Bong and the rest of the 39th would soon face.

The pilots who arrived in New Guinea that morning included several triple aces, men adept at shooting down enemy planes no matter the nationality. A few had Russian, British, Dutch, and Chinese aircraft to their credit. They were masters of the freewheeling dogfight and ready to tackle the challenge of finally putting the 5th Air Force out of business.

The Army pilots soared aloft in their graceful Hayabusas and took station with the Zeroes above the Val dive-bombers. The Japanese Army and Navy rarely got along—at times the tension between the services bordered on open hostility. A joint Army-Navy air strike was something new, forced upon them by the situation in the Southwest Pacific.

Time to see if the experiment would work.

The fighter formation topped out at thirteen thousand feet. The bombers cruised below a protective blanket of aerial firepower. Turning southeast, they sped for Buna.

Just before noon, an Aussie radar station established near Buna picked them up. The news was flashed to fighter control.

"This is Wewoka Control. Bandits inbound Buna. At least twenty-seven."

Lynch called back, "Wewoka Control, what angels?"

"Look for them at angels fourteen."[1]

Wewoka gave them a vector. Lynch altered course and led his flight off to find the intruders. Meanwhile, the other flight over Cape Hood headed their way as Fourteen Mile Drome scrambled eight more P-38s.

Five after noon, and the Americans made first contact. Spread out below Lynch's flight was an enormous formation of fighters and dive-bombers. There were at least forty, maybe more. Dive-bombers around four thousand feet. Fighter flights layered up to thirteen. Wewoka padded the altitude to make sure they didn't drop down too low and get bounced from above.

"Drop tanks, and let's go," Lynch called to his flight. He was taking four untested fighters into combat against forty-five Japanese fighters.

---

1. "Angels" was slang for altitude. One angel = one thousand feet. Angels fourteen meant 14,000 feet.

In Dick's cockpit, his hands flew across the controls. To get a Lightning into fighting trim took a blizzard of activity. Forget a step, and you'd be in trouble.

Adrenaline poured through his body. Dick struggled to remain calm and remember exactly what to do.

Switch to internal fuel.

Release the drop tanks.

Flip the gun switches on.

Switch the gun sight on.

Throttle forward.

Fuel mix rich.

Don't forget prop pitch and RPMs.

Watch manifold pressure.

Double-check the RPMs.

Coolant's in the green.

Lynch led them down in a howling dive. As Dick followed, one drop tank hung on its rack. Fighting with one of those things under the wing would leave him slow, sluggish and unbalanced. He hit the release again. No luck.

They dropped below twenty thousand, the P-38s winding up over four hundred miles an hour. The slipstream finally peeled the tank off. He felt it clear his Lightning. Now he was in fighting trim.

Down and ahead lay the Japanese. Some of the fighters were gray, some looked dirty brown. Below were the Vals, lumbering along with 550-pound bombs slung between their fixed landing gear.

Dick had never wanted to be a combat aviator. He joined the military to fly, not to fight. The sky was his home, being a fighter pilot was just the way to get there. But after Pearl Harbor, that started to change in him. Like everyone else in Poplar, he was raised to be a patriot. The Japanese struck his country, and, like others, he wanted to pay them back for the horrors they'd unleashed. On an emotional level, he wanted that chance, grew eager for it. As his skills and experience grew with the P-38, so did his confidence.

It all came down to this moment on the tip of the spear. Time to find out the kind of warrior the AAF made out of Wisconsin farm kids. This was the pivotal moment in his life.

So far, he was a flying catastrophe.

Bong prided himself on his piloting skills. He and the P-38 were one, born for each other. But Tom Lynch was a next-level combat fighter pilot. He pushed his Lightning right to the edge of its envelope, and Bong struggled to stay with him.

They ripped into the Japanese formations. Zeroes and Hayabusas scattered in all directions. Heart pounding, eyes wide, he blazed through the Japanese swarm, shooting wildly. He was jumpy, borderline panicked from the adrenaline jolt, overwhelmed by the speed and number of targets around him. Everything seemed to be happening in split-second increments. One instant, a Zero flitted in front of his nose. The next, it was gone, streaking down and away, a gray blur that became almost indistinguishable from one of the many spots of crud on his canopy.

He flew through the melee, came out the other side trying to remember all the things the veterans had told him.

Keep your speed up.

Extend away, go through 'em. One pass, haul ass.

Stay with Tom. Don't lose Tom.

Dick checked behind him and found John Mangus tacked on to him. Where was Sparks? No time to figure that out. He caught sight of the dive-bombers hitting the strip at Buna, then pulling out of their dives to the northeast. Lynch took them straight after a flight of four Hayabusas. Lynch missed his target, blew past it, and kept diving. Bong followed, watching as several Japanese planes whipped around in tight turns to get on his leader's tail.

Dick fired at one. It broke off as Lynch zoom-climbed to the left. When he came back around to dive into the fight, Dick was streaking for the deck, three Ki-43s on his tail.

Lynch pounced on the trailing Oscar and, at three hundred yards, pressed his gun trigger. The fifties chattered. The cannon thumped. A shell hit the fuselage just aft of the cockpit, blowing a hole and sending debris streaming back.

Lynch kept firing as he overran the slower Japanese plane. Finally, he eased on the trigger just as he barreled under it.

When he pulled back up, his target was nowhere to be seen. The second Hayabusa was still chasing Bong, who was rapidly running out of altitude. The situation was getting dicey. Four against forty, and already the fight was almost on the treetops. Sparks and Mangus were nowhere to be seen, but they were calling targets on the radio, so they were still alive. The sky was filled with Japanese planes, wheeling and diving and turning all around them.

They needed helped. Where was Hoyt Eason and the second flight?

Lynch fired at the second Oscar as he came up behind it. The Japanese pilot saw him and juked out of the line of the American's bullets. The pilot of the third Oscar in line tried to rescue his comrade. Damaged but still in the fight, he went after Lynch until the American was forced to break off.

For the moment, Dick Bong was on his own.

Calm down. Get control of yourself.

Dick was covered in sweat. His mouth was desert dry. He couldn't swallow. His body shook from fear and adrenaline, the jungle racing toward him. At first just a green mass. Now he was low enough to see individual trees.

The Oscars stayed on his tail, not yet in firing range, but relentless with their pursuit. Thank God for the P-38's speed.

He leveled off just above the treetops and firewalled the throttles. The engines roared with the sudden power.

Slow down. Think. Watch. Eyes open. Head on a swivel.

The radio hissed with static. Excited voice. Indistinct. Desperate calls to clear Zeroes off tails. They piled one on top of another until Dick heard Lynch yell, "We're over Maggot Beach! Get down here and get into it!"

He was talking to the first flight off that morning, Hoyt Eason's men.

"This is Wewoka Control. Zeroes at angels seventeen."

"Where? I can't see them?" Eason's voice came through the static.

Come on. We need the help.

Bong turned left and jetted out over the beach. He could see the surf crashing ashore as he gained a little altitude before settling level at 350 feet.

No enemy fighters on his tail now. Not that he could see. He twisted in the cockpit, trying to see behind the armor sheet protecting his back. Nothing.

"Can't locate..."

"...Need you down here!"

"Check your tail! Check your tail!"

"This is Wewoka Control, two Zeroes strafing Dobodura."

"We're on 'em."

A moment later, "Don't see 'em. Where'd they go?"

"Goddamnit, get down here!"

A babble of voices crashed together, drowning out any comprehensible words for the moment.

Then Eason's voice cleared the static, "Three Zeroes, ten o'clock low! Let's get 'em!"

"I got a Zero on my tail! Somebody get him off me!"

Dick had been in the fight for about five minutes. He had plenty of ammo and fuel, but no altitude. He'd need to climb back up, well out of the way of the fray, then come back into it.

Something caught his eye in front him. Was it a speck on the canopy? No. Dick watched as it swiftly grew into the outline of a dive-bomber. It was a perfect setup—he was running the bomber down from almost dead astern. The Aichi Type 99 D3A Val was a slow, awkward relic of mid-1930s technology, lacking even retractable landing gear.

Three and a half football fields away, his gun sight on the bomber's tail, he triggered his guns. The fifties ripped pieces off the Val. They spun back in the slipstream just as Bong's first 20mm cannon shells struck home.

The Val exploded and fell into the water, leaving a greasy smear of oil, smoke, and flames. No way either crew member survived.

Dick didn't think about that, too focused on what to do next.

He looked back at the coast and checked his compass. He was at full throttle heading northwest, just passing Sanananda Point, four miles up the coast from Maggot Beach. Time to get some altitude and go find Lynch.

He pulled the control column into his stomach while he twisted the yoke hard left. The Lightning leapt skyward in a near-vertical zoom climb back toward the coast. His speed drained away, but he held it as the altimeter needle spun around the dial. The wave tops grew indistinct, and the jungle trees along the beach dissolved into an endless pattern of greens and browns.

A Japanese fighter cut in front of him, also in a vertical turn. They closed so quickly, he only had time for a split-second trigger pull. The fighter rolled on its back and went under him. Still in the climb, he looked behind through the Lightning's booms to see where the Japanese plane went.

Three more fighters lurked on his tail. The main battle was now spread all over the sky for miles up and down the coast. More Lightnings piled on as Charlie Gallup's flight arrived from Fourteen Mile Drome. Now the odds seemed a little more reasonable.

Where were Lynch and the rest of the flight?

He dropped his nose and dove back out to sea, the enemy fighters in hot pursuit. Zeroes? Oscars? Did it matter in the heat of battle?

"Come on down here!" somebody called over the radio.

"Do those Zeroes strafing the field have high cover?"

"They're fucking everywhere!"

"Charlie, break! Break! Four at nine o'clock out of that cloud!"

Bong hit the wave tops. Again the P-38 outran the enemy fighters behind him. They kept up the chase, but the Lightning's Allisons pulled him clear. As he fled, he ran headlong into a flight of Vals hugging the water as he was doing.

He picked the center Val, drove straight into the formation and opened fire. His guns flared and the P-38 shuddered from the recoil. He overshot and kept going, aware that the fighters behind would pounce on him if he lingered or came around for another attack run.

Did I hit it?

He glanced back. It was still in the air, appearing undamaged.

Dick started a shallow right turn, taking him farther out to sea and encountered a lone Val straggler. The shadowing Japanese fighters saw the Val too and altered course, desperate to save their charge.

Dick drove straight into gun range. The bomber loomed in his sight. Calm and in a groove now, Dick triggered his guns. The cannon barked, then fell silent. The fifties went quiet an instant later.

Out of ammo.

The Val escaped.

Dick kept going in a wide arc, heading back for Maggot Beach, losing the fighters behind him in the process. He sped over Buna, gaining altitude, searching for Sparks or Mangus or Lynch.

He heard Lynch talking on the radio, calling that he was out of ammo and for his troops to form up on him. He gave his location. Dick altered course. Soon, he and John Mangus found Tom and started back for home.

"Anyone see Sparks?"

"There's a '38 on the strip at Dobo. On its nose."

As they flew home, the adrenaline drained out of Bong's system. He felt sick and shaky as his body went through a parasympathetic backlash. Exhaustion set in. His muscles ached. He said later, "I felt like I'd been through a washing machine with the accent on the ringer."

Lynch landed first back at Fourteen Mile. As he taxied hurriedly for the dispersal area, Bong executed two slow rolls over the field—one for each plane he thought he knocked down—then dropped into the pattern and brought his '38 back, pulling up alongside Mangus and Lynch's birds before setting the brakes and cutting the switches.

Lynch practically rocketed out of the cockpit, scrambled off the wing, shouting, "Get me another airplane! The sky's full of Japs over Buna!" The ground crew raced after him, pointing toward a '38 sitting nearby. He jumped into it and raced off alone to get another crack at the enemy. Dick and John saw him go, vanishing to the north, throttles open, the P-38 like a banshee whining through the New Guinea sky.

Shady Lane watched the entire scene unfold, frustrated that he wasn't on the flight schedule. He walked over to Bong, who was now looking at a lone bullet hole in *Thumper*'s aluminum skin.

"Guess my ship's pretty good luck after all, isn't it?"

The farm boy grinned in answer.[2]

---

2. Though this air battle has been detailed in many secondary sources, the fact that the P-38 flights entered the scrap piecemeal hasn't been well documented. Lynch's flight was especially outnumbered at the beginning of the fight. Source material for this chapter, including the radio chatter, comes from the 39th Fighter Squadron's reports, V Fighter Command's documentation of the mission, which includes some of the personal encounter reports missing from the unit records. Mission reports located at NARA, College Park, in the V Fighter Command records, also proved useful. The chatter was overheard by Army ground units around Buna and recorded in various contemporary accounts. Bong's own recollections of the mission come from his serialized interview with Lee Van Atta in 1944 and his letters home. Contemporary newspaper accounts—Bill Boni's article in particular—rounded out the sources.

13

The Man with the Broken Back

December 27, 1942
Fourteen Mile Drome, Port Moresby, New Guinea

Bill Boni smelled a story, and he was damned if he was going to let something like a broken back stop him from scoring it. He had been a sports reporter for the Associated Press, and when war came the AP made him a war correspondent and sent him to MacArthur's HQ out in Australia. Thirty-two years old and brimming with passion, he spent the fall of 1942 writing stories about the GIs fighting in the jungle around Buna, pounding out his stories on a small portable typewriter he'd set atop an overturned rations crate. Using another crate for a stool, he'd be at it for hours in his makeshift jungle office, still wearing his helmet, chain-smoking as he knocked down pages of patriotic prose.

On Christmas Eve, he was flung from an overturning jeep and fractured two of his vertebrae on landing. Even that didn't stop him. He used the time at the hospital in Moresby to interview some of the wounded soldiers there and write stories about them.

Three days later, he heard the '38s at Fourteen Mile had finally gotten into action. That would be big news back home. He limped from his hospital bed, climbed into a jeep, and sped over to Fourteen Mile, where he camped out at the 39th Squadron's grass-roofed, open-sided operations hut just before the guys returned.

Within minutes, the first jeepload of triumphant '38 pilots rolled up and the men piled out. Talking happily, they recounted their part of the mission, flying with their hands to illustrate what they'd done. The men noticed Boni, but they'd seen him around before and knew he was a reporter in their corner. He'd written several articles about 5th Air Force crews already, and his willingness to go into the Buna swamps, suffer, and go hungry to make men famous with his typewriter gave him solid-gold street cred. Later, after he was wounded in action during a Japanese air raid, MacArthur ordered that Boni receive a Purple Heart. Boni was one of the few civilians to receive it.

A Dodge weapons carrier rolled up next. More jubilant pilots poured out, laughing and chatting excitedly. They walked inside the hut, standing around its mesh sides, enjoying the midafternoon breeze that kept the ops hut from becoming stifling in the equatorial heat. The squadron's intelligence officer debriefed them, taking their reports down and furiously writing notes as they talked.

Charlie Gallup's flight returned last with Tommy Lynch. They flowed into the ops hut and joined the celebration. For all the heartache and sweat getting these birds into battle, they'd just proved their worth. As the pilots talked, the intelligence officer counted the claimed aircraft and tried to sort them out. From the looks of it, they'd knocked down over a dozen Japanese planes.

Dobodura called in to say that Ken Sparks crash-landed there in plane number thirty-six. The '38 was a total loss, shot to pieces by Zeroes and Oscars, wrecked on its nose during his forced landing. For all that, Sparks emerged unhurt. He caught a ride in a C-47 and was back at Fourteen Mile just after Charlie Gallup's flight got back.

Boni remained a fly on the wall, taking notes on the debrief. Sparks related how, with one engine shot out, he flamed a dive-bomber over Dobodura before crash-landing. As he talked, he noticed Boni nearby. Sparks was known for his mischievous grin, and he unloaded it on Boni before saying, "I wish they'd have given me another plane right away so I could go back there—that was a beautiful show, and the plane performed beautifully!"

Not all were bug-free, however. Boni listened to Charlie Gallup describe his flight's late arrival to the fight and how one of his superchargers failed. Then his guns jammed.

Gallup told Boni, "Four attacked us from the same cloud. They made the first pass, but missed."

Carl Planck, Gallup's wingman, interjected, "There's no feeling quite like sitting there and looking up and seeing a Zero on his back looking down at you. You just scrunch down behind the armor plate and give her all she's got."

"I had to run for shelter," Gallup explained after he lost his guns and supercharger. "The Zero got on my tail, but Carl picked him off."

As the chatter and hand-flying continued, Bong stepped over to the intel officer and described his role in the fight in as few words as possible. Later, while he was listening to the other pilots recount what happened, somebody told him that the Zero he'd shot up went into the water. He didn't know that, so he filed an amended report and was given credit for two kills. The rest of the time, Bong vanished into the background. Always quiet, always self-contained, he listened and answered questions, cracked a joke here and there, but was otherwise overshadowed by the exuberant Type As in the hut. Maybe he was more subdued because of the parasympathetic backlash he'd experienced on the way home. He felt exhausted, his mouth still bone dry. But part of it was just who he was—an unshowy introvert, naturally inclined to few words.

It didn't take long before the debrief turned into an impromptu celebration. Major Prentice, the squadron commander, laughed and smiled as he listened to his excited men. The others whooped and hollered, talked freely to Boni, and savored this first victory. At one point, Tom Lynch said what they all were thinking: "This was my first chance to jump some Japs from above." The days of wheezing skyward in altitude-impaired P-39s as Zeroes dropped on them were over. To the hardscrabble veterans of the 39th, the '38 more than proved itself that day. They were true believers.

While the debrief continued, a crippled P-40 with "Scatter Brain" painted on the nose above the number fifteen staggered into the pattern at Seventeen Mile Drome. The pilot, Capt. George "Red" Manning, a Darwin veteran with chiseled features and a perpetual *fuck with me at your peril* scowl, was seething with anger. His P-40 was a sieve. He flopped onto the field and parked his battered bird. Tearing his flight helmet off to reveal a thick thatch of dark red hair, he jumped off the wing and told some approaching ground crew, "I need a jeep! Now!"

They rustled one up for him, and he sped off without further word.

Manning served as the operations officer for the Seventh Fighter Squadron, 49th Fighter Group. He raced back to his squadron, which was based at another Moresby strip, and found the rest of his flight standing around a shot-up P-40. Lt. Clay Tice, another Darwin veteran, stared at Red as he rolled up in the jeep, and uttered a long string of curses.

They conferred, Red growing even more enraged when he saw the bullet holes in the back of the P-40's canopy. Another series of holes pierced the Warhawk's skin below the propeller and went into the radiator. It was amazing the engine hadn't overheated and seized. There were even a few holes in the propeller blades themselves.

Three of the four pilots who were gathered around the P-40 climbed into the jeep with Red. He threw it in gear, stomped on the accelerator, and flew down the flight line, dust pluming in his wake. He drove straight to the 39th Squadron's operations shack, where he found the Lightning pilots in full revelry.

He bailed out of the jeep and started screaming at the P-38 guys. The celebration came to a crashing halt. Bong and the others stared, stunned at the sudden appearance of four exceedingly pissed-off

P-40 pilots, a couple of whom were from Bong's assigned squadron, the Flying Knights.

"You dumb sons of bitches!" Red screamed at the 39th. "My fucking P-40's full of .50-caliber holes because of you! I got another one with a shot-up canopy. You assholes just missed taking my pilot's head off."

"What the hell are you talking about?"

"We were over Dobo. Didn't you hear us screaming at you on the radio that we were friendly? We kept telling you to stop attacking us!"

The Lightning pilots hadn't heard anyone say anything like that. Of course, at times the radio filled with so much chatter that voices just got lost in the cacophony. Either that, or the Warhawks were on a different frequency.

Wewoka control hadn't reported other friendlies in the area. The pilots of the 39th were indignant. How was this their fault? At four hundred miles an hour, how the hell do you tell a green P-40 from a green Ki-43 Hayabusa? One engine, one tail equaled an enemy plane since they didn't know there were P-40s in the area.

The situation escalated. Manning stood his ground, threatening to bring the responsible '38 pilots up on charges. That didn't go over well at all. Everyone was hyperemotional after flying combat. The stress, the terror, and knife-edge they'd just been through left both sides without filters, and their fury meters quickly pegged.

Finally, Manning's rage overcame his self-control. He reached for his holstered pistol and unsnapped its cover. The other three pilots with him saw him do it and grabbed him. He tried to fight them off, but they physically restrained him, then dragged him back to the jeep. A moment later, they drove off. Bong and the other 39th pilots sat there, shocked and shaken.[1]

---

1. Off the record, several 49th veterans mentioned this story to me. The only place it survived in print is in the 49th Fighter Group unit history, *Protect & Avenge*. It is not mentioned in the records from the 39th. While Kenney and Whitehead probably would have gone to see the 39th anyway, it may be they

Later that afternoon, General Kenney and Gen. Ennis White-head showed up to find out what happened on the mission. They conferred with Major Prentice, the squadron commander, then took each pilot's report and went off to read. Kenney noticed Bong's name on one of the reports and, remembering him from San Francisco, read it with great interest. He was surprised at its brevity. Some of the other reports went into great detail. Not Bong's. It was abrupt and contained no fluff.

The others exposed a lot of what Kenney saw were rookie errors. To his eye, they maneuvered way too much with the more agile Japanese fighters and opened fire from too far away. He and Whitehead walked back to the waiting pilots, who greeted his return with anxious looks.

The general laid into them. He was a combat pilot from World War I, he knew the score in the air—at least, he thought he did. First mistake: you want to hit 'em, get in close. Don't be shooting at fly-specks on the canopy, the real damage is done at point-blank range. Second mistake: the Japanese have it all over us with the Zeroes and their maneuverability. Turning with one, even for less than forty-five degrees, bleeds speed, makes a P-38 slow, and Zeroes will eat alive any slow American fighter.

For the old hands, he was of course preaching to the choir. For the new guys, like Bong, Carl Planck, and Mangus, the veterans had already drilled the same thing into them.

In the excitement and swirling craziness of the moment, apparently, they'd done just that.

One pass. Haul ass. Get out of the fight, climb above it, go back in for more. Anything else will get you killed.

---

got wind of the dustup and went to go investigate themselves. Officially, it was never pushed up the chain of command, though several other much more egregious friendly fire incidents later were.

Kenney made no mention of the friendly fire incident. The 49th Fighter Group's commanding officer, Col. Don Hutchison, later chose not to pursue it since nobody got hurt.

Kenney looked at Sparks, whose trademark mischievous grin was conspicuously absent.

"And you, Sparks," Kenney said, "owe me two more Japs."

"How do you figure that, General?" he asked, puzzled. His report detailed his two kills over Buna, including the Val he flamed after a Japanese fighter shot out one of his engines.

"Well, I know I promised you guys an Air Medal for every plane you bring down. But a P-38 is pretty scarce around here. So if you bring one home all shot up, you're all gonna have to get two more to even things out."

For most of them, this was the first time they'd been exposed to Kenney's sense of humor. After being chewed out, they weren't sure if he was serious.

Sparks attempted a grin, the others tried to stay out of the line of fire.

Kenney turned to Major Prentice and said, "I bet you haven't even got any liquor to celebrate your first combat!"

Prentice looked sheepish and said, "No, sir. We don't."

Kenney looked righteously pissed off. "There you are," he growled. "Robbing me of my only three bottles of scotch."

The place erupted. The scotch arrived and the bottles passed from pilot to pilot. Kenney listened to his "kids" tell and retell the story of the day, flying with their hands, laughing and joking once again, now that the tension had vanished. Kenney had a way of mock-upbraiding his young fliers to impart a lesson, but he usually ended with a bit of humor that telegraphed how much he cared about them. It was jarring to some at first, but when they understood what he was doing, his kids couldn't help but start to love him.

The friendly fire incident was forgotten as December 27, 1942, went down in history as the P-38's spectacular air combat debut in the Southwest Pacific. But not long afterward, all the ground echelons repainted all of V Fighter Command's single-engine aircraft with white tails to help avoid such mistakes in the future. Over the jungle, the white really stood out over the green, which was great if you were a P-38 pilot trying to denote friend from foe. Less great was the fact that the Japanese could see them with the same ease. So much for camouflage.

The 39th claimed fifteen Japanese planes that day. Kenney told General Arnold his kids got fifteen, but officially they were credited with ten—six Zeroes, three Oscars, and a Val. The real number was less than five, according to surviving Japanese records. In the chaos of air combat, it could be—and at times remains—almost impossible to accurately determine how many planes went down, especially when the fight took place over water or thick, impenetrable jungle that would camouflage the wrecks. In the sky, things just moved too fast, and to follow a damaged bird down to ensure its destruction usually was too dangerous to attempt. The inflated claims usually didn't reflect on the pilots' credibility; after piecing together the air battle afterward, they believed the numbers they submitted. This was true on both sides throughout the war, though the Japanese tended to be more optimistic. In this case, the Army and Navy fliers believed they destroyed seven of the new P-38s instead of the one they actually got, though Sparks's aircraft later returned to service. The actual numbers mattered little in the moment. Like so many aspects of life, perception was far more important than reality.[2]

---

2. There have been many efforts by outstanding historians to document who shot down whom on any given day during the air campaign in the SWPA. Both sides wildly exaggerated victories. What matters in *Race of Aces* is what the airmen thought at the time. The kill claims and victories used here are the ones officially recorded in the moment. Where it is important, the postwar conclusions are mentioned, but the context of the time is what mattered to the race.

Both sides celebrated victory that night after this first encounter. They also knew this battle over Maggot Beach was just the start of what was sure to be a long and bitter campaign.

Sometime after dinner, Whitehead and Kenney sat down to talk about the day at the advanced HQ in Moresby. The Fifth performed well. Between shooting down the raiders over Buna and a heavy bomber mission that damaged a couple of Japanese cargo ships, the Fifth seemed to be finding its fighting groove.

Whitehead told Kenney that the Moresby squadrons received about 10 percent of their allotted fresh fruit, less than half of the fresh vegetables they were supposed to get, and a tiny fraction of the fresh meat. It would be some time before they could unsnarl that problem. The men would have to make do. Making do while kicking ass was a lot easier than when defeat piled on defeat. The spirit was turning around.

The two generals talked long into the night. They were old comrades, having trained in France together behind the lines at Issoudun in 1918. Through the interwar years, their lives and careers intersected at times. They built a genuine rapport. Now, they were becoming close friends since Kenney had made Whitehead the commander of the 5th Air Force's forward HQ.

At length, the talk turned to aces. Fighter pilots who could shoot down five or more enemy aircraft were few and far between in the World War I era both generals experienced. It was shaping up to be no different in this war. Any given squadron would have a few malingerers who would avoid a fight whenever possible. The vast majority would carry out the missions, doing their jobs with devotion, if not always with spectacular results. The aces—they were the ones who scored the kills, did the damage, and garnered headlines back home. Fewer than 5 percent of combat fighter pilots, they accounted for 47 percent of all the enemy planes knocked out of the sky.

Kenney and Whitehead took stock of the talent in V Fighter Command. With Buzz Wagner gone, the leading active ace was national hero Maj. George Welch, who earned his first headlines by shooting down four planes over Pearl Harbor on December 7, 1941. He'd scored three more while flying P-39s in New Guinea, giving him seven altogether. Andy Reynolds, a hard-charger in the Flying Knights of the 9th Fighter Squadron ranked second, with six. Beyond them, the Fifth just didn't have many aces. Part of it was the terrible equipment the men flew. Part of it was the lack of air warning for intercepts. Part of it was lack of training—hell, most of the kids the Stateside schools sent them didn't even have any gunnery practice in fighters. The V Fighter Command resolved to solve that issue by creating its own in-theater "clobber college"—a combat finishing school for fighter pilots where they could learn tactics, shoot at towed target sleeves, and learn their assigned aircraft more thoroughly. But that would take time to get up and running. For now, the lessons would be taught by the Japanese.

All this made the fifteen planes claimed by the 39th that day over Buna even more spectacular. Days like that simply didn't happen in New Guinea with the '39s, or even the P-40s. In fact, the day's haul represented half the total score of the 35th Fighter Group's three squadrons to date. Set in perspective, the P-38 sure looked like a game changer.

An ace-creator.

"Whitey" and George Kenney speculated about the pilots they met that day. Who among those new Lightning jocks had whatever brew of psychology and talent it took to be an ace? Hoyt Eason, one of the flight leaders, seemed poised to make his mark. Charlie Gallup? Maybe. Sparks? He had the devil in his eye, so perhaps.

General Whitehead thought Tommy Lynch was a sure bet, not just for acehood, but to climb the ladder and beat Welch and Buzz Wagner to seize the lead in the theater.

Kenney couldn't help but think about Bong.

14

The Hero Makers

December–January 1943
New Guinea

Bill Boni's article about the 39th hit front pages across the country. Midsized papers ran the entire article unedited, while the larger ones like the *Chicago Tribune* chopped it down and relegated the story to the inside pages. Boni highlighted Ken Sparks and the men from Charlie Gallup's flight, but for the first time Richard Ira Bong's name hit the papers. Almost as an afterthought, the final paragraph most reproduced in the Stateside press read, "Richard Bong of Wisconsin, scored two."

Two days later, the 39th escorted a bombing raid to Lae, where Tommy Lynch destroyed two more planes. Ken Sparks actually collided with a Japanese fighter in a head-on pass, yet still managed to get home safely. Dick was credited with probably shooting a fighter down. Bill Boni poured on the ink, describing in gripping detail this second P-38 clash with Japanese fighters. His prose was filled with sports slang, such as describing Sparks's engine as, "kayo'ed" by the Japanese during the initial engagement on Sunday the twenty-seventh. His work, credited and uncredited, flew across the AP wire and into America's living rooms. He called Tommy Lynch the newest-minted ace in the Southwest Pacific Area (SWPA) and one of the most "versatile combat flyers" in the theater. With his ascension to acehood, Boni wrote, Lynch was now locked in a battle with Ken Sparks to be the reigning "King of the New Guinea's Skies," a title once held by George Welch. Other "contenders" for the top slot included Hoyt Eason, Charlie Gallup, and the oddly quiet farm kid from Wisconsin, Dick Bong. The articles earned different headlines selected by the local editors. The paper in Jackson, Mississippi, fronted Boni's work with "Speeding Planes Strike Japs Hard; Nippon Pilot Tries Smasher"—a reference to Sparks's head-on collision with a Ki-43.

Though the squadron could not be identified for security reasons, the pilots of the 39th became the darlings of the American media that December and January 1943. For a year, the press touted the P-38 as the United States' most advanced and deadly fighter. Now it finally began to live up to the hype, and the men behind their controls became household names at a time when the USAAF had few victories to trumpet. In North Africa, the fighting was going badly as the veteran Luftwaffe inflicted heavy casualties on the rookie Army Air Force. Elsewhere, the news was ho-hum. A few raids here, a few raids there in Europe, occasional news out of China, and that was about it.

But here in New Guinea, this small group of P-38 jocks was tearing things up every time they encountered the enemy. In the first part of January, they scored more headlines as they met the 11th Sentai in battle and shredded it with hit-and-run tactics. Japanese records indicate from the fifth to the tenth of January, the sixty-plane 11th Sentai lost twenty-three Peregrine Falcons and six pilots killed in action. In these first battles, the P-38 pilots shot down several of the Japanese Nomonhan veterans, including two aces.

Dick achieved ace status that month, shooting down two planes on January 7 and 8 over a Japanese resupply convoy bound for Lae. A few days later, the newspapers back home breathlessly covered the sudden burst of aces to emerge from the '38 squadron, thanks to the handful of correspondents in the Southwest Pacific Theater. Riffing off what Boni started, a blizzard of new articles emerged featuring the ace race in New Guinea. One oft-published article noted that three weeks ago, the 5th Air Force included two aces and not a single air-to-air Lightning victory. All that changed after December 27 with the rise of five new P-38 aces. Newspapers around the country ran the box scores with Lynch as the number one active pilot. Some of the papers even included all the fighter pilots in New Guinea with three or more kills. Each pilot was given a brief biography, plus the type of plane he flew.

Sparks was described as a "gangling, grinning, bashful hero," while Tommy Lynch was hailed as the "champion Zero killer." Bong was usually described as from Poplar, Wisconsin.

Being devoted patriots and careful to avoid violating operation security concerns, Boni and the other reporters kept their articles positive. Boni made no mention of the fight between Red Manning's P-40 pilots and the 39th. Issues continued to plague the P-38, including a new spate of problems with the guns. Some would break their mounts inside the nose and fire randomly until they jammed. The mechanics were driven nuts by all the weird issues that kept emerging. They'd fix one problem, and another would crop up. It was a continuous battle to keep the small number of Lightnings available in service. Yet, through tireless, thankless work, they kept the 39th in business.

Though occasional references reached the papers about P-38 malfunctions in combat, for the most part the aircraft was lionized as a Japanese killer. The press created two legends that January: the legend of the aces of the 39th and the legend of the P-38's incredible capabilities.

The truth was something less, in both cases. The aces were men, not sports heroes whose exploits took place on a baseball diamond or football field. They went into deadly combat knowing that if they went down, their chances of survival in the jungle were slim to none. If they Japanese found them, they'd be tortured and killed. In the worst cases, they would be eaten. During the missions over the Lae convoy, the men did not even carry life rafts with them. The squadron kept begging V Fighter Command to give them that fundamental piece of survival gear, but a supply of them failed to materialize. That meant if they went down over the Bismarck Sea or Gulf of Huon, all they had to stay afloat was their Mae West life preservers. It was better than nothing, but the area was known for its man-eating sharks. Without a raft, a downed pilot would probably be eaten by sharks before a friendly search-and-rescue flying boat could rescue him.

As for the P-38, its speed, rate of dive, and rate of climb gave it the edge over the Japanese fighters it faced. But any American pilot who did not adhere to the aircraft's strength would find himself desperately outmatched. The '38 was a huge and heavy fighter that bled speed in a turn at an alarming rate. Below three hundred miles an hour, the Japanese fighters held all the cards. They were lighter, more agile, lost less speed during radical maneuvers, and could turn inside any American fighter, especially the P-38.

When one Stateside newspaper proclaimed, "The P-38 Comes of Age" in New Guinea, it was not inaccurate as long as the pilots played to the Lightning's strengths. Anything less would put them at a major disadvantage.

The reporters didn't report that.

There were losses as well. The most painful one came on January 8 when the 39th escorted a bomber raid against the Lae convoy. After a fierce, sharp scrap with the 11th Sentai's Hayabusas, the squadron formed up for the return flight to Port Moresby. John Mangus failed to appear. The squadron listed him as missing in action, and a year later his family in Portland, Oregon, received word that John was killed in action that day.

It wasn't until decades later the truth emerged. As the P-38s were pulling out after the fight, John spotted a crippled bomber limping for home. A number of Japanese fighters lurked in the area, preparing to pick off the wounded bird. It was a Boeing B-17 Flying Fortress with ten men aboard.

John violated the basic rule of fighter combat against the Japanese: do not fight alone. He reversed course and dove to the rescue, driving the Japanese fighters away and saving the lives of ten Americans. Moments later, he vanished into a cloud and was never seen again. The young Oregonian who flew under the Golden Gate and was credited with two of the 39th Squadron's kills became the first P-38 pilot to die in combat over New Guinea.

After the convoy battles over Lae, several of the 39th pilots were granted leave and sent down to Australia for a break. Dick Bong left on January 10, never to return to the 39th Squadron. The Flying Knights finally received their P-38s, and the days of Dick and Carl Planck and others serving on detached duty with the Cobras were over.

Some of the men in the 39th did not shed tears over Bong's departure. Shady Lane recorded his thoughts in his diary on January 10. "Dick Bong left today to go on leave. He's a real loner and not very sociable."[1]

Yet if Bong lacked the charisma of Ken Sparks or Charlie Gallup, he did make one enduring friendship during his time with the 39th. He and Tom Lynch, flying together as a team, bonded in those initial combats. The introverted kid from Wisconsin somehow clicked with the squadron's most natural combat leader. It was an unlikely pairing, but it worked. In the air, Lynch and Bong rose to acehood and fame together. Though they ended up in different

---

1. A copy of Lane's diary is on display at the Nampa, Idaho, Warhawk Air Museum.

squadrons, their friendship endured, the only real connection Bong developed in his first five months overseas.

As it happened, Dick went to go get a tan on the Sydney beaches right as the battered 11th Sentai redeployed to the northern Solomons with the rest of the 12th Brigade. The Japanese shifted their attention to covering the withdrawal of their ground forces out of Guadalcanal. As a result, the furious level of fighting around New Guinea tapered off after the middle of the month.

The comparative lull in New Guinea did not slow the media down back home. More articles popped up in the aces' home states, detailing their exploits. While in Australia, a *Milwaukee Journal* reporter assigned to cover the state's National Guard division then recovering from the ordeal at Buna, tracked down Dick and asked for an interview. It was the ace's first of many to come.

Bong returned bronzed and well rested in early February, just as the most important air battle of the SWPA campaign took shape. The Japanese, having withdrawn their troops from Guadalcanal, now turned to reinforcing Lae. In January, the convoy John Mangus attacked on the day of his death slipped through the Allied air cordon to deliver vital supplies and reinforcements. This time, the Japanese intended to repeat that success on a larger level. Using eight transports protected by eight destroyers and five fighter groups, they intended to land a complete reinforced infantry division of over ten thousand men in one operation. The troops would come with plenty of supplies, ammunition, artillery, and even tanks.

MacArthur's staff, still reeling from the casualties sustained taking Buna, realized that a full, healthy division of Japanese troops at Lae could derail the entire 1943 Allied offensive in New Guinea. Taking the area would require far more troops than MacArthur possessed, and the losses could be devastating. The only solution was to use airpower to destroy the division while it was still aboard those eight transports.

The USAAF couldn't hit ships. The bomber units in the SWPA dropped countless bombs and killed plenty of fish, but actual damage to Japanese vessels was as rare as a lottery win. One study concluded that 97 percent of the bombs dropped on Japanese shipping missed their targets.

Yet, Kenney's future with MacArthur depended on the 5th Air Force stepping up in this crisis. Being forewarned by the code-breakers gave him one advantage. He ordered the Fifth to slow its pace of operations so the mechanics could get as many planes ready for the coming fight as possible. Next, an analysis of previous attacks on ships showed the Allies usually went after them piecemeal, a few planes at a time. Kenney wanted a hammer blow delivered with the maximum number of planes he could get in the air. That way, the Fifth could overwhelm the convoy's air defenses.

Most importantly, thanks to the legendary Pappy Gunn and his band of mechanics, Kenney now possessed a dedicated anti-ship aircraft whose crews utilized a revolutionary type of attack known as skip-bombing. Prior to 1943, most of the USAAF strikes on ships took place from above ten thousand feet. The crews depended on their legendary Norden bombsight to hit their targets, but the maneuvering ships had plenty of time to get out from under the falling bombs. Pappy Gunn changed that completely by field modifying the A-20s and B-25 Mitchells of the 3rd Attack Group with four to eight forward-firing .50-caliber machine guns. With firepower like that, the bomber crews could go in on the wave tops, strafing the ships and destroying their antiaircraft guns. They'd release their bombs, pull up and over the vessels, and be racing for the next target as their five hundred pounders hit the whitecaps and bounced back into the air and into the sides of the Japanese ships. It was a novel concept, field-tested on a hulk in Port Moresby's harbor.

Now Kenney would depend on those two squadrons of "commerce destroyers."

To escort the strike group, the 5th could employ both the 39th and 9th Fighter Squadrons—roughly thirty P-38s. The coming clash would be fought by some of the best American fighter pilots in the theater, facing the 1st and 11th Sentais, the renamed Tainan Air Group and its aces, and even the fighter squadron from the Japanese light carrier *Zuiho*, whose aircraft were transferred to Rabaul for the operation.

On the morning of March 3, 1943, the Japanese convoy was spotted in the Huon Gulf. Kenney ordered the maximum effort strike. It had been well planned to include a mix of level bombers and commerce destroyers with the P-38s up high above both groups.

The 39th led the escort force, with the Flying Knights slightly behind. Over a hundred Allied planes took off that morning. Thirty miles from the target, they ran into the first Japanese fighters protecting the convoy. Three thousand feet above the 39th Fighter Squadron, they bored in after a formation of B-17 Flying Fortresses. The 39th dropped their external tanks, poured the coals to their Allisons, and climbed after them. This was not the P-38's best fight, starting from below the Japanese like that. But Major Prentice ignored the disadvantage in order to keep the Zeroes and Oscars off the bombers.

Fourteen strong, the P-38s climbed into a force of roughly thirty Japanese fighters. After the first head-on pass, some of the Zeroes swung around to go after the P-38s, while others tore into the B-17 formation. Tommy Lynch downed a fighter, but the Japanese raked a B-17 named *Double Trouble* with cannon and machine gun fire. The B-17 staggered out of formation, flames jetting the length of the fuselage from the radio compartment all the way to the tail gunner's position. The bomb bays opened, and the men began leaping from the doomed aircraft. Seven guys got out. One fell out of his chute harness to his death. The other six opened, and the men slowly descended toward the Huon Gulf.

Three Zeroes pounced on the helpless men. Instead of protecting their convoy from the remaining bombers, the Japanese elected to machine-gun the B-17's survivors as they hung in their parachutes. The sight was witnessed by the other B-17s and by a flight of nearby P-38s that included ace Hoyt Eason, Bob Faurot, and Fred Shifflet. Enraged by the atrocity, the Lightnings waded into the Zeroes, reportedly shooting them all down. But in their rage, they failed to see another group of Japanese fighters dive after them. Other men called out warnings. Zeroes latched on to their tails. Faurot and the others twisted and juked, but then more Zeroes piled into them. In seconds, all three P-38s plummeted in flames into the gulf. Hoyt Eason may have escaped his doomed craft, as one of his squadron mates reported him in the water, swimming for shore. If he made it to the beach, the Japanese surely killed him. He was never seen again.

Meanwhile the Flying Knights spotted a second group of Japanese fighters down low, going after the medium bombers and commerce destroyers. Dick Bong and five others dove to the rescue. Bong hit an Oscar in his initial dive, pulled up and came back around to make another pass at it. The Oscar, damaged by Bong's fire, was smoking and descending toward the water. Dick closed on it and fired again, sending it crashing into the sea. He hit another one a moment later, seeing his bullets open a fuel tank. Gas streamed out behind the Oscar but did not explode.

As the fighters battled it out, Pappy Gunn's commerce destroyers waded into the convoy, their forward-firing .50-calibers hammering the ships with thousands of bullets. The fusillade blew antiaircraft guns to pieces and killed scores of men. The devastation shocked the Japanese. Entire bridge crews went down, ripped apart by the heavy machine gun fire. Seconds after the barrage of gunfire began, the bombs began shattering hulls. In a matter of minutes, most of the convoy and its escorts were crippled and sinking. Ultimately, in three days of anti-ship attacks, the 5th Air Force sank all eight transports and four of the escorting destroyers. Kenney's men succeeded in stopping the reinforcement of Lae. The bulk of the infantry division died in the Bismarck Sea, its shattered survivors spread between New Britain and the New Guinea coast. Their food, ammunition, equipment all went down with the transports. Instead of a fully equipped power force, the few hundred who made it to Lae were unarmed, traumatized men.

The Allies lost four planes over the convoy and two more in crash landings. Thirteen men were killed, twelve wounded. The bomber and fighter crews claimed sixty Japanese aircraft over the course of the next few days. Japanese records show the Zero units lost eight aircraft on March 3, while the surviving 1st and 11th Sentai records show thirteen Oscars were damaged. The next day, the Ki-43 units lost seven planes as the 5th Air Force returned in vengeance to sink any crippled ships and strafe the survivors in the water. After word of the fate of *Double Trouble*'s crew made the rounds at Moresby and Dobodura, the Allies showed no mercy to the Japanese in the water. One B-17 crew fired over a thousand rounds into lifeboats and men clinging to wreckage, burning out the barrels of the .50-caliber machine guns as they exacted terrible revenge for those men killed in their parachutes.

The Battle of the Bismarck Sea changed the entire complexion of the war in the Southwest Pacific. Allied airpower now controlled the sea-lanes into New Guinea, and the Japanese would be unable to support their troops on the island until they could defeat the 5th Air Force. *If* they could defeat it.

The Japanese would spend the next five months trying to reinforce their air units in New Guinea to wrest control of the air away from Kenney's crews. At the same time, Bismarck Sea set the table for MacArthur's advance up the north coast of New Guinea in the first big push in his planned return to the Philippines.

The victory made Kenney a household name in the United States. His face soon graced the cover of *Life* magazine. Stories of the Bismarck Sea victory were told and retold in the Stateside papers.

As the press blitz mounted, General Kenney could not have been more pleased. From the demoralized, battered bunch he inherited back in August, the air battles from December to March ignited his crews. Morale skyrocketed in the bomber outfits. While the 39th took hard losses on March 3, the P-38s proved they could be Kenney's vanguard, protecting the bombers far deeper into Japanese territory than any other Allied fighter.

With success came fame. Fame for Kenney, fame for men like Lynch and Bong and the other aces. Families back home read of their sons and husbands and beamed with pride. Prior to the fall of 1942, little ink was spilled on behalf of the New Guinea aviators. Now, between Bismarck Sea and the swelling ace race, the press couldn't get enough of Kenney's castaway airmen. The media blitz helped foster the aggressive spirit Kenney knew the 5th Air Force needed. Now, he just needed more P-38s, and more men like Bong and Lynch and Sparks to pilot them into battle.

Fortunately, thanks to Sandy McCorkle, those men were on the way.

PART THREE

Contenders

15

The Last Bottle of Yellowstone

March 23, 1943
Camp Muckley, Archerfield
Brisbane, Australia

Inside an Australian-built, unpainted barracks building, three pissed-off fighter pilots drowned their frustrations with their last bottle of Stateside hooch. Wally Jordan produced it after another terminally awful day at the hellhole bush-backwater base they landed in after arriving aboard an LB-30 transport from Hamilton Field earlier in the month.

Camp Muckley represented everything they hated about Army life. The base REMFs—"rear-echelon motherfuckers"—were a bunch of combat-shirking martinets terminally obsessed with the brainless minutiae of service. Since getting billeted here, they'd been harassed nonstop by these officers as if they were dodoes back at flight school getting hazed by upperclassmen. Bunks had to be so tight, dimes bounced off them. Hair properly cut, or the wrath of the reigning little field-grade dictator would be felt. Ties were to be straight. Long pants and a full uniform with tunic were expected. Anything less brought rebuke.

They were getting ass-chewings for not having their ties properly aligned. This from noncombat types who knew nothing of what it was like to be in battle. Their war was clean latrines and spotless laundry, not dead friends and icy crash landings. The three pilots brimmed with contempt.

"No liquor in the barracks," Wally Jordan growled as he handed the bottle of Yellowstone over to Gerald Johnson. Wally sported his trademark Clark Gable mustache. He looked like a cross between a street fighter and a rake.

Gerald took the bottle and regarded it. He was not a big drinker, but after the last few months he decided to take a long pull and feel the liquor's fire trickle down his esophagus into his stomach. He handed the bottle to Tommy McGuire, sitting next to him on a cheap, wooden barracks bunk.

"Beats Russian vodka." Tommy grinned and took a slug.

"Heard about that. Those Russians are a tough bunch," Gerald said.

"I kicked their asses!" Tommy lied shamelessly.

"By passing out on them," said Wally.

Tommy took another drink, then handed the bottle off. That signaled a change of subject.

"Never thought getting promoted would cause so much trouble," Johnson groused.

"Yeah, I almost belted that son of a bitch," Jordan said.

"What happened?" asked Tommy.

Gerald explained, "We were over at the field today, and some second lieutenant comes storming up to us and demands, 'How'd you two get first? I've been out here for a year flying in combat and I ain't got promoted yet.'"

"Jesus."

"So I said, 'Ever heard of Kiska?'"

Wally said, "Apparently the asshole never saw a newspaper."

"He shut up after Wally told him I'd gotten two Zeroes. I don't think the guy had any."

"Good thing he shut up. I wanted to belt him," Wally said again, taking a long drink from the bottle.

"The worst part of all this? I swapped Form Fives with that other guy McCorkle wanted to cut loose because I didn't want to hang around doing nothing in the States and take orders from a bunch of twenty-year-old captains—"[1]

"Who have never been in combat," Gerald interjected, "and who can't fly."

"Yeah, the foreign service guys back at Harding sure could fly cir cles around them," Tommy agreed.

"Strictly straight-and-level boys," Gerald added.

"Who would want to sit around and take that? All those people promoted ahead of us, and nobody asking any of the combat vets to impart lessons. Remember those guys we met from the Dutch East Indies and the Philippines? They were just as frustrated as us. Maybe more so," Gerald said.

"Yeah. Then we get here, and we're the assholes with the unde-served rank. How the hell did that work out?" Wally said.

"Like it's somehow our fault they've not been promoted," Gerald agreed.

"So they go around picking fights over it."

Tommy took a pull, then handed the bottle to Johnson. He held it and took a short slug as Tommy got up and started pacing between bunks.

Wally shook his head, "Tommy, you're the only guy I've ever met who can never sit still."

---

1. A Form Five was the USAAF's official flight record. Pilots kept personal logs, but every month they submitted their flight hours on these Form Fives and had them signed by a squadron clerk or officer. They were then sent up the chain of command. Many of the Form Fives survived the war, were put onto microfilm, and endured repeated moves from base to base before landing in the National Archives system.

Johnson agreed. "Yeah, I swear you run laps in your bunk every night as you sleep."

"Bet your wife loves that," Wally chortled. Then he glanced at Gerald, the only unmarried one of them.

"I'll have you know, my wife happens to love my energy," Tommy said proudly, snatching the bottle and taking another pull.

"You dog!" Wally laughed.

Johnson looked over at him and said softly, "I asked Barbara how she would like being a major's wife."

"Major? You! A major?" Tommy howled.

"Said the only second looey in the room," Wally fired back. All three erupted in laughter.

Outside, in the darkness, a kookaburra bird suddenly began calling out. Another soon answered. The air filled with their harsh, witchlike cackles. The men sat and listened in silence for a spell until finally Wally said, "Jesus, those things are loud. Make this place seem like a loony bin."

"If we do any more PT, I'll be ready for one."

The kookaburras spun up again, filling the night with their bizarre and shrill calls.

"Those things are like nails on a chalkboard. They have 'em in New Guinea?" Tommy asked.

"No idea. They have everything else."

"One of the pilots at the field told me about some poor son of a bitch who got eaten by a crocodile," said Wally.

The banter and the bonding continued late into the night, elevating their mood as the liquor flowed. The frustration they felt eased for a time, thanks to each other's company. They'd been together for most of the year now, thanks to Sandy McCorkle. Johnson got back from Alaska and his home leave only to be sent to fighter commander's school in Florida. When he wasn't promoted to captain afterward, he felt robbed, especially given the number of officers he considered useless that seemed to be clogging up every Stateside base now.

Tommy came back from leave, then married his girlfriend Marilynn, whom he'd met while in flight school down in Texas the year before. He figured they would have at least a little bit of time before he ended up overseas again. It was not to be, thanks to a request that landed on Col. Sandy McCorkle's desk.

The 5th Air Force needed experienced pilots rated in the P-38. The 54th Fighter Group was tasked with cutting loose four men for duty in New Guinea. Normally, this was an opportunity to get rid of malcontents, screwballs, and malingerers. McCorkle knew the 54th would not be going out again any time soon and would probably end up as a fighter-training unit Stateside. He decided to send four of his talented but troubled cases. One never made it past transition training; Wally Jordan swapped out with another. That left Tommy McGuire, the least popular but probably most talented second lieutenant in the group, and the promising but impulsive and overemotional Gerald Johnson.

They headed to Southern California, learning to fly the P-38 at an operational training unit outside of L.A. In March, they flew west to join General Kenney's band of jungle castaways. Along the way, they bonded as men of diverse backgrounds and personalities can only do when circumstance throws them together in unfamiliar environs.

McGuire continued to have bad luck with the '38. He crashed one during a training flight but miraculously was able to walk away.

Through transition training, Johnson pined for Barbara, always looking for an opportunity to get north to Portland to see her one more time before he departed. He never got the chance, which made him lonely and emotional. His two Alaskan friends learned to weather his moodiness, just as Gerald and Wally learned to accept Tommy's occasional barbs and acidic comments.

On the plane ride over, they even took grief from the LB-30 crew. Somewhere over the Pacific, one of them began teasing Tommy about his watch, which was stylishly large and nonmilitary. Tommy covered it with a sleeve, acting remarkably self-conscious for a man usually unafraid to fire back.

He got his chance a little later when the same crew member cracked wise and said, "Hey, how's it feel to fly peashooters anyway, especially after you've gotten to fly in a real aircraft now?"

Johnson and Wally ignored the comment. McGuire snarled, "I'd rather fly a peashooter than be a bus driver like you."

Now, stuck in limbo at Camp Muckley, they went through in-theater checkouts by some of the old hands to make sure they were competent pilots. It was an early iteration of the "clobber college" V Fighter Command wanted to establish to ensure all incoming replacement pilots received theater-specific tactical training. What worked against the Luftwaffe didn't against the Japanese. Using tactics devised to defeat the Germans over the skies of New Guinea was a sure bet to get Americans killed.

They didn't mind the flying, of course, but the base was interminable. As they shot the bull through that night in their unpainted barracks, a plan of revenge took shape. First chance they got, they would stick it to the spit-and-polish jerkweeds running the show in this backwater.

At length, they began talking shop, swapping stories about their time in the far north. Tommy related his crash-landing tale, while Johnson spoke of being so cold in the cockpit over Kiska that he had to use his entire fist to press the button atop the control stick to fire the 37mm cannon.

Tommy related a night at the Polar Bar when one of his squadron mates, drunk and sloppy, got pissed off at the owner during an argument. The pilot drew his Colt .45 and shot up the bar, sending everyone diving for cover. Moments later, as the pilot left, everyone returned to their drinks as if nothing had happened.

That brought up one of the worst memories of Adak for Wally and Gerald. The 54th included a pilot who had grown increasingly bizarre and unstable as the deployment in the Aleutians progressed. One day, at the alert tent at Adak, the pilot was sitting alone as everyone was chatting, playing cards, or reading. The pilot drew his pistol, an old-school revolver, and dumped the bullets out into his lap. Nobody really noticed this at first. Then he put one back in the cylinder and closed it with a *snick* that drew some looks. He drew the hammer back, spun the barrel, and then pointed the pistol to his head.

"The guy actually started playing Russian roulette with himself," Gerald related.

He pulled the trigger. Incredulous, the other pilots stared at him, most not comprehending what they were witnessing.

He drew the hammer back again. Pistol cocked, he put it to his head and pulled the trigger.

He blew his brains all over the back of the tent.

Long after midnight, they took their final swigs from the bottle of Yellowstone. Most of the time, the pilots maintained a front with each other. Show no fear; be the baddest, best pilot in the air. Teammates were also competition in the race to be the best in the unit. They were brash and sometimes boastful, always fueled by the ego required to get into a fighter's cockpit, but every once in a while, moments like these would come along, and if the chemistry was right, they'd get under each other's facades. That happened at Muckley that night for Wally, Tom, and Gerald. As they finally called it and headed to bed, all three were as happy as they'd been in months. That night in the barracks represented one of the best times they'd had since joining the service.

*   *   *

The next morning, the three received a summons to visit Gen. Paul Wurtsmith at 5th Air Force Headquarters in Brisbane. They arrived, quietly prepared for more frustration and grief. Instead, they found Wurtsmith to be almost one of them. Only thirty-six years old and sporting his own Clark Gable mustache, Wurtsmith looked the part of a dashing, type-A fighter pilot. In fact, less than a year before, the Detroit, Michigan, native had commanded the 49th Fighter Group over in Darwin, the only outfit in the area racking up a slew of kills against the Japanese. Kenney made him a general and put him in charge of V Fighter Command. It was a bold move that outraged countless aging colonels far higher on the promotion list. MacArthur and Kenney didn't care. Wurtsmith was an aggressive leader, exactly what the fighter pilots in New Guinea needed.

The general talked freely with the three men, plying them with food and Cokes, listening to their tales of the far north. He asked questions about the way the 54th employed its P-39s in the Aleutians and told them a bit about the fighting here.

The royal treatment continued until Wurtsmith dropped a bombshell. "We've got a glut of first lieutenants in the squadrons up in New Guinea. There's just no slots for you two," he said to Wally and Gerald. "You're going to be observers with the 9th Fighter Squadron—the Flying Knights. You'll stay for a few weeks up at Moresby, seeing how things are done, then we'll send you back to the States to share that knowledge with training command."

Gerald and Wally were thunderstruck. They stared at the general as he turned to McGuire and told him, "You're going up to the 9th as well. Plenty of slots for a second looey."

As they walked away from that meeting, Wally growled, "There is no way in hell I lied to get all the way out here, only to be sent back home for nothing."

"Agreed. I'm here to fight."

Johnson thought about a moment back in California in February. The commander of the P-38 training unit approached him and gave him a choice. "You can stay here and train pilots, or you can go on to foreign duty. What do you want to do?"

Staying in Southern California meant more opportunities to see Barbara, maybe even find a way to get married despite Mrs. Hall's continued objections. Barbara had just taken a fall at OHSU, breaking her shoulder. Gerald was worried about her. If he stayed, he almost certainly could have wangled a few days leave to get up and help take care of her.

"Foreign duty, sir," Gerald answered without hesitation. Later, when his folks found out and his mom was upset at his decision, he wrote home and pointedly asked, "What would you have chosen, Dad? Yeah, thought so, too."

To come all this way, only to be an observer, not a warrior? It felt like a kick to the groin. If the world wasn't upside down enough, in the middle of a shortage of good aviators willing to fly and fight over a primeval jungle full of Japanese, crocodiles, and cannibal natives, two pilots who only wanted to battle the Japanese now faced bureaucratic bullshit to even get that opportunity.

They found an ally in the 49th Fighter Group's deputy commander, Lt. Col. Robert Morrissey. He understood Wally and Gerald's position and recognized an aggressive spirit in both of them that would fit right into the culture of the 9th Fighter Squadron.

He told them he would advocate to get them on the roster. But then he cautioned them as well. With no first lieutenant slots open, they would be ordinary wingmen. They were not to expect to have their own element or flight. The combat pilots led regardless of rank. The new guys, blooded or not in a different theater, would have to prove themselves

"Some of the guys may be a little resentful of you too. For every first looey that comes in, it means one less in the outfit's going to get promoted. Don't forget that."

The orders went through a few days later. The next morning, the three pilots showed up to mandatory morning PT at Camp Muckley. They'd packed their bags and were ready to catch a flight to Moresby, only waiting for the transport order to come through.

The officers rotated leading the PT routines. It happened that this final morning, that duty fell to Gerald Johnson. It also happened that some of the worst of the base's martinets turned out to participate that day. They'd occasionally show up and take part, perhaps to feel like they were showing the troops they would not expect them to do anything they would not do. It was supposed to be a morale builder, seeing them there. Instead, they usually nitpicked and made asses of themselves.

Johnson seized the opportunity. A physical specimen, his body hardened from years of outdoor adventures, he possessed rare endurance. He led the group in a wicked intense regimen. The others soon clued into what he was doing and pushed the pace. The REMF officers started to fail. Johnson ran them through the ringer and left them gasping and smoked. They staggered off, furious and humiliated, but unable to retaliate since none of the rank and file fell out.

Afterward, they caught a flight to Townsville, where they transferred their bags to an Aussie flying boat tasked with returning aircrew to New Guinea after their short rest leaves in Sydney. As they settled into a crowded passenger area in the hull, a dark-eyed, curly-haired American with a bag slung over one shoulder stepped through the hatch and sat down near them. When he set his bag down, it clinked, as if full of bottles.

He was unusually skinny, carried a pair of Colt .45 automatic pistols in shoulder holsters and a gigantic knife the size of a bayonet on his belt. He wore an Army Air Force blouse, mostly unbuttoned, Aussie shorts, boots, and captain's bars. He looked like an emaciated pirate.

The man gave them a once-over, and they could almost see him mentally dismiss them as *fucking new guys*. Then he promptly closed his eyes and went to sleep.

Jordan and Gerald exchanged glances. Tommy regarded the men without expression. Finally, Gerald whispered to Wally, "Who the hell is that character?"

Another passenger overheard the question and answered, "That's Captain Tice. He's with the Flying Knights."

16

Where Everything's Trying
to Kill You

April 16, 1943
Dobodura, New Guinea
Seven Miles from Buna

The olive-drab transport plane from Moresby touched down at Dobodura, a wide, flat dirt strip engineers had cut out of the jungle at the end of the Battle of Buna. Originally, it served as an aerial resupply point for the troops, and C-47 Skytrains—prewar airliners called DC-3s—brought in troops and ammo, pulling out the wounded, sick, and psychiatric cases.

With Buna finally in Allied hands, the Japanese in Papua, and New Guinea increasingly isolated at coastal enclaves like Lae, Dobodura took on a new and more important role as the 5th Air Force's forward-most fighting outpost. On one side of the strip, the ship-killers of the 3rd Attack Group set up camp, their Pappy Gunn–modified A-20s and B-25s tucked away in revetments deep in the jungle. On the other side, the Flying Knights pitched their camp. In between, at the end of the airfield, the wrecked hulks of both bombers and fighters lay in skeletal heaps, some still with their canopies splattered with dried blood.

Wally Jordan, Tommy McGuire, and Gerald Johnson climbed out of the transport that day and were driven over to the 9th Fighter Squadron's area. The drive in sobered them. The men they saw working on the P-38s were sunbaked and stripped to the waist in the blast-furnace equatorial heat. Shoulder blades and ribs protruded, their eyes ringed with dark circles. They looked like shipwreck survivors, not a fighting outfit of the USAAF.

The 9th had built its living quarters in the jungle along the Samboga River. Initially quartered in mud-filled, boggy tents, the off-duty pilots were busy building wooden floors atop stilts to make the place more habitable.

The squadron adjutant, Jim Harvey, introduced himself and began giving them a familiarization tour. As they walked and listened, an explosion resounded across the area. The new guys froze. Harvey seemed unconcerned.

"Don't worry. The boys are just grenade fishing in the river. It's the only fresh meat we get around here."

Harvey sketched the situation for them. The Japanese were throwing everything they had at Moresby and other targets in eastern New Guinea. Over the past few days, hundreds of Japanese planes carpeted the sky. Bombers. Fighters. The Knights flew intercepts every day, the pilots bounding out of the alert shack by the side of the strip to waiting jeeps for the short ride to the Lightnings. They'd gotten good at this, able to get the aircraft started and moving in only a couple of minutes.

But the battles took a heavy toll. Instead of the twenty-five Lightnings they were supposed to have, the squadron counted only eighteen. Of those, maybe half were ready to fly. Sometimes, the squadron could only manage to get four aloft. Battle damage knocked some out. Others were constant maintenance headaches. Radios arrived improperly installed. Half the time they didn't work. When they did, the pilots heard little more than static with unintelligible voices washed out in the background. The overworked ground crews discovered the problem: the radio wiring was not well insulated. They field modified the aircraft to fix the issue.

Generators failed, engines quit. Fuel pumps died at the worst times. With no hangars, the birds sat out in the tropical sun, through downpours, and baked in the humidity. Stuff broke constantly. The ground crews threw everything they had into their tasks. They worked harder and longer than everyone else, dawn to dusk and beyond to try to make these fussy, complicated, high-tech planes stay in the air.

When one didn't, they carried the guilt of the loss with them. It fueled them to even greater outlays of energy and endurance. It also fueled their nightmares.

Around the living area, the adjutant showed the new guys to the day room, where they met some of the other pilots for the first time as they sat in homemade chairs reading or playing chess. The men didn't look happy to see a pair of first lieutenants, and there was the instant gulf between new guys and the blooded combat veterans that happens in any outfit. This caused some resentment among the new guys since they were veterans too.

Harvey took them to the officers' club next. A small thatch-roofed wood building, it was the Knights' pride. They'd built it themselves soon after arriving at Dobodura, stocking it with booze brought back from Australian leaves.

Inside, they saw the pirate from their flight to Moresby, Clay Tice, pulling bottles out of his bag and putting them behind the wooden bar. He greeted them with a scowl and a nod.

Over Tice's shoulder stretched rows of cubbyholes. Inside each was a silver drinking mug with a pilot's name inscribed in it. Johnson stepped closer, looking to see if he recognized any of the names.

Beside one that read "Dick Bong," Gerald saw an upturned mug. The name on it was Bill Sells.

"Why's that one upside down?" the Oregonian asked.

Clay just stared at him. Harvey diplomatically stepped in and said, "Those are the mugs of the boys who didn't make it back."

"What happened to Bill?" Tice asked the adjutant. Clay had been on leave when he went down.

Two days before, the Japanese had launched a raid against the airfields at Milne Bay. Somewhere between forty and fifty twin-engine bombers, covered by clouds of Zeroes. The Knights scrambled, launching all eight available P-38s. Dick Bong took one flight. Sells the other. Bill was a Darwin vet who'd been with the squadron for more than a year. Respected, with two planes to his credit, he was also a short-timer, just waiting for replacements to allow him to finally rotate home for a rest.

On the way to Milne Bay, Bong lost two of his four flight mates to mechanical aborts. Sells lost one. With five Lightnings left, they spotted the Japanese below them, their fighters stacked protectively around the twin-engine bombers. Five against at least eighty. As they dropped their external tanks and prepped for combat, Carl Planck's P-38 spewed flames straight out of its right supercharger. The engine lost power. He couldn't go down into the fight with Bong.

Dick went after the Japanese anyway. Alone, drilling straight through the fighter escort to go after the bombers. He scored his tenth kill that afternoon. He, Sparks, and Tommy Lynch were now the leading aces in the theater.

Sells and his two pilots couldn't get past the Japanese fighter escort. At one point, the others saw Sells diving away, at least a dozen Zeroes chasing him. His plane was shot to pieces, but he somehow managed to shake his pursuers and make for one of the runways at Milne Bay.

On final, something broke. The P-38 dropped into the jungle at the edge of the runway, exploded, and burned. Nothing remained of Sells's body.

"I still need to write Dulcie," Harvey said quietly.

"That's Woods's job," Tice snapped. On his last leave to Sydney, Sells married an Aussie girl he'd run into at a movie theater. A whirlwind, hyperintense wartime romance, a quick wedding, and before he headed back to Dobo, Dulcie was pregnant.

The room fell silent. Gerald noticed there were a lot of upturned mugs.

"Hey, new guys," Clay said. They looked over at him. "Remember something. First time I got a Jap, I found it to be the easiest thing in the world. To kill a man, I mean. That keeps me scared every damned day."

He paused; the new guys stared, wordless. Gerald never thought of the other pilot in the aircraft he shot down. He just saw the plane as an animated object.

"If it is that easy for me, then it is that easy for the Japs. Don't forget that when you're up there with us."

They met Sid Woods, the squadron commander, next. Another Darwin veteran, Sid was a capable pilot, an able administrator, but like everyone else, worn out and malnourished. He introduced himself, laid out his expectations. New guys who didn't listen to the old hands got killed. Keep your ears open. Stow your ego. You start at the bottom here with the Knights. Before new guys went out on combat missions, the flight leaders would take them up and see what kind of pilots they were as sort of a talent evaluation process. They were desperate for help, but a new guy who couldn't cut the mustard was a liability. Prove yourself. Earn a slot in a flight. Then earn your keep doing exactly what you're told.

The adjutant gave them a final bit of advice. "Everything here is trying to kill you. Even the birds are poisonous. Leave the wildlife alone. Stay away from crocs—they're vicious. Avoid snakes. Don't touch the centipedes—especially the ones that are almost a foot long. Keep your boots upside down at night so scorpions don't get in them. When you go swimming, watch out for the blue-and-black–striped snakes. They're deadly. Oh, and take your antimalarials regularly. If you don't, you're sure to get it."

"I heard that stuff makes you sterile," Gerald said.

"Better sterile than malaria," Harvey said, "Trust me, you don't want to get it."

As Gerald carried his stuff to his new cot inside a seven-man tent, he wondered if two days before it had belonged to Bill Sells.

That night, the squadron held a fish fry. The day's catch was cleaned and grilled in a grand cookout that was a welcome reprieve from the crap that passed for food at the chow tent. The cooks busied themselves over fires built in cut-down fifty-five-gallon drums, slinging fish from grill to mess plates with aplomb. The officers and pilots ate together beside the river, the enlisted men around them in clusters not far away. The new guys met the old hands and their flight leaders as food was passed and those not on the morning flight roster drank jungle juice from tin mess cups. At length, the men began to sing. First, the enlisted guys would serenade the officers, then the officers would offer a response. The songs were bawdy and vile. Johnson had never heard anything like them. Jordan thought them hysterical.

After the enlisted guys finished their turn, one of the old hands said, "Bastard King of England."

"Hey, you Eskimos," one of the other pilots said to Jerry, Tommy, and Wally, "listen and learn. The Aussies at Darwin taught us this one."

The pilots began singing lustily.

Oh, the minstrels sing of an English king
Who lived long years ago,
And he ruled his land with an iron hand,
But his mind was weak and low.
He used to hunt the royal stag

Within the royal wood,
Better than this he loved the bliss
Of pulling his royal pud.

Incredulous, the three new guys howled with laughter. Food and drink forgotten.

He was dirty and lousy and full of fleas.
His terrible tool hung to his knees.
God save the bastard king of England.

Wally leaned into Johnson and said in his ear, "Hey, that could be you if he only had one ball."

"I really regret telling you that now," Gerald said. Back home, his friends kiddingly referred to him as, "O.B., the Human Mystery" as a result of his missing part.

The song went on and on with verses some of the men created as inside-squadron jokes. When it ended, the enlisted men cheered a thank-you. From darkness up the riverbank, another one began. Somebody played a harmonica. It was a hot evening—a steam bath kind of heat with so much humidity that it sometimes seemed you didn't walk through it, you swam through it. Around them, jungle creatures called and cackled. In this desperate and bug-filled shithole, these young Americans found ways to mitigate their misery and keep their spirits up.

The last song of the night was a screw-you to the fate they faced.

Beside a jungle waterfall, one bright and sunny day
Beside his battered Warhawk, the young pursuiter lay
His parachute hung from a very high limb
He was not yet quite dead
So listen to the very last words

This young pursuiter said:
I'm goin' to a better land, a better land, I know,
Where whiskey flows from coconut groves,
We'll never have to work at all, just hang around and sing;
We'll have a crew of women, O death where is thy sting?

Later that night, long after lights out, the new guys awoke to the approach of Japanese engines for the first time as a night raider arrived to wreck hope of sleep. A few bombs fell, and the base's antiaircraft defenses pounded away as the Knights huddled in slit trenches, cursing the Japanese for interrupting their sleep.

This wouldn't be a summer camp.

The next morning, Wally and Gerald showed up for their tryout. Tommy would have to wait; there simply were not enough functional airplanes. Sid Woods gave Clay Tice the job of evaluating them, and he met the two Alaska vets at the flight line and gave them some further advice.

"I'll tell you the same thing I told Bing Bang Bong when he joined us. I don't care what your old outfit told you to do. Here, we do things our way, and we expect you to learn it. Don't be too daring, or too eager. There's plenty of war here and it is sure to last awhile. Don't ever forget that we are a team. We work together; we fly together. We survive. Clear?"

Gerald and Wally nodded.

"Good. Let's see what you can do."

They headed to their assigned P-38s. Left engines fired up first, right engines a minute after. They taxied to the runway and opened the throttles.

Gerald made it into the air, but Wally's P-38 suffered mechanical failure. He turned back for the strip just after getting airborne and set the fighter back down without any damage. At least he showed Tice he could handle an emergency.

Gerald played it exactly as he was directed, eager to prove his skills and demonstrate he could be one of the team. It was a good start, but he needed to learn a lot of basic tactics before he could be trusted with anything but a milk run sort of mission.

On the ground, Gerald also understood the resentment his rank caused the established second lieutenants. He worked hard to be personable, outgoing, and funny. He wanted to win them over.

A few days later, Tommy McGuire went up with a Darwin vet flight leader to get his checkout. He'd already earned a reputation among the old hands as a braggart. In the day room and the alert shack, he talked a mile a minute, sometimes carrying on conversations with two or three people simultaneously. That was how his mind worked—he simply had a faster processor than anyone else, and any lull in a conversation would bring boredom. Above all else, McGuire hated inaction and boredom. He fidgeted and paced. He talked so fast, pilots never saw him take a breath. It drove the guys nuts and disrupted the chemistry in the day room. When everyone else was relaxed and doing their own thing, having somebody unable to sit still drew attention, and annoyance.

In the air that first flight with the Knights, Tommy slipped into his assigned slot while the flight leader explained the basics of how the 9th flew in combat. Part of the evaluation process included seeing just how well a new guy could hold formation. In combat, they flew loose to give each other room to maneuver. A wide finger four they found to be the best. But on these first in-country training hops, the measure of a good pilot could be judged by how close he stayed on his leader.

The flight lead told everyone to tighten it up. The three pilots on his wing did what he asked. Tommy did it a little slower, and didn't get as close. When the flight leader started a left turn, McGuire drifted and ended up out of position.

The flight leader called out, "Come on, McGuire, close it up. Didn't you guys fly formation in Alaska?"

Stung by somebody criticizing his flying, McGuire lost his temper.

He nudged his throttles forward. Just a bit. The P-38 slid back into position. Then kept closing on the flight leader.

McGuire had already been simmering for days at the idea he'd have to undergo more training and prove himself—wasn't that what Alaska had been for? He hadn't yet shed the conceit that his experience there was nothing in the jungle, where the nature of the war was not only entirely different but was operating at an intensity level the new guys just didn't understand yet.

His P-38 pulled almost even with the flight leader. Tweaking the rudder and twisting the yoke left just a bit, Tommy's bird drifted toward the other Lightning. Yoke back to neutral now, he was mere feet from the lead's right boom.

Not close enough.

He gave the throttles another nudge and eased his P-38 even closer. The flight leader was looking left at the other element, talking to them about their positions, so he didn't notice what Tommy was doing until he heard a dull thud, then felt a vibration run through his rudder pedals.

His head swung right. McGuire's wingtip appeared to be right against his vertical fin and rudder.

"What the hell is going on, McGuire! Did you just hit me?" the lead asked over the radio, voice full of astonished fury.

"I don't think so, sir. Must have been turbulence," came McGuire's smart-ass reply.

"You're too close, you son of a bitch. Back off!!"

"Just trying to fly a tight formation, sir."[1]

---

1. This incident was related in Charles Martin's excellent biography of McGuire, *The Last Great Ace*, but more as an antic and less as a key moment with McGuire's new unit that played a significant role in his future later that spring.

Back at the field, his flight lead reamed him out and threatened to ground him if he ever did something that idiotic again.

The Darwin vets had seen men die needlessly in stupid antics. Victory rolls claimed some. Others were just tearing around on the deck and hit something. They carried the pain of seeing friends get killed because of the stupidity or mistakes of others. The vets had watched pilots with over-bloated egos kill themselves trying to showboat. Worse, those egomaniacs often killed men around them too.

This was no game, and there was no margin for stupidity or an inability to accept criticism without a wounded-ego swipe back. The 9th was short of planes. It was short of pilots. The ones on hand were battle weary, sick with a dizzying variety of tropical illnesses. Some who finished their tours went home to the States to discover their bodies were filled with parasites. Some had diseases the Stateside doctors had never seen. Combining this with the strain of constant combat, night bombings, attacking scores of Japanese planes with a paltry few P-38s, meant fuses were short, nerves raw.

McGuire decided to play a game in retaliation for a rebuke. It was one thing to joke around on the ground, but to endanger another man's life because of a wounded ego? It demonstrated astonishingly bad judgment, and it destroyed McGuire's reputation in the 9th before he even had a chance to show he could be a productive member of the team.

In the weeks that followed, Johnson, McGuire, and Wally Jordan finished their training work with the squadron, and they were eased into operations. Not sure if he was going to get sent home as a result of his "observer" status, Gerald volunteered to fly every mission Sid Woods and his flight leader would let him. In May, he flew sometimes two and three missions a day, always wanting more.

On the ground, all three men made a point of listening to the veterans as they talked tactics and capabilities. The old hands remained skeptical of the P-38 to some degree, and many times arguments broke out between the P-40 believers and the Lightning advocates. Some considered the P-38 about even to the latest, clipped-wing variant of the Zero to show up in the theater.

It was here that Gerald Johnson, Tommy McGuire, and Richard Bong got to know each other for the first time. Bong was still as quiet as ever, but he seemed to have loosened up a bit more with the Knights than he had with the 39th. His introversion was more accepted and not seen as antisocial. He and Johnson developed the makings of a friendship. When McGuire peppered Dick with technical and tactical questions, he was happy to answer.

The other pilots took to collectively calling the three new guys from Alaska "the Eskimos," while Gerald became "Johnnie Eager" for all his volunteering. Tommy became that guy who always talked himself up, who always had to one-up other guys. Fighter pilots were a naturally competitive lot, but the way Tommy went about it rubbed people the wrong way. In subsequent flights, he showed talent and natural ability in the cockpit, but no amount of talking was going to get him out from under the cloud he'd created for himself. He needed a reset, but the squadron's veterans did not forgive or forget. They left him on the bench more often than not. For a man with as brittle and prickly an ego as Tommy's, the situation could not have been more devastating. He just didn't know how to fix it.

17

"Rhumba Cardi"

June 2, 1943
Dobodura, New Guinea

Tommy McGuire stared over his cards at Gerald Johnson, trying to read the Oregonian's face. Johnson stared back, his expression blank. McGuire was the poker master, Gerald the recent devotee. Back in flight school, Gerald looked down his nose at those around him who gambled, considering it an unsavory vice. But time in the service loosened his churchgoing moral compass, and now he played poker with relish.

"Raise you," McGuire said, tossing a wad of currency onto the hood of the jeep between them. The other three players folded. Now, Gerald and Tommy kept at it, raising each other until at least eight hundred dollars in Allied currency lay between them.

The stakes earned whistles from onlookers. They were playing in the shade of an acacia tree beside the squadron's thatched-roof scramble shack. Like the 39th Squadron's, it was open on the sides with netting to keep the bugs out. Inside, Dick Bong and a few others lazed in chairs, playing bridge.

"I'll see and raise you," Gerald said, slapping a sheaf of ten-pound Australian notes atop McGuire's wad.

The two pilots studied each other. Johnson was perhaps Tommy's only real friend in the unit beyond Wally Jordan. But that friendship did not dim the competitive fire that burned in both young men. In fact, it stoked it in Tommy.

Tommy finally said, "Okay, Johnny, I call. Whaddya got?"

Gerald grinned sheepishly and laid his cards down, "King high."

McGuire erupted, "Goddamn! All I got is queen high!"

The three pilots who folded sat in stunned silence, regarding the cards Gerald and Tommy laid atop the hood. They looked like somebody just shot their dogs.

Eight hundred dollars?

The pilots watching the game burst out laughing at the sight. Both bluffing? They laughed harder when one of the other players swore loudly and announced, "I had a pair! I had a goddamned pair!"

He flipped his cards over, revealing two jacks. The howls of laughter increased.

Gerald leaned forward, and with both arms swept the cash off the hood. He savored the moment. Beating Tommy at his own game was an achievement.

Gerald dealt a new hand as somebody inside the scramble shack started winding up the squadron's portable Victrola. A moment later, a scratched-up Victor 78 was laid on the player. The pilot dropped the needle, and the tiny sounds of Xavier Cugat's Waldorf-Astoria Orchestra filled the air with a Latin rhythm.

Music from a tuxedo-wearing big band known for playing the hotel of the rich and famous seemed utterly incongruous out in the jungle of New Guinea. It was absurd in a *world turned upside down* sort of way. The men loved it, and some of the jokers in the group milked it by doing a hip-swaying dance while singing along, "Shake shake...shake those maracas..."

The men burst out with cheers and catcalls, egging the dancers on. Though trained to kill and veterans of hard fighting, at their heart, they were still just kids. In normal times, they'd have been doing these sorts of shenanigans in their college frat houses instead of beside a dirt strip an ocean away from home.

Dinah Shore's seductive voice began to sing,

With tender passion, a secret I'll impart
The Rhumba Cardi means
The rhumba of the heart.

The squadron possessed only a few 78s. They'd all heard "Rhumba Cardi" so many times as to be sick of it. In later years, for those who survived, hearing the song again would trigger them instantly, taking them back to the sweltering heat, the flies and mosquitoes, and the brotherhood of the scramble shack that they would never experience again.

Since the middle of May, the Japanese seemed to have vanished from New Guinea's skies. The alerts and scrambles flown almost invariably resulted in no sightings of Japanese aircraft. Johnson was particularly frustrated, especially after his day off, when the 9th got into a wild fight over Oro Bay, the only big one of the month. In a fury, he volunteered for and flew three missions the next day, yet didn't sight the Japanese.

For the past few weeks, boredom became their biggest enemy. Swaying hips to "Rhumba Cardi," five-card draw, and bridge games were the only weapons against the jungle torpor. Mail from home arrived in fits and starts, but that was a mixed blessing. All too often, the news conveyed in those little envelopes left the men stressed out or brokenhearted.

The phone rang. Its buzzing froze the games and sent a bolt of adrenaline through the men. The poker players scooped up cards and cash and cleared the hood. The jeep was ready for action even as one of the pilots grabbed the phone receiver, listened, and shouted, "Full squadron scramble! Go! Go! Go!"

Dick Bong rose and grabbed his gear, heading to the jeep used for the poker game. Johnson and Tommy jumped in with him, along with an enlisted-man driver and a second lieutenant, an Oklahoma native named Paul Yeager. The squadron's birds stood nearby in a long line, sixteen in all. They had twenty-two total, but five were down for maintenance. The other bird was held in reserve.

Some of the men sprinted to the nearest end of the P-38 line. The others rode jeeps the short distance to their mounts to get to them as quickly as possible. Even as they leapt from the jeeps and raced to the ladders behind the cockpits, the crew chiefs were already firing up the engines.

In minutes, they were airborne, streaking through ten thousand feet, throttles open, Dick leading one of the four flights. Wally Jordan, Tommy McGuire, and Gerald Johnson all joined him in what would become the first of many combat missions these men flew together.

Ground control told the men to climb to twenty thousand feet and head for the coast to intercept a possible incoming enemy aircraft. The Knights looped around the field, noses pointed skyward as the speedy Lightnings clawed for altitude.

As they reached twenty thousand feet, Yeager's P-38 lagged behind. The other pilots looked back at him to see Yeager's head down in the cockpit as he tried to diagnose the problem. One engine lost power, and he fell out of formation, shaking his head and signaling he needed to return to base.

The rest of the squadron pressed on as Paul Yeager traded altitude for speed and doubled back for Dobo. He was just passing ten thousand feet when his troubled engine burst into flames. Paul jettisoned his hatch, unbuckled, and jumped clear of the burning aircraft.

Yeager's chute drifted down toward a series of lakes and swamps about eight miles southeast of the airfield. He missed the lakes, only to crash down into a tree at the edge of an escarpment. With a jerk, he came to a violent halt about six feet from the jungle floor.

As Yeager dangled in his harness, the rest of the squadron reached Cape Ward Hunt and loitered around, waiting for a Japanese raid that never arrived. When the Knights returned, the pilots spotted Yeager's torn chute draped over a treetop, reported its location, and swung into the pattern. Not long afterward, a Piper Cub went out searching for Yeager and quickly found his parachute as well, only a few miles as the crow flies to the edge of the airstrip.

But those few miles between this tiny American outpost in the middle of New Guinea and Paul Yeager could be deadly; an almost impenetrable jungle, teeming with swamps, canyons, cliffs, and lakes dominated by very aggressive crocodiles. Yaeger may as well have dropped onto a different planet.

Woods decided to go out personally, taking his ops officer with him to see if they could find Yeager ahead of the main search party, which was just starting to assemble.

Woods and the ops officer took the most direct route, paddling across the Embi Lakes in a small life raft. On the east bank, they hacked a trail through the undergrowth until, toward dusk, they came to the opposite side of Yeager's ravine. They saw his chute, cupped their mouths, and shouted over the expanse below them, hoping to see if he was still alive.

The Oklahoman was indeed still alive. It took him three hours to carefully cut himself out of his chute harness. When he did, he fell the final six feet to the jungle floor, dislocating a shoulder, tearing his shirt, and ripping his pants off. As darkness approached, he covered himself in dead leaves, then wrapped the remains of his shirt around his head as defense against the clouds of voracious mosquitoes.

He heard Woods's voice and answered weakly. It was too late to negotiate the ravine's cliffs, so both rescuee and rescuers settled down for a long night in the jungle.

At dawn, Woods and the ops officer made their way to Yeager, reaching him by 0800. He was pretty banged up, unable to walk on his own. They carried him to a clearing at the top of the ravine just as some Aussie troops, also hunting for Yeager, showed up. Together, they built a lean-to as the Knights used the Piper Cub to drop food and blankets to them. They hunkered down in the lean-to as a tropical storm deluged the area.

Meanwhile the search party from Dobodura set out, taking rubber rafts and following the same route Woods used to get in. The lake was filled with crocodiles, so Dick Bong provided top cover for the rescue. Buzzing back and forth over the team in his P-38, he could see the black forms of submerged crocs pursuing the raft. Several times, according to squadron legend, he rolled into a strafing run and raked the lake's surface with cannon and machine gun fire, hoping to kill or scare off the crocodiles.

Yeager's plight was a reminder to Dick that their own aircraft were often more dangerous than the Japanese. In this corner of the world, mechanical failure could drop them not into San Francisco Bay but into the middle of a primeval world utterly foreign to them. Worse, that world surrounded the tiny little bubble of military civilization at Dobodura. They were living in an outpost at the edge of the known world, and everything beyond the airstrip was hostile, dangerous geography.

What would happen if somebody went down twenty miles from Dobo instead of eight? Or fifty? Or over Lae?

Dick and the others tried not to dwell on that.

He finished his croc patrol and headed home. The Cub buzzed back and forth, and an A-20 from the 3rd Attack Group flew over and dropped additional supplies. Then the rainstorm shut down flying for the day. The men at the top of the ravine were on their own again, shivering in their leaking lean-to.

Sometime on the morning of June 5, the rescue team got everyone out of the jungle and back to Dobo. Paul Yeager was flown to a rear-area hospital to recover from his ordeal.

The squadron was down both another pilot and another precious P-38, with no sign of the Japanese for days. The constant mechanical failures, the stress of sitting around waiting to go into battle, never knowing when the scramble shack phone would ring, had a cumulative effect on the men. They were wearing out, and the three-month leave cycle to Sydney that Kenney implemented earlier in the year was just not enough of a break to let them fully recover.

Perhaps this is why their squadron commander, Sid Woods, personally went after Yeager. Beyond the flight line lay an alien world that offered minimal survival chances should the pilots fall into it. Woods wanted to demonstrate to his men that whatever the odds, he would do everything he could to rescue them. It was an incredible display of leadership, and one of the reasons why morale never collapsed even in the worst hours the squadron experienced.

From their little bubble in the jungle, the pilots trudged between their living tents and the scramble shack every morning after a gas-producing breakfast of dehydrated eggs, tasteless pancakes, and militarized butter designed to not melt in the tropics that the men called "Marfak" after a popular type of axle grease used back home on automobiles. Each day, the pilots scheduled to fly settled down to wait, listening to "Rhumba Cardi" ad nauseam until even the hip-swaying dancers among the men failed to elicit any laughs.

For the next week, as the mechanics worked themselves to the point of collapse to get the birds combat ready, the pilots scrambled almost every day to intercept not Japanese bombers but wayward Allied planes. It frustrated everyone. Each takeoff was perilous. Each flight a hazard and every landing a gut-check moment for these young Americans. To have to undertake them without any payoff or purpose made it feel like they were flailing in futility.

Three days after a C-47 carried Yeager to a rear-area hospital, the scramble shack phone rang again. The men sprang into action, racing to the waiting P-38s. Dick, Gerald, and Tommy all rolled down the runway together, along with the squadron's thirteen other operational P-38s. Radar reported an unidentified plot over Cape Ward Hunt.

The field at Dobo was wide enough for the Lightnings to take off four abreast. It took steel nerves to pull this off knowing that if any one of the pilots made a mistake, or suffered an engine failure, the chances of a collision and a fiery death were high.

It was just before noon, a perfect day to fly, with not a cloud above—"ceiling unlimited" in pilot lingo. Tommy got off the runway and retracted his landing gear. Usually, the wheels would spin until the tires made contact with the inside of the landing gear well. When that happened, there'd be a sharp squeak as the tire ground to a stop against metal. Sometimes the pilot could even get a whiff of burned rubber in the cockpit and see a bit of smoke.

Tommy saw a puff of smoke and smelled something burning. It wasn't rubber. He sniffed, checked the gauges, and looked around the aircraft. Everything appeared normal; all his engine instruments were in the green. He wasn't leaking anything and the Allisons purred along without issue.

Tommy tucked into formation. Sixteen P-38s streaked out over the northern New Guinea coast, their pilots hoping for something to justify all this effort.

Nothing. Not even a wayward Allied bomber appeared. The sky was as empty as it was blue. Sid Woods ordered them home.

As they returned to Dobo and swung into the pattern, Sid Woods's voice suddenly came over the radio, "McGuire! Your right engine is smoking. Land immediately."

Tommy looked out over his right shoulder. A thin stream of smoke trailed from the engine cowl back over the boom like a gray-black tail. He checked the gauges. Everything was still in the green.

What the hell was going on?

He didn't wait around to find out. As the rest of the squadron watched, he prepped for landing. He lowered the flaps and hit the switch to extend his landing gear. Nothing happened. He tried again. The gear wouldn't come down. He closed the valve switch and tried the emergency system, which was a small hand pump. He pumped the landing gear doors open, but the nose door wouldn't lock. It shimmied in the slipstream, vibrating the aircraft.

He shook the wings, hoping to drop the gear and get it locked in place. The left gear extended and locked. The nose wheel didn't. Neither did the right gear. Below him, hydraulic fluid began leaking onto the cockpit floor. He tried pumping again, but he lost all pressure in the hydraulic system.

The rest of the squadron landed as Tommy struggled with this mechanical failure. He burned fuel and regarded the dirt runway. He had one gear down and locked. He couldn't get it back up for a wheels-up belly landing. He'd have to set the P-38 down on one wheel and try to keep it from spinning out into a ground loop, or cartwheeling across the runway until his '38 was nothing but a flaming debris field.

Finally, down to the dregs of his fuel supply, he lined up on final. Nose up, flaps full down, he slowed to the edge of a stall and floated down onto the strip. The left wheel impacted on the runway. Tommy fought to keep the right wing up for as long as he could. Then the gear collapsed and tore away. The P-38 crunched onto the strip, skidding along and shuddering violently. The props bent back like flower petals in a storm, their impact with the ground so sudden that both Allisons were destroyed.

He slid to a stop, crash trucks racing for him, a line of pilots and ground crew watching from around the flight line. No fire, no more smoke. As the crash crews arrived, he slid off the wing to look over his P-38. The vertical fins were destroyed below the boom. The undercarriage was toast. The engines and props destroyed. The aircraft's belly was ripped up. The plane was a total washout.

He caught a ride back to the squadron area as a truck dragged his P-38 to the boneyard to be stripped for parts to keep the remaining birds in the air.

One week, two precious Lightnings destroyed, two pilots nearly killed by their own mounts. Zero contact with the Japanese.

The Knights gathered the next morning at the scramble shack, chain-smoking cigarettes in relative silence as they settled down to play cards or read the same magazines they'd been reading for months. When somebody cranked up the Victrola and Dinah Shore's lilt wafted from the scratchy 78, nobody got up to dance.

18

Duckbutt's Groove

June 1943
Dobodura, New Guinea

McGuire didn't fly for eight days after his crash landing. As a result, he missed the only big fight the 9th got into that June. On the twelfth, the Knights and the 39th Fighter Squadron tangled with the 1st Sentai's Ki-43s, this time over a remote gold-mining strip at Bena Bena, where some Aussie troops were being resupplied. The Ki-43s bounced the 9th in scattered overcast, dropping down on the P-38s, whose pilots dove clear of their attacks, climbed back above the Japanese, and tore into them. Dick Bong and Sid Woods entered the fight a few minutes later, going after a host of Hayabusas chasing P-38s. Bong shot one down, but was hit several times as Oscars repeatedly jumped him.

The squadron returned to Dobodura without loss and with two kills claimed. Clayton Barnes, who shot a fighter down during the Battle of the Bismarck Sea, climbed out of his P-38 to find the nose and canopy streaked with the blood of his victim.

In the pattern, Dick's battle-damaged P-38 lost all hydraulic pressure. He lowered the gear by hand and settled onto the runway, only to discover a bullet had flattened one tire. He fought to keep the aircraft under control, braking as hard as he dared until finally coming to a stop. Moments later, as he taxied for the flight line, his P-38 ran out of fuel.

During the same battle, Tom Lynch knocked down another Hayabusa, giving the two aces eleven kills apiece. News of the tie came hard on the heels of a nationally syndicated article on the ace race by legendary war reporter Frank Hewlett. Frank, who had started out the war as a UPI correspondent in Manila, had seen action from the Philippines to New Guinea. He traveled around the New Guinea airfields, interviewing all the aces except Lynch, who'd been on leave in Sydney at the time. The article, which ran in mid-June, noted that Dick and Tom were tied with ten kills, Ken Sparks chasing them with nine.

Less than a week after Hewlett's profile of the New Guinea aces, the news broke that both Lynch and Bong had scored again. The race was still tied at eleven.

The fight on the twelfth left Johnson frustrated and angry. More than anything, he wanted to get into the race, but bad luck and timing seemed to keep denying him a chance to attack the enemy. His P-38 suffered mechanical failure on the twelfth, forcing him to turn over command of his flight to Clayton Barnes. It was his first chance to lead a flight and having to give it up was hard enough to take. That Barnes nailed a Ki-43 while the Oregonian was sitting on the ground with mechanics trying to fix his bird was another blow to a young pilot who never missed a chance to volunteer for a mission.

He'd get an opportunity soon enough.

After Bismarck Sea, the Japanese Army Air Force marshaled its resources for a full-scale reinforcement of New Guinea, recognizing that they could not resupply their troops on the island without defeating the 5th Air Force. The summer of 1943 was to be the season of aerial counterattack against Kenney's castaways. Since the P-38 proved superior to the Ki-43 Oscar, the latest-generation

Japanese Army fighters would form the vanguard of this new offensive, catching the Americans by surprise with their new, high-performance machines.

The Imperial Army called the fastest of the new fighters the Ki-61 Hien, or "Swallow." Built by Kawasaki, its liquid-cooled engine could pull it through the sky at over 360 miles an hour. Ruggedly built, Japanese tests against a captured P-40 showed it could out-dive, out-turn, and outclimb the American fighter. Could it do the same with the P-38? The summer of '43 would reveal whether the 5th would be fatally outclassed.

The Japanese hastily assembled two Hien groups, the 68th and 78th Sentais. Composed of a cadre of hard-core veterans from China and newbies fresh from training schools, these two outfits would be the first into New Guinea with the Hien. Together, they should have been able to field over a hundred new fighters, but production delays and mechanical problems with the new in-line engines ensured less than fifty were ready by early spring.

Getting the Hiens to New Guinea posed another major problem. The first batch arrived at Truk Atoll in mid-April, delivered there by an Imperial Navy aircraft carrier. From Truk, the Army pilots would have to navigate across the Central Pacific to Rabaul, refuel there, and continue on to the new airfield complex in northern New Guinea at a place called Wewak.

It was a journey of thousands of miles, and it did not go well from the outset. The first attempts to make it to Rabaul ended in complete failure. Bad weather, poor navigation, and engine failures caused the loss of ten out of thirteen Hiens. Eight pilots ditched at Nuguria Atoll, where the local natives killed seven of them.

Eventually, the remaining Hiens from the 68th straggled into Rabaul, while the Army sent the 78th south to Okinawa, Formosa, the Philippines, and then into western New Guinea. The 78th lost twelve of its initial forty-five Hiens during transit. They joined perhaps another twenty from the 68th Sentai at Boram Airdrome, Wewak. Instead of a massive reinforcement of these new planes, the Japanese faced the same dilemma Kenney had the previous fall. They also made the same decision: get the ones in theater into the fight.

Meanwhile, more aircraft flowed into Wewak. Three hundred arrived in June, another two hundred by the end of July. Along with the trickle of Hiens came the Japanese Army's first twin-engine fighter, the Kawasaki Ki 45 Toryu. Light and agile for a big aircraft, the Imperial Army hoped it would be a match for the P-38. More Oscars joined the reinforcement stream, as did a host of bombers, including the newest and best produced by Japan. The Imperial Army pulled out all the stops after the convoy was destroyed in March. Now, from a relatively small presence before Bismarck Sea, the Japanese Air Force in New Guinea represented a significant threat.

U.S. intelligence estimated the Japanese possessed about 485 planes in the theater that June, with the majority based at Rabaul. The 5th Fighter Command could count 214 fighters on paper, about seventy-five of which were P-38s. The rest were P-40s and P-39s. Help was on the way, but the Japanese did have a small window that summer to take the offensive against Kenney's aviators.

The end of June and early July were the calm before the storm. Johnson and several other Knights went down to Sydney on leave. Tommy McGuire left the 9th for good at the end of June, transferred to the newly formed 475th Fighter Group, which was then training in Australia. His final words to the Knights were filled with his now familiar tin-can bravado. "You guys better get as many Japs as you want before I get back to New Guinea. The 475th and I are gonna clean this place up when we get over here!"

For a guy whom the 9th never let fly an escort or fight sweep mission, it was ridiculous stuff. When he slung his gear and walked to the Australia-bound C-47, nobody except Wally and Gerald was sorry to see him go.

More changes were afoot for the Knights after Tommy left. A batch of the remaining old-timers who fought at Darwin were sent home in early July, replaced by young and eager pilots fresh from the States. There would be little time to break them in before they faced the most intense period of combat in the New Guinea air war.

For the P-38 pilots, the first hint of the Japanese buildup came on July 21, when the 39th and 80th Fighter Squadrons encountered a group of Hiens flying high cover for some bombers.[1] Gun camera film footage from the fight showed what looked to the Americans like a German Messerschmitt 109 interceptor. This was the dreaded scourge of Europe, a fighter both fast and rugged, with a climb rate that even surpassed the P-38's. In North Africa, the 109 savaged the American Lightning squadrons.

The news sent shock waves through the 5th Air Force. After having their way with the Oscars and Zeroes since December, the Hien represented a potential threat to the ascendancy of the P-38.

On July 23, Johnson was just back from leave, leading a flight over Lae at fifteen thousand feet when the squadron escorted some bombers into the area. Most of the ground below was obscured by a layer of overcast, which also concealed a melee between the 39th Fighter Squadron and the new Japanese fighters. As the battle raged below, the Knights patrolled overhead, unaware there were any enemy fighters in the area. Then an Oscar popped out of the overcast in a steep climb, executed a half loop, and dove back into the scud. Johnson saw it and others twisting in and out of the clouds.

---

1. The 80th was known as the Headhunters. After flying P-39s and P-40s through much of 1942 and '43, V Fighter Command finally had enough P-38s on hand to convert them. The Headhunters went on to become one of the most aggressive, best-led, and highest-scoring units in the USAAF. Over the next two years, the 80th and 9th consistently battled it out for top-scoring honors in theater.

He punched his tanks, ordered his troops to follow him, and dove down after the fleeing enemy.

A Lightning broke out of the cloud layer in steep climb, racing for altitude as an Oscar climbed hard after him. Gerald altered course and went after the Japanese fighter. The Oscar pilot saw the Oregonian coming and pulled into a tight half loop, pointing his guns at the onrushing Lightning in a head-on pass.

Johnson fired. The Japanese pilot fired. Tracers laced the sky between both aircraft.

But no bullets found their mark. The Oscar tore past Johnson, flipped upside down and dove away in an inverted half loop known as a split S.

Gerald kept diving, remembering not to maneuver with these far more agile Japanese planes. Ahead and below, a pointed-nosed fighter emerged from some clouds, climbing straight at him. Was it a P-40?

Gerald dipped his nose and put his gun sight on the onrushing aircraft. No radiator under the nose, which was the distinctive characteristic of the P-40. Whatever this was, it wasn't American.

It opened fire on him at about a thousand yards. He triggered his fifties and the 20mm cannon. From long range, the two pilots hammered at each other, even as they closed at over six hundred miles an hour. Gerald missed. So did the mystery pilot, who fired low and under Johnson's Lightning. But in the final seconds of the head-on pass, Gerald saw some of his bullets strike home. The pointed-nosed aircraft ducked under the P-38 as they passed each other.

No turning back. To do so meant maneuvering with the Japanese. Johnson kept going, leveling out of his dive gradually to keep his speed well above 350 miles an hour. When he looked back, he could see an aircraft burning on a hillside through a hole in the cloud cover.

Get back up high, then turn around, dive back into the fight. That was the P-38's game, and Johnson was sticking with it. A moment later, a P-38 appeared in the distance, another Oscar on its tail. Gerald banked and went after them, firing at long range. The sudden stream of fiery red tracers passing his Oscar spooked the pilot, who broke off his attack, rolled upside down, and dove away.

The Knights returned from that fight without any losses and several claims. Johnson received a probable credit for the in-line engine fighter. That new fighter elicited a lot of curiosity among the pilots, who looked over intelligence bulletins and recognition silhouettes after the fight to learn more about the Hien. Early in the war, U.S. intel had discovered the Japanese had imported several Messerschmitt 109s from Germany and may actually have put the 109 into production. That aircraft was given the code name the Type III Mike.[2]

The Knights assumed they encountered those Japanese-built 109s that day. In Europe, the 109 matched or exceeded the P-38's performance, leading in part to a mediocre kill-to-loss ratio against the Germans. Their seeming arrival in New Guinea concerned the Knights. Nobody in the squadron had served in Europe before coming to the Pacific, so there was no institutional experience against the 109. Would they have to develop new tactics to defeat it? If so, they didn't have time to work them out. The pace of operations at the end of that July was so intense that Major Woods didn't even have time to break in the replacement pilots with easy missions. The new guys went straight from Australia into combat around Lae.

Everyone flew on the twenty-fourth and twenty-fifth. Bombers needed protection, transports to Bena Bena and Wau required escort. Though other units ran into the Japanese, the Knights missed those battles.

---

2. It took Allied intelligence time to realize the Ki-61 was an entirely different, native Japanese design powered by a license-built version of the German engine used in the Bf 109. When that discovery was made, the Ki-61 was given the code name "Tony."

On the twenty-sixth, the Knights were lounging around the scramble shack getting to know the new guys as they sat through alert duty. Dick Bong and Gerald sat beside each other in wooden chairs, talking about home and hunting trips with Bob Wood and Stanley Johnson, two of the replacements. The two Johnsons hit it off, especially after Gerald discovered Stanley was married to a woman named Barbara. Same last names, same romantic partner's names. That was enough, it turned out, to spark a fast friendship between the U of O Duck and the new kid, who'd been a bank teller back in his Montana hometown.

At length, somebody started sharing photos from home. Family snapshots, pictures of their girlfriends went from hand to hand around the shack. Somebody noticed Dick's kid sister Jerry in one of the photos. She was beautiful and young, which triggered a whole new conversation about dating each other's sisters after the war. Laughter filled the hut and the new guys relaxed—just a bit.

Capt. James Watkins sat down to join the two Johnsons and Bong. An old hand from the squadron's Darwin days, he'd been a hard-core devotee of the P-40. The P-38 frankly scared him at first. Between engine failures on takeoff and the threat of losing a fan from mechanical trouble or battle damage once aloft, he spent the spring flying it tentatively. This was unlike him. Five foot six, cocky, and usually quite wild on leave, the twenty-two-year-old grew up in rough-and-tumble rural Mississippi, where he had his nose broken twice, once while boxing and again while playing high school football. He tried college, hated it. All he really wanted to do was fly. About the same time Johnson and Bong enlisted, Watkins went in as well.

After seeing him waddle between scramble shack and his waiting fighter, his parachute pack swinging side to side on his rear end, the Knights nicknamed him "Duckbutt." He was beloved by the other pilots for his irreverent and blunt sense of humor, which often trended to the profane, and his Southern storytelling abilities.

He was a short-timer now, a fact that made most men far more aware that they just might make it through this horror show after all. It tended to make them cautious, more fearful. But when Jim Watkins woke up one morning that July, he shoved thoughts of Mississippi out of his head and cast his lot with the P-38 completely. No fear. Instead, he adopted an uncharacteristic *live or die, I don't give a fuck* attitude. He asked Sid Woods to extend his tour, and was granted a few extra weeks, serving as the squadron's executive officer. His swagger, gone since the Knights began flying the Lightning, returned with a vengeance.

The alert phone rang. Somebody answered. The 10th Fighter Sector detected a large incoming Japanese raid over the north coast. Full scramble. The joking about sisters and postwar plans went silent as the pilots grabbed their gear and ran to their aircraft. Crew chiefs strapped them in and clicked the canopies shut. Four at a time in three waves, they hustled into their planes, panting, and rushed into the cloudy afternoon sky.

Twelve P-38s, broken into Red, Blue, and Green flights, sped toward the coast. One pilot aborted with mechanical failure; another got lost in the clouds. The others continued with the intercept: Dick Bong leading Blue Flight with Bob Wood on his wing, and Duckbutt Watkins leading Green, which included the two Johnsons.

They reached Salamaua just before two that afternoon. The three flights spread out line abreast, Red in the middle led by Capt. Larry Smith. The 39th Squadron was nearby, but nobody could see them in the cloudy sky yet. The ground controller diverted the 39th from a transport escort mission to help with the intercept. Apparently, their radar was full of bogeys.

The Knights saw nothing. Smith led them up the coast to Lae. Still no sight of the enemy. Their ground control turned them around, sending them back to Salamaua over the Markham Valley at sixteen thousand feet.

Bong with his eagle eyes spotted the enemy first. Dead ahead, at least twenty of them a few thousand feet below Blue Flight, the controller had set them up for a perfect bounce. The enemy was coming straight at them, seemingly unaware of their presence.

"Bandits! Twelve o'clock low!" Dick called over the radio. Watkins saw them a moment later and called them out as well. The men went to work in their cockpits, prepping their Lightnings for the battle ahead. Heads dipped briefly as they reached down with their left hands to turn on the fuel boost pumps, then reach farther back to switch to internal fuel on the left side, then right side. Heads back up now, scanning the sky as they flipped their gun sight light bulbs on.

Seconds passed. The two sides closed on each other. The P-38 guys kept working furiously in the cockpit. Punch the external tanks—nobody wanted to fight with those gigantic hundred and fifty gallon monsters slung under the wings. Next step: fuel mixture. While cruising, the mixture was set to "auto lean," this had to be set to "rich" by pushing their controls forward. Then the engine's RPMs had to be increased. Finally, manifold pressure—or the throttles—were shoved to the stops. War emergency power, technically known as sixty-five inches of manifold pressure, set the Allisons howling.

A belly tank hung up on Smith's P-38. He tried to shake it loose, but it stubbornly stayed on the shackles. Unable to fight like that, he headed for high altitude to try to get it loose, the rest of his flight covering him.

That left Bong's four and Watkins's three P-38s to start the fight. The pilots hunkered down behind their sights, diving to make their initial head-on passes. The aircraft grew closer, resolving into dirty green Oscars and the new in-line fighters, Hiens misidentified as Messerschmitt 109 Mikes. In the chaos, it was hard to tell how many, so the men later estimated ten of each type.

"Bandits, three o'clock high!" somebody called out seconds before the merge.

"Six o'clock high! Six o'clock!"

Gerald and Dick glanced right. Five or six of the new in-line engine fighters were over there above them, swinging wide around their P-38s to try to bounce them from the rear. Even more of those Mikes were already behind them, diving to the attack.

They'd been boxed in. The new Japanese fighters held all the advantages: height, position, surprise.

Watkins knew the situation was a desperate one. Blue Flight, already committed to attack in the Oscars, was about to get hit from the rear. He rolled his wings and banked hard, turning his '38 one hundred eighty degrees to get his guns on the diving Japanese Mikes. He led Green Flight in a headlong uphill charge.

Go right for the center. No fear.

The three Knights careened right through the diving Japanese formation, guns blazing.

Behind them, it was too late for Bong and his flight to break off their attack. They tore through the Japanese ahead of them in a slashing pass. Bong fired on a Hien. He missed, kept going, shooting his way through the Japanese formation. Then he was clear, looking to extend out and come back around for another run.

Bob Wood stayed on his wing through that first pass, watching Dick take shots as the enemy planes sped around them. Seconds into the fight, his left engine cut out. He looked over to see torn metal petaled around a gaping hole in the cowling, smoke pouring out of it.

Bong edged ahead as Wood's speed fell off. One engine, surrounded by Oscars and Hiens eager to get on his tail, was no way for anyone to fight, let alone a pilot a week into his first combat tour. He took quick head-on shots at five different Oscars as he dove out through the fight, his left propeller windmilling. When Bong pulled out to go around for more, Bob stayed in his dive until, down on the deck, he looked back, saw no pursuers and feathered the prop. He limped home to discover he'd skipped a step in the complicated cockpit ballet required to get the '38 ready to fight. In all probability, he forgot to switch the mixture, or increase the RPMs. When he went to war emergency power, he caused the left engine to backfire, blowing the intake manifold off and probably throwing a rod. The engine was a total write-off. It was a rookie mistake that many made, thanks to the P-38's complexity.

Without his wingman, Bong cleared the fight and turned back for another pass. By the time he did, the sky was filled with diving, turning planes, tracers coursing between them. So many things were happening at once so quickly that no human could keep track of it all. An Oscar appeared in front of him, turning to make a head-on pass. Bong put his guns on him and waited to get close before triggering them. The fifties and 20mm ripped into the lightweight fighter. It exploded in flames, tearing past him while he searched for another target.

He hit a Hien from behind and saw pieces fall away from it as his bullets did damage. A moment later, he bored in on another one, firing until it began to burn and dropped out of the fight. In another head-on pass, he went nose to nose with an Oscar, blowing off its canopy with cannon strikes. More hits caused part of the engine cowling to disintegrate, sending pieces streaming backward. He took one more shot at a Hien, missed, and broke for home low on fuel and ammo.

As Bong fought on alone, Watkins and the two Johnsons climbed right through the diving Hiens trying to close the trap on the Knights. It was a wild fight, with the Americans heavily outnumbered, clearing each other's tails as the more maneuverable Hiens got behind them.

Early in the action, Stanley Johnson stayed with Gerald despite some radical maneuvers that would have shaken loose most other green pilots. But he too made a rookie mistake prepping his '38 for combat. Seconds after the initial pass, he lost his left supercharger. Then his right one failed a moment later. His Allisons lost power as their manifold pressures dropped to twenty-nine inches. Crippled, he had no choice but to abandon Gerald and climb for some clouds a few thousand feet above the fight. He ducked into them and turned for home.

Watkins and Gerald fought on, a team of two relentless tigers who tied up the second group of Hiens long enough to keep them off Bong's flight. Watkins shot a Japanese fighter off Gerald's tail. The Oregonian returned the favor a moment later. They climbed and dived, weaving through the Japanese as they made their passes and kept each other alive. It was brilliant teamwork, and Watkins flamed three more fighters. Then he lost Gerald in the swirling fight.

The Oregonian had turned into an attacking Hien. Nose to nose, the two fighters sped toward each other, the Japanese pilot matching Gerald's determination and aggressiveness. The American opened fire first; Gerald's bullets stitched holes in the Hien's cowling and wings. The Japanese returned fire, sending tracers over Johnson's P-38 high and to the left. In an eyeblink, the two planes sped to point-blank range until Johnson's cannon did its deadly work, blowing the Hien's wing off. The doomed Japanese fighter spun crazily, out of control—and straight for Gerald, who tried to juke out of the way. He pulled up, but the Hien either exploded or spun right into his tail boom, catching the bottom of the vertical fin. Gerald heard a thump. The '38 shuddered violently. He held his climb, trying to figure out what just happened and whether his Lightning could still be controlled.

About this time, the 39th Fighter Squadron entered the fight from the east. The sudden arrival of more Lightnings turned the tide decisively against the now scattered Japanese. Those who could, disengaged, but not all got away. Tom Lynch, now commanding the Cobras, hit an Oscar and claimed it probably destroyed. One of his other pilots, Charles Sullivan, knocked one more Japanese plane down, becoming an ace and ending the scoring for the day.

Back at Dobodura, the Knights straggled home. Red flight returned without getting into the fight. Stanley Johnson and Bob Wood limped in to land. Bong set his bird on the runway and taxied to the flight line, where he was greeted by Elwood Barden, his crew chief. Excitedly, they looked over number seventy together. The P-38 didn't have a scratch on it. Bong lit up at this, smiling broadly. Frequently, he brought Barden a battle-damaged bird after a scrap. When his crew chief asked how many for the day, Bong held up four fingers almost as an aside. He was far more excited to get through the fight without any holes in their Lightning than he was with the four kills, though he wasn't beyond noticing that they made him the top-scoring USAAF ace in any theater. He was the number one Army pilot in the world. Only a few Marines, led by Joe Foss, had higher scores thanks to the 1942–1943 Guadalcanal campaign.

Last to return was Johnson, whose P-38 flew like a wounded duck. He came straight in, using almost full rudder on the side opposite the damaged boom to keep the Lightning on the approach. He sideslipped and crabbed the aircraft onto the runway. At the flight line, he killed the engines and shut the aircraft down, gathering himself as his ground crew surveyed the damage. Bathed in sweat, heart still pounding, and the adrenaline flushed from his system, he began to tremble.

Jack Hedgepeth, Johnson's crew chief, climbed onto the wing to assist him out of the cockpit. Gerald popped the canopy hatch and felt Jack's hands unstrapping him from his shoulder harness. Hedgepeth, a tall, skinny NCO, lifted Johnson up and helped him out onto the wing, where the Oregonian shucked off his helmet and stood regarding the damage to his left boom.

Wires dangled down from torn aluminum. Holes peppered the boom. Most of the lower half of the vertical fin was gone. It was remarkable that the aircraft held together.

Lockheed tough.

Johnson scurried down the ladder and ran off to get a camera. He returned to snap pictures of the damage with his crew chief standing beside it. Smiling and laughing, he seemed to take the dance with death in stride.

By now, the local war correspondents in New Guinea were keeping close tabs on the 39th and 9th Fighter Squadrons. The 9th was now the top-scoring squadron in the entire Army Air Force, and the Knights were developing a following back home, thanks to all the newspaper accounts of their exploits. On this day, Vern Haughland, an Associated Press reporter, happened to be present when the men gathered for their debriefing. Haughland was another gritty veteran correspondent, a man who survived bailing out of a B-26 Marauder the previous summer. He had spent forty-three days wandering through the New Guinea jungle before finally reaching safety. After a long hospital stay, Vern was awarded the Silver Star by MacArthur, becoming the first civilian to be decorated with that medal. The Knights spoke candidly to him as they waited their turn to give their statements to John Spence, the squadron intel officer.

Bong and Watkins were the day's stars, of course. Bong now had fifteen planes to his credit. Watkins was the newest Knight ace with five. Yet it was the black-haired kid from Oregon who drew the reporter's attention. Vern chatted with Johnson, who described the fight in detail to him.

"I caught an in-line engine fighter in my fire—saw it practically explode in the cone of my guns. It caught fire and exploded. I was going to hit it, but pulled up just in time...I looked back, and what was left of the Jap plane looked just like the leaves of autumn falling."

Vern filed his story that night. The next day, newspapers across the country recounted the Markham Valley fight, noting Bong's new status and the two rising stars in Watkins and Johnson. Overnight, Kenney had two more national heroes, and the ace race was the talk of the town from Oregon to Pennsylvania.

Duckbutt Watkins slung his chute over a shoulder and, after giving his debriefing statement, headed for a waiting jeep. Funny, after a year in combat, he found his groove by giving up hope. Not caring if you lived or died turned out to be an act of psychological libera tion. It unchained him, allowed him to trust his P-38 and the tactics the squadron developed. It stuffed thoughts of home and Charlcie Jean, his girlfriend, into a locker deep in his heart.[3]

Don't think about them. Don't plan on returning. Surrender to the moment, to this battle completely, and victories will come.

Watkins had found his groove.

---

3. Watkins named his P-38 *Charlcie Jean* in his girlfriend's (his future wife's) honor.

19

The Innocent Killers

July 28, 1943
Dobodura, New Guinea

Altitude meant life to any fighter pilot, but especially those flying the P-38. With the high ground, a Lightning jock could pick his time and place to fight the Japanese. He could keep his speed high so the enemy could not pursue him after he made his slashing attack. So when the order came down from V Fighter Command to protect a 3rd Attack Group B-25 strafer squadron from low altitude on the morning of July 28, 1943, the Knights must have felt more than a little uncomfortable. To double their discomfort, the mission order called for them to provide close escort for the Mitchells. Usually, the fighter escort was layered with a top cover of P-38s to make sure the close escort didn't get bounced. Fighters are at their best when not tied up. Ranging free ahead or to the sides of a bomber stream, able to attack any incoming interceptors, worked the best to keep the bombers safe. The Germans learned this the hard way in 1940 over Britain. The 5th Air Force knew it too, but there would be no available top cover for the day's mission.

The Knights would follow the bombers to an airfield and naval anchorage at Cape Gloucester on the western tip of New Britain. The B-25s that day were all modified by Pappy Gunn's crew in Australia—except one. The one was flown by Pappy Gunn himself.

Straight from the North American factory, this Mitchell incorporated a 75mm howitzer in the nose, along with four .50-caliber machine guns. Generals Kenney and Whitehead wanted to see how the new cannon-armed aircraft performed in combat. Pappy Gunn, always eager to hammer the Japanese, was determined to prove the howitzer could be devastating.

By the summer of 1943 Pappy Gunn was a pivotal figure in the 5th Air Force. He was the mad genius who backyard-engineered the strafers that destroyed the Bismarck Sea convoy. Kenney put him to work solving a wide array of issues with the 5th Air Force's aircraft. Back in Australia, he was always elbow deep in grease, tinkering with some new idea to give the line squadrons more range, more firepower, or more capabilities. His imagination knew few boundaries—he once mounted a lighthouse's light on a B-25 for use as a night anti-ship strafer.

He was a VIP in the SWPA, and Whitehead wanted him protected. Wurtsmith gave the job to the Knights. Stay tight to the strafers, keep the fighters off them. The P-38s would be a barrier, not a rapier.

They left Dobo just after dawn, the B-25s racing along the wave tops for New Britain, nine Knights stacked above them in three flights at four, six, and eight thousand feet. Watkins led the trailing flight, with Bong as his element leader.

The strafers hit the coast of New Britain just as a Japanese transport plane touched down at the airstrip. Offshore, the Americans discovered two Imperial Navy destroyers. The B-25 squadron split, some going after the warships, Pappy and another crew going after the airstrip. Pappy's 75mm howitzer boomed, its shells exploding around the transport as its passengers jumped out and began running for cover. The cannon fire blew them to pieces and set the transport ablaze. Coming off their gunnery run over the airfield, Pappy and his wingman turned their firepower on the destroyers.

The attack savaged the two Japanese ships. The B-25s swarmed in, strafing and skip-bombing. Pappy's howitzer scored a direct hit on the *Ariake*'s smokestack and a second on the bridge, killing the skipper and much of the crew stationed there.

Overhead, the Knights watched the attack unfold, circling the B-25s as they scanned the sky for any enemy aircraft. Ten minutes passed. Then thirty. The B-25s continued their runs, expending their bombs and ammo on devastating passes.

"Bandits, eleven o'clock high!"

In the western sky, a dozen dots materialized above the Americans. The Knights furiously prepped their P-38s for battle. Tanks punched, they fluttered away shimmering like fishing lures in the midmorning light.

The Japanese held all the tactical cards. Five thousand feet above the lowest flight of P-38s, they dove to the attack. The Knights shoved the throttles to the stops. They needed all the power their Allisons could give as they banked left and climbed into the attacking Japanese planes.

The two sides merged, red and green tracers lacing the sky in long ropes between them. In seconds, Bong lost his wingman, Lieutenant Hyland, who as the squadron's last man quickly attracted four Japanese fighters. *Zeroes? Hayabusas?* In the crazy chaos of air combat where pilots covered hundreds of feet in seconds, identification came a distant second to survival. The two planes looked similar enough and had similar performance, so the tactics would always be the same for the P-38s: speed high, one pass, and haul ass.

Hyland dove away, heading for the wave tops with those four fighters chewing at his heels. Bong and Watkins blew through the Japanese formation, shooting as they went. Watkins stayed nose to nose with one fighter until his guns set it afire. It exploded right in front of him, and he maneuvered wildly to avoid the debris.

After that pass, Watkins dove away, leveling off at four thousand feet, intending to zoom-climb and reenter the fight. When he looked back to clear his tail, Bong was nowhere in sight. No time to worry, a pair of Oscars were coming straight at him.

Bong lost Hyland and Watkins in the mad dash through the Japanese fighters. Diving clear, he climbed back up to eight thousand feet too early. He spotted five other Knights working together to drive the Japanese away from the B-25s and started to wing over to go after them, when suddenly his P-38 shuddered. A sound like hail on a car roof filled his ears.

He checked his tail and what he saw sent a paralyzing chill down his arms. A Hayabusa was parked right behind him, sending a stream of bullets into his Lightning.

Bong proved quicker than the Japanese pilot. Five rounds struck his fighter, but with sweat dripping into his eyes he jinked out of the line of fire and put his nose to the water. The P-38 dropped out of the sky, leaving the Hayabusa far behind.

Watkins pointed his guns at the onrushing Oscars. Head-on passes were mostly lose-lose affairs for the Japanese if the American possessed any marksmanship abilities. The concentrated cone of death created by the 20mm cannon and four fifties could blow apart the lightly constructed Japanese planes. In return, Oscars carried only two rifle-caliber machine guns. They were outmatched, and the two Japanese headed toward Watkins seemed to know it. One broke off the head-on pass by pulling up in front of Jim, intending to half loop over him and roll back down onto his tail. The other one went low.

Watkins reached the looping Oscar just as it began to flip on its back. Watkins drilled him. The fighter caught fire and dropped for the sea.

Unable to join with the other P-38s because of that lone Oscar's attack, Bong tried to clear the fight and get some altitude. Then he spotted two Oscars chasing a B-25. He pulled out all the stops, bending around after them and firing a long, concentrated burst at the lead plane from forty-five degrees behind and above the Japanese pilot. His bullets sawed into the Oscar. The pilot had one chance: break hard right into the attack. It would give Bong a much more difficult shot, and set the Japanese up to pull a quick 180-degree turn and get behind him.

Bong crippled him before he could do that. The Japanese fighter fell off on its right wing and splashed into the Bismarck Sea. The other one abandoned its pass on the B-25.

Down low, with no other P-38s around him now, Bong decided it was time to get home. He turned south, only to get bounced by two more Japanese fighters. They dove after him, chasing him across the whitecaps. Bong trusted in his P-38, throttles wide open. The Lightning was almost a hundred miles an hour faster than the Oscar on the deck, and the Japanese simply couldn't catch him even with the extra speed gained in the dive. They fell behind, perhaps hoping he would turn back and make a mistake. He didn't, and at length they gave up their pursuit. Bong headed for home, encountering the B-25s on the way, fresh from crippling both destroyers. He climbed above them and protected them back to Dobodura. Both warships later sank.

The Knights claimed seven Japanese planes that day. Watkins bought the drinks that night at the bar they'd built in the jungle at Dobodura, having scored three kills altogether that day. In two days, he vaulted from obscurity as a one-kill P-40 devotee to one of the leading aces in theater with nine kills. It was an amazing accomplishment, one that Gerald Johnson hoped to emulate. The squadron celebrated and morale lifted. Winning always did wonders for the mood, which was often tense on the ground. The men lived a pressure-cooker existence in a primitive space filled with physical misery. Kicking the enemy in the teeth meant an escape from that. For the moment, nobody scratched his jungle rot or minded the dreadful food while gathered in the O club, toasting the latest ace within their ranks.

As they partied, the weather turned ugly. Dark clouds dumped buckets of rain on the men at Dobodura. Over the next few days, they sat in the tents, listening to thunder cracking around them. Missions were scrubbed and the men resigned themselves to a bout of New Guinea cabin fever.

In the meantime, things were changing within the squadron. By now, almost all the Darwin vets were gone or getting ready to leave. The 9th would soon say farewell to its core leadership group. Sid Woods, Larry Smith, and Duckbutt Watkins would need replacing. Gerald Johnson impressed all of them, not only with his tenacious flying and constant volunteering, but he was also settling down into a capable leader. They pulled him into the leadership core, giving him a chance to prove himself as an administrator on the ground and a flight leader in the air.

On the night of August 1, 1943, Sid Woods sought out the young Oregonian and told him the morning mission would be his. He'd brief and lead the squadron. The torch was being passed. The old hands were letting the now not-so-new guys of spring take the reins.

They'd be escorting strafing B-25s again. Down low, a repeat of the twenty-eighth, except this time, the P-38s from the 80th Fighter Squadron would give them top cover from fifteen thousand feet. Johnson spent the evening planning the mission, helping assemble the roster. He picked Stanley Johnson to be his wingman, and Jump O'Neil would have his second element. Johnson gave Wally Jordan Blue Flight, his first shot at an aerial command. Watkins would be the old hand looking after everyone from above and behind.

The next morning, Gerald gathered with the other pilots and went over the mission. The B-25s would run along the coast from Lae up toward Saidor on the Huon Peninsula, shooting up any

Japanese shipping they found. These were called "barge hunt missions." After the Bismarck Sea, small coastal convoys of landing craft and luggers proved to be the only way to get supplies to Lae. General Whitehead wanted to choke this route off too and leave Lae starved and running out of ammunition in the final weeks before the scheduled Allied invasion there.

Johnson led the 9th aloft at the van of a sixteen-plane formation. They linked up with the 80th, found the B-25s, and headed for the coast. The weather cooperated for a change, with a sixteen-thousand-foot ceiling and scattered clouds below. Gerald positioned his flight ahead of the B-25s and above them at four thousand feet. Wally Jordan's flight covered his back, two thousand feet above and behind him. The remaining two flights were stacked up behind Blue to eight thousand. Should any Japanese try to intercept the bombers, they'd have layers of P-38s to get through first.

They made contact with some Japanese shipping near Lae, and the fighter pilots watched in awe as the B-25s ripped the ships apart with their incredible firepower. Those eight machine guns in their noses shredded wooden-hulled boats as if they were made of paper. Johnson later wrote that nobody could have survived such an onslaught. Given what they knew of the savagery the Japanese troops displayed toward the Aussies and American troops fighting in the nearby jungle, few of the Knights lost any sleep over the sight of this carnage.

The bombers continued on, blowing apart barges and landing craft they found hiding in coves and inlets. Johnson kept Captive Red Flight in the van, ready to engage any fighters trying to make a head-on run against the strafers.[1] They pushed up the coast, heading for Saidor on the Huon Peninsula, the B-25s leaving columns of smoke like funeral pyres in their wake.

------

1. "Captive" was the 9th Fighter Squadron's call sign in the air.

At But Drome, Wewak, that morning, the veterans of the 24th Sentai took off on one of the most important missions of their careers. The 24th was a storied unit that had been in near-continuous action since the late 1930s. The unit flew the latest Ki-43 Oscars, up-armed with two 12.7mm heavy machine guns and a slightly more powerful engine. It still could not catch a P-38, but it was an upgrade.

Forty-year-old Lt. Col. Hachio Yokoyama, the sentai's commander, led the mission that day. Yokoyama had joined the Imperial Army in 1931 and was already a seasoned sentai commander by the time he led Japan's most famous unit into battle against the Russians in 1939. He became an ace in that bitter border war, commanding the 64th Sentai. Shot down and wounded, he evaded capture and returned to Japanese lines. After he recovered, he served as a test pilot before taking the 24th to New Guinea. Yokoyama was a legend in the Army Air Force, a national hero back in Japan, and one of the most experienced fighter leaders in New Guinea.

His best squadron commander, ace 1st Lt. Mokosuke Kashima, flew in the formation with him, along with the most talented veteran pilots left in the 24th. The unit arrived in New Guinea from the Dutch East Indies in May, and its men knew all too well the danger posed by Kenney's P-38s. They would be extra alert that day, for their job was to escort Lt. Gen. Hatazo Adachi's plane to Lae for an inspection trip. Only a few months before, P-38s in the Solomon Islands shot down and killed the Japanese commander of the Combined Fleet, Admiral Isoruku Yamamoto. Adachi was the senior Army general in the Southwest Pacific, and the Japanese could ill afford to lose him.

Flying in a mid-1930s fixed-gear reconnaissance bomber, Adachi's pilot hugged the coast at less than five hundred feet. The escorting Oscars stacked around their charge from five hundred to five thousand feet.

Just after lunchtime, the escorted general ran headlong into the strafing Mitchells and their protective layers of P-38s. The collision between the two groups caught everyone off guard. Adachi's recon plane broke hard and ran east out to sea in a desperate attempt to get away from all the P-38s. Meanwhile, Yokoyama's high cover at five thousand feet was sandwiched between Gerald's flight and Wally's. Some of the Oscars rolled inverted and did a split S down on Captive Red. Others went after Jordan's pilots.

Wally saw the threat to Red and dove after one of the Oscars, his wingman, Grover Fanning, trying to follow despite his external tanks hanging up. Wally was always a tiger, aggressive and bold with his flying. Now, he finally had an opportunity to get a kill, and he followed this Oscar relentlessly. The Ki-43 pilot saw him diving behind and banked hard left to avoid his attack. Normally, the P-38 pilot would keep going, blow past the turning Ki-43 and extend out of the fight. Not this time. Wally wanted this Oscar. He twisted the yoke, his wings rolling perpendicular to the water below, and he tucked into a tight turn after the Japanese plane.

Right then, Fanning saw Wally had set himself up. Other high-cover Ki-43s hadn't dropped down into the attack yet. Now one rolled in on Wally from behind and to the right as he turned after his quarry. Fanning could have dived on and tried to tear his external tanks loose, but the Knights were about teamwork, and his leader was in trouble. So Fanning threw caution to the wind and yanked his P-38 into a hard right turn. His speed bled off. The P-38 felt sluggish with the drag of the drop tanks still under the wings. Yet, he pulled around tight enough to get his guns on that attacking Oscar. A long burst and his cannon shells blew the canopy apart. The Oscar rolled over, flames streaming from the engine, and fell toward the Huon Gulf.

Seconds later, after a complete 180-degree turn, Wally took a shot at his Oscar. Few Lightning pilots could have followed a far more maneuverable Oscar around in such a turn, but somehow Wally pulled it off. His aim was hot straight and true. The Ki-43 exploded and spun wildly downward, out of the fight.

Meanwhile, the two Johnsons and Jump O'Neil reacted to the bounce by turning in to the attackers and sticking their guns on them. O'Neil's tanks refused to release too, but he stayed with Gerald and Stanley through the initial climbing, head-on pass. Right then, two Oscars, wreathed in flames, spun past Gerald and Stanley on either side of the Lightnings, victims of Blue Flight's handiwork. Seconds later, they lit into the reaming Japanese fighters. Gerald went after one, trying to take a ninety-degree deflection shot at it. These were among the toughest types of shots in aerial combat, as the lead required was considerable. Johnson, a crack shot with rifle and shotgun back home, led the Japanese fighter, closed, and pressed his gun triggers.

Nothing. He pressed again. Nothing. The Ki-43 loomed in front of him. As Gerald tucked under it to avoid a collision, he saw the Japanese pilot wave at him. He sped past, checking behind him to see the Japanese fighter rolling right and turning onto his tail.

Speed saved him. The Lightning zoomed out of range before the agile Oscar could swing behind him. A quick look over his shoulder revealed it falling well behind. Stanley Johnson was right there with him, like a shadow. Where was O'Neil? Gerald scanned the sky for his other pilot and saw him diving away, one tank still stuck stubbornly on his wing, an Oscar behind him, but it was losing ground.

It would be him and Stanley. He banked and came back around for another pass, charging and recharging his guns, hoping they'd fire. The Oscar pilot accepted the challenge and bored headlong at the two P-38s, firing furiously as they merged.

Gerald triggered his guns again. Nothing. The fight of his life, and he had no way to fight. Still, he stayed in the head-on pass, playing chicken with the Oscar as Japanese tracers zipped past his P-38.

A split second later, they merged, the Ki-43 already turning to get on the Oregonian's tail.

Stanley put an end to that. The former bank teller caught the Ki-43 in its turn and blew it apart with a deadly accurate deflection shot.

Stanley had saved Gerald's life. It was a wake-up call for the Oregonian. Without working armament, Gerald had no business going nose to nose with the Japanese. That was just too reckless. When Duckbutt Watkins and his men piled into the melee, Gerald dove to the whitecaps and ran for home. Behind him, Watkins flamed three Oscars in quick succession. Other pilots knocked down seven more.

One Ki-43 escaped on the wave tops. But within minutes, only one Japanese fighter remained in the air. Practically all the remaining Knights went after it. The pilot dodged every attack, refusing every attempt the Americans made to go head-to-head with him. Experienced enough to know the dangers of the P-38's concentrated firepower, he chose instead to dodge and juke, taking snap shots whenever he could. Pass after pass, the 9th missed this canny Japanese pilot, who'd whip his fighter around in incredibly tight turns to try to get his guns on the slashing Lightnings after they sped by. The Ki-43 didn't have the speed to run away. All the pilot could do was keep fighting until he either died or the P-38s gave up. Eventually, the 9th, low on fuel and ammo, let the Japanese pilot go and turned for home. It was an epic one-versus-many dogfight that ended in a draw. Exactly who that lone aviator was will never be known, but he might have been Warrant Officer Chiyoji Saito, a veteran ace with over twenty kills to his credit.

The 24th Sentai's survivors straggled back to Wewak. The ground crews waited anxiously for hours, hoping more planes would return. Toward dusk, they gave up, and the 24th sank into despair. Both Lieutenant Colonel Yokoyama and Lieutenant Kashima had died in the fight. The battle gutted the 24th Sentai's leadership and dealt a stunning blow to the Imperial Army's fighter units in New Guinea. A national hero made famous by his exploits against the Russians four summers before was gone.

General Adachi survived, his plane reaching the strip at Cape Gloucester that Pappy Gunn had strafed with his cannon-armed B-25 on the twenty-eighth. He continued on to Rabaul, where he reported by radio back to New Guinea that he was safe. The cost to keep him alive had been a steep one indeed.

If August 2 was a dark day for the Japanese, it was a spectacular victory for the 9th Fighter Squadron, whose pilots claimed eleven kills without a single loss. One pilot aborted the mission with hydraulic failure and crashed back at Dobodura, but he survived unhurt. Watkins was the star of the day again, having scored ten kills in eight days. He passed Tom Lynch and now was the second-ranking ace in New Guinea, within striking distance of Dick Bong.

This time, Lee Van Atta of the International News Service scored the scoop. Lee was a fearless combat journalist only two weeks past his twenty-first birthday. Before going into journalism, he'd been a teenager in Hollywood, appearing in six films, including *Dick Tracy*. Lee was the same age as the pilots he wrote about, and he was well known for an almost reckless desire to see the war firsthand from their perspective. When he sought out Jim Watkins, the Mississippi native gave him a surprisingly candid interview. He also talked to Lee about killing. "It's funny, though—when we're up there scrapping, I never think of killing a man. My only objective is to destroy another Jap plane. I never want to be a killer, but when I remember what the Nips have done to Americans, I'm glad to see them get what they deserve."

He added, "I am actually beginning to enjoy watching those Japs bail out with chutes that don't open."

Bong and Gerald Johnson were the same way, as probably most of the fighter pilots were that summer. Their war was remote, a standoff duel of guns and machines. They rarely saw the enemy they killed and never thought of the pilots in the planes. It was a coping mechanism for young men a year removed from civilian jobs, Sunday church services preaching peace, and a world away from the sudden death they faced every time they climbed into the cockpit. Yet, they embraced their role in the war effort and loved being fighter pilots, something civilians often did not understand.

After Gerald received a wave of press back home, Barbara wrote him, "I think you like your job too much." Gerald bristled at this. To him, dedication to the war effort was the reason he volunteered for so many missions, but in his most honest moments he recognized that Barbara hit a little too close to home. Being a fighter pilot was the biggest high he'd ever known. Proving he was better than the other pilot shooting at him fed something in him he didn't understand, and the more he thought about it, he realized he didn't want to. He'd prefer to go on thinking he was only destroying machines.

Bong did the same, though he probably ruminated less than Gerald did on the human cost of their work. More than Gerald, though, Dick was acutely aware that his score was bringing him increasing attention and that Stateside fame may lead to some paparazzi and fangirl moments when he got back home. For an introvert, this terrified Dick. He didn't want attention, felt awkward in its spotlight. He avoided drawing attention to himself when he could, but at times V Fighter Command ordered him to talk to the press. There were rumblings that he would be sent home on a war bonds tour, like other aces were doing. Joe Foss, Marion Carl, John L. Smith—the Marine hero fighter pilots of Guadalcanal—roamed the country on such a tour after they got back from combat earlier in the year. That was way too far out of Bong's comfort zone. He knew he was awkward and lacking as a public speaker. To his mother, he wrote, "I don't want to come home to make speeches to any hero-worshipping public. Not that I don't want to come home, but I don't want it under those circumstances. I would much rather get home without anyone knowing about it."

Stateside adulation and media attention were par for the course for anyone knocking down Japanese planes. In Jim, Gerald, and Dick, a competitive fire burned that drove the rivalry between them. It also helped the 9th Squadron's sense of esprit de corps to know that they were Kenney's elite, the best of the best, with the kill flags on their aircraft to prove it. Their score was important, and they watched the ace ladder as carefully as they would a sporting event. All three wanted to be number one. Gerald lagged behind, but he'd also matured that summer in a way that earned him a promotion to captain. He'd seen firsthand how teamwork in the air kept men alive. One P-38 was vulnerable, but two P-38s working together? Almost unbeatable. The August 2 fight drove the point home. Without Stanley sticking to his tail, he may not have come home. He'd gone from the moody kid intent on proving himself to a respected leader who always looked after his team. As he matured as a fighter pilot, he never chose personal score over what was best for the men around him. What was best was keeping everybody alive first, shooting planes down second.

Wally Jordan, ever the wild one, would be Gerald's right-hand man in the weeks to come. The two were fast friends, though total opposites in many ways. Gerald, the adrenaline junkie, couldn't match Wally's *live hard, play hard* ethos, which was underscored when he and Dick were granted leave together. Along with several other undernourished, tired pilots, they would soon be flying south to Sydney and the squadron's seven-room flat in the Buckingham Building.

Dick was looking forward to eating real food—steaks and ice cream, time on the beach, and the chance to enjoy life without constant fear and tension for a few days. But Wally had other plans. "We're gonna eat, drink, and screw! And we'll have no trouble doing any of that!"

By now, Bong was an accepted if not entirely understood member of the Knights. He'd never felt fully like a member of the 39th, but after all the fighting and scoring, he was a Knight and liked by most everyone. He rarely confided in those around him, so he formed no deep bonds. That wasn't his way. In that respect, he was very much like his father, distant and quiet, a throwback sort of person who never shirked from hard work or dangerous duty.

Despite the combat and the killing, he was still an innocent farm kid. He barely drank, didn't smoke, and had never been with a girl. He didn't even have a girl back home, unlike most of the guys in the squadron.

Wally Jordan resolved to change all that and corrupt the Wisconsin farm kid with booze, women, and smokes. They headed off to Sydney in early August, where they lived with a waterfront view from Point Piper and the parties at the Buckingham never ended. They were wild, carnal days and nights filled with male bonding, a few brawls with other squadrons or Aussies, and lots of alcohol. They ate like there was no tomorrow and tried to live a lifetime in a ten-day leave. They were coiled tight, combat aviators who lived on the edge of death, who had seen the worst of human behavior and suffered the grief of friends killed or maimed. At the Buckingham, they let out all the tension. They celebrated life. They experimented. They chased women, and some fell in love. Those ten days were lived on the opposite extreme of their existence in New Guinea. From want to plenty. From celibacy to sexual indulgence their parents would have been shocked to learn of. The polarities seemed somehow to bring them into balance and prepare them for the grueling psychological challenges ahead.

Wally returned from Sydney with a girlfriend named Ruby, who promised to hook up with him every time he got leave. Dick climbed off the transport with a big grin on his face and a cigar stuck between his lips, two massive bags slung over his shoulders. One held two cases of beer, the other a dozen bottles of the finest alcohol he could find on the Aussie black market. He was worldly, no longer the unknown Midwest innocent who looked up in awe at the St. Francis Hotel the year before. Wally watched his brother Knight climb into a waiting jeep, exhaling a cloud of cigar smoke as he settled in, and thought, *Mission accomplished.*

Bong carried his score of alcohol to the squadron's bar and began pulling the bottles out one at a time. Everyone who drank did their best to restock the bar with black market booze from Australia. That August, the pickings behind the counter were getting pretty thin, so the reinforcements were much appreciated by everyone. When one precious bottle slipped from his fingers and shattered on the wooden floor, Dick looked down at the wasted liquor and almost started to cry.

20

Return of the Outcast

August 18, 1943
Fourteen Mile Drome, Port Moresby, New Guinea

As his aces cut a swath through the new Japanese Army Air Force units, General Kenney wanted to know from where all the new planes were coming. Through the summer, his photo recon squadrons buzzed over New Guinea, searching for the Japanese buildup. They found it, of course, at the airfield complex around Wewak. Photo reconnaissance showed Japanese aircraft crammed into the five airdromes there, none of which were properly developed enough to handle the hundreds of planes sent from the Home Islands. Without dispersal areas, the planes sat around the runways, and the influx of personnel to fly and maintain them lived in filthy, primitive conditions that took a heavier toll than the 5th Air Force could. Amebic dysentery, malaria, jungle rot, fevers, scrub typhus, and dozens of other diseases felled about 60 percent of the men at Wewak.

Kenney recognized the threat the new Japanese units posed and resolved to knock them out with the most destructive force he possessed—Pappy Gunn's strafers. The Japanese, thinking Wewak was out of range of American fighters and medium bombers, did not adequately protect their own airfields. A sense of bizarre complacency had set in for them. The Japanese felt safe.

Pappy Gunn changed that. He devised an auxiliary fuel tank for his modified B-25 strafers that could be ejected from the fuselage through a trapdoor installed where the Mitchell's belly turret was usually located. The extra three hundred gallons gave the Mitchells the legs needed to get to Wewak.

To protect them, Kenney wanted every single P-38 in theater overhead, knocking down any Japanese planes that rose to defend the airfields. Through the first part of the summer, he possessed three P-38 squadrons: the 39th, 9th, and 80th. Collectively, they fielded about forty fighters on any given day. That would not be enough to keep the B-25s safe.

In June, Kenney formed the 475th Fighter Group in Australia. This was his baby, and it was staffed with a mix of veteran talent from the three established Lightning squadrons and a raft of well-trained newbies fresh from the West Coast. They spent a month and a half assembling newly arrived P-38s and melding into a combat outfit. By early August, Kenney could wait for the 475th no longer. Wewak needed to be destroyed. He ordered the 475th to New Guinea. The number of P-38s available to the 5th was now over a hundred.

On the seventeenth, two hundred aircraft gathered at Port Moresby. Gerald Johnson led the Knights over the Owen Stanleys to refuel as the B-25s took off from nearby strips. With everyone concentrated in one place, the intricately timed strike went off flawlessly.

The strafers hit the Wewak airfields just after the Japanese brass came for an inspection trip. Brand-new Ki-61 Hiens and Ki-43 Hayabusas stood wingtip to wingtip as if on display at a peacetime air show. The strafers went in, dropping parafrags and blowing aircraft apart with their awesome firepower. When the day was done, scores of Japanese planes lay wrecked and burning on the strips.

That afternoon, Kenney ordered Wewak hit again. The entire mission was to be repeated on the eighteenth. They'd hammer at Wewak until their bombs had only broken wreckage to rearrange.

On the morning of the eighteenth, Tommy McGuire looked up from a cup of lemonade as another wave of B-25s thundered overhead. These past two mornings he had seen more planes concentrated in one place than at any other time in his life. He took one more swig and handed his cup to a waiting Red Cross volunteer. She smiled at him, and he thanked her. Nearby, his former squadron mates in the 9th were finishing their lemonade, munching on doughnuts, and flirting with the women running the Red Cross trucks.

He'd heard about the fights over Lae and the Markham Valley. He knew Bong's score now, and how Duckbutt jumped to second place in the race. His old Aleutian pals were in on the scoring too. But what really got Tommy was Gerald Johnson's rank. Promoted to captain now, his friend had gone from a first lieutenant with no authority or official slot in the 9th Fighter Squadron to its new squadron commander. Twenty-three years old, same as he was, and his friend would be a major before Halloween if he did well with the Knights.

What a difference eight weeks makes.

When Kenney called for veteran pilots to form the cadre of the 475th, he underscored that he did not want the deadwood. He wanted proven pilots who could fight, and teach others to fight. The 475th was to be the elite fighter outfit in the Southwest Pacific. Amazingly, by and large, the New Guinea squadrons abided by their commander's wishes and sent great pilots to the 475th.

Tommy was a talented pilot, of that nobody had any doubt, but he had been bounced out of the 9th as a problem child. He came to the 475th under a cloud, made worse by the fact that he was assigned to the group's 431st Fighter Squadron, which happened to be full of guys from the 9th. His reputation followed him.

When he tried to ingratiate himself with his new command, he was transparently sycophantic, which turned his peers off. At other times, the snark and sense of superiority burned through the new affectation, and he once again got under more than a few skins. He was on the skids again, and if he was bounced out this time, there'd be nowhere else to go but home. He'd be a combat pilot with no combat experience, sent Stateside in disgrace.

As he struggled in the 475th, his mother died on July 22, 1943. Still living in the hotel where he'd visited her on his last home leave, she drank herself to death, though the official cause was "heart failure." Perhaps the official cause was true; she died of a broken heart abetted by alcohol and years of alienation from her family and neighbors. She wasn't found for days. In fact, the hotel staff couldn't get into her room after repeated attempts to check on her. Finally, they called the fire department, raised a ladder to her floor, and went in through a window. Tommy's mother was found dead, naked on the floor, survived by the family poodle.

Word spread over town, and her death was reported salaciously in the local papers. Tommy's wife was summoned to help deal with the scene, but nobody in Sebring knew how to contact Tommy directly. He found out much later that he was on his own, a fact underscored by a document his war bride discovered among his mother's personal effects. His dad had given up legal custodianship of him years ago and terminated his parental rights.

All he had waiting for him back home was his wife, with whom he'd lived for bare weeks before leaving for the Pacific.

The sense of isolation and grief must have taken its toll on him. He took to spending most of his time with the squadron's P-38s, and he understood these machines so much more, it seemed, than the people in them. He tried to be kind and helpful. He got branded a suck-up. He fired back when provoked, and was then judged an asshole. He couldn't win.

Two things happened that saved him from ignominy. First, the squadron commander made him the assistant engineering officer, which required working closely with the mechanics and armorers.

Enlisted men were no threat to Tommy's prickly personality since he outranked them. That position of superiority put him at ease, and he grew friendly with them. He worked hard and learned more about the P-38's design and construction than probably any other pilot.

Marion Kirby became the second half of Tommy's salvation. Kirby was an Airacobra pilot from the defense of Port Moresby days with a probable kill to his credit and reputation for being a no-nonsense, blunt tiger. He ranked Tommy by both experience and date of promotion. When he came to the 475th and was given a flight, Tommy initially ended up in it.

Kirby saw considerable talent in McGuire's flying and intellect. He wanted to shape that talent into something useful, but he watched McGuire shoot himself in the foot time after time. At length, he pulled Tommy aside and called him out on his behavior. He gave him a choice: shut up, learn from him, and stay in the squadron, or get sent home. His way or the highway.

The tough love worked. Tommy had never really seen anyone stand up to him like that. He fell into line and did what the former Texas Aggie demanded of him. Kirby's mentorship laid the seeds of McGuire's transformation, and by the end of the squadron's workup, Tommy was given his own flight to command. The ground echelon came to respect and admire McGuire so much that they picked the best P-38 in the squadron and gave it to Tommy as a gift for all the hours he'd sweated beside them in those Australian hangars. He named it *Pudgy*, his wife's college nickname.

Finally, a step in the right direction.

The last B-25s passed overhead, turning north for the Owen Stanleys. The morning's raid would cross through the heart of New Guinea's interior, avoiding the coast and all the Japanese bases dotted along it, to delay detection for as long as possible. As they sped onward, the ground crews at Moresby worked to pump the final gallons of gas into the P-38s. Almost a hundred Lightnings launched in the wake, forming up and climbing to their escort altitudes. Whitehead and Wurtsmith worked through escort tactics that layered the '38s in front, above, and behind and on the flanks of the strafers. Any waiting Japanese fighters would have to fight their way through a Lockheed blanket stacked from four to fifteen thousand feet. The 431st provided close cover that morning, with McGuire's flight catching up to the B-25s and pushing thirty seconds ahead of them to clear their path.

The strike group flew through thick overcast, weaving around towering mountains and dark clouds. The bombers held tight formation. It was a miracle nobody collided in the soup. One B-25 from the 3rd Attack Group narrowly missed a rocky outcrop. As they swung around it, a black mass erupted in front of them. Swirling, swarming bats—thousands of them—filled the sky so completely that the pilots opened fire with their nose guns to try to clear a swath through them. Too many. They impacted against the bomber, leaving bloody, furry smears and severely damaging one engine. As fast as they appeared, the bats vanished in the squadron's rear. Wewak lay ahead.

Patrolling Japanese fighters spotted the inbound raid and called in a warning to their base. Ki-61 Hiens were already warming up, their ground crews throwing buckets of water on their engine cowlings to keep the temperamental in-line engines from overheating. As the pilots got them out on the runway, steam rose from their noses. They opened their throttles and sped into the sky.

The strafers hit them in mid-scramble. A wave of B-25s passed over the fields like a threshing machine, mowing everything before them. Planes exploded. Antiaircraft guns were torn apart. Men dove for cover, including one who found refuge in a cesspool.

The patrolling fighters, Oscars from the newly arrived 59th Sentai, dove to the defense of their bases. The 431st saw them coming, and a wild, low-altitude dogfight erupted in the middle of thick antiaircraft fire.

An Oscar bounced McGuire's fight, diving in from two o'clock high. The Americans punched their tanks and prepped their '38s for combat, all while banking up and into the attack.

"Let's get him! Zero at two o'clock," McGuire called out. He was shaky, filled with fear and adrenaline. He fired twice before the Oscar blew past him. Then the smell of cordite from his own guns filled the cockpit. Something about that flipped a switch in McGuire. The nerves vanished. His knees quit shaking. He felt a sudden warm calm flush away the fear.

"Tommy!" yelled his wingman, Francis Lent. "Zero on my tail!"

Tommy dove toward Dagua Airdrome, fires burning everywhere along the runway, smoke rising from bomb craters. People ran back and forth. Antiaircraft cannon blazed, filling the sky with deadly black puffs as their shells exploded. He checked his tail, saw the enemy fighter closing on Lent. It was an Oscar, misidentified as a Zero. Either way, the dictum was clear: never maneuver with the more agile Japanese fighters.

Tommy hauled the P-38 into a left wingover, turning impossibly tight. Tommy pushed the bird right to the edge of its envelope and beyond. He knew the P-38 was overengineered and could take more G-forces than the tech manuals said. He put that knowledge to use now as he sped to his wingman's rescue. It was a risky strategy, as he didn't know just how far past the manuals he could push the plane before he'd spin out of control.

But until he found himself past that line, the strategy would work. The Japanese pilot, taken by surprise by Tommy's incredible maneuver, dove away for Dagua.

McGuire tenaciously went after him, snapping out bursts every time the Oscar crossed his gun sight. He saw his bullets striking home, sparks flaring on the fuselage near the cockpit. He scored another hit. The Oscar engine began to burn. The Japanese pilot stood no chance. Another fusillade from McGuire's Lightning shattered the cockpit. Pieces of plexiglass streamed back over the Oscar's tail. Pilot dead or wounded now, the Japanese plane rolled and crashed at the edge of Dagua Drome.

Tommy and Francis Lent chased another Oscar, but were foiled when another Ki-43 came to its rescue. The Japanese tacked onto McGuire's tail, but Lent saw him and scraped him off with a long burst, saving his flight leader's life.

The fight waxed and waned around Wewak as more fighters joined in and a wave of bombers sped through the flak. The 431st fought on around the B-25s, chasing Oscars to the treetops and keeping the strafers safe.

Lent and McGuire worked as a team, keeping their tails clear and shooting up anything that crossed their noses. Whenever a Japanese fighter made a run at them, they'd turn and offer a game of chicken. Head-to-head, they rushed at their enemies, guns barking. Some of the Japanese had no stomach for such a contest and would break off their runs. One Oscar pilot took the challenge. Firing all the way in at McGuire, the two stubborn pilots refused to break. At the last instant, McGuire tried to duck under the Japanese fighter as its pilot rolled to avoid a collision. Both waited too long, and their wingtips smashed together. The Japanese plane dove away. McGuire went looking for more trouble until the last of the B-25s finished their runs. They spotted three, running on the deck for home and rolled in after them to give them cover. Ten minutes out of Wewak, the weather started to clear. The two Americans swiveled their heads, searching for threats.

Above them, a lone Ki-61 pilot saw the B-25s. He dove to the attack, his fast in-line fighter gaining speed quickly. He blew past Lent and McGuire and shot at the bombers, the two P-38s in furious pursuit. As fast as the Ki-61 was, the P-38 was faster, and Tommy caught up to him. The silver and mottled yellow-green fighter swelled in his gun sight. He'd been careful with his ammo use, but he'd fired a lot already and wasn't sure how much he had left.

He pressed the gun triggers. The cannon boomed. The fifties chattered. The cockpit filled with smoke and the Ki-61 began to burn. He held course, making instinctive corrections with his rudder and yoke before firing again. His tracers disappeared into the fleeing Japanese plane. Oily black smoke belched from the engine cowling. The fighter rolled over and went into the jungle, its courageous lone pilot wounded. He would be rescued, only to die in a jungle hospital four days later.

Back at Moresby, McGuire's crew chief, Sgt. Frank Kish, helped him out of the cockpit. "Frank, can you take a look at the left wing? I think I had a midair collision with a Zero."

The crew chief scrambled down the ladder behind the cockpit and went to go take a look. McGuire joined him a minute later. Soon, a small crowd gathered to check out the streak of Japanese green paint along McGuire's scuffed-up wingtip. A few bullet holes peppered *Pudgy*'s aluminum skin, but neither the collision nor the Japanese lead did significant damage.

Tommy McGuire hit five fighters that day. His squadron saw three of them go down. A fourth also went into the jungle, but another pilot in the squadron was shooting at it the same time McGuire was putting rounds into it. In other theaters, this would have been a shared kill, half credit for each pilot. But the 5th was an all-or-nothing outfit, and only one man could get the credit. The intelligence officer took everyone's statement, and the situation couldn't be resolved from what everyone had seen. The men settled on a coin flip. McGuire's poker luck failed him; the other pilot won the toss and got the victory.

It didn't matter at the time. McGuire just made a statement, one that quickly made the rounds through every tent at Moresby and Dobodura: the outcast was back, and kicking ass.

21

The Jug Driver

Summer of 1943
New Guinea

Kenney flung the 5th Air Force against Wewak repeatedly through the end of August, using his P-38 force to cover both heavy bombers and the Pappy Gunn modified strafer B-25s. The attacks destroyed hundreds of Japanese planes on the ground, while the few that got airborne to challenge the Americans were knocked out of the sky by the eager Lightning jocks. It was one of the most lopsided aerial victories of the war, and it changed the entire complexion of the New Guinea campaign. The strafers tore the heart out of the Japanese Army Air Force, blowing apart on the ground the planes that took so much effort to get to Wewak from the Home Islands. Hundreds of Japanese aircrew were killed, and the new fighter units were almost completely destroyed. In early September, some of them could count only a half dozen available Oscars and Hiens. The rest lay in jungle craters, or broken and burned on the sides of the Wewak runways.

There would be no further Japanese Army Air Force counteroffensives in New Guinea. The 5th ruled supreme.

Beyond the strategic implications of the raids, the Wewak air battles created a host of new American aces and gave the current leaders a chance to extend their scores. Tom Lynch shot down three more fighters, bringing his total to fourteen at the end of the month. George Welch, the Pearl Harbor hero who spent the better part of the last year flying the hated Airacobras, finally talked his way into the 80th Fighter Squadron, which reequipped with P-38s earlier that summer. Over Wewak, he made a huge statement, flaming three fighters on August 20. He and Lynch were neck and neck, battling for second place and striking position to catch Bong.

Dick missed the Wewak raids. Johnson, who took formal command of the Knights on the twenty-seventh, assigned him to cover other strikes around New Guinea and the western tip of New Britain. While he flew what turned out to be milk runs, his competition racked their scores up, and Vern Haughland breathlessly documented their kills. At the end of the month, Vern wrote a story about George Welch's return from Airacobra obscurity, highlighting his three-in-a-day battle over Wewak. Being one of the first American air heroes of World War II made him a favorite back home, though in the 5th he was less revered by the senior leadership. He could be an acerbic person, one who didn't hold back with the press. When asked what the best aspect of the P-39 was, he quipped, "Eleven hundred pounds of Allison armor." It was a reference to the engine being behind the pilot. Not a stellar thing to say to the people back home building them. Whether the senior brass kept reporters away from Welch or he simply wasn't covered much while he was not scoring in his Airacobra unit after late 1942 is unknown. Either way, he wasn't a Kenney favorite.

Tommy McGuire destroyed two more planes at the end of August to become one of the 475th Fighter Group's first aces. Back home, nobody noticed. Vern and the other reporters covering the ace race ignored him, though in Australia the papers did carry an account of his first fight over Wewak. He was lost in the crowd of new aces rising with the P-38's ascendancy, and the fact that he still was not well regarded by his peers—despite his astonishing success that August—had done him no favors.

With the Japanese units at Wewak in shambles, Kenney turned the 5th Air Force against Cape Gloucester, New Britain. The massive Japanese base at Rabaul lay on one end of that island, a secondary airfield on the other. To support the impending amphibious invasion around Lae, Kenney wanted to make sure Cape Gloucester couldn't be used as a staging base by the Japanese.

The strikes triggered a strong Japanese reaction. The Knights tangled for the first time with the new Japanese Army Air Force twin-engine fighter, the Ki-45 Toryu. They made easy work of the slower, if more agile, aircraft. Johnson shot down one Toryu on the second of September, achieving ace status with his two kills from the Aleutians. On the same day, George Welch returned home with two more victory claims, both of which V Fighter Command confirmed. That tied him with Dick Bong, and for a month they shared top ace honors.

But George Welch's tenure with the 5th Air Force ended right after the September 2 air battle. He developed a severe case of malaria and was medically evacuated to Australia, never to fly in combat again.[1] Upon recovery, he returned home and was sent on the war bond tour circuit, giving speeches all over the country. It was a job he loathed so completely that in 1944, he asked Gen. Hap Arnold personally for permission to leave the Army Air Force so he could go be a test pilot for North American Aviation. Arnold let him go, and the first American air hero slipped into civilian clothes a year before Hiroshima.

---

1. There were suggestions in postwar interviews with veteran Headhunters that Welch's malaria attack was used as an excuse to get him out of theater. He had earned few friends over the past months and alienated many of the old hands in the 80th Fighter Squadron with his behavior.

He left behind a unit that soon challenged the Knights for primacy in the Southwest Pacific. The Headhunters of the 80th Fighter Squadron had languished at Moresby for over a year flying Airacobras. Now, with their new P-38s, the unit cut a swath through the Japanese in every aerial encounter. Jay Robbins was their star ace, having scored seven kills in two fights in July and September to vault him ahead of Johnson on the ace ladder.

As the P-38 pilots competed against each other and crushed the Japanese in nearly every battle, Kenney's latest special project arrived on the scene and totally changed the dynamics of the ace race at a time when the 5th was gearing up for its greatest challenge: destroying Japanese airpower at Rabaul.

Back in the spring of 1943, Kenney returned to the States briefly following the Battle of the Bismarck Sea. He returned a national hero, a general in a backwater theater whose men scored the AAF's biggest victory of the war. Kenney's face now graced the cover of *Life* magazine. Reporters clamored to interview him. He was on everyone's A-list for dinner in the Washington elite set when he arrived in the capital to personally brief Hap Arnold. During that meeting, Kenney asked his commanding general for reinforcements. He needed more fighter groups, more P-38s, and more bombers if MacArthur's drive to the Philippines was to get under way. The P-39s in the 5th needed to be discarded.

Arnold told Kenney he didn't have the planes to give him. As for any new fighter or bomber groups? The ones working up Stateside were all earmarked for Europe. The conversation proceeded stiltedly from there.

Eventually, Arnold slammed the door to further discussion, leaving Kenney to process the fact that his theater would continue to get everyone else's scraps.

He'd made good use of scraps, though, thanks to ingenuity and a whole lot of outside-the-box thinking. Kenney decided to do the same thing in Washington.

Thanks to the Bismarck Sea victory and his status as America's latest hero general, President Roosevelt asked him to the White House to discuss the situation in the Pacific. During the meeting, FDR asked him if he needed anything. Kenney seized on the moment and told the commander in chief he needed more fighter and bomber groups. Roosevelt listened, then promised to send him the reinforcements.

Kenney learned a valuable lesson that day. Publicity, accolades, and victory could be used as political currency to get what he wanted for his theater. He'd executed a masterful end run around Hap Arnold, who could not have been pleased with his insubordination. But the commander in chief ordered Arnold to send Kenney reinforcements, and dutifully he picked several about to head to England and directed them to Australia instead.

That's how Lt. Col. Neel Kearby, commander of the 348th Fighter Group, found himself getting off a transport in Australia instead of the UK. A father of three young boys, he was a bantam of a man with charisma to burn and flecks of gray in his dark hair. At thirty-three, he'd spent his entire life dreaming of only one thing: becoming America's ace of aces. When he met General Kenney for the first time, he looked at his new commanding general and asked, "Sir, who are the high scorers here? I need to know who to beat."

Kenney smiled broadly. As he wrote later, "Kearby looked like money in the bank."

22

Rebels in Thunderbolts

Summer of 1943
Eagle Farm, Brisbane, Australia

While the Lightnings turned the summer into a scoring fest, Kearby's men arrived in Brisbane along with their factory-fresh Republic P-47 Thunderbolts. Broad-legged, squat, and enormous, the P-47 looked less like a graceful fighter and more like an aged boxer gone to seed. Around Brisbane, Aussie and American pilots took one look at the Republic and started laughing. Anything that big would be meat on the table for a Zero. It looked like a milk jug on its side with splayed legs. In bars and officers' clubs, the veterans mocked the new aircraft right to its pilots' faces.

It didn't help that when Kearby first showed up in May, ahead of the group's arrival, he tried to demonstrate one of the first P-47s to reach the theater, only to be unable to get it off the ground after a seven-thousand-foot takeoff run. The bird's massive Pratt & Whitney R-2800 radial engine could produce unparalleled horsepower, but early versions also contained plenty of bugs.

Kenney and Whitehead were not sure about the new fighter's value. They wanted more P-38s, or the new P-51 Mustang. Beyond the 475th Fighter Group, though, more P-38 outfits were not in the cards. The Jug was what they would get, and now they had to figure out what it could do for them. Its short range soon became another black mark against it. Just warming up the engine before flight consumed forty-seven gallons of gas. Once in the air, the 5th learned, it possessed the same radius of action as a P-39 with a drop tank—only a few hundred miles. This was no power-projection weapon. At best, on its internal fuel, the 5th figured it could serve as a point defense interceptor, protecting bases from Japanese attack. In the meantime, the innovative geniuses in Australia went to work figuring out how to extend its range.

Unlike everyone else in the 5th, Kearby and his men believed in the P-47 with almost religious zeal. The Texan had trained his men thoroughly—most of his guys had almost two hundred hours in P-47s during their Stateside workup. They were proud of the plane and their role in being the first to fly it in the Pacific, so when they caught flak from other pilots, they bristled and grew defensive. After the P-47 pilots ran into a bunch of Aussie Spitfire pilots at a pub one night, things grew more charged. The Spitfire was one of the extraordinary fighters of World War II, agile, fast, with graceful lines. The British-built aircraft served as the gold-bar standard to the Commonwealth pilots. If the Spitfire was the prom queen, the P-47 was the fat kid trying out for ballet. It couldn't climb. It couldn't turn. It was nothing more than a bigger, uglier P-39—a dog of a plane sure to get its pilots killed.

One of the Jug pilots finally had enough of the Aussie attitude toward the new fighter. The next morning, he took a P-47 up over Brisbane, found the Aussie alert shack at their airfield, and dove down on it. If the Jug couldn't maneuver or climb, the one thing it could do was dive. The pilot pushed it past 550 knots, pulled up at the last second and blew the radio antennae off the Aussie hut.

If his pilots bristled at the criticism, Kearby didn't endear himself to other pilots outside the 348th either. The 348th was his team; everyone else could go to hell, as far as he cared. He didn't hold back his opinions, even when they offended his audience. He also didn't suffer fools. While his men were getting the P-47s ready in Australia, he flew back and forth to New Guinea in an appropriated B-26 bomber. Known as the "widow-maker" for the high number of accidents its hot landing speed caused, the B-26 was not well loved in the 5th Air Force. It was tricky to fly, even for an experienced bomber pilot, especially from the jungle strips around Port Moresby. The 5th was busily getting rid of them from the only frontline group equipped with them.

One day, after forgetting to set the elevator trim for takeoff, he narrowly averted crashing on his way back to Australia. When he landed and popped out of the fuselage hatch, he overheard the other guys aboard talking about the near calamity with other members of the 348th. Kearby walked up, listened to the conversation and said, "Those bomber guys—they're a bunch of sissies!" After all, if a fighter pilot with less than five hours in twin-engine aircraft could fly the socks off the B-26, anyone could. Right?

It was not a popular opinion, but it was a solid introduction to Neel Kearby's swagger. He'd been flying since the depths of the Great Depression, starting out when some of the kids he now led were mere tweens. In those prewar years, Kearby racked up thousands of hours in every fighter plane used by the Air Corps. Piloting a bomber, even with virtually no twin-engine time, was cake to him.

Pilots love their planes like car guys love their cars. A lot of the needling was the fighter pilot equivalent of the Ford versus Chevy debates that have raged in gearhead circles for generations. But part of it was also based on real-world experience in combat against the Japanese. Deep down, the 348th knew that, and the constant barrage against their beloved aircraft started to erode their confidence. As it did, they grew increasingly defensive and angry. Kenney saw the wedge between his pilots growing and knew something needed to be done. He ordered Kearby to give the P-38 guys a lesson in the Thunderbolt's performance. The Texan took to the assignment with relish. He'd been a fighter pilot his entire adult life and had more time in them than any pilot in the SWPA. He came of age in the Depression-era Army Air Corps, flying everything from the Art Deco–era P-26 peashooters to P-40s and P-39s. When kids like Bong and Johnson were going to their first junior high school dances, Kearby was training other pilots on fighter combat tactics.

At thirty-two, he should never have been flying combat. The legendary Greg Boyington, the Marine ace portrayed by Robert Conrad in the *Baa Baa Black Sheep* television series, was dubbed "Pappy" for being the old man in his squadron at thirty-one. The fighter game was seen as a young man's realm. A pilot like Kearby was seen by the early twenty-somethings outside the 348th as a regular officer relic, suited for a desk job or command above the fighter group level. Kearby was not a desk guy. He was a pilot to his soul, a man who grew up in a wealthy Texas family obsessively reading about the World War I aces. He collected everything he could find about them and built dossiers on the great ones like Rickenbacker and Frank Luke, keeping them in binders in his room as a kid. When he finished college, he wanted only one thing out of life: to fly fighters and be the next American ace of aces. It wasn't his fault that the next war started after he passed thirty. Stateside posts may have kept him close to his family, but he was a man built to fight.

He sought out Dick Bong and challenged him to a one-on-one duel over Port Moresby. A crowd gathered to watch the scrum. They started with the head-to-head pass, merged, and the game was on. The two extraordinary pilots put on an exhibition of flying skill that dazzled the men on the ground. Both pushed their planes to the limits of the envelopes, roaring in after each other in furious simulated slashing attacks. They juked and shook each other off their tails, went back for more as they battled relentlessly. Neither gave up, and for the rest of their lives the witnesses of that battle would argue over who won. The P-47 guys claimed it was Kearby's fight. The P-38 guys refused to concede and said Bong had the edge.

Kearby chose Johnson next. The Knights' commanding officer didn't have the score Bong did, but he was widely considered to be one of the finest pure pilots in V Fighter Command. Kearby bounced him at twelve thousand feet over Moresby, and the two pilots went at it with every trick they possessed. Kearby learned these young pilots had plenty of game and skills. Johnson and the others learned that as long as the Jug pilot stayed in his plane's type of fight, it was almost as good as the P-38. It could out-dive the Lightning, it was probably a little faster at high altitude, and it was well suited for the slashing attack tactics the 5th used against the Japanese.

The Knights who watched that fight against Johnson claimed the Oregonian put the professional in his place. The 348th said it was no contest: Kearby ran rings around him. Whoever was right will never be resolved. What followed from that fight, though, was a mutual respect and budding friendship.

In mid-July, Kenney wrote Whitehead and told him to get the 348th into New Guinea. He was concerned about the group's eroding morale in Australia and thought the pilots were stagnating. Even though they did not possess drop tanks yet, he wanted the Jugs up there, getting some scalps and building morale. Just as the Japanese counteroffensive began that summer, the Jugs showed up at Moresby to begin flying local missions to get the pilots familiar with the weather and terrain.

One day in August, Johnson was out with the Knights and spotted a formation of blunt-nosed fighters below them. It was a perfect setup, and he rolled in at the head of his squadron, thirsting for the fight. At the last second, somebody called out, "They're Jugs! They're Jugs!"

Kearby's men saw the Lightnings dropping on them, and their frantic calls on the radio were finally heard by the Knights. They narrowly averted a tragedy, and Johnson felt bad about the incident.

He went to see Kearby and apologized personally, handing him two precious bottles of gin to underscore his sincerity.

The two men, though a decade apart in age, shared a lot of common attributes. Both looked after their men with complete devotion. They were seen as coaches, with Johnson a bit more of a cheerleader with his eagerness and pep talks at briefings. Both men were there to fly, and flew far more than the required missions. In July, Kearby flew twenty-two missions alone. None resulted in an encounter with the Japanese, but still his men knew that he would lead from the front. Many group commanders stayed on the ground, focusing on the administrative duties required to keep their outfits functional. Kearby hated that stuff, as did Johnson. Their place would always be at the tip of the spear.

A few days after that near–friendly fire incident, Kearby talked his way onto the first two Wewak raids. His Jugs didn't have the range to get to Wewak from Moresby, so the 348th carried out secondary duties elsewhere while their commander went rogue. No matter what his group was doing—or flying—Kearby refused to be left out of a big show, and that became one of the hallmarks of his combat career. Quite possibly, he leveraged his friendship with Johnson and flew with the Knights on August 17 and 18—in one of their P-38s. Whichever squadron he joined, he'd never flown a P-38 before. On one of the missions, he lost an engine and was forced to turn back. That he didn't kill himself flying combat in a twin-engine fighter was a testament to his skill and experience as an aviator.

Though Kearby flew nearly every day that August, he missed his group's first fight with the Japanese. In a span of two days, while the 475th was going into action around Wewak, his Jug pilots shot down one Oscar, losing two pilots and three planes. When stacked against the 475th's incredible run of well over two dozen kills over Wewak, the aspersions cast on the P-47 seemed to be justified. The unit's morale took another hit.

Bringing an untested fighter group into action is a difficult enough command challenge, but doing so with a new aircraft of questionable use in theater elevated that challenge to a near crisis after those first losses. What saved the group was the steely confidence of their Texas commander and his squadron leaders, including a quiet New Englander named Maj. Charles H. MacDonald.

Kearby relied on "Mac" not just to lead and fight with his squadron; Mac had become one of his closest friends within the group while in training on the East Coast. Though wildly different— Kearby was brash, often abrasive, and plainspoken, whereas Mac-Donald was an introvert—they shared commonalities that pulled them together. Both were family men, older than the other pilots and more established in life. Both were prewar regular officers who chose to make the Army Air Corps their life. They were the yin and yang of the 348th, fire and ice. Together, they kept the troops from losing heart, drilling into them the tactics they believed would make the Jug a success and keep them alive.

In the middle of their introduction to combat, tragedy struck Neel's family. He learned that his older brother had been killed in a Stateside plane crash. Maj. John G. Kearby had always been the scientific mind in the family. He graduated with a master's degree in physics in 1931 and spent the Depression years prosperously employed while traveling around South America, doing research for American engineering companies. As war approached, he volunteered to serve in the Army Air Force at age thirty-six. He was sent to Wright Field to begin researching high-altitude pressure suits. He was a rising star in engineering circles there and soon set several records. He was the first man to reach sixty thousand feet in a pressure chamber, as he insisted on testing his experimental suit personally. He never talked to his family about his work, as it was all highly classified, but they knew he was doing something revolutionary and very important. Ultimately, his research laid the groundwork for the first American space suits produced a decade later.

On August 4, 1943, John Kearby was returning from a series of high-altitude flight tests with his new suit when his plane crashed, killing everyone aboard. The Kearby family back in Texas was devastated by the news. John was married and had a young daughter. When the news reached New Guinea, it rocked Neel to the core. Yet he could not show his pain to his men, especially when they were losing friends to the Japanese. He was an emotional man, prone to outbursts of anger when provoked, yet always an inspiring figure to his men. He could be magnetic, charming, the personification of a leather-hard Texan willing to lead from the front into whatever odds the enemy threw at them. This resonated with his men, and they admired him. As the rest of the 5th Fighter Command's pilots treated them and their aircraft with contempt, they had rallied behind Kearby and put their faith in his leadership. Failing them due to his own personal hardships was simply not an option. He pushed the news away. Home was remote, news from it unreal. Until he returned home, he would keep that loss bottled up. In the meantime, he turned to his friendship with MacDonald, and the shared bond ensured he never felt alone.

He threw himself into his work, flying constantly, advocating for the P-47, and keeping his men focused. They went back to basics as Kearby sent officers to each squadron to give additional instructions. They covered intelligence procedures, radio discipline, tactics, and strafing methods for ground attack missions. The classes helped get the group over the sense of alienation, not just from the other fighter groups, but from the very terrain they flew over every day. New Guinea was a different world to kids fresh from the States. Kearby drilled them until they knew every course and reciprocal to enemy bases and friendly ones.

As they studied on the ground in their spare time, they flew backwater missions, covering the P-38 bases when they were out on long-range flights and escorting transports to new airfields being constructed in the Ramu Valley. Kearby barraged General Wurtsmith for a chance to show the 5th what his men could achieve. His pleas fell on deaf ears.

On September 4, 1943, the invasion of Lae began. Aussie troops carried in American landing craft poured ashore along a stretch of beach at Hopi Point. Kenney turned to Wurtsmith's fighter pilots to keep the amphibious fleet safe from air attack. All day long, the 5th's Lightnings and P-40s patrolled over the Navy's ships steaming off the invasion beaches.

That afternoon, a Japanese raid swept in from New Britain. Radar spotted it, and the word went out to the 348th to get planes aloft. Twenty Jugs waddled into the air, with Kearby leading one flight of four. They sped northwest for the action, but many of the P-47s fell out along the way due to mechanical issues. The new birds continued to threaten the lives of those who dared to fly them.

By the time the remaining Jugs reached the scene, the P-38 squadrons had broken up the attack and downed several planes. The fighting scattered the Japanese, and their formations broke down. Now, clusters of a few bombers and fighters sped this way and that, ducking for home or making runs on the Allied ships.

Kearby spotted a bomber down low, escorted by a greenish-gray fighter on either wing. He was high above them, in a perfect position to bounce. He called the bandits in over the radio, then rolled into a diving pass on the fleeing Japanese. The Jug fell out of the sky like a chunk of concrete, its speed passing four hundred miles an hour within only a few thousand feet.

In all his childhood research on the Great War aces, Kearby read that some of the best could knock down multiple planes in a single pass. It was hard enough for most pilots to hit one; getting two or more was an incredible feat. He decided to see just how good he was after all the years of training and simulated dogfights.

He wanted the bomber and one of the fighters. He lined up with his gun sight's pipper between the two as his P-47 dropped down on them. The Japanese seemed totally unaware of his presence. Or perhaps they saw the snub-nosed P-47 and thought it was a friendly aircraft. Either way, they flew on serenely.

Three hundred yards out, Neel Kearby unleashed the P-47's secret weapon: the same firepower as Pappy Gunn's strafer B-25s. Eight .50-caliber machine guns ripped into the closest fighter, filling the air around it with hundreds of bullets traveling twenty-seven hundred feet a second. Kearby held the trigger down, eased back on the stick and watched his fire slide from the fighter to the bomber it was escorting. The fifties ripped into its wings and fuselage, setting its internal fuel afire. As he pulled up and over the formation, the bomber, wreathed in flames, fell into the sea. The Japanese fighter spun in after it, seen by Kearby's wingman.

Neel looked back just in time to see the bomber impact with the water. His flight followed him up in a zoom climb to regain position before coming around for another pass. The lone remaining Japanese fighter, probably a Mitsubishi A6M Zero, ducked and weaved, maneuvering violently to avoid the new American fighters. The Japanese countered every pass Kearby made with a sudden chandelle.[1] Unable to follow the trick, the Americans remained disciplined, using speed and altitude as the Zero tried to turn avoidance into advantage. Each chandelle ended with a steep, diving turn to get on the tail of a P-47. Each time, the Zero pilot found himself slow and

---

1. A chandelle is a climbing turn. Japanese pilots used sudden, steep chandelles to avoid the slashing attacks they endured at the hands of American pilots, usually hoping to pull around and get a snap shot off on the American fighter as it extended away.

too far behind the Jugs to get a shot at them. They stalemated each other, and both sides disengaged.

When Kenney heard the news of Kearby's two-in-one-pass day, he cut orders awarding the Texan a Distinguished Flying Cross. About the same time he heard the news of his own award, his family back home learned that the Army Air Force posthumously awarded his brother the same medal for his high-altitude test flights.

Kearby's victories provided a solid morale boost to the 348th. He proved they could be effective in battle—the Jug just needed to be employed properly. The major hamstringing of the P-47's use in New Guinea remained its short range, not its combat attributes. Fortunately, not long after Kearby's kills, two hundred belly tanks, produced by the Ford Motor Company of Australia, arrived at Thunderbolt Valley, the 348th's home at Moresby. With these range-extenders, they could take the fight to the enemy. Kearby's boys were ready for the big time.

23

The New Guy

September 6, 1943
Dobodura, New Guinea

The 9th Squadron's alert P-38s stretched along the flight line at Dobodura, a new crop of pilots waiting at the alert shack thumbing through the same worn magazines the Darwin vets had read last spring. Now that Duckbutt Watkins had rotated home, several of the new guys split time flying *Charlcie Jean*, his old P-38. Other Lightnings, still carrying names that meant something to the old hands, stood ready on the flight line. They looked beat-up and war weary, their olive-drab paint scuffed and scratched. Some were checkerboarded with aluminum patches that covered bullet holes picked up during the fierce summer fighting.

Amazingly, despite the constant skirmishes, the Knights had not lost a pilot since July, and Gerald and Wally, now running the squadron with veteran Harry Lidstrom as the deputy commander, intended to keep the streak going.[1] This would be tough, as they had no time to ease the new kids into combat. After the lull in June, the

---

1. When Gerald took over the squadron, Lidstrom become his XO and Wally took the operations officer (S3) slot. They formed the core leadership for the Knights going into the fall's brutal battles over Rabaul.

pace of operations never slowed down. Now, with the invasion of Lae in full swing and the Japanese trying to bomb the amphibious task force offshore, the 9th pulled double duty: flying offensive missions as well as sitting on alert duty.

Gerald did the best he could to integrate the new guys and keep them alive. He teamed the greenest new guys with the most experienced pilots so they could be mentored and protected. Dick Bong, now one of the longest-serving guys in the squadron, was promoted to captain, and Gerald gave him a flight of his own to command. He also gave him one of the youngest pilots in the squadron to be his wingman. Second Lt. Jim Fagan hailed from upstate New York. He grew up near Lake Ontario in Monroe County, volunteering for the Army Air Force in 1942 at age nineteen. While in primary training in Arizona, he fell in love and married a local woman named Nancy White. She moved with him as he bounced from base to base finishing his training. After only six months together, he received orders sending him overseas.

Fagan arrived to join the Knights at the end of August, to do his time at the alert shack with the rest of the squadron. Whatever precombat jitters he might have had were eased by his assignment. Dick Bong was becoming a legend and inspiration to young pilots heading into combat. They looked up to him; some revered him. To be paired on his wing was like a kid from the minors being mentored by Lou Gehrig.

Mail, as always, was slow to arrive on both ends of the Pacific, but a few letters from home finally caught up to Jim at Dobo. He kept one tucked away like a prized possession. In it, Nancy told him she was pregnant. He spoke of his impending fatherhood to his new squadron mates, who offered hearty congratulations to the new guy. He was a stalwart kid, eager to learn and anxious to contribute.

Word came that morning the Knights were to put a full squadron up over the Lae beachhead. Just before noon, fourteen pilots climbed into the waiting P-38s. Bong offered his flight a few last-minute words of advice, though his element leader, a Utah Mormon named Ray Swift, had already seen plenty of combat and knew the ropes. They'd be Blue Flight on this mission.

Over Lae, a Navy controller reported an inbound strike at sixteen thousand feet. He coached the Knights onto the Japanese planes, following the action on his radarscope. He set them up for an excellent bounce. The Japanese planes, Mitsubishi G4M Betty bombers, flew a tight formation under a protective blanket of over a dozen Zero fighters.

The Americans prepped their P-38s, dropping their tanks and working up to full throttle. The old hands did this far quicker than the new guys, and soon they were diving after the Betties.

Bong drove straight for the enemy, singularly focused as he set up a run on the left side of their formation. Behind him, one of Fagan's drop tanks failed to release. Imbalanced, still with all the drag those huge fuel nacelles created, he should have climbed above the fight to try to shake it loose.

Instead, he followed what all the old hands told him: a wingman never abandons his leader.

He sped after Bong, his P-38 unable to keep up with him as the ace's P-38 flashed after the bombers. Just then, the Zero escort hit the squadron, breaking up much of their attack. Zeroes tacked onto fleeing Lightnings, whose pilots steepened their dives in a bid to escape. Others stayed and fought. Soon, a swirling, chaotic battle unfolded around the tight formation of bombers.

Bong ignored the confusion and bored in on his targets, hitting a Betty even as machine gun and cannon fire struck his own P-38. He blew through the formation and came around for another pass. This time, he swung directly behind his target. The tail gunner, armed with a 20mm cannon, unleashed a fusillade at his P-38. Bong narrowed the range, firing controlled bursts that peppered the Betty's wing and fuselage. Then he dove away, Zeroes streaking around him, chasing P-38s, as their pilots desperately tried to protect the Betties.

His right engine coughed and sputtered. Smoke boiled out of the cowling, streaming behind him like a "kick me" sign to the Zeroes overhead. His speed fell away as the engine lost power. No sign of his flight, or Jim Fagan. Crippled, alone, and vulnerable, he found himself over Huon Gulf, miles from land. He'd seen the sharks feasting on the Japanese on the water during the Bismarck Sea. No way was he going to risk a water landing. Instead, he feathered his right prop and limped for the nearest base, which was the freshly constructed one at Tsili Tsili west of Lae.

Over Tsili Tsili, he went straight in for the runway, his left engine starting to cough now from the strain of getting the bird home. Bong tried to drop his gear. Nothing happened. The Japanese gunners had knocked out his hydraulic system. He lowered the gear manually at the last possible minute. Just as his wheels hit the runway, his left engine seized. The P-38 slewed and sped off the runway and slid into a bomb crater, where it came to rest with its nose in the mud.

A few tense moments passed as Bong remained hunkered in the cockpit, calming himself down. After seeing so many others die in P-38 crashes, he was under no illusions as to how close he'd come this time to burning alive in the cockpit, or ending up with the sharks in the Huon Gulf. At length, he popped the canopy hatch and emerged to greet the crash crews rushing to his battered bird.

It took three days for Bong's plane to be fixed. When he flew back to Dobodura on the ninth, Gerald and Wally were waiting for him. They asked him if he'd seen what happened to the new guy, Jim Fagan.

Bong was thunderstruck. From the moment he'd engaged the bombers, he lost track of Fagan. Only Ray Swift had seen Jim during the fight as he lagged behind Dick, one tank still under a wing.

Johnson spent three days leading search-and-rescue efforts, combing the Huon Gulf for signs of their lost man. They returned without sighting anything on the water.

Fagan had simply vanished.

Dick felt responsible for his death, and he took it exceptionally hard. After a year of flying and fighting in theater, Bong was at the edge of his endurance. He was worn out, and even the leave in August hadn't brought him all the way back. It was the same with all the high-time pilots in theater. The months of bad food, jungle diseases, and constant tension and fear affected everyone at a different rate. The commonality was how everything they experienced was cumulative and began to weigh on them. The farther the pilots flew past their outer edge of endurance, the more mistakes they made. At least one squadron leader in the 5th recognized he'd reached the point of no return. He couldn't think as quickly or clearly; his reactions started to slow. He realized he was a danger in the air to the men whose lives were entrusted to his judgment and skill. He pulled himself out of combat and asked to be reassigned elsewhere.

Dick withdrew even further, his introversion masking his grief to his fellow pilots. He talked to Gerald and Wally, asking to be allowed to fly solo so he didn't have to carry the responsibility of another life on his shoulders—and in his conscience. Johnson reminded him the Knights fought and won as a team. There'd be hard days, but nobody in his squadron was going to freelance. That did nothing to restore Dick's frame of mind.

Others who served with Dick sometimes talked about how cold-blooded he was. Losses seemed to leave him unaffected. It gave rise to very nasty talk that he didn't care about anyone but himself. They saw the stoic farm kid, not the man who internalized everything. Gerald, who was closer to Dick than probably anyone else that September, could see beyond the expressionless face in the alert shack. Johnson's own emotional nature gave him considerable emotional intelligence. He sensed his friend was not going to pull out of this at Dobo. He gave him a week before pulling him off flight status. A few days later, Gerald sent Bong back to Australia to get away from the fighting and bring back a fresh P-38 from Eagle Farm.

This time down in Australia looked nothing like his trip in August. After losing a wingman and nearly getting killed while crash-landing, other pilots would have drunk themselves into a stupor and stayed that way for the duration of their time in Australia. Alcohol was at once a coping tool, a social lubricant, and a way to blot out memories. For some, it was the only way they could sleep after coming out of combat. Dick was a lightweight—two whiskey and Cokes would leave him lit. Truth was, he hated its effects and didn't like the taste. Without Wally to corrupt him, he eschewed the party scene, preferring solitude instead. He stopped writing home. He didn't go out much at all, even spending his birthday on the twenty-fourth lying in bed at his temporary quarters in Brisbane. There, deep within himself, he imagined a summer home he wanted to build for his family. In his orderly mind, the house took shape. Each room he detailed with furniture and fireplaces. He wanted a game room for the kids he would raise someday, complete with pool and Ping-Pong tables. He even envisioned a bowling alley running along the side of the game room. Of course, the place would have a hangar and a small grass strip, so he could fly whenever he wished. He wanted the latest audio tech, too: a combination radio and record player, which would never, ever play "Rhumba Cardi."

How much would it cost? He guessed eight or ten thousand dollars. He'd squirreled away two grand. He suspected he could swing it when he got home.

For a lonely young aviator fresh off his twenty-third birthday, such flights of fantasy were the only way he knew to handle what was happening to him. He never opened up. There were no military counselors to help him handle the grief. This was something he did alone.

In the end, he did what he knew. He fell back on his farm years and the way he coped with the loss of his sister. He pushed the grief and sense of responsibility down as deep as he could. Jim Fagan's daughter would grow up without a dad. He owned that now, it was a part of his combat life, and he would carry the guilt silently. Now, all he wanted to do was get home. It had been two years since he'd last seen the farm when he first left for training. He was the old hand, the short-timer just trying to survive to see his family again. In that context, the ace race mattered not at all.

He did not go home. Instead, he returned to the Knights at the end of September, at most only half healed. Maybe later, if he got home, he could work through it all. For now, the only path to Wisconsin lay through more dogfights with the Japanese.

24

The Original Freelancer

October 10, 1943
Thunderbolt Valley, Port Moresby, New Guinea

Neel Kearby flew ninety-two hours of combat time in August, and another sixty-five in September. This represented almost twice the number most of the junior officers were flying at the time. Combat veterans later reported that more than forty hours of combat flight time a month ran the aircrew into the ground. Kearby was a machine, flying almost nonstop, whenever the weather allowed. Yet, in September he encountered the Japanese only one other time, scoring his third kill on the fifteenth. Despite the arrival of the external tanks, the 348th was still given the second-string missions. The P-39 squadrons were getting more action than the 348th.

Kearby grew irritable. After one milk run, he landed back at Moresby and ordered the 342nd Fighter Squadron's line chief to get his bird, *Fiery Ginger*, prepped for another flight. When the NCO made a snarky remark that he'd get to it if he could, Kearby wheeled on the man and shot him a look that could have melted steel. "You'll get it ready, or it'll be your ass!"

It didn't matter how many missions he flew; without opportunity, there would be no victories. He suffered through the month, thinking through his options. In the mid-1930s Army Air Corps, he'd been known as the fighter tactics guru of the service, a pilot virtually unbeatable in a dogfight. Legend had it that he would school new pilots in air combat tactics in a Seversky P-35, the grandfather of the P-47. The new guys would be sweating and flinging their birds all over the sky, unable to shake Kearby's P-35. They'd give up, waggle their wings, and look back to see Kearby coolly eating an apple or smoking a cigarette. He'd beaten them one-handed.

All these years of simulated combat flying would be for nothing if he didn't get his shot at climbing the ace ladder. He knew a thirty-two-year-old light bird was not going to remain in combat long.[1] His combat shelf life would be nowhere near the typical yearlong tour. The window to complete his life's goal was a narrow one. Yet, the rules of the game seemed stacked against him.

What do you do when the rules are stacked against you?

Change the game.

With the 348th at Moresby, there were few Japanese targets in range of the P-47s. However, a new strip had just been constructed at Tsili-Tsili, which put both P-40s and P-47s in range of Wewak. The 8th Fighter Squadron was already there, along with part of one other group. Perhaps in time, the 348th would make the move up there, but for now, they were stuck in Thunderbolt Valley.

In August, Kearby left his group and flew a P-38 to Wewak twice. He was a lieutenant colonel in a world of junior officers; nobody was going to challenge him or tell him to stay in his own lane. He'd been in the service long enough to know he could leverage his rank to try to get more action. After he flew the Wewak strikes, he saw an opportunity. Tom Lynch, the second-ranking ace, went home on leave. He'd be out of combat for at least two or three months while he sold war bonds and saw his family back in Pennsylvania. One competitor was out of the race. Bong, Johnson, McGuire—they

---

1. "Light bird" was slang for lieutenant colonel.

were all still flying, but Bong was coming up on a year in theater, which meant he'd be going home soon too.

Kearby saw that he had a window to catch up to them, but only if he could find the opportunity to score. With Wurtsmith still sending the 348th on milk runs, the opportunity eluded him despite all the flying hours he accumulated in New Guinea.

He decided to make his own opportunities.

On October 10, 1943, Neel Kearby and one other pilot took off from Moresby, probably headed for Tsili Tsili to refuel before going to Wewak. They ran into bad weather and instead turned north, linking up with two other P-47s from the 342nd Fighter Squadron. The four Jugs gassed up at Dobodura, then crossed the Bismarck Sea to stir up trouble over Cape Gloucester. There'd been a series of big fights there over the past few weeks, so this seemed like a good secondary hunting ground.

To Kearby's extreme disappointment, they found no enemy planes. Instead, derelict barges littered the beach, victims of summer strafing attacks. They circled overhead until lunchtime, punching their external tanks as they ran dry. Finally, with no other targets in sight, Kearby led the quartet down to strafe the barges. A few looked functional, and their .50-caliber firepower made short work of their wooden hulls. One of the Jug pilots noticed a fuel dump just off the beach. They wheeled around, set it afire, and called it a day.

The mission was reported as a "recce" to Cape Gloucester. Nobody at V Fighter Command seemed to notice or care that this run was off script, so the next day, Kearby tried again. This mission may not have been officially authorized either.

This time, he cherry-picked some of his best pilots. Major Gallagher, the 342nd Fighter Squadron's commanding officer, would lead the second element. Captain Moore of the 341st would be Kearby's wingman, while Captain Dunham of the 342nd would fly on Gallagher's wing. One group commander, one squadron leader, two

General George Kenney (center left) took command of MacArthur's air force in the summer of 1942 when morale had hit rock bottom. Part of his effort to build a fighting spirit included frequent visits to front-line squadrons, where Kenney was subjected to Japanese bombing raids. Here he chats with some of his aviators beside the head of his V Fighter Command, General Paul Wurtsmith (center right). *USAF*

Gerald Johnson became the first of the five aces to see combat. Flying the quirky Bell P-39 Airacobra on missions against Japanese-held Kiska island, he detailed in his diary shooting down two Japanese aircraft. While he was awarded a medal for one of those kills, they were never officially confirmed, the paperwork being lost. Here, one of the squadron's P-39s undergoes repairs at Adak Island in September 1942. *USAF*

A quiet, self-effacing farm kid from tiny Poplar, Wisconsin, Richard Ira Bong became in only a few weeks of combat one of the leading P-38 aces in Kenney's Southwest Pacific Theater. The ghastly food and sleepless nights—owing to the Japanese bombing raids—that he endured at Dobodura, New Guinea left him grizzled and emaciated. *USAF*

"The Eskimos"—Gerald Johnson, Tommy McGuire and Wally Jordan—all joined 9th Fighter Squadron, the Flying Knights, in April of 1943 and flew combat with Dick Bong. Tommy's behavior alienated many of the Flying Knights of the 9th, and he was transferred to the 475th Fighter Group in June as a result. In this photo, taken a year after his transfer, the Eskimos had been reunited shortly before the invasion of the Philippines. *Barbara Curtis*

Colonel Neel Kearby (center) and Colonel Charles MacDonald (right) arrived in New Guinea with the 348th Fighter Group in the summer of 1943. Neel, a hot-blooded Texan whose men practically worshipped him, was utterly committed to beating all comers to take the ace of aces crown. "Mac," one of his squadron commanders and a close friend, was an introverted, enigmatic character who engendered tremendous loyalty among his pilots. *475th FG Assn.*

As a flight leader, Dick Bong (left) lost two wingmen in the summer of 1943. Their deaths affected him so completely that he asked Gerald Johnson (right) to let him fly solo so he did not bear the responsibility of another pilot's life. Gerald, who had risen quickly to become commander of the Flying Knights, refused and sent Dick on an extended leave to Australia to let him heal from the trauma. This photo from October 1943 shows Dick shortly after he returned to the squadron from that leave. *Barbara Curtis*

Neel Kearby and his group introduced the P-47 to combat in New Guinea. Much maligned by the Lockheed P-38 devotees, the heavy Republic fighter, as Neel was determined to prove, could be just as effective as the beloved Lockheed. After some harsh growing pains, the 348th developed into a deadly force under Neel's dynamic leadership, eventually taking a heavy toll on the Japanese. *USAF*

Gerald Johnson poses with reporter Lee van Atta and bomber leader Dick Ellis after the Bloody Tuesday mission against Rabaul. Lee was one of the principal image makers in the race of aces and originally planned to write Bong's memoirs for him. Ellis later became the vice-commander of the air force, recalling in later years that he considered Gerald the best pure fighter leader of the war. L-R: Gerald Johnson, Lee Van Atta, Dick Ellis. *Barbara Curtis*

Tommy McGuire named his P-38 "Pudgy" after his wife's college nickname, and he went through several Pudgies, mainly due to battle damage. A ferociously aggressive pilot, Tommy could push the P-38 closer to the edge of its capabilities than anyone else in the Fifth Air Force. *475th FG Assn*

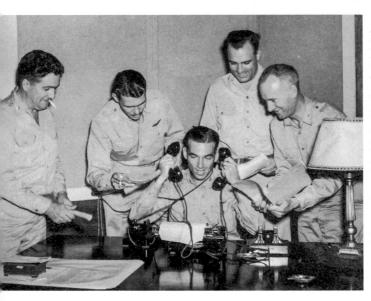

After being put in for the Medal of Honor by MacArthur and Kenney, Neel Kearby (holding the phones) was transferred out of the 348th and into what should have been a non-combat slot as the deputy commander of V Fighter Command. He hated the staff work, as this photo was intended to convey. As soon as Paul Wurtsmith went home on leave, giving Neel temporary command over all of MacArthur's fighter squadrons, Neel got right back in the cockpit and continued racking up kills. *USAF*

Tom Lynch, who would become one of the top aces in contention for the crown, returned from home leave in November 1943 and rejoined the Cobras of the 39th Fighter Squadron. He was there for only a few days into early December when Kearby transferred him to V Fighter Command headquarters and sent him to Australia on non-combat staff duties. He returned to combat in February 1944, flying with Dick Bong in what was dubbed "The Flying Circus." *USAF*

Reporters surround Dick Bong after his 27th confirmed kill, which crowned him America's ace of aces. When reporters wrote about the bet that sparked the race, and the two cases of alcohol Dick was now due from Kenney and WWI great Eddie Rickenbacker, temperance organizations back home furiously protested the prize. Dick was happy enough to have the bet paid in full—with cases of Coca-Cola instead. *USAF*

Dick returned home that spring to a hero's welcome. He was feted all over the country and embraced as a celebrity back in Wisconsin. It was that leave home where he fell ever harder in love with Marge, and by the end of his time Stateside, they were determined to get married. Their small-town romance resonated with the country, and for the next year they were America's sweetheart couple. *Bong Memorial Veterans Center*

Among the many publicity events Dick (front and center) participated in during his time at home was this one at the state capital, where he was made honorary Governor of Wisconsin for a day. Though a good sport about such things, he was never a dynamic speaker and felt ill-at-ease. *Bong Memorial Veterans Center*

While Johnson and Bong remained Stateside during the summer of 1944, Tommy McGuire never left the Southwestern Pacific (SWPA). He continued flying missions without a break from August 1943 through January 1945. Few of Kenney's fighter pilots stayed so long in combat without a home leave. *475th FG Assn*

Gerald and Barbara pose as newlyweds in front of the St. Francis Hotel in San Francisco in the late summer of 1944. It was here that they found out Barbara was pregnant. The news that Gerald would be a dad was the capstone on what he thought of as the happiest summer of his life. *Barbara Curtis*

McGuire (left) and the Killing Tourist, Charles Lindbergh. Lindbergh's bizarre tenure with 475th represented one of the only times a civilian non-combatant was allowed by the U.S. Army Air Force to hunt and kill enemy personnel. After using his fame to talk his way into the SWPA, get to a line unit, and fly missions, Lindbergh nearly got himself killed and the fiasco damaged Charles MacDonald's promising career. *475th FG Assn*

McGuire prepares for another mission in the cockpit of his P-38. His crew chief helps to strap him in while wearing two caps—his own, and McGuire's beloved talisman. At the start of every mission, McGuire handed the cap to his crew chief for safe keeping. It sits on display at the *USAF* Museum today. *475th FG Assn*

In December 1944 at an impromptu ceremony at Tacloban Airdrome, Leyte, Douglas MacArthur personally awarded Dick Bong the Medal of Honor. Dick would stay in theater for another couple of weeks, before Kenney sent him home to another hero's welcome with forty confirmed kills as his final score. *US Army*

Charles MacDonald steers his P-38 over the Philippines. The battle for Leyte and Luzon culminated in some of the most brutal and continuous aerial fighting seen in the Pacific. Mac's 475th and Johnson's 49th Fighter Groups shot down hundreds of Japanese planes, but took what were at times devastating losses. *475th FG Assn*

Tommy McGuire (sitting in the cockpit) prepares to launch Pudgy from Leyte for a mission over Clark Field in 1944. Though he trailed Dick by eight kills, two successful missions put him within two kills just as Dick left the theater. Instead of giving him a chance to beat Bong, Kenney grounded McGuire so that Dick could be hailed as the ace of aces upon his imminent return home. McGuire ignored the grounding order and surreptitiously continued to fly combat missions in hopes of bagging three more planes and stealing the crown. *475th FG Assn*

In June 1945, Jerry Johnson, Gerald's son was born. His crew chief surprised the ace with a full repaint of his P-38, complete with a baby portrait rendered on the nose. *Barbara Curtis*

Tommy McGuire's widow receives her late husband's Medal of Honor from George Kenney while Tommy's dad looks on. The post-war event was attended by dozens of photographers and made national news. Tommy's widow, still mourning the loss of her husband, coped with the scene as long as she could. Then Lindbergh, who saw she was struggling, stepped in and escorted her from the event. *USAF*

captains—it was a brass-heavy flight of four that probably received no clearance from V Fighter Command.[2]

The quartet took off from Moresby on the morning of the eleventh, refueled at Tsili Tsili, and climbed out to twenty-eight thousand feet. The Jug was built around a massive supercharger system that gave it exceptional high-altitude performance. Where other fighters skidded around and could barely maneuver at high altitude, the P-47 possessed power to spare. Nothing the Japanese had in New Guinea could match the Jug above twenty thousand feet. Kearby knew it, and banked on that advantage.

At 1035, the little American formation reached Wewak. The sky was empty, aside from a few scattered clouds down below them. Kearby led them around in a loitering orbit near Boram Drome, watching as an aircraft taxied on its runway but did not take off. Other planes lined the strip there as well. For thirty minutes, the four P-47s hovered over Wewak, looking for trouble. They drained their external tanks and dumped them. They'd have perhaps two and a half hours of flight time on internal fuel, if they carefully managed it.

Another ten minutes passed. Though Wewak had been hit hard in August, intel reports suggested they were rebuilding their demolished units there. Still, Kearby and his three other hunters didn't see a thing.

---

2. Missions were assigned to the squadrons from the top down. V Fighter Command would be given a list of missions to support, aircraft to escort, and they would task the available squadrons accordingly. Usually, if a squadron wanted to run its own mission—say a search for a downed pilot—V Fighter Command would be notified and the mission cleared. That way, those in V Fighter Command HQ could see the status and number of available planes at any given point during any given day. If a crisis emerged, such as a surprise incoming Japanese raid, V FC could flex to meet the threat based on the aircraft available. It is unclear whether Kearby notified V FC of his freelance missions, but from the available evidence it looks unlikely. At times that fall, he took pains to cover up what he was doing and where he went.

Even freelancing wasn't bringing the kills he wanted. What a bust.

The pilots kept one eye on their fuel gauges, one eye on the air around them. Kearby decided to stretch their gas just a bit longer and stick around for a few more minutes. That decision paid dividends at 1115 when the Texan detected movement below. A single Japanese fighter sped along at their eight o'clock about eight thousand feet below them. It looked like a Zero to the Americans, but was really a Ki-43 Hayabusa, loafing along and heading northwest.

Kearby called it out and led the formation in a dive turn to get behind the Japanese plane and upsun to it.[3] It was a perfect bounce. *Fiery Ginger*'s radial engine roared as Kearby opened the throttle and rolled in to the attack. Moore and the others followed, covering their leader.

Kearby didn't wait to get close. He'd been a crack shot back home before the war, spending hundreds of hours making simulated runs on target sleeves. Behind and above, he sped down on the Ki-43 from its seven o'clock. The pilot never saw him, and never had a chance. At fifteen hundred feet, Kearby triggered his fifties. The guns spewed lead. He held the trigger down, a second, two, eased the pressure and fired again. The Hayabusa burst into flames and spiraled toward the water.

One down, now back to the perch. He pulled back on the control stick, sending his Jug racing for altitude. His speed bled off, but that didn't matter. They were safe up here. He leveled off at twenty-six thousand, only to discover Major Gallagher was missing. He'd seen another Japanese fighter farther off the Wewak coast and dove after

---

3. Putting the sun to your back was an old World War I trick Kearby no doubt learned about as a kid when he was obsessed with the aces of the Western Front. This was not a tactical detail that pops up much from other American combat reports in New Guinea, but Kearby used every possible advantage, including this one. A plane diving out of the sun is exceptionally difficult to detect due to glare, so it was an effective way of achieving complete surprise.

it. The enemy pilot saw him coming and raced for a nearby cloud. The two planes plunged into it at ten thousand feet and lost contact with each other. Gallagher was out of the picture after that.

The three remaining P-47s continued the looping patrol over Wewak, waiting for Gallagher and looking for more targets. Ten minutes later, a big formation appeared on the horizon to the east. Thirty-six Japanese fighters, stacked from ten to fifteen thousand feet in flights of four covered about a dozen bombers tucked into a tight formation below them. They seemed to be coming back from a raid, but none were carried out against targets in New Guinea that day. They'd either aborted their attack or the bombers were part of the reinforcement stream coming from Rabaul, and the fighters were escorting them to their new base.

Kearby assumed they were coming home to land. Thinking they were in safe airspace, their situational awareness was low and they had no clue American fighters lurked in the area.

As they ran along the coast, the Texan led his two wingmen around behind them. The layers of fighters between them and the bombers looked too thick to get through with certainty, so Kearby went for the easiest target. One flight of Ki-43s covered the rear of the entire strike group, flying above and behind everyone else. To its left was a flight of Ki-61 Hiens, but they were fairly far away and a little lower.

Tail-end Charlie was the most vulnerable position to fly. How many times had Kearby read about that in his World War I studies? The last guy in the last flight of a formation was always the one the Germans tried to kill first over the Western Front. Manfred von Richthofen, the top ace of the war, preferred to hunt just like this. Stay high, swoop down, and pick off the weak links.

Kearby positioned his guys perfectly. Eleven thousand feet above the trail Hayabusa flight, behind, and upsun. They checked their tails, then dove after their quarry, Kearby in the lead.

The number-four man in the formation seemed to almost be asleep. Perhaps he was a new guy, more concerned with staying in formation than he was making sure he and his wingman were safe. Or perhaps he looked into the sun and couldn't see the trio of snub-nosed fighters dropping on him like olive-drab banshees.

Kearby opened fire at fifteen hundred feet again, closing on him fast at four hundred miles per hour. The big Jug was a solid, stable gun platform. Perfect for this kind of aerial sniping. The Hayabusa, flayed by the eight heavy machine guns, staggered, caught fire, and fell out of the formation. Kearby adjusted, closing now on the number-three man. The Japanese were still oblivious to the danger. Kearby raked him and the Hayabusa's internal fuel tanks exploded. It too, fell out of formation.

Two left in the flight and Kearby was closing fast. The Japanese still were clueless. He hit the flight leader's wingman, smothering it with .50-caliber fire. The light Japanese fighter erupted in flames, rolled over, and went down.

One more to go. Kearby was closer now, furiously trying to line up on the flight leader. Suddenly, the man awoke to the danger. He pulled up in a tight climbing turn, then dove for the safety. Kearby took a shot at him, but it was a high-deflection angle and a split-second opportunity.

Right then, three Hiens rushed into the attack, speeding in from the left and slightly above. They'd been the nearest flight to the Oscars, saw the American attack, and chandelled up and around to the rescue.

A Hien skidded hard, trying to get on Kearby's tail. Bad move. He exposed himself to Dunham's guns. The young captain took the shot. A wall of .50-caliber lead slammed into the Hien, blowing a hole right below the canopy. There was little chance the pilot could have survived that burst without being hit. The Hien fell away from Kearby's tail as Dunham sped past.

Moore went after the other two Hiens, chasing them off Kearby and shooting one down after stitching it from cowling to cockpit. He pulled up, trading speed for altitude while searching for Neel. A moment later, head pivoting from side to side, checking his six to make sure there were no fighters in pursuit, he saw three fires burning on the water off Wewak. He turned east, heading back down the coast for Allied territory, searching for Kearby all the way.

After that initial pass, the Texan climbed back above the Japanese and turned east as well. The odds were heavily stacked against them—three against thirty-six—and the only thing that would keep them alive was rigid adherence to their tactics. Staying above the enemy was crucial.

Twenty miles east of Wewak now, Kearby ran into six Hiens at twelve thousand feet. Alone, he dove on them, his Jug rocketing along. He unleashed his guns and saw tracers disappear into the enemy fighter he targeted. Pieces fell off, and the Hien broke hard and tried to dive away.

The other Hiens gang-rushed Kearby as he tried to extend away. Moore watched as three latched on to his commander's tail. The Hiens were faster and more capable than the Hayabusas, and they were more evenly matched with the P-47. It was a dangerous situation.

Moore shot one off Kearby's tail with a thirty-five-degree deflection pass from above and behind. As he dove past, two Hiens rolled away from Kearby and tacked onto his tail. They were close behind, but not quite in shooting range yet. Moore went to full military power and stayed in a shallow dive. The Hiens hung with him, not losing ground but unable to get in range.

Distracted by their fleeing quarry, they never saw Kearby swing back around to go to his wingman's rescue. Diving fast and steep, his airspeed blowing past four hundred miles an hour, Neel arced down behind the two Ki-61s. Once again, he opened up at long range—fifteen hundred feet—and saw hit sparkles erupt along the Hien's wings and fuselage. It caught fire, fell off its right wing, and went into a steep dive.

Moore held his own dive, watching as Kearby cleared his tail. The remaining Hien tried to evade the Texan's attack with a hard right, breaking dive. It was a tough shot, but Kearby judged the lead and held his trigger down. Tracers bridged the two thousand feet before the two aircraft and the fifties ripped pieces off the Japanese fighter. Moore saw it fall off into an uncontrolled spin.

By now the fight had spread from Wewak to Richthofen Point and lasted twenty minutes. Hard fighting and flying at full-military power drained much of the remaining fuel the Americans carried. With Hiens and Hayabusas still in the sky around them, Kearby decided enough was enough. He dove into a nearby cloud, extended away at full-military power, and called his troops to disengage. They met up farther east, unable to get back to Tsili Tsili with the fuel they had left. They'd have to go to Lae, where the Aussies had recently captured the old Japanese strip there. They touched down at 1245 with about fifty gallons of fuel left. None of the four American planes had taken a hit. They gassed up and returned to Port Moresby, where already word had spread that something big had gone down over Wewak.

Kearby, perhaps trying to conceal the freelancing over Wewak, wrote in his flight log that he'd patrolled the Lae area and made no mention of camping over the Japanese base. If he was trying to obscure what he'd been doing, there was no way the cover-up could last. Too many ears on the ground heard the combat chatter on their radio frequency. Tongues wagged. Kenney, who was at Moresby with Douglas MacArthur that day in preparation for a major attack set for October 12, heard the scuttlebutt. He sent word to the 348th for Kearby to report to him as soon as he got back.

When Neel got back to Moresby that afternoon, he went to see General Kenney at once. To his surprise, he found himself describing the mission not only to his commanding general, but to Douglas MacArthur as well. The two generals listened intently to the pugnacious Texan detail the encounter. When he finished, Kenney told MacArthur that the only other time anyone had shot down five or more planes in one mission was Butch O'Hare's Medal of Honor flight that saved the USS *Lexington* from a Japanese bombing raid in February 1942. Kenney probably didn't know that a Marine named Jim Swett claimed seven in a mission over Guadalcanal in April 1943. No matter, Swett's fight earned him the Medal of Honor too. Kenney told MacArthur that if the claims held up, he wanted to get Kearby an award.

Back at Thunderbolt Valley, Kearby's ground crew pulled the gun camera footage from *Fiery Ginger* and sent it off to be processed. They also noted that collectively the four pilots fired thirty-five hundred rounds at those Japanese fighters, most of which came from *Fiery Ginger*'s eight fifties. When the film was developed and viewed, it corroborated the witness statements the other three Jug pilots gave at the debrief but ran out just as Kearby was firing on the seventh aircraft. After that, Kearby almost always flew with a second camera mounted next to his gun sight.

Postwar Japanese researchers could identify only two losses that day. One was the commanding officer of the 14th Flying Brigade, and the other was a squadron leader in the 68th Sentai, who was also a ranking ace. Both men died in their cockpits, dealing yet another body blow to the morale of the Japanese units at Wewak.

Exactly how many planes the four Jug pilots shot down will probably never be known for sure. What matters isn't the postwar research, though, but what the men in the moment believed. Fifth Fighter Command gave Kearby credit for six kills. The other three pilots received credit for three more. With those six, nine kill flags were painted on the side of *Fiery Ginger*, vaulting him ahead of Johnson and McGuire. He was climbing the ranks of active aces now, and he was not about to stop freelancing when it proved so fruitful.

It almost got him killed the next day. The 5th Air Force threw its full weight against the Japanese air bases at Rabaul, New Britain, on October 12, 1943, in a one-two strike where high-altitude bombers pounded the fields while Pappy Gunn's strafer-modified B-25s went in on the deck. The maximum effort required maximum escort. Every P-38 squadron put up as many birds as their mechanics could get functional. Where most days they were running missions with between twelve and sixteen P-38s, Johnson led the Knights at the tip of a twenty-one-plane formation. The 39th managed eighteen that day. Even the headquarters element of the 475th Fighter Group was thrown into the raid. Instead of going with the group's three squadrons, it was formed into what was called the 1st Provisional Squadron, filled out with other P-38s, and put sixteen more fighters over the bombers that day.

Kearby was not about to be left out of this mission into the heart of the largest remaining concentration of Japanese aircraft in theater. Yet, the 348th didn't have the range to get to Rabaul. Somehow, he got ahold of a P-38 and either flew with Johnson and the Knights again, or went out with the ad hoc 1st Provisional Squadron.[4]

The raid caught the Japanese totally by surprise, but for all the Lightnings in the air that day, only a few pilots saw enemy interceptors. The 1st Provisional shot down a lone Betty bomber caught trying to escape from the area south of Rabaul. A few other fighters were seen and shot down. The rest of the Japanese planes never had time to even scramble before the 5th's bombers rampaged over their runways.[5]

---

4. From the available evidence, it seems most likely he went with the 1st Provisional.

5. This mission was the only one in which the 1st Provisional is mentioned in any V Fighter Command records. Its presence on this mission, combined with later ideas suggested by Kearby to Whitehead and Kenney, may have set the stage for the much more famous Flying Circus that came into being briefly in early 1944.

Over the target area, Kearby suffered catastrophic engine failure. His right Allison exploded. His left began to trail smoke, which found its way into the cockpit. Chances are good that Neel made the same mistake so many rookie P-38 pilots made during their first combat missions. When prepping his Lightning for battle, he probably missed a step and blew the right engine. It was the price of audacity for flying a plane into the heart of Japanese territory with only a few hours worth of experience in it.

Kearby turned back for a staging base at Kiriwina Island off New Guinea's eastern shore, barely able to stay aloft with the one remaining engine guttering and threatening to quit at any moment. He made it back to Kiriwina, lined up for a single-engine landing, and despite his minimal experience in the P-38, defied the odds and got the crippled bird on the ground safely.

He returned to Thunderbolt Valley the next day, shrugging off his close call. To him, the opportunity was worth the risk.

He found Bill Boni waiting for him, eager for the straight scoop on Monday's Wewak fight. Kearby obliged with a self-effacing, straight-talking interview where he derided his own marksmanship skills and pointed out his own mistakes.

"We came in from behind and they didn't know we were there until we'd gone through. That didn't take any real shooting."

Boni's article hit the AP wire that night. By Thursday morning, Kearby's own account of his six-in-a-day mission greeted morning readers across the country, and the folks back home learned a new pilot had thrown his hat into the ring. From here on out, with Kearby in the hunt, the ace race would go high octane.

25

The Warrior's Path

Late evening, October 13, 1943
Dobodura, New Guinea

Gerald sat in his cot, penning a letter home to Barbara with the aid of a single bare bulb dangling from a wire over his head. The tent was quiet. Somewhere in the darkness beyond that bulb, the squadron's harmonica player picked up his instrument, filling the air with a tune from home. Gerald's pen stopped as he paused to listen, closing his eyes.

Today had been the worst day of his life.

Kenney's maximum-effort strike on Rabaul on the twelfth was just the start of a concentrated campaign to destroy the Japanese aircraft and shipping based there. Time was short: a new Allied invasion was scheduled for November 1, 1943, that would be well within range of enemy bombers using Rabaul's airfields. If those bombers weren't destroyed, the invasion fleet could suffer heavy losses. More pressing for the 5th was the lack of P-38 replacements coming into theater. Kenney heard rumblings in September that the heavy losses in the European theater triggered a shift in production priority. The B-17s couldn't survive in the sky against the Luftwaffe without long-range fighter escort, so the P-38, the longest-legged type the Army Air Force possessed, was sorely needed in Europe. The flow of new P-38s to the 5th slowed to a trickle. The ones in theater were pieced together and kept flying with the sweat and ingenuity of the ground crews, but the numbers available slowly dwindled. If the replacement flow was curtailed any further, the 5th would not be able to keep its six P-38 squadrons in the air.

Timing and capabilities meant the aircrew would carry the burden on their shoulders. Rabaul would be attacked every time the weather allowed—and even sometimes when it didn't.

Another maximum-effort strike force sallied from New Guinea's airfields that morning, only to run into fierce tropical storms. Tommy McGuire, flying with the 431st, suffered mechanical failure and landed back at Dobo only thirty minutes after takeoff. The rest of the squadron tried to get through the weather, couldn't find any holes, and turned for home. The rest of the 475th followed suit and aborted the mission.

Johnson did not. Over the summer, he'd made fast friends with some of the bomber leaders, especially Jock Henebry and Dick Ellis in the 3rd Attack Group. An old friend from Eugene also happened to be in the 3rd. There were more than three hundred Japanese planes at Rabaul; if the bombers reached the target without fighter escort, Gerald knew they would be savaged.[1]

They made the rendezvous with the bombers, along with the 39th and 80th Fighter Squadrons, but the weather worsened. The bombers flew through thunderclouds, dodging and weaving through the worst of it until they were spread out and scattered. The weather grew steadily worse until the men were flying practically wingtip to wingtip just to be able to see each other in the thick soup. He should have called it right there, somewhere off the south

---

1. Don Good was Gerald's old friend from Eugene. Don had briefly dated Barbara before she met Gerald, taking her to a dance at the U of O. In June 1943, he suddenly appeared in Gerald's tent, having heard through the grapevine about his fellow Oregonian across the runway from the 3rd Attack Group.

coast of New Britain. Instead, Johnson pushed it, risking the squadron to try to make sure the bombers could be protected.

A recall order was broadcast over the American radio frequencies. The bombers heard it and turned back for New Guinea, as did the Cobras and the Headhunters. The 9th didn't hear the recall. By the time of the broadcast, the Knights were flying through torrential rain, searching for any way to continue.

They passed through one squall, came out the other side to see a veritable wall of thunderclouds ahead of them. Gerald, with Stanley Johnson on his wing, tried to go around to the left, diving for what looked like a hole through the storm. The rest of the squadron, following behind Gerald, emerged out of the rain, saw the front before them, and broke hard right to avoid it.

Johnson lost everyone after that. He passed through part of the storm, ice accumulating on his aircraft, which closed his pitot tube and knocked out his airspeed indicator. Enough was enough. Heavy heart, he keyed his microphone and ordered the squadron home.

Four and a half hours later, half the squadron was missing. Gerald's flight returned to Kiriwina, refueled, and went home to Dobodura. A few others straggled in that afternoon. Wally and his entire flight remained unaccounted for through the early afternoon. Three other pilots from Green Flight, including Theron Price in Watkins's old mount, *Charlcie Jean*, were also missing.

Despite the weather, the Knights mustered four aircraft and went off to search for their missing friends. They found nothing, though Wally's flight finally reached Kiriwina and reported in that they were safe.

Theron Price, Ralph Hays, and Frank Wunder vanished in the storm. As best as could be determined, they'd collided with each other in the clouds.

It had been Gerald's decision to continue, and he knew he was responsible for their deaths. These were his men, and however noble his intentions, his call still got them killed. At least, that's how he saw it that night, sitting alone in his tent.

He put his pen down and walked out into the night. Most of the pilots were over at the O club, nursing drinks. The ground crews labored on the remaining P-38s a few miles away at the flight line. The squadron functioned well. They were a great team. Today, Gerald felt he'd let them down. He wouldn't go to the O club that night. Instead, he walked down to the river and stood regarding the moonlight playing across its surface.

I can't do this. I'm done.

He felt hollowed out, consumed by guilt. He'd failed, and now he would have to write three letters home. The thought of that drove him deep into despair. He knew these lost men like he knew his brothers back home. Their survival was his mission. Killing Japanese was a distant second to that. He worried that he had somehow lost sight of the order of these priorities.

I can't be their leader. My nerve's gone. I don't deserve this responsibility.

This was the most brutal part of the warrior's path, these moments in the dark after fatal decisions. At twenty-three and over a hundred and thirty combat missions, Gerald reached that point in his combat journey where he'd either grow or break. By the river, his heart hung in the balance.

The best warriors, the ones men will follow through all manner of hell, are the men with heart. They don't live emotionless lives. They are not automatons, or wantonly careless. To the core, they are invested in their fellow warriors. That is the core of their bond.

Gerald's men knew what he was trying to do. They knew his heart and believed in his judgment no matter what happened that day. They were still with him.

But was he still with himself? In the moment, it didn't feel like it. Confidence blown, judgment second-guessed, he was on the verge of collapse. Other men broke under this kind of pressure and pain.

It was more common than the military wanted to reveal. It takes a unique combination of character traits to be twenty-three years old and give orders that could kill your closest friends. When the worst happened, some simply couldn't hack it and were reassigned out of combat.

Gerald had grown up in a devout family. Under that New Guinea moon, he thought of those Sundays back in Eugene spent downtown at the First Christian Church. He'd never lost his belief in God, but so many times the warrior road he traveled diverged from the path of the righteous. In that context, he felt he'd lost his way a long time ago, straying from the path his parents and Barbara expected of him.

He looked up at the moon, shining between roving clouds, thinking of that first kiss with Barbara, those nights he'd crept onto her roof to whisper for hours with her through the window. How could he ever return to her after all he'd seen and felt? How could he return, knowing that combat had killed the boy his family knew and loved? The battles here were changing him. He knew it, could feel it. He didn't know what he was turning into and, next to losing men under his command, that was his greatest fear.

He glanced back down at the water as a thought struck him. He couldn't change what happened today. The best decisions were thrown into the chaos of combat and often were milled to dust.

He could control his response to it.

Gerald began to pray. He closed his eyes and listened to the sounds of the river burbling over stones and windfallen branches as he dug into the well of his faith. The torment he felt eased with a rush of newfound strength. He would never outlive the guilt of this terrible Wednesday, but he could grow around it and learn from its pain.

I remember the men who served their fellows—soldiers, poets, doctors, they served the greatest and the least. The emptiness vanishes and I am alert, alive, filled with a spirit that my task shall be completed. I ask not for wealth, or fame or long life, only that I may have the strength and courage to get to my objective and hit it, and hit it, and hit it.

This would become his soldier's mantra, and in the many difficult nights ahead, he resolved to close his eyes and mediate on this humble prayer. When he returned to his cot later that night, he knew this ordeal would not break him.

26

Four Days in October

0800, October 15, 1943
Dobodura, New Guinea

Captive Red, bandits inbound Turnbull Ninety, heading southwest. Angels unknown. Probably high."

Gerald's P-38 streaked for altitude, the rest of his squadron behind. Dobodura was under red alert status, and every squadron available was getting into the air. The Japanese were coming at them in force, determined to avenge the October 12 strike on Rabaul. Exactly how many planes could not be determined by the radar plot alone, but to the controllers, it looked big.

Back at Dobo, the duty pilots of the 475th Fighter Group waited at their alert shacks, ready to go as soon as the intercept controller ordered them aloft. With them that day was a curious figure, new to the group. Slim, balding, and quiet, he wore the oak leaves of a major. Whispers among the pilots suggested he was their new group executive officer. In three months of fighting, the 475th had been like a chainsaw to the enemy, knocking planes down at a rate unseen in the 5th Air Force. If it continued, then one of its squadrons would surely overtake the Knights for highest scoring in New Guinea. That said, most of the command element at group HQ had been in theater for well over a year. They were exhausted, and it was time for a change. This major lounging with them was one of their new replacement leaders.

His name was Charles MacDonald, Kearby's closest friend and a former squadron commander in the Jug outfit. The other pilots figured he'd come down from group to observe the men and learn a little bit about the outfit. But he wasn't asking questions or even saying much. He sat with barely a word, a lone field-grade in a group of lieutenants and captains, minding his own business.

The alert phone rang, a pilot calling out, "Full squadron scramble! Oro Bay!"

Before any of the other pilots could react, the new major flung himself out of his chair and sprinted to the nearest P-38. He beat all the other men to their aircraft, and before the assigned pilot could object, Major MacDonald was already strapping into the cockpit.

A moment later, the 475th took off in hot pursuit of the incoming Japanese.

Johnson and the 9th reached the enemy formation first over Oro Bay. They were Imperial Navy aircraft, stripped from their fleet's carriers to reinforce Rabaul. Below, a flock of Zeroes lumbered a tight vee of aged Val dive-bombers.

Against P-38s, those bombers would stand little chance. Getting to them through the Zeroes would be the biggest challenge. Johnson ordered his men down into the attack. In seconds, flaming planes tumbled out of the sky to splash into Oro Bay around Allied shipping. Bombers ducked and weaved, desperate to avoid the Lightnings as Zeroes challenged the Knights at every turn.

The fight spread out into a multi-altitude brawl as the 475th and other squadrons piled onto the Japanese. Tommy McGuire winged a Val, then hit a Zero, which escaped, though badly damaged. The new major, Charles MacDonald, proved the old adage that the quiet ones are the most dangerous. In short order, he hit two Vals and shot down two others in furious, close-range gunnery runs. The new man was a pro, a veteran of the prewar Air Corps who'd been one of the few fighter pilots to get aloft at Pearl Harbor on December 7, 1941.

Unknown to any of the men flying with him, this Japanese attack was deeply personal to him. The dive-bombers were trying to go after the ships in Oro Bay—transports and cargo ships covered by destroyers. MacDonald's brother was a naval officer in the South Pacific who commanded a squadron of tin cans. He'd already become a war hero to their native Pennsylvanians after his ships fought several night surface battles against the Japanese in the Solomon Islands.

The Vals were simply massacred by the P-38s and P-40s. In return, they inflicted no damage on the ships targeted by their bombs. It was a resounding American aerial win.

The men of the 9th and 475th returned to Dobo to find part of Kearby's Thunderbolt group covering the airfield for them. Second-string duty for the Jugs yet again. On the ground, a wild celebration followed as the men recounted their exploits. When it was all tallied up, the intelligence officers concluded the fighter pilots shot down twenty-six Vals and eighteen Zeroes that day. Gerald flamed two Vals and Zero, plus probable credit for a third dive-bomber. That gave him eight kills, counting the two in the Aleutians. McGuire's Val put him square on Bong's tail with ten.

Charles MacDonald's first combat mission with his new unit left a lasting impression on the men. This major was no staff officer. As quiet as he was on the ground, he was a tiger in the air. That he beat the other pilots to a waiting P-38, then downed a pair of dive-bombers in the fight, demonstrated to all that he was there to fight right alongside them.

As was usually the case, the American claims were too high. The Japanese lost fourteen of fifteen Val dive-bombers along with five Zeroes out of an escort of almost forty. Conversely, the Japanese thought they had sunk several ships and shot down eight American interceptors, but no damage was done to the vessels in Oro Bay. Only one American fighter was lost. The lesson from the postwar recounting of losses was how difficult it was to be certain a plane was destroyed in the middle of a wild, swirling dogfight where a moment's inattention to the sky around you could result in swift death.

Once again, Bill Boni got the story, and the Sunday editions of newspapers throughout the United States regaled their readers with the stunning success in New Guinea. The aces feasted, and the theater-wide count for the day was given at over a hundred Japanese planes.

Kearby missed it all as his men flew second-string missions, covering Dobo and other bases including Tsili Tsili. There was no trouble to be had. Either way, Johnson was a kill behind him, McGuire a kill ahead. He was thirsting for action and wanted a good mission.

Through mid-October, Kenney was determined to keep the pressure on the Japanese. If he couldn't hit Rabaul because the weather turned bad, he planned to hammer targets in New Guinea. On the night of the fifteenth, as it looked like the weather wouldn't cooperate for another Rabaul raid, three main B-25 attacks were laid on against Madang, Alexishafen, and Wewak. Of the three, the Wewak attack was most likely to be intercepted, so Wurtsmith tasked four P-38 squadrons to provide escort.

Kearby saw the orders for the 348th that night and must have been disappointed. Instead of going to Wewak, Wurtsmith ordered the Texan's 340th and 342nd Squadrons to cover the B-25s to Alexishafen. His other squadron was to fly escort for transports—another second-string day for them.

Kearby could have led the escort to Alexishafen, but that was usually a pretty quiet place. Instead, he decided to go to Wewak again. This time, he pulled three other pilots from the 340th and 342nd, including the Maj. Hervey Carpenter, the commander of the 340th. The next morning, the four-plane hunting flight took off at 0750, an hour before the escort mission to Alexishafen began.

The four Jugs set down an hour later at Lae to refuel, then got on their way after forty minutes. The timing was very important. The P-38s and B-25s heading to Wewak reached the target area at 1055. About fifteen enemy aircraft tried to intercept. The Lightnings shot down five of the Japanese planes before the fight ended at 1120 and the Americans withdrew for home.

Five minutes later, Kearby's flight reached Wewak, cruising with their drop tanks at twenty-three thousand feet. Neel was a master tactician, and as a group commander he must certainly have known the details of the Wewak raid in advance. It seems likely that he timed his arrival over the Japanese base just after the main strike turned for home. On the eleventh, the Japanese planes he shot down were coming back to land. After intercepting the Americans on the sixteenth, the Japanese would be scattered and streaming back to rearm and refuel. It was a perfect moment to drop down on them from above.

For twenty minutes, the Jugs patrolled around Boram Drome, sighting one single-engine fighter down too low to make a worthwhile target. When no others appeared, it looked like the patrol would be a bust. Then the Texan sighted a better target: a single Ki-43 cruising along at eighteen thousand feet. He led the flight down, the other three pilots covering him as he made a surprise attack from dead astern. At the last minute, the Japanese pilot awoke to the danger and broke hard right in a climbing turn to face the onslaught.

He was too late. At fifteen hundred feet, Kearby opened fire, and his long-range marksmanship was dead-on. The burst destroyed the Oscar's engine, and the aircraft fell away on fire. A moment later, the pilot bailed out, his chute opening above him.

Without any other targets, the Americans returned to Lae, refueled, and got back to Port Moresby that afternoon after six hours and fifteen minutes in the air. When they arrived home at Thunderbolt Valley, the rest of the group was celebrating the end of their biggest day ever. It turned out, while Kearby and Major Carpenter were over Wewak, their commands were intercepted en route to Alexishafen. The Japanese threw almost twenty planes at the Jugs at medium altitude. The men claimed thirteen destroyed and five more probables, virtually wiping out the intercepting force. It was a tremendous statement, one that resonated up the chain of command and led to a more aggressive employment of the P-47. The aircraft's capabilities had been validated. The 348th would soon be given bigger and better missions.

Exactly why Kearby chose Major Carpenter for his Wewak hunt will probably never be known. He had pulled the 340th's commander away from his squadron on what turned out to be its biggest day in combat to date. Either Kearby was trying to rotate his Wewak flights between his squadron commanders to get them familiar with the area, or he chose to fly with the best pilots in the group. Whatever the case, Neel Kearby's single-minded determination to run his score up was pushing the boundaries between personal glory and command responsibilities. He was taking risks. He was flying missions away from his group, cherry-picking the time and place to go hunt on his own. Yet, he possessed an electric charisma that smoothed all this over. His men saw him as larger than life, a hero in waiting Stateside before they came over, a defining one now that they'd seen combat. With his enormous energy, he was able to multitask, flying constant combat missions while taking care of all the myriad issues a fighter group commander at the front faced on the ground. There was no denying the man was a special kind of type A leader, but after the eleventh of October, his urge to repeat that six-kill performance dominated everything else. He would continue to hunt at Wewak, taking bigger and bigger risks to catch the high scores he had set his eyes on when he first arrived in theater.

27

The Battering of the *Pudgy*s

October 17, 1943
Dobodura, New Guinea

In three months of combat, Tommy McGuire proved to be as hard on his aircraft as he was on his peers. The kid from Florida who used to run from bullies and cry in the school bathroom when punched in the nose was dead, replaced by a man who always piled into the middle of a Japanese formation. He had grown reckless, wild, and supremely aggressive at the controls of his P-38s, which is how he ran his personal score to ten in such a short time. There was a cost: at the end of August, he limped out of a fight over Wewak with a burning engine shattered by Japanese cannon fire. He barely made it to Tsili Tsili, where the aircraft was deemed irreparable. He was given a new, precious P-38, which he named *Pudgy II*. The Japanese quickly drilled it with bullet holes.

At times, he returned to base with an overstressed airframe, having pushed the plane beyond its g-limits. The cost of that extra maneuverability was not trivial. At a time when P-38s were in critically short supply, he often returned from missions with his P-38 suffering from significant structural damage. The aircraft would be down for days as the ground crews replaced cracked spars and bent wings. Once, after being taunted by a Spitfire pilot in Australia, he challenged the Commonwealth pilot to a duel. The two went at it furiously, McGuire throwing his P-38 all over the sky. When he landed, the brand-new aircraft was so badly damaged from over-stressing that it could not be repaired.

For all his faults on the ground, what ultimately mattered in a fighter squadron was performance in the air. That fall, McGuire's combat record earned him considerable respect within the 431st. In the air, he was a totally different person. Selfless, always watching out for the men around him, he went to the rescue of fellow pilots and beleaguered bombers several times, ignoring the personal risks in doing so. Yet, even in combat he could annoy. In the heat of the moment, he talked incessantly over the radio, battling the Japanese while babbling at such speed that not only was he hard to under-stand, but his chatter sometimes stepped over warning calls to check six. That habit did nothing to win his peers over.

On the ground, success in battle made him even less well liked, as he morphed back into a braggart. He'd finally been able to back up his talk, and after a short period of toning down that obnoxiousness over the summer, he'd rebounded with a vengeance. Now he had street cred with the kill flags on the side of his P-38's nose. He lectured. He needled those around him whom he considered lesser pilots and men. At the same time, he was flying more than almost anyone else in the outfit, and doing more for the pilots than perhaps any other junior officer. Every morning that he was not slated for a combat hop, he'd go down to the flight line and spend the day test-flying repaired birds to make absolutely sure they were in top condition. It was a risky job, and one he did so the other guys wouldn't run into a life-threatening situation when they took the repaired birds out on missions.

When not flying, McGuire personally boresighted the guns in every plane in the squadron. In fact, he was the only pilot who knew how to do that in the 431st. Usually, this was the ground crew's job.

Through the end of summer and early October, the 431st flew nonstop combat missions, racking up an incredible tally right along with the rest of the 475th Group. By the time the Rabaul raids started, the group had claimed a hundred and fifty Japanese planes against the loss of ten pilots.

The success came with a cost. The grinding pace, the pressure-cooker atmosphere of a fighter squadron existing on a razor's edge in the middle of a primeval jungle put the men on edge and shortened tempers. Drama flourished, personality differences grated even more, and the squadron coalesced into a series of close cliques. McGuire didn't fit anywhere, as usual. It also didn't help that on those sporadic days when they received their pay, he would quickly bankrupt anyone willing to play poker with him. Again, whispers of his cheating at the game swirled around him.

As his score rose, his press did not. In the wake of mission after mission, Boni and the other chroniclers of the ace race ignored his rise, mentioning him only in passing. His personality on the ground probably had a lot to do with that, and while he didn't appear to care about the press at all, he had always been the kid eager to draw attention to himself. It was a deeply contradictory part of his personality: an externally validated young man who tended to alienate everyone around him with his behavior. The truth was, he wanted connection. He wanted the comradeship others experienced. He just didn't know how to connect after a lifetime of outsider status. So on the ground, he pretended not to care, though inside he was devoured by his lack of recognition, baffled by what he could be doing wrong.

Marion Kirby and a couple of other senior pilots rode herd on McGuire, trying to develop him further. Though a stubborn man, McGuire learned everything he could from them. Their mentorship transformed him into a team player in the air.

On the morning of October 17, 1943, McGuire rose early to get working on the squadron's birds. *Pudgy II* was down for maintenance, and he wasn't on the flight schedule that day. At this point, even his work ethic pissed off some of the other pilots. Those not on the day's roster wanted to sleep in. McGuire made that harder, getting to the line at the crack of dawn to test engines and aircraft.

McGuire was hard at work when radar picked up a confusing number of contacts to the north. Some seemed to be stationary, some seemed headed to Oro Bay. The controllers concluded the Japanese were trying to jam their radar systems with reflective metal chaff, a trick the British developed during their night bombing campaign of Germany.

The radar operators stayed glued to their sets as the controllers sent an alert to Dobo to be ready to scramble at two minutes notice. McGuire saw the duty pilots rushing to their cockpits and realized something big was afoot. When he asked around, word had it another big strike was inbound.

A good plot finally resolved on the scopes that morning just before ten. The radar guys estimated perhaps thirty-five to forty Japanese planes, altitude unknown. The controller scrambled all available aircraft.

Marion Kirby led the squadron that day, as General Wurtsmith had summoned Major Nichols to V Fighter Command headquarters. As a perk of rank, Nichols kept his own P-38 and gave standing orders that nobody else was to fly it. McGuire glanced along the flight line and saw it was the only unoccupied bird. He rushed over to it, shouting to the crew chief, "Get Major Nichols's plane ready!"

The NCO objected, reminding Tommy of the commander's standing order. Tommy told him he'd take full responsibility. The Japanese were inbound, and every plane was needed in the fight. He sped aloft to join the other P-38s, already climbing over the field, taking over as a flight leader when he caught up to them.

Kirby followed the ground controller's directions and stayed over the field at first. The 431st would cover Dobodura and backstop other squadrons, including the Knights, as they went directly for the Japanese raid. Soon word came to turn north and go hunting. Apparently, there were a lot of Japanese.

The 431st sped toward the contact, leveling off at twenty-three thousand feet. Normally, this would be more than high enough, as the Japanese tended to fly below twenty. Not this morning. A cry of alarm sounded over the radio.

"Bandits! Eleven o'clock high!"

Nearly twenty Zeroes resolved ahead of the Americans. Before they could react, the Japanese dove after them. The Americans dropped their tanks and banked into the Japanese attack. They were at a terrible disadvantage. Slow from their most economical cruise speed, they went to full power but were forced to climb to get their guns on the Japanese.

The two formations merged, guns belching flames, tracers lacing the sky. Tommy hit a Zero on that first pass, turned, and dove to finish him off. As he did, his wingman broke out of the fight, unable to shake one of his fuel tanks loose. He couldn't climb above the action, so he power-dived out of it.

At eighteen thousand feet, McGuire gave up pursuit of the Zero he'd damaged and zoomed for altitude. He was alone now, his second element somewhere in the sprawling furball above him. Tommy looked for any friendly P-38s to join, and spotted Kirby's quartet still together, working to keep each other alive. He sped for them, intending to link up, when two Zeroes dove on Kirby's men from behind and off to the right.

Still climbing, bleeding speed off as he went, McGuire banked hard and went after the attacking Zeroes, spraying enough lead that both abandoned their gunnery runs on the other P-38s.

The move to save Kirby's flight cost him dearly. Before he could extend away and gain critical speed, four more Zeroes dropped on him from dead astern. With position and speed, the Japanese had McGuire cold. He couldn't turn, couldn't climb. All he could do was roll into the steepest dive he dared, running the P-38 to the edge of compressibility. The controls grew stiff as he plunged downward at ever increasing speed. The Zeroes refused to give up the chase. They hung in there after him even as he began to pull away, hoping he'd run out of altitude before he could get completely clear of them.

Oro Bay's blue-gray water lay ahead. McGuire pulled the yoke back, gradually forcing the Lightning's nose up until he finally came out of the dive at a thousand feet. The Zeroes now lay far behind.

With the fight twenty thousand feet over his head, stray Zeroes lurking between him and the battle, most pilots would have called it a day and turned for home. But McGuire refused to cut and run. Instead, he traded the enormous speed he'd built up in the power dive for altitude, zoom-climbing back into the fight.

At eighteen thousand feet, he ran into three more Zeroes. He made several passes, but missed. As he came around again, three more dove on him, and his borrowed P-38 shuddered from bullet strikes. A machine gun round punctured the cockpit and ricocheted around him. He dove away, but one of the Zero pilots hung with him long enough to hit him again. Another bullet cracked past him into the cockpit. The Zero was close, blazing away at him. He dove almost vertically and, pushing the Lightning beyond its engineering limits, risked compressibility again.

At seven thousand feet, he looked back and saw his tail was clear. He sped on, entering a shallow climb to have another go at the Zeroes. As he passed angels twelve, movement below him drew his eyes. One of his squadron mates was running for his life in a crippled P-38, seven Zeroes on his tail. The closest was almost in firing position. McGuire had no help nearby. The American would die if he didn't go down and help. Even if he did, the seven-to-one odds did not bode well.

What kind of man risks near-certain death to save a squadron mate who probably dislikes him just like most of the others? There was nobody else around to see him run or fight. McGuire could have saved himself without backlash.

A split-second choice needed to be made. McGuire never hesitated.

He rolled his wings and broke hard down after the Zeroes, ignoring the trailing ones to get after the leader who was the biggest threat to the crippled '38. It would be a tough shot; he dove at a ninety-degree angle off the Zero's right wing, closing fast. He opened fire and held the trigger down, hosing the air with tracers and lead. Normally, McGuire used short, controlled bursts. Instead of easing off the trigger, he kept firing as he closed, making instinctive adjustments as he saw his tracers edge toward the Zero.

The Japanese was in firing range now. The cripple was easy meat.

The Zero exploded. McGuire thundered past the flaming debris, bending his P-38 around in an impossibly tight turn to tack onto another Zero. He was going faster than the Zero even with the tight turn, and now he climbed right up its tail. At a hundred feet, he cut loose with cannon and fifties. The lightweight fighter stood no chance. Twenty-millimeter shells exploded along its fuselage and wings. The fifties added to the carnage. One of its fuel tanks erupted, sending a sheet of flame back toward McGuire's Lightning. The Zero rolled over and went straight into Oro Bay like a comet.

Two kills cleared the Lightning's tail, but McGuire's attack was a sacrificial act. By making that turn and putting the remaining Zeroes directly behind him, he'd set the table for the Japanese.

Bullets tore into his P-38. A cannon shell exploded in the radio behind his seat, the blast concussing him and sending shrapnel into his buttocks and hip. He tried to maneuver, but a quick glance behind him revealed a Zero less than thirty yards back, its wings and nose afire as the pilot triggered his guns. A bullet punctured the side of the cockpit, went through McGuire's wrist, and spanged into the instrument panel with a metallic thud. Another cannon shell exploded behind him, sending shrapnel into his right arm.

The Zero had him. No chance of escape. The Japanese pilot closed for the killing shot at absolute point-blank range.

McGuire tried to dive away as both engines took hits. The right one started to smoke, the left one vomited flames. Time slowed and the scene became surreal. Tommy looked down to see the symmetrical hole in his wrist and his concussed brain briefly marveled at its perfect shape.

He tried to maneuver, pulling the yoke back to exit the dive and throw the Japanese pilot's aim off. The controls didn't respond. No chance to save the aircraft; he could only try to save himself now.

Tommy reached up with a wounded arm and released the canopy hatch. The plexiglass piece tore away from the aircraft as he fumbled to unbuckle his shoulder straps. The Lightning passed four hundred miles an hour, flames tailing behind both engines as it dove. He cut the throttles, but he'd be going out against a vicious slipstream anyway. He got the shoulder harness unbuckled and stood up. The wind force hit him like a concrete wall, tearing his goggles off and pinning him to the back of the canopy. Everything went black for an instant as his oxygen mask slammed into his brow, covering his eyes. He clutched at it and pulled it away. The 400-mile-an-hour slipstream struck his face full force now, seeming almost to tear his eyes out of their sockets. Furiously, he tried to get the rest of the way out, but something snagged his chute harness in the cockpit. He was trapped as the P-38 went into death gyrations. Slammed from side to side and thrown repeatedly against the back of the cockpit, he fought to save himself, the engine fires spreading to the wings and booms.

Suddenly, he was free, falling clear of the doomed Lightning. Oro Bay was about five thousand feet below him now. With his wounded wrist, he reached up, grabbed his parachute's D-ring, and pulled it.

The chute didn't deploy. Instead, the D-ring came away in his hand, its cable severed by cannon shrapnel. Tumbling and spinning toward the water, with no reserve chute, Tommy groped around for the other half of the cable dangling by his side, praying he could find it before it was too late. He yanked it hard. The chute billowed out over him and opened. He swung once and slammed into the water with such force that it broke ribs.

Many pilots died in the water when their parachutes pulled them under. Getting out of the chute harness quickly was the only way to avert that fate. With bullet- and shrapnel-wounded hands and arms, broken ribs, and black eyes so swollen they were half closed, it must have taken a supreme act of will to get clear of the chute. Somehow, Tommy was able to do it, and then triggered his life vest, which was known as a "Mae West." One side inflated. The other did not. It was barely enough to keep him afloat.

Then he tried to inflate his life raft. He popped the CO_2 canister, heard air hissing, but the thing didn't inflate. He looked it over, found it full of shrapnel holes. It was useless. He cast it aside, shucked off his Australian boots, and began treading water. A moment later, he realized he was bleeding; the water around him was turning inky red. His mind was occupied with a single thought—the images of pilots he'd seen downed in the oceans and encircled by sharks. He reached back for his life raft, rummaging around until he found the survival kit lashed to its interior side. He pulled it clear, cracked open the shark repellent and yellow dye marker that would help search planes see him on the water. By now, the adrenaline rush that got him through the ordeal began to drain away. His wounds began to ache. The pain grew worse. His concussed head throbbed. He could barely keep his chin above the water. He unstrapped his pistol, let it sink, and pulled off every other piece of gear he could reach. Feebly, now, he began trying to stem his bleeding with direct pressure, fading closer and closer to unconsciousness.

Hands grabbed at him. Dazed, he heard an engine sound as he was pulled out of the water and dragged onto the deck of a Navy PT boat. He lay there as the sailors dressed his wounds, jabbering away at how they'd seen him knock down two Zeroes, then go straight in himself. "Damnedest thing we've ever seen," one kept saying.

Did he save the cripple? Nobody knew.

McGuire was taken back to New Guinea and flown to a hospital at Port Moresby. Major Nichols found him there a short time later, lying in a clean bed, arms and hand covered in bandages. His eyes were shockingly blood-filled and blackened. His face looked like a hell-bound raccoon's.

When he saw his squadron leader, he apologized at once for losing his aircraft. Nichols was pissed at that and had intended to chew Tommy out for it. But the moment he saw this twenty-three-year-old kid so badly hurt, that anger vanished.

"You know, if you took better care of your aircraft, things like this wouldn't happen," Nichols chided lightly. Then added seriously, "To hell with it, I don't care about the airplane. I'm just happy to see you alive."

As he listened to Nichols, McGuire felt a sense of comfort long absent. After losing his mother, bouncing from unit to unit as the man nobody wanted to fly with, he'd lived an unsettled, sad life separated by his quick tongue and braggart's mouth from his squadron mates. Now, despite the pain pushing through the fog of morphine in his IV drip, he felt the warrior's bond for perhaps the first time since drinking that bottle of Yellowstone with Gerald and Wally. It was a shame it had finally taken root now, when he would probably never see the 431st again. Nichols figured he'd be lucky to even get back in the air. He had a long and difficult convalescence ahead. They both knew that. But as Nichols told him how the squadron learned his fate and self-sacrifice from the PT-boat's crew, how word was out that Tommy McGuire had taken on the entire Japanese Air Force alone, shooting three more planes down before they got him—well, the ordeal seemed worth it. It was the price of loving his brother warriors.

28

The Race over Rabaul

Mid–October to Mid–November 1943
New Guinea

Two days after McGuire went down, Kearby destroyed a pair of Japanese floatplanes on another hunting mission over Wewak with his "Musketeers" flight, as his handpicked group of four tigers came to be called by the reporters covering the race. Kearby was the one constant; the other Musketeers changed often. In this fight, Neel took Bob Rowland, Capt. Frank Oksala, and Capt. Meade Brown. The leading active aces in theater now included Bong with seventeen, Kearby with twelve, Danny Roberts of the 475th Fighter Group with nine, Gerald Johnson with eight, and Jay Robbins of the 80th with seven.

With the invasion of Bougainville in the northern Solomons fast approaching, Kenney needed to get his Rabaul blitz underway. Weather defeated most of the attempts, but on the eighteenth the B-25s got through, with Johnson leading the 9th fighters as part of the cover for the raid. The Knights of October 1943 were a vastly different outfit than the one Gerald and the Eskimos had joined six months before, during the spring. He and his peers were the institutional experience now, and all the leadership slots were filled with pilots who had been in New Guinea about the same time as Gerald.

Between May and September, the squadron lost two pilots killed in action. In two October missions, Gerald's command lost three pilots to weather and its executive officer, Harry Lidstrom, to combat. Wally Jordan took over as XO after Harry's death on the sixteenth. Four men missing in less than a week battered the squadron's morale, especially when the unit counted probably less than thirty-five pilots on its roster.

Replacement aircraft for those lost proved in short supply. The Knights made do with P-38s that the ground crews kept patching and repatching together with parts stripped off wrecks. At the moment, when Kenney demanded the utmost of them, the Knights could not field anything close to a full squadron of fighters. The birds were old, worn out by months of service in terrible jungle weather. They sat outside during thunderstorms. The humidity and moisture caused electrical issues. The gun sights failed. Tanks hung. Crashes took out even more birds, the worst of which happened to Clayton Barnes, who was nearly burned alive in his cockpit after losing an engine on takeoff. He had been evacuated to Australia, never to fly again.

Gerald faced one other issue that October. Though Dick Bong remained the top ace in theater, he had not really come back after losing Fagan in September. In fact, the short trip down to Eagle Farm hadn't done much good. He flew a few more combat missions after he returned, shooting down a Mitsubishi Ki-46 Dinah reconnaissance plane. Gerald sent him down to Brisbane on leave again. In the past two months, Dick had spent almost three weeks out of combat in Australia. He was at the end of his combat effectiveness, fighting his own demons, and just needed to rotate home with the other pilots who'd been in theater for a year. That would come, hopefully soon. For now, Gerald needed his best-functioning pilots to get the squadron through this ordeal.

On the twenty-third, the Knights reached Rabaul as high cover for heavy bombers targeting the airfields. The weather closed in yet again, but that didn't stop the Japanese from trying to intercept.

Gerald, leading fifteen other P-38s, ran into about ten Zeroes at twenty-six thousand feet. The Japanese made diving attacks on the heavy bombers below. Johnson led the Knights down to keep the bombers safe. In the fight that followed, the Knights sent the Zeroes diving away from the bombers, damaging one that broke clear of the fight while trailing thick, black smoke. Johnson swung in behind another Zero that had just finished a gunnery run on a B-24 Liberator. He hammered the Japanese plane with all guns as he zoomed into point-blank range. He cut the throttles to keep from overshooting the fighter. Then an explosion rocked the Zero. A second one followed, blowing debris back into Johnson's P-38. The Zero flipped inverted and went straight, as observed by Gerald's ever-faithful wingman, Stanley Johnson, who confirmed the kill.

The 475th got into a similar fight that day, and Charles Mac-Donald shot his third plane down while protecting the bombers. Danny Roberts got two more. The next day, when the 5th returned to Rabaul for a low-altitude B-25 strike, Jay Robbins of the 80th bagged four Zeroes in a wild scrap over the Japanese base. Danny Roberts also scored. Rabaul was serving as high-octane fuel for the ace race. With McGuire out of action, George Welch home with malaria, and Bong at the end of his tour, the chance to gain fame and catch the leaders was never better.

Bong flew on the twenty-fourth but failed to encounter the enemy. It was his first combat mission in almost three weeks. The next day, he wrote home, acutely conscious of the contenders nipping at his heels. "As for the number of planes I have, why I actually have nineteen, but only have official credit for seventeen. It's still more than anyone over here has ... Received orders on the Distinguished Service Cross today, so that makes four medals I have received. The Silver Star, Air Medal, Distinguished Flying Cross, and the Distinguished Service Cross."

To keep the squadron functioning through these brutal long-range missions, Gerald had to balance the daily duty roster with a mix of experienced veterans whose leadership he could trust. He and Wally flew every other day. On days when they weren't aloft, Capt. Bill Haney led the squadron, with Dick Bong one of his flight leaders. As a result, Dick and Johnson did not fly together through the last week of October. It was something Gerald later had cause to regret.

On the twenty-ninth, Haney led the Knights to Rabaul as high escort for the bombers. This time, Dick flew with a young Greek-American pilot named George Hanniotis on his wing. George had arrived in the squadron only a short time before these maximum-effort strikes began, but already he'd proven himself a brave and reliable pilot. He was also popular on the ground, easygoing with a great sense of humor. He was also a workout warrior, always lifting weights or exercising in some way while off duty.

Over Rabaul that day, the Knights protected the bombers as they targeted the Japanese airfields near the harbor. A veritable cloud of Japanese fighters rose to intercept, climbing for the Americans north of the bombing area. They turned south and dove through the P-38 escort blanket and hit the bombers. Haney rolled in after them, leading the entire squadron down in a furious chase to save the B-24s. Zeroes began to fall in flames as bombs exploded on their runways. The fight started at eighteen thousand feet and quickly spread all the way down to the waves and treetops as the P-38s spiraled and zoomed after fleeing Japanese fighters. Bong caught a Zero after it went through the B-24 formation, but missed it as two more Japanese pounced on him. George saw the Zeroes getting behind his flight leader and tried to scrape them off. Bong was forced to dive away, Hanniotis sticking with him as the P-38 ace extended clear of the Zeroes and pulled up at three thousand feet. He whipped around and went after one of his pursuers, Hanniotis hanging on to his lead with dogged determination.

The Zero went head-to-head with Bong. After one pass, it fell in flames before the merge, its fuel tanks set afire by the farm boy's cannon. Two more Zeroes joined the fight, and soon a low-altitude, high-speed steeplechase ensued. Bong nailed one from dead astern, sending it into the water of Open Bay. The other he tried to catch, but he ran out of ammunition after scoring a few hits. He broke for home, George Hanniotis still right with him despite all the wild maneuvers.

Back at Dobodura, the Knights returned without loss and with six kills under their belts. It was a big morale boost to a squadron on the ragged edge of exhaustion. When word spread that the 475th and 80th were having big days too, that Danny Roberts, Charles MacDonald, and Jay Robbins were all running their scores up over Rabaul, Bong took comfort that he'd padded his lead with two more Zeroes. He wrote home, "Got two more, so that makes nineteen. That puts me three up on anyone over here."

It was a good day, but the string of maximum-effort strikes continued to take their toll on the squadron's aircraft. For the next three days, the ground crews worked day and night to repair the aircraft left to the outfit and get them ready for the biggest Rabaul raid yet.

On November 1, 1943, Allied troops went ashore at Bougainville Island, only about 250 miles from Rabaul. If the Allies could build an airfield complex here, the Japanese base would be in easy range of dive-bombers and fighters. Rabaul would become unusable to the Japanese Navy. Recognizing the urgency of the moment, the Japanese sent a task force of cruisers and destroyers to obliterate the Allied amphibious task force off Bougainville in a night battle. The U.S. Navy was waiting for them, and, in what became known as the Battle of Empress Augusta Bay, dealt the Japanese a stinging defeat. Their cruiser task force turned around and limped back to Rabaul, where it dropped anchor just in time to be attacked by the full might of the 5th Air Force.

Tuesday, November 2, 1943, went down in history as the largest single air battle of the Southwest Pacific campaign. Kenney ordered every B-25 and P-38 in his command to strike at the airfield and shipping in Simpson Harbor. Whitehead and Wurtsmith tasked Johnson with leading the escort force that day.

The attack was a complex one, with lots of moving parts that demanded exceptional timing. The 3rd Attack Group would take its B-25s around the coast of New Britain to attack the shipping from the north. Two other B-25 groups would bomb and strafe the airfields while laying a smokescreen to blind the land-based antiaircraft gunners. The 475th, 80th, and 39th would cover the bombers hitting the airfields. Johnson's Flying Knights would have the extraordinarily difficult task of staying with the 3rd Attack Group as they skip-bombed the ships in the harbor. They'd have to be low to cover those B-25s, which would make the P-38s vulnerable to getting bounced from above by any patrolling Japanese fighters. This made surprise an essential part of the plan.

Weather delayed the mission for several hours that morning. The Knights assigned to fly sat around the alert shack, waiting for the "go" order and reading copies of *Reader's Digest* magazine that Gerald's family had sent to the squadron. Blev Lewelling, a new pilot with the squadron, sat beside Gerald, talking with him of home. Blev grew up in Oregon, in a little mill town called Albany, about fifty miles north of Eugene. His dad was a judge, and as the two pilots talked, they grew convinced that their fathers must know each other, at least professionally.

For this mission, Gerald pulled together his most experienced leaders along with his freshest remaining pilots. Bill Haney, who usually took the squadron on alternate days when Gerald didn't lead it, would take a flight on November 2. Johnson would take Captive Red. Wally Jordan had Captive Green. Significantly, Gerald left Bong off the roster that day. Why, when all his other best pilots were slated to fly, did he leave the USAAF's top ace off the mission? In fact, Bong hadn't flown since the twenty-ninth, a clear indication that Johnson was starting to see him as a liability—to himself and those around him. He was combat weary, still hurting over the loss of Fagan. Wurtsmith needed to send him home for a long rest. Every man can only take so much combat, stress, and repeated adrenaline rushes, and Bong didn't need any more of those. He needed a ticket back to Wisconsin.

At ten, the phone rang. Gerald snatched it up, listened, and told his men to get to their ships. The mission was on.

They sped to Kiriwina, landed, and refueled, only twelve strong. Despite all the work and sweat the weary ground crews put in, a half-strength squadron was the best they could do with the aircraft left to the Knights.

Back in the air, Wally Jordan's P-38 soon suffered mechanical failure. Cursing with frustration, he reversed course and headed back to Kiriwina as the rest of the squadron linked up with the 3rd Attack Group. The B-25s stayed right on the water while Gerald kept his squadron above them at a thousand feet. If the timing worked right, the 80th Fighter Squadron would go in first on a sweep, clearing a path for the two B-25 groups slated to hit the fields and lay the smoke. Thirty seconds later, the 3rd Attack Group would go into the harbor.

The entire raid swung around the east coast of New Britain, following the shore northward and past Rabaul. They turned left, then came down at the Japanese base between two volcanoes.

The timing was perfect, but at the last possible minute, the Japanese saw them coming. They scrambled every available fighter, and the Headhunters plowed right into them as they lifted off from their airfields. In seconds, the 80th faced over a hundred Japanese fighters. A wild, desperate fight broke out even as the other two B-25 groups rushed over the jungle, between the two volcanoes and down into Rabaul proper, covered by the Cobras and the 475th Fighter Group.

Last in came the Grim Reapers, the 3rd Attack Group. Jock Henebry, one of the great veteran skip-bombing pilots of the war, led the bomber force. Dick Ellis, with daredevil reporter Lee Van Atta in his B-25, led one of the 3rd's squadrons that day. They raced right into the teeth of the storm. Zeroes filled the sky ahead of them. Antiaircraft fire stitched after the strafing B-25s, whose crews flayed the airfields with hundreds of thousands of .50-caliber bullets.

The smoke screen rose along the shore behind another formation of B-25s from the 38th Bomb Group. The 3rd Attack Group's B-25s reached the harbor and went after the shipping. Cruisers, destroyers, cargo vessels, luggers, and troop transports lay at anchor, all with guns pointed at the onrushing twin-engine bombers.

The B-25s opened fire, raking the ships from bow to stern in hopes of suppressing the incoming flak. Bomb bays open, targets swelling before them, the Mitchell crews pickled their bombs. Jock Henebry pulled up over a merchant ship to discover the Japanese heavy cruiser *Haguro*, right in his path, its profile dotted with muzzle flashes. Flak pounded his B-25 as he fought to get the nose down and suppress the guns on that warship. He ran out of time and space, passing right over the ship, so close he could see the bridge crew gazing up at him as he thundered past.

The 3rd was getting hit hard by the ship-based flak. Overhead, Johnson's Knights rushed into the scene at three thousand feet.

"Bandits! Six o'clock high!" somebody called out. Gerald twisted in his seat just in time to see about a half dozen Zeroes above and behind, dropping their belly tanks in preparation to attack.

Feverishly, the Knights worked to prep their P-38s for battle. They shed their tanks, milked their engines for full power, then chandelled right into the diving Zeroes. The squadron raced at the threat in the worst possible tactical position. The Japanese, strung out in pairs a few thousand feet apart, saw their targets turn into them but did not break off their attack. Head-to-head, the two forces collided in a fury of tracers and booming cannons.

Blev Lewelling stayed tacked onto his flight leader, Carl Planck, as they made the turn into the Zeroes. Bob Wood, flying with them, lost them in a low-hanging cloud. The Zeroes loomed. Guns blazed. Carl held his course and refused to break first. Blev watched in horror as he flew straight into a Zero, the two planes exploding with all the violence of a 500-mile-an-hour collision.

As the formations merged, Gerald opened up on a Zero in a forty-five-degree head-on pass. Pieces blew off his target. The pilot rolled his crippled bird down and out of the fight. Haney and Glade Hill both saw it go into the side of one of the volcanoes.

The fight devolved into a low-altitude slugfest. More Zeroes and Japanese Army fighters dove into the battle, forcing the Knights into the defensive. Blev Lewelling found Bob Wood just in time. Zeroes were everywhere, slashing past, then flitting up and away with their remarkable agility. The two young pilots weaved and covered each other's tails, ducking through clouds and taking snap shots at speeding Japanese fighters.

Gerald and his wingman, the dauntless Stanley Johnson, kept each other alive the same way. Teamwork overcame tactical disadvantage, but they were overwhelmed too. Zeroes dashed in and among them, guns blazing, while the two Americans tried to turn into these attacks. They couldn't outrun the Zeroes, couldn't dogfight them, and they couldn't dive clear and reengage. All they could do was get their guns in the enemy's face.

Meanwhile, the Grim Reapers streaked across the harbor, heading south for home after expending all their bombs on the Japanese shipping. Zeroes broke through the fighter cover, and with the 9th totally defensive now, Henebry's B-25s were subjected to repeated fighter attacks. A running battle ensued, with the Knights trying to break clear of their fight to go help the Reapers.

The two Johnsons were trapped by Zeroes on the northwest side of the harbor. Gerald took a snap shot at one, setting it afire, and Stanley saw it crash. A moment later, as he ducked and weaved right on the deck northeast of Vunakanau Airdrome, Stanley tacked onto a Zero's tail and chased it until his guns set it afire. Gerald covered him and watched the Mitsubishi plunge right into a coconut plantation and explode. He whipped past the coil of smoke rising from the wreck and bull-rushed another group of Zeroes entering the fight. By now, Gerald had only two guns firing. He snapped out bursts, watching pieces fall off a few of the Zeroes, but no lethal damage was done. In each case, though, the Zeroes broke off their attacks, giving Stanley and him another minute of life.

The Johnsons broke clear at one point, speeding after the rest of the American planes, only to see a crippled P-38 with one engine out about to get attacked by another Zero. The two Johnsons raced to the rescue, driving the Japanese fighter away. Together, they headed for Kiriwina.

The staging base was chaos. Desperate pilots with wounded men aboard their bombers ignored the pattern and set down any way they could. A P-38 exploded short of the runway. Jock Henebry, his B-25 crippled by Japanese, crash-landed in the surf short of the runway, his crew rescued by a PT boat. Another P-38 careened into a jeep parked on the flight line. By the time Gerald and Stanley returned, the field was covered with crippled B-25s and P-38s, bleeding oil and hydraulic fluid into the ground. Crash crews pulled wounded gunners out of the B-25s while the P-38 pilots gathered to see who was still alive.

On the flight line, Dick Ellis ran into Gerald. The two men embraced. They'd become good friends over the past few months. On previous escort missions, Gerald would sometimes drop down beside Dick's squadron, flipping inverted, and flying along with them upside down. Such antics were Gerald's hallmark—he never outgrew that wild adrenaline rush he'd get from such flying. But he also did it to give the bomber crews a moment of levity in an otherwise tense moment. He also reassured them that their escort leader was a tiger of an ace.

Lee Van Atta appeared beside Dick. He'd spent the entire run home typing up his bird's-eye view of the mission in the navigator compartment of Ellis's B-25, *Seabiscuit*. Now the three men took a moment for photographs, the reporter snapping away at Gerald and Dick beside a P-38. Gerald held up two fingers for the pair of Zeroes he shot down. He smiled broadly, showing the trademark grin that Barbara found so irresistible. Then, the PR moment over, he went off to see after his squadron.

He found the Knights bone-weary and depressed at the loss of two more of their brothers. As they talked through the raid, the chaos around them gradually diminished while the last planes staggered home. The wounded received treatment; the ground echelon went to work trying to patch together the damaged planes. It had been a hell of a day. Seventy B-25s and seventy-eight Lightnings battled more than a hundred Japanese fighters in twelve minutes over Rabaul. Nearly fifty American aircrewmen were killed, wounded, or missing. The 80th lost two P-38s; the 9th lost two as well. The 475th lost five over Rabaul and another at Kiriwina. The 5th claimed sixty-seven Japanese fighters shot down by the B-25 gunners and P-38 pilots, two destroyers sunk, and over a dozen other ships damaged. The truth was, the raid was largely a bust. Only a couple of merchant vessels were sunk, and the claims against the Japanese interceptors were unrealistically high.

Part of the squadron flew home that afternoon. The rest remained behind until the ground crews finished working on their P-38s. Bob Wood was one of those who stayed behind, sleeping in a transient tent with P-38 pilots from other squadrons. The next morning, he struck up a conversation with one of those pilots. The two sat on their cots, chatting away about the previous day's mission. Suddenly, the other pilot's arms flailed up and he pitched backward off the far side of his cot. Bob stood up and rushed to him, finding the man convulsing on the tent floor. His body twitched and writhed, his arms jerking uncontrollably.

Bob rushed out of the tent, looking for medical help. He quickly returned with medics in tow. The man's seizure had passed. He was sitting tranquil on his cot again. A doctor arrived, and while he seemed to be completely healthy, the attack wiped the P-38 pilot's memory completely. He had no idea who he was, where he was, or what he was doing. Confused and frightened, he was led away by the medical staff.

Everyone had a breaking point. Rabaul pushed the Lightning pilots to the brink and beyond. As Bob watched the pilot go, he wondered how close to the edge he was.

A lot of pilots spent the night after November 2 thinking the same thing. The raid went down in 5th Air Force lore as "Bloody Tuesday." It was a catastrophe for the Lightning squadrons, whose birds were now on their last legs. The Knights managed to scrounge together a mix of aging P-38Fs, some Gs that reached the theater almost eight months before, and a few newer H models. That was it. And there were no replacements for the Lightnings lost. Rabaul was slowly bleeding the squadron to death. Even the better-equipped 475th was suffering the same shortage. The 80th and 39th were down to about half strength as well.

Kenney, seeing the beating his men were taking, tried to turn Bloody Tuesday into a major victory. With Lee Van Atta's first-hand account leading the way, the press blitz went into full gear, filling Stateside papers with action-packed accounts of the destruction wrought on the Japanese that day. Kenney's inflated shipping claims earned him considerable resentment from the Navy, whose squadrons battled Rabaul from bases in the Solomons. Between the services, it earned Kenney a bad reputation for showboating, and the Navy's bias against the maverick general never waned.

Was the press blitz designed to pump Kenney up back home and earn him more headlines? Or was it a concerned general's attempt to bolster morale among his men by getting them recognition back home at a time when their last full measure was not enough to overcome the Japanese at Rabaul? Only General Kenney knew the answer to that question, though plenty of postwar historians have speculated on his motives and sided with the Navy's view.

Whatever the case, morale among the fighter pilots was fast reaching a crisis point unseen since Kenney first arrived in theater. Building that dispirited force up into the powerful, Japanese-thrashing command had been an incredible achievement over the past year. Now, the repeated raids against such a well-defended target using tactics that put the P-38 pilots at a significant disadvantage threatened to undo all that progress.

Meanwhile, the attacks against Rabaul continued. On November 5, General Wurtsmith ordered his P-38 pilots to take the bombers back to Rabaul. This time, a Navy aircraft carrier raid was laid on for the morning against the shipping in the harbor. The 5th was to strike the airfields with twenty-seven B-24 Liberators escorted by all available P-38s shortly after the Navy cleared the area. The six Lightning squadrons put sixty-seven birds in the air, with many aborts. In the 475th, one squadron had four of eleven P-38s turn for home with mechanical trouble. Kenney had moved the group temporarily to Kiriwina, and the pace of operations was clearly overtaxing the ground echelon there.

The Knights managed to get a dozen P-38s aloft. Johnson returned the unit to the staggered schedule, resting his pilots when he could. By now, losses had so drained the unit, he had no choice but to send Bong on this mission. He flew with George Hanniotis on his wing. One aircraft aborted en route, leaving eleven to stay with the B-24s.

Stacked in three flights from twelve to twenty thousand feet, the Knights were spread thin over the B-24s when the Japanese intercepted them over Rabaul. All the P-38 squadrons ended up in the fight that followed. The 9th went after about fifteen Zeroes spotted below them. Bong dropped behind one Zero, whose pilot never saw him coming. Closing to a hundred yards, Dick held his fire until absolutely sure of the setup. Dead astern, point-blank range. The Zero filled his sight. He triggered his guns. The Zero blew up as the Lightning's concentrated cone of fire tore into it.

Bong dodged the debris, chased after the Zero's wingman, and opened fire again. This time, he held the trigger down, hosing his target until it began to smoke. The pilot rolled the plane upside down and dove away into a split S. He didn't get far. As he dove away, a fuel tank exploded, blowing the plane to pieces.

Two kills, in a matter of minutes. Bong checked the sky around him. Hanniotis was nowhere to be seen, but there were still Zeroes engaging P-38s all around him. He went after another Zero. As he did, Hanniotis showed back up and tacked onto his wing. Bong shot at the Zero, but failed to inflict fatal damage. A moment later, George was gone again.

The fight continued, but Bong soon ran out of ammunition and turned for home.

A voice cut through the radio chatter. "Dick, where are you? Are you still in the area? I'm in trouble." It sounded like Hanniotis. Bong keyed his microphone and replied.

George called for help again as if he hadn't heard Bong's response. He tried again. No luck. George was nowhere in sight. A few more calls for help, and the radio went silent.

The squadron linked back up outside of Rabaul and headed for Kiriwina. As they did, Hanniotis's voice came over the radio one last time, giving his position somewhere off the southern shore of New Britain near Arawe.

Back at Kiriwina, Blev Lewelling reported seeing George's P-38 diving out of the fight, one engine trailing smoke. Search-and-rescue planes were dispatched to search for him, and over the next four days the Knights flew search missions of their own. They found him several times, adrift off the south coast of New Britain. Each time, they reported his position, but some snafu fouled up the rescue attempt. Finally, four days after Hanniotis went down, Johnson pulled seven members of the squadron together, including Blev, and told them they were going to go find their downed man and stay over him until a flying boat came and picked him up.

They found him again, deeper out to sea this time. Eight P-38s circled overhead while Johnson tried to get a PBY flying boat to their position. No luck. Finally, a PT boat responded that they were on the way. The Knights, low on fuel, waited overhead as long as they dared. Finally, they were almost to the point of no return and Johnson was forced to order the squadron home. He and Blev stayed over George's raft, nursing every bit of endurance out of their Allisons until the PT boat at last appeared on the horizon. Johnson talked them onto George's raft. The crew reported seeing it. Gerald and Blev broke for home and barely got back to Kiriwina.

George Hanniotis was never recovered. Shortly after Gerald and Blev cleared the area, the PT boat lost sight of his raft in the swells. They searched the area and couldn't find him.

The raft washed ashore near Cape Ward Hunt, New Guinea, three weeks later. Deflated, it bore no signs of its occupant. George Hanniotis had simply disappeared.

Since Gerald joined the 9th Fighter Squadron in the spring of 1943, Dick Bong had lost three wingmen. Lieutenant Sibly disappeared out of his flight on July 10—nobody saw what happened to him. Fagan went missing in September. Now, Hanniotis. There was considerable talk in the squadron about the pattern, and the men were aligning around several opinions. One group believed that the issue wasn't Bong but circumstance—war happens, guys die. Others thought Bong's flying was so much better than the new guys' on his wing that they couldn't stay with him. The skill sets were too far apart, so in the wild heat of combat, Bong's maneuvers threw them off, and they were killed by the Japanese.

But the harshest critics spoke bitterly about the trend. Most of the men did not see how Fagan's death affected Dick. They just saw his stoic exterior. And some concluded he was coldhearted and didn't care about others, only his score. The selfishness was highlighted by the whispers that he kept asking Gerald and Wally to let him fly alone.

Bong's critics were right to the extent that he didn't *want* responsibility. He didn't want to be in charge of other people's safety. He wanted to fight, but he didn't want to lead. Fagan's death took that out of him.

As the squadron kept trying to rescue Hanniotis, another Rabaul mission was laid on for the seventh. Gerald couldn't fly the mission that day. Bong asked if Stanley Johnson could fly his wing. Gerald was very nervous entrusting Stanley to Dick in his current condition. He reluctantly agreed, but told Dick he'd better bring Stanley home in good shape. Dick promised he would.

The Knights went out only eight strong that day, Jump O'Neil leading the squadron. Over the target area, they ran into a patrol of Zeroes and dove to the attack. Dick's edge was gone. He went after several targets, missed them, then saw Del Moore's P-38 being chased by nine Zeroes. Dick charged in to save him, Stanley tight on his wing. The two pilots broke up the attack and saved Moore. But Dick lost Stanley in the attack. Last seen, Stanley was diving out of the fight with four of the Zeroes on his tail.

Dick returned to Dobodura and faced Gerald. He told him the news. Gerald was devastated. They both were.

The Montana banker's fate would never be confirmed; his remains and aircraft were never found.

The death of one of the most liked and loyal members of the squadron was a grim capstone to Dick's first tour of duty. He'd been hurting over the other men he'd lost on his wing all fall. This ripped those wounds wide open.[1]

Dick never wanted to fly with a wingman again. He couldn't take feeling responsible for another death. Every man had his breaking point. Stanley's disappearance pushed Bong beyond his. Gerald saw that and knew he had to get him out of combat.

Gerald's relationship with Bong would also never be the same. Part of it was probably guilt. Gerald knew Bong shouldn't have been flying and he'd let him go to Rabaul anyway. Part of it was the pain he endured over Stanley's death.

Bong, never one to show much emotion, hid the depths of his despair from most. Gerald knew him perhaps better than anyone and saw beyond that hardened farm-boy facade. Others didn't, and whispering around the squadron characterized Dick as coldhearted and uncaring. Nothing was further from the truth. He'd been crippled by these losses.

Enough was enough; the Wisconsinite needed an extended rest. Two days later, Dick flew to Moresby and back, probably to meet with Kenney. Kenney wrote after the war that he ordered Bong home. This undoubtedly came as the result of a strong recommendation from Gerald. However it happened, Bong packed his gear and headed for Australia. The top Army Air Force ace was finally going back to Wisconsin, twenty-one planes to his credit.

Neel Kearby learned of Bong's departure and knew the ace race was now his to lose. Unknown to Neel, though, Kenney had other plans for him.

---

1. The death of Stanley Johnson was a terrible blow to the squadron's opinion of Richard Bong, and the black mark of so many lost wingmen would haunt him for the rest of his career. Postwar, most of the guys glossed over the rift, not wanting to cast aspersions on a national hero. They also were proud of the fact that the ace was part of their heritage and accomplishments. Off the record, however, some talked in their last years about the resentment and fury felt by some pilots over what happened in those final months of his first tour.

29

The Relentless Rogue

November–December 1943
New Guinea

When Bong left for home, the entire complexion of the ace race changed. McGuire was still in the hospital recovering from his wounds, so he was out of the picture. Danny Roberts, Jay Robbins, and Gerald Johnson were Neel Kearby's competition now. This was his chance. His childhood dream of becoming America's new Eddie Rickenbacker required only one thing: opportunity.

The 348th hit its stride in October, shooting down more than fifty planes, a convincing display of skill that finally put them on Wurtsmith's first team. With new airfields being built above Lae and in the Ramu Valley around Gusap, the Jugs would soon have a home close enough to Wewak that they would no longer need to stage out of another base to get into the fight.

On November 9, 1943, Danny Roberts died in action when he collided with another P-38 during a battle over Alexishafen. His squadron saw him shoot down another Japanese plane, giving him fourteen confirmed. Danny was an atypical fighter pilot: he didn't smoke, he didn't swear. He was low key, just like the 475th Fighter Group's commander, Charles MacDonald. The loss of their beloved commander tore the heart out of the 433rd Fighter Squadron. It would take weeks for the unit's morale to recover.

Meanwhile, Japanese reinforcements into New Guinea increased the number of air raids hitting the new fields in the Ramu Valley. It was a hunter's game, and the P-47 was now the ascendant fighter in the theater, thanks to decisions back in Washington. Replacement P-38s dried up completely in October because General Arnold shifted all of Lockheed's production to Europe in an effort to stave off the defeat of the daylight bombing campaign. Arnold wrote to Kenney and told him not to expect any P-38s until a few months into 1944. This was a catastrophe to the six Lightning squadrons. While some Lightnings remained in the pipeline between Burbank and Australia, there would be no way to field all six after the crucible of the Rabaul raids.

Kenney decided to convert the Knights and the Cobras to P-47s. Their remaining P-38s would be used to plus up the Headhunters of the 80th Fighter Squadron and the 475th Fighter Group. The P-47 was almost universally detested by the dual-engine pilots forced now to fly what they derisively nicknamed "Republic's Abortion." With the 9th and 39th out of the long-range power projection picture, their pilots' scoring rates declined. The 80th soon caught up and surpassed the Knights as the top-scoring outfit in the theater, a distinction they would cling to for almost a year.

Kearby was tasked with selling the Knights and the 39th Fighter Squadron on the P-47's virtues. At one point, he quipped, "If you can't shoot Japanese planes down with one engine, what the hell are you gonna do with two?" They weren't won over. Neither were some of the P-40 units who received Jugs around the same time—some actually converted back to the Warhawk as soon as possible. Scoring rates declined, mission capabilities diminished, and the range at which the 5th could pound the Japanese with its full force shrank along with the number of P-38s.

As cold as it sounded, the field was clear for a run to first place for the ace so inclined. Neel Kearby had flown fifty-six combat hours in

October, many of them to Wewak with his Musketeers. He finished the month with twelve confirmed kills. After four months at such a pace, he went down to Australia, probably on leave. When he came back, he relished the chance to make his push to catch Bong.

It would be an extraordinary month for the 5th: the fighters were flying constant missions now to Cape Gloucester ahead of the Marine invasion slated for December. Wewak remained a major target, and all of the outfits alternated between the New Britain missions and escorts or sweeps to Wewak. In between, intercepting Japanese raids remained a staple of the unit in New Guinea; the Japanese still had plenty of fight, though the quality of their aircrew continued to decline as their losses mounted.

Unbeknownst to Kearby, General Kenney had plans for his high-octane Texan. After his six-kill mission over Wewak, Kenney put Kearby in for the Medal of Honor, America's highest award for bravery in combat. This was not like giving out a Silver Star or Distinguished Flying Cross. Only a handful of aviators earned the MOH, and most had died in action. Rather, a living fighter pilot wearing the Medal of Honor transcended the norm into a national asset. Back home, the medal meant war bond tours, speeches, radio appearances, newsreel clips, and lots of ink. Most went from warrior to morale builder, something they universally detested.

Kenney simply could not have Kearby in combat as the award write-up navigated through channels back in Washington. He decided to pull him out of the 348th and put him in a desk job at V Fighter Command headquarters.

That role would ensure Kearby continued to play a hand in the war from a safe perch. There he would work with General Wurtsmith, who directed the V Fighter Command, assigned squadrons to missions, approved missions requested by the units themselves, and worked closely with V Bomber Command to task enough escort assets for strikes on the Japanese. In other theaters, this was an enormous organizational and logistical effort that demanded large numbers of experienced staff officers. In New Guinea, V Fighter Command ran lean—exceptionally lean. In early November, V FC, as it was called, counted in its ranks only General Wurtsmith, seven lieutenant colonels, twelve majors, and sixteen captains. A scattering of about two dozen lieutenants and two hundred enlisted men rounded out the ranks. These men were responsible for managing fifteen fighter squadrons in five groups, each carrying out anywhere between one and four missions a day.

There, Kearby would be riding a desk for his duration in theater; then he'd return to the States to a hero's welcome and get to work propping up the home front. In the meantime, the 5th Air Force's masterful public relations officers got busy making Neel a household name. The publicity would give the push to get him the Medal of Honor that much more heat.

On November 13, 1943, after Kearby returned to the 348th to fly an uneventful escort mission to Alexishafen, he was given the news. When he got back to Moresby, he received orders to report to Wurtsmith as his new V Fighter Command chief of staff. He must have been bitterly disappointed by this. His unit was just getting into the groove, and he was looking forward to many more scraps with the Japanese. Now he would replace Lieutenant Colonel Morrissey, who was in desperate need of a Stateside leave having been in theater since March 1942.

The desk awaited. Kearby packed his gear and flew to Port Moresby, reporting for duty the following day. After racking up dozens of hours of combat flying every month, Kearby barely touched a control stick for the next eleven days.

Normally, when pulled up to a fighter or bomber command headquarters, officers elsewhere in the AAF stopped flying combat missions. The 5th was different. Kenney's first bomber command leader, Gen. Ken Walker, repeatedly ignored orders from Kenney to stop flying combat. He led from the cockpit and couldn't in good conscience send his crews on missions he himself would not fly. In January 1943, after arguing against a B-17 strike on Rabaul and losing to Kenney's insistence that it be carried out, he deliberately disobeyed a direct order from his commanding general and flew the mission. He was shot down, fate unknown.

Rumors persisted through the war and beyond that Walker survived a bailout to be captured and executed by the Japanese. Intelligence reports during the war hinted at this, and that must have given Kenney some very tense moments. As one of the top three generals in the 5th Air Force, Walker would have been an intel gold mine for the Japanese, had they captured and interrogated him. That sort of security breach could not be tolerated again, and Kenney tried to clamp down on his senior staff officers flying on missions. For the most part, he succeeded, though rumors abounded that Lieutenant Colonel Morrissey would sometimes sneak back to his old command, the 49th Fighter Group, to fly with his remaining friends there.

That there were aggressive field-grade officers in headquarters who wanted to lead from the front was a blessing and a curse for Kenney. He needed men like that to infuse the 5th with its aggressive spirit. Wurtsmith, Walker, and Morrissey certainly played a key role in developing the culture of the 5th. The trade-off was that they sometimes disobeyed orders and flew missions. Kenney lived with it, though when he heard Walker disobeyed his direct order in January, he reportedly said that if Walker returned, he'd court-martial him, and if Walker didn't return, he'd put him in for the Medal of Honor. Walker's family received his posthumous MOH later in 1943.

Kearby must have had some hope that he might still be able to dip a toe in the flying game, given this atmosphere. Still, as he came up the staff officer learning curve, there was no opportunity to sneak back into combat.

That was, until General Wurtsmith went home on leave. "Squeeze," as Kenney called him, had been in theater since almost the start of the war. He was one of the first outstanding fighter group leaders of the Pacific War, a member of the old Darwin crowd of the 49th Fighter Group. After a year and a half of constant combat, stress, and bad food, he asked Kenney for a break. Kenney granted him a thirty-day leave plus travel to go home to Detroit and see his family.

In his place, Kenney put Neel in charge of V Fighter Command, effective November 25, 1943. In less than three weeks, the Texas ace had gone from leading the 348th Fighter Group to one of the top three command slots in the entire 5th Air Force. He would waste no time in using his new position to his advantage in the race.

When the cat's away...

That morning, Kearby got hold of a P-38. Along with one other Lightning pilot, he linked up with two friends from the 348th and flew a combat patrol to Arawe, New Britain. Officially, he wrote in his flight records that they were "local" flights. The strange formation of two P-47s and two P-38s reached the coast of New Britain, saw only a single aircraft down low, then came home without getting into a scrap. V Fighter Command reported the mission to 5th Air Force HQ without mention of the pilots involved. Kenney probably had no idea his new acting commander of V FC was out hunting.

Kearby was in charge now, and he intended to use the position to both take a crack at Bong's score and develop some ideas for future fighter operations. Kearby was a man comfortable with being in charge—he'd always been called "Boss" by his men. He loved to lead and he loved to innovate. If Kenney intended Kearby to be merely a caretaker for Wurtsmith's command while he was gone, the ace didn't know it. He immediately set about implementing ideas, crafting strategies, and enlisting some of his favorite leaders into the effort.

Still, he hated being a staff officer and sometimes complained to his ground crew that he never should have accepted the job. Each day before Wurtsmith left, he and the general would sit down for staff meetings that sometimes lasted for hours. If doing paperwork was bad enough, sitting in a plywood room at Port Moresby, talking on multiple phones at once while surrounded by REMFs, was almost unbearable to the ace.

He was also offered up to the press for interviews. More than once, he was spotted at V Fighter Command HQ surrounded by the likes of Lee Van Atta, William Boni, and Lorraine Stumm of the *London Daily Mirror*. Gary Sheahan, the *Chicago Tribune*'s legendary artist, painted him as he described his air battles, flying with his hands as he recounted his exploits.

He didn't hide his displeasure at being behind a desk. Other members of the headquarters noted that he never seemed to be around when they needed his signature on a document or had a meeting for him to attend. Instead, since Wurtsmith left, he was off flying. And some of those flights at the end of November may very well have been off the books. There's considerable evidence to show he tried to cover up what he was doing.

Lee Van Atta wrote a profile of Neel that ran in the Stateside papers at the end of November. The lead began, "If there is one 'weak link' in General Douglas MacArthur's fighter command, it's the chief of staff. He can never be found anywhere but in combat."

The day after Lee's article began running in the States, Neel escaped from headquarters to spend over five hours in the air at the controls of *Fiery Ginger*, quite possibly on a hunting mission over Wewak that encountered Japanese aircraft, but he scored no kills.

On December 3—officially—he flew two hops in the P-38s at Port Moresby. Unofficially, he put the band back together and went to Wewak with three 348th pilots, Lt. Col. Bob Rowland, Capt. Frank Oksala, and Capt. Meade Brown—his Musketeers. Once again, he felt at home at the controls of *Fiery Ginger*, his beloved P-47. Over Wewak, the Jug quartet patrolled at twenty-eight thousand feet, hoping to drop down on the Japanese once again in the same fashion that Manfred von Richthofen did on his opponents during the Great War.

This time they ran into plenty of trouble. Captain Brown, flying wing on Kearby, called out bandits low and ahead. About two dozen fighters spread out in flights of four were coming down the coast, heading southeast toward Allied bases at twenty-two thousand feet. They were higher than usual—perhaps in response to the many times the Jugs had played this game.

Despite the odds, Kearby intended to attack. He took his time, positioning his flight upsun from the enemy and behind them. During the setup, though, Rowland somehow lost the rest of the formation.

Kearby was undeterred. He led the remaining Musketeers down in a screaming dive behind and slightly to the right of one flight of four Japanese Hayabusas. At fifteen hundred feet, *Fiery Ginger*'s guns boomed. The Japanese plane burst into flames and rolled over in a death dive. Still on his initial pass, he banked left, intending to line up on the next Ki-43. Suddenly, four more Japanese fighters ahead and to the left of his target detected him. They broke into hard chandelles, reversed course, and dove straight for the P-47s even as Brown and Oksala blew up two more Ki-43s.

Neel went nose to nose with the four fighters coming at them. He hit the leader with a short burst, seeing hits in the engine and wings. Still in the head-on pass, he tweaked the rudder and walked his fire into the Japanese leader's wingman. That aircraft took serious hits as well. Still locked in that aerial game of chicken, Kearby thought he had just enough time to get his guns on the tail-end Charlie.

He didn't. The Ki-43 careened right at him, and only a last-second juke saved both pilots from death in a flaming collision.

Kearby dove away, the Musketeers right with him. One pass, and they were done. Stay disciplined and live to fight another day. That was Kearby's way of doing business. It was smart, and he used all the advantages he could to negate the odds and inflict damage.

Dean Schedler, one of the former *Manila Bulletin* reporters who followed MacArthur from Corregidor to Australia, scored the scoop on Kearby's latest victories. "Japanese fighter pilots are probably sitting around their rice bowls at Wewak angrily discussing ways to stay clear of *Fiery Ginger*," Dean wrote in a widely circulated AP article. Headlines like "*Fiery Ginger* Dusts Off Two More Planes" prefaced Dean's article, which went into detail on the Japanese kill flags on the side of Kearby's P-47 he used to fight against tremendous odds and still emerge victorious. One paper printed a photo of Neel with the caption beneath reading "Has Jap Chopsticks Shaking."

"It isn't like I like to kill anybody," Kearby told the reporters, "but I do like to hunt."

For all his aggressiveness, Neel found comfort in the same psychological barrier to the killing as the other aces in the race. It was the plane he was destroying, not the pilot inside it. He didn't think of that man, just the machine. That he did most of his firing at long range—fifteen hundred feet—gave him an additional buffer to the reality of what his weapons did to the men he battled.

Kearby was the hottest ace in theater. With the press lined up behind him, he grew bolder and did not seek to hide his combat flying later in December. Kenney, while trying to keep Kearby safe, had unintentionally created a monster. Kearby was running V Fighter Command, he was a star back home—even his plane was famous—and he flat-out refused to live the life of a noncombat staff officer. Kenney found himself boxed in by his own PR campaign. He couldn't demote Kearby. He couldn't fire him or send him home. Doing any of those would have generated a PR nightmare. Instead, he entreated Kearby to keep the combat flying to a minimum and not to be chasing records.

Kearby griped about it to the reporters hanging around Port Moresby. He told them that General Kenney had rationed him to two combat missions a week, or less. "With an emphasis on less," Kearby added with some bitterness. The press turned the odd situation into a highlight. "Jap Killer Put on Rations" quipped the *New York Daily News*. "Flying Colonel Takes Jap Hunting Junkets," crowed another paper in Nebraska. That Kearby was now being rationed to a pair of missions a week continued to be reported in dozens of papers through much of December. In fact, that month, stories about Kearby appeared back home on eleven out of thirty-one days. Not even MacArthur was getting that level of hype.

Kearby ignored Kenney's rationing demands. Through December, he flew fifty-six combat hours on nineteen missions. Nothing short of his being wounded and knocked out of combat, or Kenney's taking the political/PR hit, would get the Texan out of the sky. With his Medal of Honor nomination now under review in Washington, had Kenney relieved him at this point, the award might not have been approved, and surely there would have been a firestorm of bad publicity over it. Kenney decided to let it ride, urging Kearby to be cautious.

Kearby considered his tactics cautious. Picking off a few planes with a single high-speed pass from upsun, then dashing away, seemed almost foolproof. The slower Japanese planes could only react and get out of the way, or turn into his P-47 to try for a head-on pass. Two rifle-caliber machine guns versus the eight fifties in the Jug was a challenge the Texan would always take.

Speaking of challenges...

At the end of November, as Wurtsmith headed home, Maj. Tom Lynch returned from his fall leave to Pennsylvania, where he had married his college sweetheart. His hometown had welcomed him with great fanfare. He was hailed as a hero with sixteen kills to his credit. He was also considered one of the best squadron commanders in the 5th Air Force. Beloved by his men, he repeatedly put their safety and well-being over his own while leading from the front. He was also an exemplary fighter pilot, one of the most experienced combat aviators in the theater.

In early December, he flew to Port Moresby and rejoined the 39th Fighter Squadron at a time when his replacement, Charles King, was getting ready to go home on his Stateside leave. His old job as squadron commander of the legendary Cobras would soon be open again. It was not a stretch to think that he'd relish the chance to lead his men in combat once again.

A normal progression for a fighter leader usually went like this: command a two-plane element, then a flight of four. If successful, the pilot would be pulled into the squadron's command element, usually as operations officer or deputy CO. Once given command of the squadron, he would be promoted to major if the pilot did a good job. From squadron leadership, they'd be pulled up to group headquarters, usually once again as the operations officer. From there, commanding a fighter group was the next step, followed by an assignment at higher headquarters.

This didn't happen to Tom Lynch, whose return made him the theater's leading ace. Exactly why his career path took a strange turn will probably never be known for sure. He spent only a few days back with the 39th, learning to fly the P-47, before Neel Kearby issued Special Order 326/5 transferring Lynch to V Fighter Command headquarters. Usually, such additions to the HQ element included the specific role that officer would perform. In this case, Lynch's role was described as "A-3 Section, Principal Duty."

The A-3 Section was the operations department. This was the busiest part of V Fighter Command headquarters, a place where the assigned officers planned the daily missions for all fifteen fighter squadrons. If Kearby had wanted to keep Lynch out of combat, this was an excellent place to put him. Even more unusual, Lynch spent most of December moving back and forth between Port Moresby and Eagle Farm on administrative duties. Whatever operations he was assisting on, they didn't seem to have much to do with frontline combat. Of course, being in Australia ensured Tom could not borrow an aircraft and go hunt Japanese.[1]

On December 18, Charles King went home. Capt. Harris Denton, a veteran Cobra who fought with Bong and Lynch in the first P-38 dogfights a year before, took command of the 39th Fighter Squadron. Instead of going home after the typical twelve months in action, Denton extended his tour six months and remained in command until June 1944.

As Lynch rode a desk far from the Wewak scraps, Johnson and the Knights went into action over Gusap on December 10 in their detested new P-47s. Johnson shot down a Hien in the fight, giving him twelve kills, only three behind the Texan. Kearby redoubled his efforts to find the enemy. On the sixteenth, he spent eight hours in the air hunting, to no avail.

Stuck at fifteen kills, he couldn't catch Lynch and Bong if there were no Japanese to shoot. Over the course of the next two weeks, Kearby flew almost constantly in search of a fight. In nine days, he recorded twelve combat missions. This was pushing it, even for the ace with boundless energy. But he felt it was what he had to if he wanted to stay in this race. After all, Tommy McGuire was back.

---

1. Every secondary source consulted for this book places Tom Lynch back in theater in either January or February, as that's when he and Bong were reunited and started making headlines. However, Lynch actually returned to Australia in November, flew a B-25 up to Port Moresby on December 4, 1943, from Townsville, then spent December 6 and 7 checking out at Moresby in P-47s. His Form Five flight records document this. It is significant in that he very well should have taken over the 39th again as Charlie King was heading home. His arrival was perfect timing. Yet, he was pulled out of his unit by the acting commander of V FC, which looks suspiciously like Kearby administratively sidelined his biggest rival in the ace race.

30

The Ignored One

November–December 1943
Dobodura, New Guinea

The day after Bloody Tuesday, Tommy McGuire limped into the 431st Fighter Squadron's area at Dobodura, appearing gaunt and unwell. Still bandaged, his face a mass of yellow-blue bruises around his eyes, McGuire was nowhere near a combat-ready pilot. His ribs still ached. His wounds were half healed. He didn't care. He wanted to fight.

He was twenty-three, a double ace who had proved himself over Wewak and earned grudging respect from those who disliked him on the ground. Now, he would wear the Purple Heart as a reminder for the rest of his life that when split-second decisions had to be made, his instinct was to save others.

He could have gone home. In fact, he probably should have. His squadron commander certainly thought so, and wrote McGuire's wife telling her Tommy would be back in the States soon. He'd done his part: paid the price, so honor and duty were served. Going home, though, was the last thing on Tommy McGuire's mind.

Nichols took one look at him and sent Tommy back to Australia. He may have talked his way out of the hospital, but there was no way he was going to talk his way into the cockpit in his current condition. He spent the first half of November on leave in Sydney, recovering his strength with good food and lots of rest. Not all the rest was good. As with almost any combat veteran, the idle hours led to a restless brain that dwelled on the trauma and close calls he'd experienced. At times, it got under his skin. Would he be the same pilot once he got back to the 431st? Or would he be hesitant, lose his edge, and be overcome by fear? The time off gave him plenty of license to ponder this. It made him brittle and impatient. Best to find out fast, rather than linger with the uncertainty.

When he returned to New Guinea later in November, the squadron flight surgeon refused to clear him for combat. Nichols put him in charge of the chow hall and told him to figure out a way to improve the muck being served to the men. He did as ordered, chafing as he watched the squadron take off each morning while he stayed behind to ride herd on cooks who were already doing their best with the dreck available to them.

It took a month of further healing before the flight surgeon relented. McGuire returned to flight status on December 12, 1943. He spent four hours in the air, getting reacquainted with the Lightning and checking out replacement pilots over the course of the next few days. On the sixteenth, he flew almost nine hours in combat, got into a fight, and damaged a Zero over Arawe, New Britain.

Those in the game knew just how good a fighter pilot McGuire became after he joined the 475th. While home on leave, General Wurtsmith gave an interview and listed those he thought were the best combat aviators in his command: Dick Bong, Tommy McGuire, Danny Roberts, Ed Cragg (the Headhunters' commander), and Neel Kearby. It was the first time in print that Bong and McGuire were mentioned together.

With only Johnson nipping at his heels, Kearby may have thought he had an open field to catch Bong while he was back in Poplar with his family. With Lynch down at Eagle Farm most days, the rush to best Bong would be a horse race between McGuire and the Texan.

Both men flew with ridiculous intensity. Tommy spent upward of six hours a day in the cockpit after his mission over Arawe. He flew one day on, one day off for the rest of the month. Between December 12 and the 31, he put in seventy combat hours, matching Kearby's energy, stride for stride.

On the twenty-second, both men ended up over Wewak. Kenney wanted another low-altitude suppression strike flown against the Japanese airfields there to knock out the Japanese reinforcements to the area, like mowing the grass every time it started to grow. Once again, V Fighter Command's entire P-38 force took part in this attack. They were ordered to go in low, as close cover, just as Wurtsmith had ordered over Rabaul. The 431st led the way, and at four thousand feet over the target, they were bounced from behind and out of the clouds by almost forty Japanese fighters. A P-38 went down. Another crash-landed back at base, the pilot surviving. McGuire was leading Green Flight, and it was all he could do to protect his pilots until they were able to escape. He took snap shots at a pair of Hayabusas but scored no killing hits before attacking Japanese planes forced him totally defensive. It was a near-run thing, and a reminder that protecting the strafer B-25s with these tactics came at the expense of the Lightning pilots.

Later that afternoon, Kearby took a hunting flight over Wewak composed of pilots from the 341st Fighter Squadron. Not his usual Musketeers, but aggressive and capable pilots nonetheless. They encountered a small formation of six Hayabusas trundling along well below them at six thousand feet. Using their tried-and-true tactics, Kearby surprised them, and his flight downed half the enemy formation. Kearby returned with his sixteenth kill. He was now tied with Lynch as the top active ace in theater.

The next day, the B-25s returned to Wewak with only the Headhunters as escort. A fight erupted over the target area lasting from 0945 to 1030, when the final B-25 made its escape.

As the 80th covered the bombers as they came off their runs and raced for home, Kearby and his Musketeers arrived over the area. It was brilliant timing based on the acting V Fighter Command leader's intimate knowledge of the missions laid on for the day. He'd taken a look at the board, and had seen that the 475th and 348th were slated for missions over western New Britain at Cape Glouces- ter and Arawe as part of the run-up to the Marine invasion, now scheduled for the twenty-sixth. The Wewak strike looked like a per- fect opportunity to sneak overhead after the main battle to pick off returning Japanese planes low on fuel and ammunition.

Over Dagua Airdrome at twenty-eight thousand feet, the quartet of Jugs patrolled for fifteen minutes, looking for trouble in a sky full of scattered clouds. Kearby caught sight of two Ki-61 Hiens running below the cloud cover. They were approaching Dagua at about two thousand feet and looked like they were going to land.

In the past, Neel refused to go after such low-altitude targets. Trading twenty-six thousand feet for a crack at a pair of fighters didn't make much sense, especially if there were others in the clouds nearby. The ace race was starting to bend his judgment. He wanted kills, and if they were down that low, why, he'd take the risk and go after them.

The Jugs skinned their external tanks and spiraled down after the Hiens at 350 miles an hour indicated. The American aircraft dropped out of the sky, went through the scattered clouds at around ten thousand feet, and lost the Hiens in the weather. Kearby caught a fleeting glance of a bomber landing at Dagua, but before he could go after it, he reacquired his original target. At eight thousand feet, he pressed his attack from behind and off to the right. This time, he closed fast, firing from fifteen hundred to five hundred feet with a long, four-second burst. He saw hits on the Hien, but it ducked away into the clouds and everyone lost sight of it.

In his earlier attacks, Kearby would have headed upstairs after this pass. Instead, a Hien on final approach at Dagua caught his attention. It was right on the deck, the Japanese pilot probably clueless to the American fighters in the area.

The Texan dove after him, ignoring the risks that other Hiens may be nearby. Bending around behind the Japanese, he set up a dead-astern attack from above. It was a perfect tactical move, except Neel was overtaking the Hien so rapidly that he'd have only seconds to get the kill shot.

The Texan did something he'd never done before: he throttled back, slowing his Jug down so he could get just a bit more time to aim and shoot. At 250 miles an hour, he hammered away at the Hien. Normally, pilots fired short, controlled bursts lasting no more than a couple of seconds to keep the guns from overheating or jamming. This time, Kearby gave him everything his guns possessed in a thunderous ten seconds of firing. The Hien rolled over and crashed in the trees at the edge of the strip.

He looked back. The Musketeers were right with him, but the sky behind them was filled with Hiens and Oscars—ten to twenty of them. A well-flown Ki-61 was a formidable opponent for a Jug pilot, especially down low and below three hundred miles an hour. The Americans were in a precarious spot, with all their usual advantages squandered. The Japanese smelled blood and piled onto them.

Kearby and the other pilots firewalled their throttles and tried to run away. They sped over Dagua Drome, the antiaircraft gunners below them hammering away, thinking they were under attack again. The diving Ki-61s must have looked like P-40s to those gunners, who'd been under siege for months now by the 5th. They turned their guns on their own comrades. The Hiens twisted out of the line of fire, giving the Jugs a precious few seconds to make their escape. A single Ki-61 broke through the antiaircraft fire and tried to catch the Americans, but by then their two thousand horsepower R-2800 engines pulled them well out of danger.

The men flew to the 348th's new base at Finschhafen, where Kearby refueled before heading back to Moresby and all his administrative duties. He received credit for one kill, the Ki-61 the flight saw crash into the jungle at the edge of Dagua Drome. It was his seventeenth kill, which put him one ahead of Lynch and four out from Bong's twenty-one.

The kill had come at a cost. It was the first time Kearby violated his own tactical rules. Perhaps if he'd thought back to his World War I reading, he would have remembered how the Red Baron did the same thing in April 1918. He sacrificed all his carefully measured tactical advantages to drop out of a fight and chase an Allied pilot on the treetops. Another Allied plane got on his tail, and anti-aircraft fire erupted around him. Who killed him is still debated, but the eagerness for a victory overcame his tactical sensibilities. He took an enormous risk, and it killed him.

The truth was, Kearby's similar gamble could have ended in disaster, had the Japanese flak not intervened and shot at the wrong aircraft. He was starting to push, feeling the pressure to score. With McGuire chasing him, Bong's leave set to end sometime in January, and Lynch growing increasingly agitated by his noncombat role, Kearby felt plenty of heat. Even worse, his days as boss were numbered: Wurtsmith would be coming back to resume command soon, and Kearby's combat time was short. Wurtsmith would make sure he went back to his desk.

On the twenty-sixth of December, Kearby took his usual hunting trip to Wewak, found nothing, and returned to Finschhafen, where he and his Musketeers refueled and took off on a second mission to New Britain. Though he flew six hours that day, most of it over Japanese territory, Kearby never sighted the enemy.

But McGuire certainly did. That morning, he led the 431st Squadron over the coast of New Britain to cover the 1st Marine Division's invasion task force steaming off Cape Gloucester. The 348th was also up, covering the vulnerable ships as well. Just before noon, USN radar picked up an inbound strike and vectored McGuire's squadron for it. The Lightning pilots climbed to twenty-three thousand feet and ran headlong into a formation of Japanese Zeroes at roughly the same altitude.

McGuire committed the squadron to a head-on pass on the Japanese fighters. As they went nose to nose, somebody called out Japanese bombers below them. McGuire glanced down and saw them too: perhaps thirty Val dive-bombers in tight formation, just about to reach their attack points over the Allied ships.

Protecting those vessels was the day's mission. McGuire made a split-second decision and ordered his men to switch targets and go after the Vals. The Lightnings rolled down on the slow dive-bombers as ordered, but the move gave their Zero escort a perfect setup on the P-38s. Soon, the Americans maneuvered furiously to avoid the Zeroes while still getting to the Vals before they could start their dive-bombing runs.

It was a crazy, twisting race down to medium altitude. McGuire lost his wingman but stayed on the bombers. They were seconds too late. The Vals peeled off and dove on their targets, pursued by a rush of P-38s and Jugs from the 8th Fighter Group whose pilots had just arrived to wade into the fight. McGuire caught up with a Val at eight thousand feet, shot it to pieces, and kept going. Pulling out just above the water, he slipped behind a bevy of dive-bombers fleeing the scene now. He drove right up behind one in a dead-astern attack and unloaded on it. The Val exploded just as a flaming Zero tumbled past McGuire's P-38 and plummeted into the water nearby. He banked to avoid the fire and debris, spraying bursts at the remaining fleeing bombers before sliding behind a laggard and sending it into the water.

The sky around him was filled with diving P-47s, his fellow Lightning pilots slashing through the dive-bombers with Zeroes furiously scurrying after them. More P-47s piled into the fight, these from the 36th Fighter Squadron. In the chaos, McGuire and a P-47 pilot went after the same Val. It crossed the beach at Gloucester, racing east for Rabaul. Both men opened fire. McGuire was certain his bullets struck the plane, which dipped down suddenly and careened right into a tree to explode with no survivors.

Back at Dobodura, McGuire found that all members of the 431st had returned safely, claiming eleven Japanese planes in the fight. It was a tough one, and nobody would have faulted McGuire for staying after the Zero fighter escort had he chosen that route. Instead, he risked a great deal going after the bombers, doing his best to protect the thousands of sailors below.

Such was the life of a fighter leader. To keep safe those ships or aircraft they were entrusted to cover often meant making a terrible decision: sacrifice fighter pilots, or let the ships and bombers get hit by the Japanese. It was the sort of choice few Americans have ever made. The best leaders make the right call. In this case, McGuire had risked his own life, and his men, for the greater good.

Later that evening, he learned the 8th Fighter Group was claiming his last dive-bomber. He firmly believed his bullets drove it into the trees, but the P-47 guy wasn't going to cede the kill. Once again, since the 5th did not give partial credit, the two pilots had to decide who would get the Val.

A coin flip didn't work for McGuire the last time, so this time they drew cards. McGuire's poker luck evaporated. The Jug pilot got the kill. Tommy was so bent over it that he ordered his crew chief to paint an extra kill flag on his P-38 as a sign of protest. It stayed on *Pudgy's* nose for weeks to come. That was the second time he felt robbed by fickle lady luck.

For Neel Kearby, McGuire's not getting credit for the kill was a break. That fourth kill would have put McGuire even with him. Instead, Tommy was now one behind. To gain ground and catch Bong, Neel flew relentlessly through the end of the month. Yet, while the 348th ran into two large formations of Japanese bombers over Cape Gloucester later on the twenty-sixth and again the next day, Kearby missed those fights. Every mission he undertook ended up being a dry hole.

The year ended with Bong still in the lead with twenty-one, and the pack behind him stalled for lack of opportunity. Wurtsmith was due back at Moresby any day, and the race was closer than ever. Kearby knew he only had a few days left to score.

31

Off the Rails

January 1944
New Guinea

On January 2, 1944, Allied forces hopped up the New Guinea coast and invaded Saidor, where engineers quickly built an air base within P-47 range of Wewak. The move cut off some six thousand Japanese combat troops, who were forced to try to escape the Allied cordon by marching through the Finisterre Mountain Range. Most starved or died of disease during the trek. The Saidor landing was a major Allied success, costing the Allies less than fifty men killed in return.

The 5th Air Force supported the landings by providing fighter cover and bombing secondary Japanese airfields between Saidor and Wewak. The drive toward the Philippines up the New Guinea coast was shifting into high gear at last.

As the troops went ashore at Saidor, Kearby gained a reprieve. Wurtsmith's travel back to New Guinea had been delayed, and he was not expected back for at least another week. Neel seized the moment and made one more furious push to catch Bong. On January 3, he showed up at Finschhafen with *Fiery Ginger*, grabbed three pilots not assigned to the squadron's escort mission for the day, and took off for Wewak.

There were no strikes scheduled against the Japanese base that day, as the 5th was pounding targets elsewhere as part of the Saidor operation. At twenty-five thousand feet, they arrived over Wewak as a Mitsubishi Ki-21 "Sally" light bomber took off from one of the airstrips. Kearby punched his drop tank and dropped on the vulnerable target. He'd learned a lot since October, using the same manifold settings and speed range as he made his diving approach. At fifteen thousand feet, he began a wide corkscrew-like spiral turn as he dove into the warmer air. He discovered in previous attacks this kept his windshield from fogging over as he sped from subzero temperatures back into the tropical heat.

With his musketeers covering him, he dropped down right on the Sally's tail and blew up both its engines with his eight machine guns. The Sally twisted out of control and crashed just offshore.

The Jugs flew to Gusap and quickly refueled at Gerald Johnson's airfield there. The Knights, once given the toughest and most combat-intensive missions, were currently relegated to boring standing patrols over the Ramu Valley. They had seen little action since Johnson shot down a Hien over Gusap on December 13.

Kearby wanted more action that day. He took off with three P-47s, bound for Wewak. The fourth plane in his flight stayed behind with mechanical failures. En route, one of the remaining Thunderbolts suffered another mechanical gremlin. The pilot turned for Gusap.

With just his wingman, Kearby pressed on to Wewak at twenty-seven thousand feet. Over But Airdrome, they passed a single Hayabusa, cruising along at about four thousand feet. Kearby went after it, his wingman protecting his tail. Three hundred and fifty miles an hour on his airspeed indicator, he dove dead behind the unsuspecting Japanese pilot. At a thousand feet, he hammered it with a controlled three-second burst. One of the Hayabusa's fuel tanks exploded as Kearby overshot, climbing and turning to get a look at his quarry.

The Japanese pilot dove for the trees and the fuel-tank fire went out. The Texan would not be denied. He violated a cardinal rule: don't turn more than ninety degrees in a fight against the Japanese.

It bleeds too much speed and they can turn inside any American fighter.

He made a tight 360 and went after the Hayabusa. The pilot was either wounded or so green he froze at the controls. Either way, he took no evasive action as the P-47 climbed up his tail and Kearby laid on the trigger. Six seconds and 450 bullets later, the Hayabusa staggered and caught fire a second time.

Down to a thousand feet just off the Wewak coast, Kearby blew past the crippled plane and pulled into a zoom climb. In the past, he would have let it go, getting back upstairs as fast as he could. This time, he saw the fire go out again and turned around for another pass. As he dove for a killing shot, the Hayabusa pilot lost control of his aircraft, and it careened into the sea.

Kearby returned to Gusap, refueled, continued on to Finschhafen and then back to V Fighter Command Headquarters, which had just moved up to Nadzab. Both kills were confirmed. He was now undisputed number two in theater with nineteen planes. He also knew he was almost out of time.

On the eighth, he sat down and drafted a report for General Whitehead, the deputy commander of the 5th Air Force (his current immediate boss) and detailed an operation against Wewak he hoped to be able to lead. He called for using the 9th Fighter Squadron's P-47s at Gusap to run four-plane hunting missions over the Japanese base—exactly as he had been doing since October—in order to "partially" deny the airfields there to the enemy. He did not sugarcoat the dangers and advocated using only volunteers who truly believed in the Jug's capabilities. He mentioned the 348th would be better suited for this special operation, but they were farther away at Finschhafen. Gusap was only a hundred and ninety miles from Wewak.

He ended the report by offering to go to Gusap and "teach" the Knights how to execute this mission personally. It was a naked ploy to try to stay in the race after Wurtsmith returned. Exactly where Kearby would go and what position he would have at V Fighter Command headquarters was an open question. He may return to his deputy commander status, or Kenney may use the opportunity to stash him out someplace where getting into combat would be even more difficult.

The clock was ticking. Before dawn the next morning, he flew to Finschhafen, grabbed three pilots, and sped toward Wewak. They made it halfway before the weather closed in. They turned around, refueled, and went out a second time late that morning. The weather was still bad, with rainsqualls and thunderheads filling the sky around them. By the time they reached Wewak, the weather forced them down to eighteen thousand feet.

They patrolled over the target area, weaving around scattered clouds below the main overcast, seeing nothing but a solitary ship offshore, shrouded in a smoke screen. Suddenly, roughly eighteen Hiens bounced them from three o'clock high. Arrowing down out of the base of the overcast, they caught the Americans completely by surprise. Kearby reacted quickly, turning toward the attackers as his Musketeers followed him. The Japanese didn't break away. The two formations closed as Kearby opened fire. He hit a Ki-61 that went down before the merge. Seconds later, the Jugs were scattered and fighting for their lives. Two Hiens went after a lone Jug, diving down on the exposed pilot who was trying to extend out of the fight. Kearby turned and went after those two Hiens, trying to save the Jug, which was flown by Capt. Walter Benz. His wingman followed, the Ki-61 pilots broke away. The Texan gave chase, following them into a tight, spiraling climb. He opened fire, hit the Hien, but the Japanese wingman whipped around and charged him, forcing him to abandon his attack and point his guns at the onrushing fighter.

Both Japanese and Americans opened fire. The in-line fighter flew right into Kearby's bullet pattern, transforming it into a flaming comet. Benz saw it roll over and go straight in, tailing a long plume of red-orange fire and smoke.

Kearby was alone now, not something that ever happened before on these hunting flights. He searched for his wingman, saw a swarm of Hiens instead. He was running out of altitude, and they were above him. He dove, poured the coals on, and ran for his life, pulling out right above the jungle as he pointed *Fiery Ginger* for Gusap.

The fight was a near-run thing. The Americans all survived, though one Jug force-landed at Gusap with a wing full of cannon- and machine gun holes. Kearby also picked up two more kills, tying him with Bong. Yet, the Japanese weren't stupid. By now, they caught on to Kearby's game and were hunting for his high-flying Jugs with their best aircraft, the Ki-61. Had the Americans not seen the attack coming when they did, disaster would have ensued. Neel was living on the ragged edge, sacrificing his earlier tactical caution for a shot at the brass ring.

Now he was only five kills away from being the first to catch Eddie Rickenbacker. He wanted that distinction more than anything. Back in the States, his Medal of Honor nomination was approved. Neel was not only the leading active ace now, he was soon to wear the highest medal for bravery the United States bestows on its warriors.

Wurtsmith landed at Nadzab on January 13, relieving Kearby as commanding officer of the V Fighter Command. Neel returned briefly to his status as chief of staff and deputy commander. When word reached 5th Air Force of Kearby's MOH, Kenney saw an opportunity to get him out of harm's way. Initially, the plan was to have President Roosevelt award the medal personally at the White House. It was a perfect way to get him out of combat and home safely.

That same day, Lieutenant Colonel Morrissey returned to V Fighter Command. Wurtsmith made him his deputy commander and chief of staff—Kearby's position. With a lieutenant colonel junior in rank to him taking his spot as second-in-command, there could be no place for him in V Fighter Command Headquarters. The ace would soon have his Medal of Honor, but now he had no job. His days in theater were numbered, and he knew it. He was sent down to Australia on leave, where he reported to Kenney's headquarters in Brisbane. When the idea of a White House ceremony was broached, Kearby would have none of it. He refused to leave the combat theater. Years later, Kenney framed the Medal of Honor ceremony that took place as an ad hoc affair on January 20, 1944. It may have been, and Kearby got his wish: he was not sent home. General MacArthur personally decorated the Texas ace with only a few staff officers present.

There remained what to do with a senior officer who hated staff work and only wanted to fly combat. Kenney later wrote he told Kearby he wanted to send him home for a month's leave. Another attempt to get him out of the combat theater. According to Kenney, Kearby balked and said he wanted to stay until he got his fifty kills. Kenney reportedly told him to cool it, and keep it to "one Nip a week."

He had two national heroes out of his fighter pilots now that helped create and inspire the aggressive fighting spirit he knew the 5th needed. The papers back home spent much of January and early February running wire stories about how Bong and Kearby were now tied for top ace status. His Medal of Honor award broke back home on the twenty-second. He was photographed and featured in newspapers in every state. *Life* magazine prepared a major story about him. The Texan with the lopsided, impish grin had become the face of the air war in New Guinea.

Kenney could not afford to lose him in combat now. With the MOH awarded and no staff position, this was the perfect time to send him home, but Kenney couldn't quite bring himself to order it. Part of it was probably his natural sympathy toward an aggressive fighter pilot. He was once himself an aggressive combat aviator. He knew that inner fire well. Sending Neel home would have broken the man's heart. He would have felt like Kenney had denied him his life's ambition. The general likely intuited this. They liked each other. He couldn't do that to the man.

Later historians concluded that Kenney wanted Kearby to run his score up and stay in the fight to become the undisputed ace of aces, but if that was the case, the assignment he received made hunting much more difficult. In all probability, Kenney needed a fiery leader, a colonel who could get things done out close to the front. Close to the front, but not over it. He decided to give Neel what he wanted— a command in theater—but hoped the new assignment would minimize his combat flying.

Meanwhile, Johnson and the Flying Knights returned to battle again after almost a month of boring holes over the Ramu Valley. While still committed to those missions, Johnson was able to get at least one sweep or escort mission every few days for his men. On the eighteenth, while they were flying a full squadron fighter sweep over Wewak at twenty thousand feet, a lone Oscar bounced them from behind. The Japanese pilot dove through the trailing flight of four P-47s, took shots at the tail-end Charlie, then tried to escape. Essentially, the Japanese tried to use Kearby's tactics against Johnson's squadron.

The Oregonian saw the Hayabusa diving away and rolled after it. The Japanese pilot stayed committed to the dive, which proved a fatal mistake. Johnson easily caught up to it and closed to point-blank range. The aircraft exploded almost the instant he triggered his guns, leaving a fan of aviation gas trailing in the doomed aircraft's wake. It was Johnson's thirteenth kill and was witnessed by two full squadrons from the 49th Fighter Group.

Two days after Kearby received his Medal of Honor, Maj. Tom Lynch climbed out of a fabric-covered Beech Staggerwing biplane in

New Guinea. He'd been using the old airliner as his personal transport as he traveled between bases in Australia and Port Moresby. That morning, he walked into V Fighter Command Headquarters for the first time in weeks. There, he met with Col. Bob Murtha, the A-3 operations chief.

Lynch asked him a particularly odd question, so odd that Bob later sent a radio message to General Wurtsmith about it. Lynch wanted to find some extra P-38 pilots who could be pulled out of the 512th Photographic Reconnaissance Wing (Provisional)—the eyes of the 5th Air Force—and loaned out for some unspecified task.

There was no shortage of P-38 pilots in January 1944, nor were there shortages of veteran P-38 pilots stuck in P-47 squadrons willing to chew off their own hand to get back in a Lightning's cockpit. Why inquire about Lightning drivers in the 5th's photographic reconnaissance outfit?

To be fair, the 512th included an element that had flown photo recon versions of the P-38 called the F-4 and F-5, so it was a plausible request. Murtha called the commander of the recon wing, who told him that none of his guys had any P-38 experience. That was a skillful answer that parsed details—he did have Lightning pilots, just none of them had flown the fighter variant. Clearly, the 512th's commander didn't want to part with any of his men.

Murtha reported this back to Wurtsmith, who was at Lae that afternoon. The tone of his message suggested he thought the idea was crazy, and he recommended dropping it. Murtha must have been confused by his subordinate's inquiry.

Just what Lynch was doing wasn't clear until a few days later, when General Whitehead approached Kenney with an idea first floated by Neel Kearby when he was still the acting head of V Fighter Command. The Texan had advocated culling the line squadrons for the best and most aggressive aces and forming them into an elite killer group that could take the fight to the enemy unencumbered by any routine missions. It would have been the first (and only) special operations fighter unit in USAF history.

The idea probably stemmed from his World War I knowledge. Through the 1920s and '30s, the American aviation literature and war movies were filled with lurid depictions of Manfred von Richthofen and his Flying Circus of elite aces. Dubbed the circus for their mobility and use of large tents, the Red Baron and his legion visited terror on Allied aviators wherever they were sent. Kearby, taking a page from the Germans, wanted to do the same thing. No doubt, he also wanted to be its commander.

Denuding the fighter squadrons of all their most experienced aces made no sense to the senior leaders in 5th Air Force. Those men were the backbone of V Fighter Command's aggressive spirit. They were keeping the new guys alive and mentoring them as Sid Woods had done with Johnson, and Marion Kirby had done with McGuire. Concentrating those men in one group would degrade the capabilities of the other units significantly. The idea seemed to have never been taken seriously.

That was, until somebody developed a modified version of it. Whitehead's spin on Kearby's idea was to find a small cadre of P-38 pilots and pull them into V Fighter Command as a special mission unit that he dubbed "the Flying Circus Squadron." The trick was to do this without degrading the efficiency of the line outfits who were all fully committed to the fight against the Japanese in both New Guinea and New Britain. In all probability, he sent Lynch to go overturn rocks in search of some P-38 pilots who could form the core of the squadron. The recon wing was a natural place to look.

In January, General Arnold had informed Kenney while he was briefly back in Washington that the first shipment of the latest model of P-38s would soon be sailing for Australia. Over fifty would arrive in the first batch, with more to follow in February and March. These new P-38s included more mature technology, with hydraulic boost controls, making them easier to fly and more maneuverable. They also had significantly longer range with the addition of more gas tanks. Overall, they were significantly better Lightnings than what the 5th possessed. Due to their additional fuel capacity, the 5th's leadership called them the "Long-Range P-38s."

These were desperately needed. The P-47 was still loathed by units outside the 348th. That loathing was made worse in January when modifications Neel Kearby suggested to extend the Jug's range turned out to cause fires through the supercharger when hit with gunfire. Kenney ignored those tests and ordered the modifications to be fielded, noting the "kids" would soon be putting fuel in the extra tanks when they found out how far they needed to fly. This sent a message to the pilots who interpreted it, right or wrong, as Kenney's willingness to send them to fiery deaths to get a little extra range out of an aircraft they already didn't like. Whitehead noted the precipitous drop in morale among the P-47 pilots outside the 348th as a result.

A new P-38 with longer legs could not have arrived at V Fighter Command at a better time. MacArthur was planning to make a huge jump around Wewak to land troops deep in the enemy's rear at Hollandia, which was currently serving as a massive staging base for the Japanese Army Air Force. To make this leap, the hundreds of planes at Hollandia would need to be destroyed. Problem: from the current airfields, the older P-38s couldn't get there and stay overhead very long. The new Lightnings could with plenty of time to loiter and fight.

It is quite possible that Whitehead wanted the Flying Circus Squadron to be equipped with the new P-38s, with, as he and Kenney called them, "picked crews." The new unit would function exactly like the 1st Provisional Squadron did during the October 12, 1943, Rabaul raid: as a force multiplier against very important and heavily defended targets.

On February 12, 1944, Kenney wrote to Whitehead:

The news about the formation of the "Circus Squadron" is just right. Go ahead with the setup as you have planned it. I am particularly glad Lynch has gotten back in the swing and believe that placing him in the Circus outfit is an excellent thing. If he once gets started I honestly believe he will give Bong and Kearby a little competition.

Seven days earlier, Dick Bong arrived at Nadzab with orders assigning him to V Fighter Command HQ's operations section. He'd been sitting for a few days at a replacement depot in Australia waiting for orders, unsure if he would be sent back to the Knights again or not. He was the 5th's other great national hero now, but he was also a man who wanted nothing to do with command, or responsibility for the lives of others while in battle. He'd met Stanley Johnson's widow while home on leave, and the meeting had not gone well. It was a dreadful reminder of the final weeks of his tour.

The Circus Squadron seemed a natural place for him. He'd be given opportunity to hunt without the overhead of normal duties a captain would carry out. He wouldn't need to be a flight leader. His talents could be maximized, and he could continue his push to beat Eddie Rickenbacker.

Meanwhile, Kearby returned to New Guinea, anxious to score, but without a formal assignment. He couldn't stay at V Fighter Command. He was a full colonel and outranked the executive officer who replaced him, so that situation was not tenable. He managed to sneak away one day in early February for two missions over Wewak. On the first, he and the Musketeers saw nothing. On the second, they ran into weather and turned back.

On February 14, 1944, Kearby transferred from V Fighter Command and joined a new advanced field headquarters called the 308th

Bomb Wing. It wasn't a bomber outfit at all; rather, the 308th served as a flexible headquarters element designed to operate as far forward as possible while being tasked with special missions. Units were assigned or withdrawn as needed. For now, the 308th would spearhead the air operations for MacArthur's invasion of Manus plus the upcoming Hollandia operation. Kearby would be out of the fight for a while, though he remained the darling of the press back home. Instead, he was saddled with administrative and PR duties. The latter included showing John Wayne around Saidor when the actor showed up in theater as part of a USO ensemble meant to bolster morale.

It wasn't combat flying. While he enjoyed having his picture taken around *Fiery Ginger* by *Life* magazine photographers and meeting famous actors, he was there to get his fifty and lead men in battle. Every day he missed his 348th Fighter Group, regretting not holding out to retain command of it the previous November. Looking ahead, a normal combat tour lasted a year. Neel reached the theater in May. No matter how much he resisted, Kenney would almost certainly use that opportunity to get him home. He had to find a way back into the air.

32

Whitehead's Flying Circus

February 10, 1944

Two shiny new long-range P-38Js awaited Tom Lynch and Dick Bong at Nadzab. The books on both were cooked, as Bong's was assigned officially to the 49th Fighter Group, Lynch's to the 39th Fighter Squadron. Their old units were still flying P-47s, and the Knights wouldn't convert to the new P-38s until the second week of April. The Cobras wouldn't get new Lightnings for months.

If the original intent of the Flying Circus was to create a fully staffed and equipped squadron, it wouldn't happen in February. The shortage of P-38s was still acute. The two Lightnings reserved as VIP rides for Lynch and Bong came at the expense of the 475th and the 80th, whose birds were showing their age. It would be at least another month before there were enough P-38s in theater to not rob the line squadrons to feed the Circus.

While they waited for more planes, Bong and Lynch received clearance to fly combat missions. Though officially assigned to the operations section at V Fighter Command, they did little, if any, staff work. The days of Lynch flying a desk while his boss was flaming Hayabusas at Wewak were over. The boys were unleashed to go hunting.[1]

---

1. Some postwar historians have written that Bong, Lynch, and Kearby were all pulled into V Fighter Command HQ by Kenney to "audition" for top ace status and allowed to freelance at the higher HQ simply to rack their scores up. The truth

For Bong, this was the perfect assignment. He couldn't go back to the Flying Knights—the cloud of the final weeks of his first tour still lingered there. Besides, Tom Lynch had been his closest friend while he was attached to the 39th Fighter Squadron, at the start of his combat career. Lynch was an outstanding pilot, aggressive, cagey, and tactically disciplined. Together, they wouldn't need to worry about rookie pilots and taking care of men who couldn't push their P-38s as hard as they could. Bong and Lynch trusted each other completely. Plus, Bong would not feel so alone.

They had their own preserve handpicked for them by Wurtsmith. For the past year, the Japanese had been busy building a series of airfields along the north coast of New Guinea that were used as transit points for reinforcements heading to Wewak. The airfield complex at Hollandia was the largest of these, but an airfield at Tadji, about midway between Hollandia and Wewak, was often full of Japanese aircraft. Reconnaissance missions had shown that to be the case, but V Fighter Command had yet to send any P-38s over it, in part because it was so much farther away than other targets.

With the longer-legged P-38Js, Bong and Lynch could reach Tadji from Nadzab without any problem. The 475th and the Headhunters were busy with missions either to Wewak or to Kavieng, New Ireland, so Tadji would be a virgin hunting ground, a place the Japanese probably felt was comfortably far enough behind the lines to be free from marauding American fighters. It was an excellent place to test the Circus concept—and run scores up.

On February 10, Bong and Lynch flew together on a two-Lightning variant of Kearby's Wewak missions. They discovered a

---

is more nuanced. By the time the Circus stood up, Kearby was off with the 308th and was no longer assigned to V FC HQ. Kenney was doing his best to utilize Kearby while minimizing his opportunities to get into dogfights, while Lynch and Bong were marking time while waiting for the planes and pilots to be available for the full Circus squadron.

lot of activity at Tadji that afternoon. About a half dozen fighters were taking off just as they arrived over the strip at fifteen thousand feet. As they watched the fighters, a twin-engine Kawasaki Ki-48 Lilly bomber took off from the opposite direction as the fighters.

The American duo dropped their tanks and rolled into a dive. The P-38J could dive faster and steeper than earlier versions of the P-38. They used this additional performance to sweep down behind the Ki-48 and catch it at a thousand feet. Lynch was senior man, soon to be a lieutenant colonel, so he was leading the element that day. He got first shot, which blew the bomber's right wing off. The plane crashed about two hundred yards off the coast.

They went back the next day, looking for trouble, but the sky over Tadji proved empty of Japanese aircraft.

They flew together again on February 15, this time tacking onto the 80th Fighter Squadron en route to Kavieng. Wurtsmith tasked the Headhunters with escorting an A-20 strafer strike against Japanese shipping there. Kavieng was a high-threat area and a likely place to run into enemy planes, hence the mission selection on Lynch's part.

The two silver P-38s joined the 80th's formation en route to target and covered the bombers from medium altitude. While the A-20s found transport vessels to shoot up and bomb, there were no Japanese planes to be found. Disappointed, they headed for home. Just north of Cape Hoskins, Bong noticed movement below. A single Ki-61 Hien was scuttling along eastward toward Rabaul at twelve thousand feet. Bong rolled into a 180-degree diving turn and came down on the Hien's tail as Lynch covered him.

Bong closed to seventy-five yards, dead astern, no deflection, and pulled the trigger. At such close range, the P-38's cannon and machine guns pulverized the Hien. The Japanese pilot never knew what hit him, the plane exploding in midair, pieces dropping into the sea.

Lynch now had eighteen; Bong had twenty-two. He'd taken the lead away from Kearby and was only four away from matching Rickenbacker's record. Only Marine fighter ace Joe Foss had reached twenty-six so far in World War II. Nobody had bested the World War I legend's record—yet.

The next day, February 16, it appears Lynch flew a mission on his own to Tadji on a solo hunting flight. That morning, Bong was back at Nadzab, checking out in a B-25. If Lynch encountered any enemies, he didn't report them. Over the next two days, Bong did the same thing while Lynch did no flying. Unfettered, without any concern for a wingman, Dick flew deep behind enemy lines in search of quarry.

These two missions were straight out of the lone wolf days over the Western Front circa 1916. In World War II, it simply was not done. The lone wolves of the Western Front all died by 1917. After that, teamwork became the essential element of air combat.[2]

As Bong probably knew, the lone wolves of the Great War had been picked off one by one until the last of them, Werner Voss, died in one of the epic fights of air combat history when he ran into British ace James McCudden and part of his Number Fifty-Six squadron. For Bong—and possibly Lynch—to be out doing this alone was an extraordinarily dangerous risk that not even a full-blooded tiger like Neel Kearby would take.

In the meantime, one of their duties at V Fighter Command HQ included interacting with the press. Either Lynch avoided much of that or the reporters there didn't devote as much time to him. Either way, Bong was the pilot they covered. After his lone wolf flight on the nineteenth, he returned to Nadzab to find a newspaper

---

2. On the seventeenth and nineteenth, the two days Bong flew these lone wolf patrols, there were no other V Fighter Command squadrons assigned to Tadji as a target. The P-38s were all tasked with missions elsewhere.

artist waiting for him. He sat for a portrait, which made him wonder about the press coverage back home. While on leave in Poplar back in December, the 1940s' version of the paparazzi had mobbed him. Photos of him walking through the two blocks of downtown, surrounded by wide-eyed, hero-worshipping kids, hit the wire services. More photos of him with his family, hugging his mother, and preparing for a hunting trip filled inside pages for days. *Collier's* prepared to run a big story on him.

He wrote home that night wondering about the *Collier's* piece. It was one of the first times he expressed any interest in his press back home. In the past, it made him uncomfortable thinking about giving interviews and being the object of such attention. After the adulation he received when he got home, he was growing more comfortable and more curious about it.

Other duties and bad weather restricted their flying after the twentieth. Bong went down briefly to Australia, while Lynch slipped away on one combat mission on the twenty-fifth. They didn't team up together again until February 26, a mission that proved to be a dud.

The next day, Lynch checked the operations board at Nadzab and saw his old squadron was assigned to escort a B-24 raid to Wewak. He and Bong decided to tag along. But even over this once lucrative hunting area, the sky was empty of Japanese aircraft. Reality began to set in: the Japanese Army Air Force had been shredded in the brutal fighting since the previous summer. Its aircraft lay smashed and broken on the sides of runways all over the theater. The Japanese aircrew was starving, disease-riddled, and decimated by losses. Morale was generally low, and the quality of the remaining pilots was nothing like the skilled veterans of Nomonhan the Knights faced in the summer of 1943.

An ace race cannot be run without opportunity to score. By now, some pilots in the line units were flying all their assigned missions without ever encountering an airborne enemy aircraft. The pickings were slim, which meant the only way to score was to maximize the opportunities that came along. And to do that meant taking greater and greater risks.

By this point, Neel Kearby was anything but risk averse. Bong was a plane up on him, and he couldn't stand being second again. He wanted to fight but found few opportunities to get away after his assignment to the 308th. At least once, however, he flew into Finschhafen looking to join a good mission. He sat on the runway, his P-47's engine warmed up, listening to what the other squadrons were doing over the radio. When the 342nd got into a scrap, he took off and sped after them to see if he could get in on it. He did not score.

On February 26, General Whitehead transferred Kearby to the 309th Bomb Wing as its acting commanding officer, a caretaker slot he'd hold only until Maj. Gen. St. Clair Streett arrived to take over. The 309th served a role in the 5th Air Force similar to that of the 308th, functioning as a flexible air task force headquarters. Kearby was living an itinerant life at this point, frequently packing up his meager belongings and bouncing from base to base. This time, he moved to Lae, home of the 309th's headquarters element.

He was the boss again, even if for only a few days. He seized the opportunity to get back into the air and find what Japanese fighters were left. The next afternoon, while Bong and Lynch were over Wewak, Kearby found his old friend Lt. Col. Bob Rowland and prevailed upon him to head out on a two-plane circus of their own. They left Finschhafen together, climbed to high altitude, and went hunting over New Britain. Not far from where Bong shot the Hien down on the fifteenth, they ran across a Japanese bomber running low over the jungle. It was just a dark speck to them, moving over the dark jungle, but it was opportunity. They headed downstairs, Kearby in the lead.

At fifteen hundred feet, Kearby's standard attack range, the Texan hammered the bomber from dead astern. Hits flared along the fuselage and wings. A fire erupted. The bomber looked doomed as Kearby finished his run and climbed past it. Rowland, still behind the bomber, recording Kearby's potential kill for him with his gun camera, noticed the fire began to subside. He closed in and hosed it down before climbing after Kearby. They lost sight of the bomber and returned to base, each claiming damage to it. Weeks later, the V Fighter Command intel section reviewed the footage and saw the bomber crash. Rowland received full credit.

After this mission, members of the 348th recall hearing the news that Kenney had come down hard on their old boss, warning him if he continued to fly combat, he would be sent home. With Bong and Lynch hunting together and running their scores up, being sidelined in the middle of the race must have been supremely frustrating to the great ace.

On March 3, Maj. Gen. St. Clair Streett reached New Guinea and added the 309th to his various command responsibilities. Kearby was ordered to take over the wing's advanced echelon at Saidor, where work on the airfield continued to go poorly. Kenney needed that strip in working shape so the 348th could make the jump forward from Finschhafen. Saidor would put the Jugs 130 miles closer to Wewak. It also meant they'd be just behind the Australian troops fighting in the nearby mountains. It was an ideal point from which to launch ground support missions for them.

The field was nowhere near operational yet. Heavy rains had turned it into a bog. The 348th sometimes used it as an emergency strip when low on fuel, and their Jugs would get mired down in the dispersal area just sitting on the waterlogged ground. Kearby was ordered to straighten the situation out and get the Army's engineers to build a proper drainage system for the strip and the dispersal areas. The Texan packed up his gear and flew to Saidor, where he was part of the most forward element in the 5th Air Force. It was rugged, wet, and miserable. His tent was only a few miles from the Aussies fighting in the jungle. In a letter home to his wife Virginia, he wrote about that experience:

> *I am now ten miles back of the front and can hear firing. We are being bombed every night, sometimes three times a night. Our wounded are pouring in camp. Up until this time, war had been a pleasant experience. But now, it has become gruesome.*

He longed to be back in the cockpit, above the jungle, where he could pretend his hunting missions were duck hunts with airplanes. Fifty was a pipe dream now, but he could still be the first to beat Rickenbacker.

33

Walking with the Beast

March 5, 1944
Saidor, New Guinea

Kearby awoke in his primitive surroundings in a foul mood. He was having nothing but problems with the engineers, the strip wasn't fully operational, and the food was terrible. He'd been exiled from the ace race at a time when it was the most competitive. To add insult to injury, he'd learned the night before that Whitehead's Flying Circus had run into enemy planes over Tadji on the day he took over the advanced echelon at this hellhole. Bong and Lynch both scored. The farm boy claimed two bombers, while the Pennsylvanian hit four, claimed two. Not only did Bong pull ahead again, Lynch was catching up to Kearby.

He looked around his spartan quarters. Muddy floor, mosquito netting draped around his cot, boots overturned beneath him to keep scorpions out. Still, as he got dressed, he banged them together and waited to see if anything would come tumbling out before pulling them on.

Bong had twenty-four. Lynch nineteen, maybe more if the intel guys decided to upgrade his probables over Tadji to confirmed. For Kearby, it all felt like it was slipping away. Never mind the Distinguished Service Cross, the DFCs, and the Air Medals sitting in a small box engraved with his beloved fighter group's number. The medals weren't enough. Even the Medal of Honor wasn't enough. It was in that box, too, a reminder of his unfettered hunting days in October.

He remembered his first days as an Air Corps cadet back in 1937. He was fresh from his college graduation, frat parties, and the life of a hardworking son of a well-to-do Southern family. All he wanted to do was fly. His career almost ended before it began. Throughout training he kept suffering bouts of tonsillitis that sidelined him for days on end. Sheer force of will pushed him forward.

That internal drive became one of his greatest assets. He was relentless, determined, and singular in focus when a goal lay in his crosshairs. He'd been an outstanding fighter pilot, working his way up through the prewar ranks among careerists who enjoyed the trappings and comfort of their status as officers. He didn't care about those things. The airplanes. Flying. Tactics. Learning from the men who came before him—those things mattered. He had few hobbies, and the job always came first.

He looked over at his desk. Beside the 348th box rested a photo of his wife Virginia—the original Fiery Ginger—and their three boys. On the other side was a photo of his parents.

He could have stayed with them, training a new generation of warriors from the safety of some Stateside base. But that wasn't him. He coached and mentored those in his unit, preparing them for combat because he would be at the tip of their formation. No warrior would ever want to be left behind. For all his upper-class heritage, inside Kearby beat a warrior's heart.

His parents would never understand. He knew that. He could have given Rowland the 348th in August and gone home without any blemish to his honor after his brother had died. After the deaths of the five Sullivan brothers aboard the USS *Juneau* in 1942, the military made a point of pulling the sole surviving sons out of combat so families were not devastated.

Kearby had opted to stay, to lead his men, fight his own war on the side. Long ago, that private war came to dominate his life, defining the risks he took in battle and the way he functioned as a field grade. Nobody but Neel will ever know what truly lay inside his warrior's heart, but whatever it was burned with such fire that he kept evading his commander's intent to go hunting with his favored Musketeers.

The acclaim and publicity seemed not to matter to him. His pilots and ground crew practically worshipped him, though some in the other outfits in the 5th found him abrasive and arrogant. That was the P-38 versus P-47 controversy talking, though. Kearby would always be the biggest advocate of the Thunderbolt, which made him unpopular among those who only wanted to fly Lightnings. He may not have been liked by everyone, but among his fellow warriors, he was respected.

Perhaps what fueled his ambition wasn't fame or glory but a more elemental need: the need to prove he was the best of the best. As good as Bong and Lynch and Johnson were, he believed he was better. After all, he had spent his childhood dreaming of becoming an ace and his entire adult life in uniform, training for this opportunity here in the Pacific. Now he had proven beyond a doubt he was one of the great aces of the USAAF. He could make a pass on an enemy formation and knock down multiple planes—something only the very best could do. His tactics worked. His shooting unerring.

Yet he stood at the cusp of realizing all he wanted to achieve, only to be sidelined. The score was what would matter in the years ahead. No matter how good he was, if he didn't have the kill flags on the side of the cockpit, the best of the best would always be a disputed title. To be considered number one, the kill board on *Fiery Ginger*'s fuselage would have to have no peer.

He finished getting dressed, took a final look around to make sure he hadn't forgotten anything. Sitting next to a bottle of perfume he'd purchased for Virginia lay his Ray-Bans. He considered grabbing them. They'd been with him through many fights and countless flights. Today's battles would be administrative and on the ground, not in the clouds where he belonged. He turned and exited the tent, his sunglasses left behind beside the box that held his Medal of Honor.

Over at Nadzab, as Kearby was getting to work at Saidor, Bong and Lynch took off on a two-plane hunting flight to Wewak. The pickings had been slim there for a while now. Since August, the Japanese Army Air Force units in New Guinea lost over seven hundred aircraft. There just weren't many left, though reinforcements continued to trickle in. During February, one of the last of the elite fighter units reached the theater. Down to less than three dozen Ki-43 Hayabusas, the 77th Sentai had fought against the Flying Tigers in Burma in 1942 and in the defense of the Dutch East Indies the following year. Led by a kernel of excellent, high-time fighter pilots whose careers predated Pearl Harbor, the 77th began flying missions out of Wewak on the twenty-seventh of February.

Over Dagua Drome, the two Lightning pilots encountered a patrol from the 77th. With altitude and surprise, the P-38s held all the cards. They dropped down on the Japanese planes. Lynch shot one Hayabusa down and damaged another, while Bong knocked pieces off two more. The 77th learned a hard lesson that morning: when flown with tactical discipline, the P-38 was the most dangerous opponent its pilots had ever faced.

Word of the fight probably reached Saidor in the early afternoon, after Bong and Lynch returned to Nadzab to report their encounter. This was too much for Kearby. He went looking for pilots and found Capt. Bill Dunham and Sam Blair ready to go with him. There was no fourth Musketeer available, but Kearby didn't care. Blair was a tiger with six kills to his credit, and Dunham was one of his oldest friends in the 348th. The two had first met when Kearby commanded a squadron in defense of the Panama Canal Zone back in 1941–42. When the Texan moved on to take the 348th, he pulled Dunham into the Thunderbolt outfit with him. A former University of Idaho student, Dunham was a fighter pilot's pilot. Aggressive, capable, a crack shot, he'd flown on Kearby's wing during many of the Musketeer flights in October. The fuselage under his cockpit was adorned with seven Japanese kill flags.

The three aces took off at 1600, climbing west to their typical attack altitude above twenty thousand feet. They would have two and a half hours until sunset, just enough time to slip over Wewak, patrol for a few minutes, and get home to land in twilight.

They reached Wewak an hour later, running up the coast at twenty-two thousand feet, all eyes in the Jugs scanning the sky around them. Kearby called out the first contact, a Ki-61 Hien down low approaching Dagua Airdrome. As they watched, the Japanese fighter dropped its landing gear and alighted on the runway. No point in going after it now. They continued on into the setting sun.

About five minutes later, better quarry appeared. Three bombers flitted south toward Dagua, coming in from the seaward side right on the water. It would mean trading twenty-two thousand feet of altitude for a crack at them, but Kearby decided to risk it.

They let down, spiraling at fifteen thousand feet to keep the temperature change from fogging their windscreens. The aces kept their eyes on those bombers as they reached Dagua and entered the pattern in preparation for landing. This was going to be a tougher show now. Even if they reached the bombers, they would be in the airdrome's flak envelope. Dagua was heavily defended by antiaircraft guns, a fact Kearby knew all too well from previous hunting missions.

Sun at their back, the Jugs caught the bombers at five hundred feet on the north side of Dagua as they ran east, parallel to the field. They closed fast, clocking their established 350 miles an hour with Kearby in the lead, Dunham perhaps a thousand feet behind him, covered by Blair bringing up the rear. They were committed now, the bombers aware of their presence.

From his vantage behind the other two, Blair glanced right just in time to see a formation of Hayabusas over Dagua at a thousand feet. He counted four. They turned and dove after the streaking Americans. At the same time, eight Ki-61 Hiens were taking off from the strip. The first one was just getting airborne, the pilot sucking up the landing gear as he banked hard left to take a desperate, high-deflection shot at the Jugs as they sped by.

Too late to break away, Kearby stayed on his target, picking out the lead bomber and uncharacteristically holding his fire as he raced right up the plane's tail. At two hundred feet, sheets of flame erupted from his wings as he cut loose with his fifties. The bomber staggered. Kearby switched targets, taking a snap shot at the bomber on the right side of the formation before zooming over them in a climbing left turn. He sped up and out to sea, away from the flak now coming up from Dagua.

He also put the diving Hayabusas directly behind him as he climbed, bleeding speed in a tightening turn.

Despite the intensity and uncharacteristic accuracy of the anti-aircraft fire, Dunham and Blair pressed into the bomber formation, taking the one on the leader's left. Dunham sent it down in flames, and pulled up and to the left, looking for Kearby. Seconds later, Blair reached the final bomber, knocking it down as a Ki-61 took a snap shot at him. Seconds later, two of the Hayabusas overhead latched onto his tail.

The Americans were in real trouble. The men in the Hayabusas were some of the 77th Sentai's best pilots.

One pass, haul ass. It was axiomatic, embedded in the fighter tactic DNA of 5th Air Force pilots. It had served Kearby well, allowing him to repeatedly beat the odds with his speeding, slashing attacks and sudden escapes.

They should have stayed low and run for home. They were already going east when they first attacked the bombers, but Kearby wasn't sure he got his. He wanted that kill, so he violated the core precept of his own teachings and came back around, low and slow, for a second pass.

The Hayabusas were on him in a flash. Far more maneuverable, with the speed advantage now, one took a beam shot at Kearby as the Texan broke hard right in an aileron roll, searching for any way out. The Hayabusa slid behind his tail, closing for a kill shot.

Dunham came around in a 180-degree turn, saw Kearby climbing toward him with the Oscar trailing. His old friend was in trouble. Dunham raced to his rescue. He pitched his nose down and made a furious front-quarter pass, all guns blazing. The Hayabusa's canopy shattered and fell away. Dunham kept shooting until the merge. Blair saw the Oscar explode and crash as Dunham blew past.

Blair skidded and dodged as the two Hayabusas pressed their attack on him. But he didn't break the cardinal rule, hadn't started a second pass, so his speed was high and the Oscars couldn't catch him. To avoid the flak, he banked left and sped out to sea in a long looping turn that set him up for a headlong rush back to the coast on the west side of Dagua. Low clouds hung over a valley there, and he ducked into it, hoping the hills and overcast would mask him from the dozen or so Japanese fighters boiling around Dagua.

Just then, a radial engine fighter went straight into the jungle off the end of the runway, exploding into a roiling fireball as it impacted the ground.

Blair reached the valley. A moment later, Dunham swung down into it as well. Together, they poured the coals on, hugged the trees, and ran south for five minutes, calling to Kearby over and over.

There was no response.

Neel was hit. Either in the beam attack or when the Hayabusa got behind him, his P-47 was riddled with machine gun bullets. He streaked over Dagua, flak filling the sky around him, another Hayabusa in hot pursuit.

The plane was finished. Crippled. He may have been wounded. There was no way he'd make it home. He jettisoned the canopy and bailed out. *Fiery Ginger* plunged into the jungle six hundred yards off the west side of Dagua.

But Neel was alive. His chute opened despite the low altitude of his jump. He swung hard and plummeted into a huge tree. The chute caught in the branches, and he found himself trapped, dangling beneath it.

The Hayabusa saw him and banked for the tree. Kearby looked up and saw it coming, nose afire as the Japanese pilot triggered his guns. His aim was true. A rash of 12.7mm bullets shredded the tree, tearing away branches and leaves. Bullets riddled Neel's body. One round probably hit his left cheek and blew out the back of his head, killing him instantly.

Two hours later, several Japanese pilots found his body, hanging limp in his chute harness. They ordered a New Guinea native to climb the tree and cut him down. The native did as ordered, noting the bullet strikes on the tree and the many wounds to Kearby's body. After he fell to the jungle floor, the Japanese stripped everything off him, including his boots, watch, clothes, jacket, and dog tags. They left his naked body unburied, sprawled facedown at the base of the tree, his parachute still entangled in its branches like a canopy for his anonymous grave.

Dunham and Blair returned to Saidor heartsick. They'd gone back briefly to search for Kearby but could not raise him on the radio and had to head for home. They were running out of fuel and daylight. They landed at sunset and jumped out of their planes to talk over what had happened. Neither was sure what had occurred, just that a fifth plane had gone into the jungle toward the end of the fight. Dunham, almost frantic, tried to get into another P-47 to go find Neel. It was dark now. There would be no point to search for him at night and only serve to risk another P-47. It didn't matter. Bill's friend was out there somewhere, and he could think only of going to his rescue. Blair and some of the ground crew physically restrained him from getting in the cockpit.

That night, as the moon rose and the jungle animals called around them, Kearby's ground crew refused to give up on their beloved colonel. They waited for hours as a gibbous moon lit the runway, ignoring the fact that his Jug's fuel would have given out long before. It didn't matter. They stood watch in the moonlight, straining to hear the reassuring growl of Kearby's R-2800.

The sky remained silent.

34

The Casualties

March 8, 1944
New Guinea

Late on the night of March 5, General Whitehead wrote Kenney and broke the news that Neel Kearby went missing over Wewak. He informed his commanding general that Dunham and Blair would fly into Port Moresby at first light to personally report what happened. Then a coordinated search effort could begin to find him.

Unfortunately, administrative red tape clogged up the search efforts. While Dunham did go back to the Wewak area in search of the crash site either the next day or day after, the 348th did not participate in a search initially, as the group didn't realize Kearby's P-47 was still on their books. Administratively, the 348th thought the search would have been carried out by the 309th Bomb Wing. A flurry of messages between headquarters eventually unfurled this mess, but of course any search was too late anyway.

The pilots and ground crew of the 348th were devastated by the news of Kearby's loss. Nobody had advocated harder for them or their aircraft. He'd taken care of the 348th from its inception. His leadership and inspiration had left a lasting impression on it. He was larger than life, the "old man" with a devil-may-care grin and a sense of invulnerability that gave new pilots into the theater a boost to their morale.

It was a double-edged sword. Now that he was gone, those who found inspiration in Kearby's example suddenly questioned their odds of survival. In the days following his loss, many young pilots asked the same question: *If the Japanese can get a man like Kearby, how am I going to make it through this?*

At 5th Air Force Headquarters, the news of Kearby's disappearance must have rocked Kenney hard and reminded him of the nightmares he faced when Gen. Ken Walker went down the year before over Rabaul. If captured alive, Neel would have been an absolute gold mine of intelligence to the Japanese. As tough as the Texan was, few men endured the savagery of Japanese torture sessions without breaking and telling what they knew. If he'd been captured, the inner workings of V Fighter Command would be revealed to the Japanese sooner or later.

Beyond the security issue of his loss, Kenney's personal affection for Kearby filled him with grief. For all the headaches he'd caused him these past few months, Kearby was still Kenney's kind of man: a pilot to the core who lived to fight the enemy. Losing him was like losing a part of himself—the man he once was over the trenches of the Great War's Western Front.

Kearby was also a national hero, the wearer of the Medal of Honor. Of all the aviators fighting around the globe, few had the sort of household name recognition Kearby did in early 1944. Explaining his loss to the country was going to be a painful process, one that might attract scrutiny from Washington. The decision was made to wait to release the news of his missing status. In the meantime, searches would try to determine what happened to him, and coordinate a rescue if possible.

On either the sixth or seventh, Dunham led a flight that returned to the Wewak area, sighting small tendrils of smoke coiling over the wrecks of the aircraft the Jug pilots had shot down. Of *Fiery Ginger* there was no sign. He circled the area, the Japanese conspicuously absent, before giving up and heading for home.

The mood at V Fighter Command remained a mix of shock and grief for several days. Kearby's fighting spirit had long infused the headquarters with an esprit de corps, a sense that they were different from all other rear-echelon commands. Neel had been well liked at HQ, and his loss came as a terrible personal blow to its men. Out of the entire USAAF, theirs was the only fighter command headquarters where staff officers routinely flew combat missions. Now, a point of pride suddenly looked like it might become a point of scrutiny.

The bleak mood picked up a bit on the seventh, when General Wurtsmith announced Tom Lynch's promotion to lieutenant colonel. The promotion was richly deserved. Tom's magnetism and natural leadership abilities made him one of the most popular and respected officers in V Fighter Command. He'd always been like that, from his days as an Eagle Scout back in Pennsylvania to his first days in combat. He was a man others instinctively followed. He wasn't the outgoing, brash type like Kearby. Instead, Lynch was quiet and unassuming. Each word he spoke carried weight. In the 39th, his men learned to trust his judgment. He was never just about scoring kills; Lynch was a man with his eyes on the bigger picture, and the responsibility of leadership never seemed to test his core.

Lynch's promotion served as an excuse to celebrate. The headquarters staff had been so down, a blowout party was exactly what the men needed. That night, they indeed celebrated—even the usually reticent Bong attended. How much alcohol flowed will probably never be known, but both Tom and Dick were not known to drink much. Still, the party was a great success, one that lifted everyone's spirits and would be talked about for years after.

The next morning, the Flying Circus went searching for kills over Tadji. Lynch had twenty kills, Bong twenty-four. The race to beat Eddie Rickenbacker's twenty-six riveted readers back home, who knew that Marines Joe Foss and Pappy Boyington had tied the great ace's record earlier in the year. Pappy went missing in January. Joe Foss was home and out of combat. Now, the race to beat Captain Eddie's record boiled down to four pilots: Bong, Lynch, and two 8th Air Force pilots flying from England against the Luftwaffe: P-51 ace Don Gentile and P-47 pilot Robert S. Johnson.

Bong and Lynch had the inside edge, since they could fly whenever and wherever they wanted. The only issue they faced was opportunity. There just weren't many Japanese planes left east of Hollandia.

That day over Tadji, they found the strip as empty as the sky. Lynch led Bong back east down the coast, hoping to run across something with wings. A few minutes later, they approached Aitape, a small Japanese base with a primitive harbor and airstrip. Three small cargo vessels lay at anchor there, a couple of barges chugging along nearby.

It was a strafer pilot's dream. Three vessels at anchor, their decks clogged with stacks of supplies and drums of fuel—a single flight of the Pappy Gunn–modified B-25s could have destroyed all three in a matter of seconds. Had the two fighter pilots simply continued on with their hunting mission, returned to Nadzab, and reported the shipping, nobody would have thought anything about it.

Lt. Col. Tom Lynch didn't hesitate. His mission was the destruction of the enemy, be it on the water or in the air. It didn't matter. He and Dick had the firepower to inflict major damage on those vessels, and that was all that mattered to him.

They would attack.

Lynch gave the signal and rolled into a sweeping dive, Dick following his leader. They picked out the *Yashima Maru* as their target.

Down low, the P-38s indicating over three hundred miles an hour, they raked the vessel with cannon- and machine-gun fire. The fusillade killed the lugger's captain, wounded three others, and caused fuel drums to explode and pour flaming gas all over the deck. The Lightnings flashed overhead, streaking past their targets, noses pointed toward Nadzab. When the pilots looked back, they saw the *Yashima Maru* wreathed in flames and starting to sink.

One pass. Haul ass.

They should have kept going, climbing back to patrol altitude as they worked their way home. Long ago, Allied pilots learned never to make a second strafing run on the same target. The first pass—the enemy usually would be surprised and have trouble responding. A second pass gave the enemy ground gunners a do-over, and they invariably would be waiting to exact revenge. The single pass that had for so long been a part of V Fighter Command's tactics, both for aerial targets and ground ones, seemed to have fallen by the wayside.

Lynch led Bong around in a looping left-hand turn out to sea. He came back around and dove to the whitecaps, his P-38 only twenty feet off the water. Throttles forward, the two Lightnings sped straight for the other two luggers, fangs out, ready to inflict even more punishment.

Aitape had just been reinforced by a fifty-man detachment from a naval garrison force. They arrived at the end of February with two 7.7mm and three 13mm antiaircraft machine guns, which the detachment commander emplaced along shore to cover the harbor. As the P-38s came back for a second pass, they barreled straight toward those guns, giving their crews minimal deflection shots.

The Japanese opened fire. Tracers webbed the sky around the two Americans as they began shooting at the cargo vessels. Bullets skipped across the whitecaps. Others zipped past Bong's P-38. Then the gunners found the range. Tom's P-38 shuddered with direct hits. A split second later, Bong's was hit as well. Rounds thumped into

Dick's right engine, tearing holes in the nacelle and boom. His left wing took further hits, and a line of bullets stitched across his vertical stabilizer.

As he fought to control his stricken fighter, something flew off Lynch's P-38. Part of the nose exploded, streaming debris. Tom's right engine burst into flames. He pulled up suddenly, abandoning his run in a bid to gain altitude. Bong saw him arc up and to the left, trailing flame and smoke as he crossed the coastline.

"Dick! Can you see me?" Lynch called over the radio.

"Yeah. You're on fire, bail out!"

Dick went after his friend, the sky still filled with tracers. His P-38 was hit repeatedly. His right engine started to lose power. Still, he chased after Tom, catching up to him at twenty-five hundred feet, perhaps a mile south of Aitape.

Lynch's '38 was doomed. The engine fire was spreading along the right wing. He'd lost power and the zoom climb that got him to twenty-five hundred feet cost him most of his airspeed.

"Bail out, Tom!"

Lynch struggled in the cockpit. Bong saw him jettison the hatch and start to go out the left side, away from the flames. The P-38 fell into a steep dive. He had only seconds left. Still, he couldn't get out of the cockpit. The Lightning plummeted toward the jungle, Bong following, watching as his friend remained in the cockpit.

The P-38 dropped through a thousand feet, flames engulfing the entire right side of the aircraft now. Part of the canopy suddenly tore away, the P-38 now only a few hundred feet from the trees. Lynch fell free of the aircraft, his chute trailing behind him.

The P-38 exploded directly beneath him. Lynch's body was blown skyward, flung like a ragdoll over the fireball. Bong saw his best friend's body pinwheel through the air, losing momentum as his chute streamed uselessly behind him. A second later, Tom Lynch fell into the jungle.

Dick circled the area, desperate to see any sign of life below. The P-38's wreckage burned and smoked nearby, but of his friend, he saw no trace. He made a final pass, then realized he was in dire straits himself. His right engine was coughing, crippled by the burst of machine gun fire on the second pass.

He limped toward Gusap, sick at heart, hands trembling. The oil pressure in his left engine started to drop. The right engine gave out, and he feathered its prop. Somehow, the Lightning held together long enough to get him to Nadzab, where he set the crippled bird down. Not a minute too soon; the left engine probably had moments left to live, as a bullet had pierced an oil line.

The ground crew rushed to Bong's P-38 after he landed and used a little tractor to tow it from the runway to the flight line. They found America's ace of aces stricken and shaky, hardly able to contain his grief. One of his mechanics recalled years later that this was the only time he'd seen Bong "nervous" after a mission. Bong climbed out of the cockpit and went off to report the terrible news as his ground crew counted eighty-seven bullets in his P-38.

Word of Tom Lynch's death spread through V Fighter Command squadrons like wildfire. It devastated those who had flown with him and found so much to like about the introverted Eagle Scout. It did not take long for rumors to form, and many of those turned the rage and grief on Dick Bong.

It is a strange psychological aspect of life in combat that the enemy cannot be given credit for a win. If a friend dies, often the men in his unit will blame one of their own for his death long before they blame the enemy for it. It is an especially easy thing to do if there is an unpopular officer or NCO who can be assigned the blame. In the 39th, whispers swirled around Bong. Rumor was he had made a mistake. He made a bad call. He got their friend killed. Grief turned to venom, and for some, the years after the war never dimmed that emotion. To their last days, they were convinced Bong somehow got Lynch killed.

The rumor mill was fueled by the lack of documentation surrounding the mission. When an aircraft went down in combat, usually a missing aircrew report (MACR) was filed, detailing as much information on the fate of the plane and its occupants as was known at the time. This usually included witness statements of those who survived the mission. In Lynch's case, no missing aircrew report was ever filed. Dick reported everything he'd seen, which was synthesized into a V Fighter Command summary of Lynch's last flight. For those inclined to see conspiracies, this smacked of a cover-up. As if some part of Bong's role in the mission was being sanitized in order to protect the AAF's current ace of aces.

To the Cobras and others, it looked very shady. The gossip further damaged Dick's reputation within V Fighter Command and more thoroughly isolated him from his peers.

Was there a cover-up? The Japanese sources agree with Bong's story. They credited Leading Seaman Amano with Lynch's P-38. He was one of the recent arrivals at Aitape, serving under the detachment commander, Warrant Officer Hideo Ezawa. Ezawa's machine gunners had plenty of ammunition—seven thousand rounds—and they used it liberally as the P-38s came back for a second pass.

The mistake the Americans made was that second pass. But Lynch was leading the Circus that day, so Bong had no say in it. Like everyone else who ever flew with Tom Lynch, Dick trusted his friend's judgment instinctively.

The 5th's official summary of the mission includes details of the second pass. Later, Bong spoke of Lynch's last moments to Lee Van Atta in a serialized collection of articles detailing Dick's life and combat career. Either he didn't mention during the interview that they'd gone back for a second pass, or that detail was edited out of the final article. That was the only real cover-up.

The 5th Air Force kept silent on this double loss for a week. At Whitehead's forward HQ, the staff received intelligence that Kearby did not survive his crash around March 9. Yet it was not until Thursday March 16 that 5th Air Force HQ released near-simultaneous statements reporting that Kearby and Lynch were both missing in action.

The day before the official announcement, Virginia Kearby answered the door at the family home in San Antonio to find a Western Union deliveryman holding a telegram from the War Department. She signed for it, stepped inside, and read the words, "Missing in Action."

It seemed unreal to her. Even more unreal when five days later, the mailman brought her a letter Neel had written, explaining how he'd now joined a bomb wing and was eager to go back into action with it. His mood and tone sounded different than the previous letter touching on the horrors he'd seen at Saidor. He seemed happy, eager, and back to his normal self.

Now he was missing?

Simultaneously, Neel's parents received the same news at their home in Arlington, a Dallas suburb. His mother never understood her son's obsession with hunting Japanese planes. She couldn't fathom why he insisted on staying in combat after all he'd already done. He'd more than met the threshold for duty fulfilled. Everything else to her seemed needless risk. Later, she wrote to General Kenney and confessed she would never grasp what drove Neel be a part of the ace race. In her pain-wracked world, the ambition to be the best cost her family their sole remaining son.

Around the state, the papers reported Neel's death and interviewed his family. Virginia refused to accept her larger-than-life husband was gone, telling an interviewer, "Until Neel is reported dead, I'll not give up hope."

In Catasauqua, Pennsylvania, the dreaded yellow telegram from the War Department arrived at the Lynch household almost at the same time the Kearbys received theirs. Within minutes, the news traveled all over town, and people rushed to offer their assistance. The police chief arrived with the family's parish priest. Neighbors poured into the house. Cars lined the street out front, and people stood in shock, talking in hushed voices in the yard, on the porch, and in the house. They were there because the Lynches were beloved members of the community. Their son was the greatest hero to emerge from Catasauqua during the war. When he'd returned home the previous fall, he was feted and welcomed with much acclaim and joy.

At lunch, Tom's sister Catherine walked home from the high school, unaware of what was going on. As she reached the house, seeing all the people consoling each other set off alarm bells. She rushed through the back into the kitchen, only to find a neighbor doing the dishes. She looked up from the sink and told Catherine to talk to her mother at once.

She found her mom in the living room, surrounded by townsfolk. Her dad was sitting next to the radio, listening intently above the commotion around him.

"They told us we lost your brother," Alice Lynch said to her daughter, "but we don't believe it."

For days after, Tom Lynch's dad refused to leave his seat next to the family radio. Searching, praying to hear a newscaster report that his son had been found alive and well. The days passed, and no such report was heard. In the stress and grief, not knowing what happened, Tom's dad suffered a stroke. Though no bullets struck the Lynch home in quiet Pennsylvania, father and son were equal casualties of war.

35

Longer-than-Long Legs

March 1944
Nadzab, New Guinea

Dick Bong lay on the cot in his jungle quarters, listening to the sounds of the night animals moving beyond their camp. The silver light of a full moon shone through the gaps in the tent flaps, periodically obscured by passing clouds.

He ached with grief. Tom Lynch had been his only real friend in New Guinea, and he had watched him die horribly. He tried to squeeze the sight of his last seconds out of his mind, bury it alongside that long-ago memory of holding his sister for the last time before their father drove her to the hospital in Superior. But this one was too fresh and too raw. It hung in his mind's eye like a movie screen, replaying the scene on an endless loop.

Why had he come back? He could have stayed home, requested assignment Stateside to support the war effort in some other way. He could have stayed on the war bond circuit, urging factories full of Rosies to give just a bit more for the troops overseas. That would have been easy; he was a national celebrity now, he could have asked for anything and received it. That was the power of acedom and fame in wartime America.

Yet he never asked. It never occurred to him to cull special privileges from his success in combat. So he came back. Just like Tom.

Following orders, yes. Was that the only reason he did it, not the hunting, not the Circus? Where was the line between duty and personal ambition?

He focused his thoughts on home. The return bore no resemblance to his anonymous departure in 1942. Last fall, he was followed everywhere by well-wishers and worshipful autograph seekers. The newshawks photographed his every move, from hugging his mother to going hunting with his family, to simply walking through downtown Poplar. He tried to stay even-keeled, but the truth was he had little patience for the constant flash of their cameras.

There were bright spots. He was ordered to New York, then Washington, D.C., to meet with members of Congress. In New York, he stayed at the Waldorf-Astoria and was treated like royalty. This was the kid who a year before had stood before the St. Francis Hotel in San Francisco, just another farm boy in uniform, unable to even afford a room. Now, senators hung on his every word.

He longed for home. Not the Waldorf, where he'd done a radio appearance for the news show *Report to the Nation*, nor of the halls of power in Washington, D.C. He missed the farm. And Marge.

She was a gorgeous sorority girl from his old school, Superior State Teachers College. When he first got back to Poplar, she and her posse from their chapter of Lambda Sigma Lambda drove out to the Bong family farm to invite Dick to come crown the school's homecoming king and queen. Her circle of friends called themselves the "Scintillating Six" and they had a monopoly on the queen's crown. Marge had won in in 1942. Her friend Violet scored it the following year.

Dick showed up at the college's gym with an old friend and two of his sisters. With great fanfare he crowned Violet homecoming queen. Afterward, he tried to escape from the autograph hounds, taking Jerry, Nelda, and his old friend "Pete" Peterson to a late-night grill on Tower Street in Superior. The place was packed, but they found a spot in back.

Dick thought about that moment a lot. He wasn't the sentimental type. Nostalgia, which so steeped Gerald Johnson's personality, never thrived in Dick's heart. But that moment when he looked up from the booth to see Marge coming through the diner's front door? That changed everything for him.

Her raven hair and easy smile, they shined at him through the crowd. She and her friends looked around the place, but there were no empty seats. Dick seized the moment and waved them over.

She didn't ask him for his autograph. She didn't ask him any of the inanities he'd been subjected to by countless strangers.

What's it like to shoot a Jap down?

You gonna break Rickenbacker's score?

How many Japs have you killed?

What's it feel like to be a hero?

God, how he hated that last question.

Through the meal, people of all ages descended on the table. Men in uniform asked Dick to sign their short snorters. Teenagers asked him to autograph napkins. One girl flipped up her dress and begged him to sign her slip. But this was not Sydney, and he was not with wild Wally Jordan. The normal social rules applied back here, and he refused. She settled for an autographed napkin.

In the middle of this circus, Marge treated him like a person, not a celebrity. It was disarming, and Dick warmed to her immediately. She soon saw parts of him nobody else did. They double-dated. They went out with Dick's sisters. The normally stoic and unassuming fighter ace was transformed into a goofy big brother around Jerry and Nelda. He'd tug their hair, tweak their noses. He'd kid them. He teased his sister Jerry and called her "Long Legs." After he started falling for Marge, he had dubbed her, "Longer-than-Long Legs" since they were almost the same height. In heels, Marge was taller than him. That lightness and warmth he showed his family shone toward Marge, and she was captivated.

They had fallen in love, and Dick found solace in their connection on more than one occasion. Just before Christmas, he got word that Stanley Johnson's widow was in Superior, visiting her pregnant sister for the holidays. When she learned that Dick was home, she called the Bong house and asked to see him. He rushed to meet her, unsure of how he would be received. The meeting left him grief-stricken, and he turned to Marge for comfort. He told her that Stanley's widow was a brave woman who tried valiantly to hide her despair as Dick recounted her husband's last mission.

The meeting ripped open half-healed wounds in Dick. He saw in her eyes another cost of war he'd not considered much. The connections back home, when severed by loss—well, those folks would never be the same. He resolved then not to put Marge through that. No wartime marriage for them. If he died, he did not want Mrs. Johnson's pain etched into her eyes.

Love still finds a way. Even as he traveled the country, he thought of her. He wrote her. Missed her. They shared a final tearful good-bye in January, and then their episodic moments together became a consistent long-distance affair, held together by the words penned under a bare bulb dangling from the ceiling of Dick's quarters.

He wished he could see her now. Maybe then, Tom's death could be tamped down deep, airbrushed out of the moment filled by the love growing between them. For now, the sleepless nights would be filled with a battle between the grief of loss and the longing for his connection with Marge.

The next morning, he went to see a staff officer in the intelligence section that he'd gotten to know and handed him a small print of Marge's high school graduation portrait. He asked him if he could enlarge it so he could put it on the side of his P-38. In due course, the intel section's photo lab produced a 20 x 24 copy, which Bong had glued and varnished to the side of his P-38. If he couldn't be with her through this ordeal, at least she'd be there in spirit, on the side of his Lightning's fuselage, like a talisman against trauma. Marge's name was painted on the nose, and twenty-five kill flags adorned the aluminum skin behind her photo. Dick's count was high—he actually only had twenty-four confirmed. But in due course, he knew he would fix that.

The Flying Circus was dead. With Lynch gone, there was no point to try to continue the experiment. If it really was intended to be a full squadron of elites attached to V Fighter Command, that idea never got off the ground. The next batch of new P-38s arrived in Australia a few days after Lynch's last mission, and it took the depots over a month to assemble them and get them combat ready. Had Lynch lived, perhaps the Flying Circus may have been fleshed out. Instead, it would be remembered only as an excuse to let two aces hunt and rack their scores up.

Without Lynch, Bong had nobody to fly with. Instead of simply turning to a desk job, he received permission to fly with the other P-38 squadrons in the area. He'd pick a mission that looked like it would probably encounter Japanese planes, and he would attach himself to it. He flew with squadrons in the 475th Fighter Group and with the 80th. Usually, he'd catch up to them en route to target, tacking himself onto the formations. The squadron would be told in advance to expect him, but it appears Dick rarely attended the pre-mission briefings. From his position at V Fighter Command HQ, he knew the details of the missions and simply tagged along.

It was a strange way to continue fighting the Japanese. Dick was no longer part of any squadron. He was a gunman who joined up for a potential fight with men he only passingly knew. To them, Bong was often seen as a VIP or a brass hat coming down from high to get a little combat time. There was no bond between them. Rather, Bong put as many barriers between those he flew with and himself as he could. It was his way of defending against further pain of loss, but it often resulted in resentment on the part of the squadron he joined. It also isolated him physically as well as emotionally from his fellow pilots. He led an itinerant and lonely life in the weeks after Lynch's death.

Toward the end of the month, Kenney grew concerned about Dick's mental health. The ace had lost noticeable amounts of weight, more so than the normal effect New Guinea had on the men. It was a warning sign that the stress and grief were taking a heavy toll. Kenney decided to send his top ace down to Australia for a short break.

He returned on the thirty-first. His aircraft with Marge's portrait on the side had been lost by another pilot on a reconnaissance mission. Three days later, while flying another P-38, he joined up with the 432nd Fighter Squadron, 475th Fighter Group, during a low-altitude escort mission to Hollandia. Charles MacDonald led the group that day at eight thousand feet with the group stacked above a formation of A-20s.

Over Hollandia, the P-38s encountered a string of Japanese fighters running west at about a thousand feet. The pilots punched their tanks, prepped for combat, and dove to the attack. Once again, the men of the 475th earned their reputation as one of the best outfits in the entire Army Air Force. In a furious, low-altitude brawl with the Japanese, Satan's Angels knocked down twelve fighters. Dick repeatedly attacked a Ki-43, whose pilot dodged every pass. Another flight of P-38s went after it, then Dick swung in behind the elusive fighter and saw some hits. The Japanese pilot twisted hard left, burst into flames, and flew into a hillside near Lake Sentani.

P. J. Dahl, an ace with the 475th Fighter Group, arrived at the post-mission debriefing and listened to the other pilots recount their perspectives of the fight. Another pilot in the group described how he shot down the same aircraft Bong thought he got. Dick showed up in the middle of the debriefing and was absolutely convinced he was the one who got the kill. The pilot, seeing Dick's rank and not wanting to fight about it, gave him the credit. After all, he was a bigwig now from HQ. At least, that's how some of the P-38 pilots felt about the situation. It was officially awarded to Dick as his twenty-fifth victory.

With Bong only one away from Eddie Rickenbacker's score, the press focused on this threshold and glossed over the loss of Kearby and Lynch. Though it was already lost, Bong's plane with Marge on the side became an instant hit in the papers. Where many of the Army Air Force's planes were decorated with naked women and filthy names, here was the ace of aces in an extraordinary departure from the norm who adorned his P-38 with a picture of his girl back home. It was such a beautiful small-town angle for the reporters that photos of the original Marge spread across the country long after it had gone down.

Nearly every day, newspapers ran an article or a photo of Dick, frequently standing beside Marge. In early April, the news of the day included word that Dick's official score had been revised downward to twenty-four, but that didn't last long. Two days after the Hollandia mission, news reached home that he'd knocked another plane down. The race to twenty-six grew superheated. Papers ran box scores showing the top ten aces under headlines like, "Three U.S. Air Aces May Trump Rick's Record."

The pressure was on. He wrote to Marge of the race and the pressure, asking her, "Do you think I can get to the top?" Marge's reply was unequivocal, "I know you will."

Bong had transcended the typical role a fighter pilot played in New Guinea. He was a bigger asset to the 5th Air Force than just another captain in a fighter group. He was a media sensation, and the more press he garnered, the better it was for the war effort and morale back home. America needed heroes. Bong fit the bill perfectly. He was an everyman, the unassuming boy next door who embodied the warrior spirit of America's citizen soldiers.

His fame was also an asset to the 5th Air Force and Kenney's efforts to wheedle reinforcements out of Washington. That Bong didn't want to return to any squadron and bear the onus of his rank played into this and gave Kenney an excuse to leave him in place, freelancing with whomever he wished. Bong received tacit carte blanche to beat Rickenbacker's score. He could fly whenever he wanted with whatever squadron he chose.

He was also told that once he broke the record, he'd be sent home, whether his tour was complete or not. The path back to his flesh-and-blood Marge led through formations of Japanese planes. If he ever lacked motivation, there was no question about it now. As it was, he found most of military life boring and unrewarding. Staff work was anathema to him. He was a farmer, not a desk jockey. Combat flying, on the other hand, made everything pale in comparison. He never squared it with killing, seeing it from the same psychological buffer as the other aces. It was a game. It was sport. Hunting, just like back home in the woods around Poplar.

On April 12, 1944, Dick attached himself to the 80th Fighter Squadron for another mission to Hollandia. This time, he joined the squadron on the ground and flew one of its planes, a P-38J named "Down-beat." Ace Jay Robbins led the mission that day. Dick acted as tail-end Charlie and did not fly with a wingman. He was the lone gunman in the back of the pack, holding the most vulnerable position in the formation.

Over Hollandia at fourteen thousand feet, about fifteen Japanese fighters intercepted the Americans. Dick went head-to-head with one Oscar, missed it, and sped clear of the engagement so he could come back around for another pass. As he did, the Hayabusa pilot entered a dive, heading for some clouds a few thousand feet below. Dick gave chase and easily caught up with the fleeing Japanese plane. He opened fire just before they reached the cloud cover. The Ki-43 began to smoke and rolled into a steeper dive. Dick dove through the clouds, came out the other side, and watched the Oscar crash into the sea off the coast of Hollandia.

That was twenty-six. He was tied with Rickenbacker, Boyington, and Joe Foss.

He sped for altitude, looking for targets as he traded his airspeed for position. When he leveled out over the sprawling fight, he noticed two Japanese fighters together heading for the cloud layer. He pounced on them, shot them both up until they started smoking, but they escaped into the clouds before he could finish them off. Instead of going after them, he turned and made a fifty-degree deflection run on another Ki-43 that was tacked onto a P-38's tail. His bullets raked across the fighter, which twisted into a spin and went into Tanahmerah Bay.

Another Oscar darted below his P-38. Dick rolled in on it, but the pilot saw him coming. The Japanese dove to the water, pulling up at only a few feet. Dick chased him, snapping out bursts. Another P-38 swept in and shot at the Hayabusa, then pulled up in a zoom climb. Dick stayed on him, boring in for the kill. The Japanese saw he was pinned between the water and the onrushing Lightning. Out of options, he did the only thing left to him: he tried a tight, sudden turn to the left.

He was too low and too unskilled. He dug his left wingtip into the whitecaps and cartwheeled nose over tail, shedding pieces and bursting into flames. Dick blew past the wreckage and went searching for more targets. After a final scuffle with a very aggressive Oscar pilot, he sped for home with the rest of the Headhunters.

He claimed three that day, but his second kill went unwitnessed so 5th Air Force could not give him credit. Yet, he was so sure of where it hit the water that he pinpointed its location. Kenney promised to send divers out to look for it once Hollandia was in Allied hands. That happened a month later, and the divers found the wreck. Bong would eventually be credited with three planes as a result. For now, he returned to Nadzab with twenty-seven kills, where Kenney immediately promoted him to major for beating Rickenbacker's score and becoming America's all-time ace of aces.

He'd won the first leg of the race. The image-makers surrounded him, Bill Boni and Lee Van Atta and all the others piled on with questions. He sat patiently trying to answer them, uncomfortable with the spotlight as ever. Somebody snapped a photo of the moment, and in later years some judged Bong to be "holding court" in it. The truth was more nuanced. Kenney had sent the reporters to tell the story, and Bong dutifully played his part. He'd run the race, remained humble and likable as always, which made him a picture-perfect war hero for the thirsty public back home.

Word of the new record spread quickly across the United States. The *Los Angeles Times* put the news above the fold on its front page under the heading, "Pacific Ace Tops Rickenbacker Record." He was lauded as the "Wisconsin farm lad" who had broken the three-way, two-war tie to become the new all-time leading American ace. Hard on his heels were Robert S. Johnson and Don Gentile, both aces flying with the 8th Air Force out of England.

The news was echoed and amplified by scores of papers from coast to coast. Eddie Rickenbacker congratulated Dick and spoke to the press about the deal he and Kenney had made back in the fall of 1942. Kenney promised a case of scotch to whomever broke Eddie's record. The Great War ace had promptly doubled down and offered a second case to the winner. The aging warrior took interviews from his Eastern Airlines office, where he served as the company's CEO, telling reporters, "Where I will obtain the scotch or how I can get it to Major Bong is as yet unknown. But I will not leave a stone unturned to fulfill my part of the bargain."

Later, temperance groups protested the promise of liquor to honorable servicemen. It kicked up such a dust storm that the case of scotch was changed to a case of Coke. In due course, Bong received his bounty. While others may have been disappointed, Coke suited him just fine. The press ate it up, casting Bong in an ever more small-town, boy-next-door kind of light. In this moment, the media morphed Bong into something even larger than a war hero. He'd become a symbol for young Americans whose mettle had been proven as the nation's citizens put down their plows to go to war.

General Arnold, meanwhile, watched the news from New Guinea with growing concern. The death of Lynch and Kearby particularly alarmed him. As the nation took a victory lap, celebrating's Bong's new status, Arnold wrote to Kenney about losing senior-level fighter leaders and aces. It was the first hint of Washington scrutiny to the craziness that had gone on all year at V Fighter Command. The subtext in Arnold's message was *Keep Bong Safe*. Kenney prohibited Bong from further combat missions, and at the end of April made good on his promise to send him home. After a tour of less than sixteen weeks, the ace of aces returned to the United States, the media tracing his every step. He was the man of the hour, and everyone wanted a piece of the hero. But the hero only wanted to see his Marge and his family.

Not a week after Bong returned home, Maj Gerald Johnson stepped off a plane at Hamilton Field to no fanfare and caught a ride to Eugene. Though he had not scored a kill since January, he'd been flying combat throughout the first four months of the year as part of the 49th Fighter Group headquarters element. He was being groomed for command of the 49th, and part of that job meant getting to know the men in the 7th and 8th Squadrons. He'd dutifully performed his staff duties and had flown with all three squadrons in the group, assessing the men and leaders and making sure they knew he was not going to be a field grade who led from a desk.

In the two years since he'd left Portland after his failed attempt at marriage, he'd been transformed by his experience of war and flying. He'd left Oregon an overemotive boy on the threshold of manhood, still clinging to romantic notions of heroism and derring-do. He returned a man defined by combat, his uniform carrying all the trappings of his own hero's journey. The Distinguished Service Cross, the Silver Star, the DFC awarded many times over, the Air Medal with many oak leaf clusters—the salad bar of medal ribbons on his left breast stretched down, row after row. Though he couldn't care less about medals, they symbolized the man he'd become: a warrior leader who knew his place was at the tip of the spear, where he had shot down thirteen Japanese planes, proving he was among America's fighter pilot elite.

He came home with all the gravitas and strength of a leader revered by his men, confident in his abilities, proud of his achievements. His feud with Mrs. Hall—those days of feeling impotent to her will and meddling? They were over. He made Barbara his June bride. Mrs. Hall never stood a chance.

After the wedding, he and Barbara packed up his old Plymouth and set off for Fort Riley in Kansas to attend Command and General Staff College, the Army's training facility for officers destined for a shoulder board of stars. There was no doubt what this meant. General Kenney was grooming him for great things to come.

He finished the accelerated course there later in the summer, just in time for the Johnsons to return to Oregon and honeymoon in the rugged Steens Mountains. For two weeks, they lived in a primitive cabin, bathing in the local streams, fishing for their dinner, and hiking the hillsides together. Gerald wore a ridiculously garish red hat when they went fishing, which provoked Barbara to howl with laughter.

Most importantly, five years after that illicit moonlight kiss, they finally, joyously made love at every opportunity.

In that glorious summer of 1944, while the men and women in uniform carried the flag forward on all fronts, Gerald lived the life he'd always wanted: a husband and a man whose life's work would not include being chained to an office job and consigned to anonymity. Now, if he could only be a father before he returned to battle, his life goals would be complete.

36

The Two Macs

The men of the 475th earned their reputation as Kenney's warrior elites. The unit's three squadrons were filled with hard-charging pilots with racks of kill flags on their P-38s. The leadership cadre was tight-knit, capable, and loyal to the men. The 475th was perhaps the best-run and -led unit in the 5th Fighter Command that spring, thanks in large part to Col. Charles MacDonald.

Mac arrived shrouded in mystery the previous October. He made a statement that first day when he snagged a P-38, scrambled with the alert squadron, and shot down a couple of Japanese dive-bombers. He was a colonel who led from the front. Where many other group commanders let their admin duties keep them on the ground, MacDonald struck a balance. He flew the boring missions; he flew the most dangerous ones. He set the example, but did it without fanfare. Where Johnson was a gregarious and outgoing leader, MacDonald was the quiet professional. His economy of words gave each word heft. When he spoke, his men listened.

He kept a professional officer's distance between himself and his pilots. It meant few got to know the man behind his rank. What the rest of the 475th did know about MacDonald was that he always was in their corner. Do your job to the best of your ability, and the colonel would be your biggest supporter.

He handled disciplinary issues with the same low-key approach. Once, when it became clear that a pilot's frequent aborts during missions had nothing to do with mechanical issues, he swiftly removed him and sent him to the rear. There would be no place for cowards in the 475th. The morale and culture he'd helped create within its ranks demanded nothing less than giving the last full measure for their brotherhood.

He was fair. He never asked his men to do anything he would not. He listened to them, advocated for them when necessary, and gave them the benefit of the doubt. They responded with loyalty and their last full measure.

In the air, he proved himself a tiger every time they encountered the enemy. By May, his aircraft, *Putt Putt Maru*, carried ten Japanese kill flags. He was a fighting leader who'd shown he was among the best at the craft.

That spring, he revealed another side of himself to some of his pilots. The group had been flying and fighting for months without much respite. With the 9th and 39th still flying Jugs, the burden of the long-range missions fell to Mac and his men. Their brief leaves to Sydney provided their only real escape from the meat grinder.

Charles MacDonald went to Sydney far less often than his pilots did. The work of keeping the group running demanded his presence, plus his own devotion was part of the example he set. But even a leader like Mac needed a break now and then. That spring, he flew to Sydney with a group of his pilots, who set up shop in the 475th's flat and commenced to party.

There was nothing like fighter pilot parties—frat keggers were kindergarten tame in comparison. The only rival to the legendary levels these parties achieved could be found where the infantry partied. And though soldier benders may not be possible to top, the fighter pilots sure tried.

MacDonald attended the first parties but behaved strangely aloof at the same time. He was older, that was one difference. At twenty-seven, he was an established professional Army Air Force officer with a wife and family back home. He was more settled, but there was something more than that. Perhaps he didn't want to be seen out of control and drunk by his men. In his mind, that might have lessened his leadership authority. Perhaps he never was much of a partier. That fit the rest of his character. He wasn't one who ever wanted attention drawn his way. He shirked the spotlight, wanted nothing to do with the press. And in that flat at the start of the week's revelry, he simply took a seat and nursed a drink, watching his men uncoil like overstressed springs.

Acquiring liquor in wartime Australia remained a tricky proposition that required cultivating contacts among Sydney's black marketeers. The Americans used a particularly odious character, who would arrive at the flat with their liquor order and charge them ridiculously inflated prices for the hooch. The men pooled their money to keep the liquor flowing, so they tolerated the fleecing for months. Each successive group of pilots to come down would be armed with their black marketeers' contact information, so they could get all they needed and bring some back to New Guinea.

After a couple of deliveries, the pilots around MacDonald grew angry and restless. The booze they'd ordered had been watered down, even as the price for it was jacked higher. When their contact showed up at the flat again, they confronted him. A loud, drunken argument ensued. The black marketeer never stood a chance. Several pilots picked him up, carried him down the hall, and tossed him into the building's elevator shaft.

MacDonald peered out the flat's door, turned to P. J. Dahl, who was watching nearby, and said, "Well, I don't think we'll be seeing that guy again."

Mac returned to his chair, nursed his drink, and observed as the festivities reignited. Later, the men began bringing women back to the flat. The party really kicked off then. One pilot brought Mac a gift, two gorgeous Australian women, who promptly sat on his lap.

In the live-for-the-moment bubble the pilots existed in, the normal morals they abided by back in the States did not apply. Infidelity was rife as they clutched onto slivers of life against the backdrop of the death they faced to the north. When you don't know if you will be alive in a week, or a month, the rules of living tend to evolve.

MacDonald would have none of it. As the women sat on his lap, he looked uncomfortable. He fended off their hands, politely refusing to engage. P. J. Dahl saw this and felt a rush of sympathy for his commander. Here was a married man with the chance to live out whatever fantasies he wished. But what he wished was to remain a loyal husband.

He pulled Mac away and asked him if he wanted to go get something to eat. They fled the flat in search of a steak dinner. When it was over, Mac checked into a hotel for the rest of the week.

A man with a moral code that could not be broken, not even by the threat of death or freedom from consequence—that was a rare thing. It was also one of the reasons why the 475th came to love their enigmatic leader so much. He was their rock in a fluid world of violence and chaos.

Back in New Guinea, the 475th was undergoing some serious changes. Losses had been heavy, with fourteen pilots killed or missing in the first four months of 1944. The replacements sent to the group were considered extremely raw. Lots of potential, but they would need a lot of mentoring if they were going to survive.

Tommy McGuire, who was still the operations officer in the 431st Squadron, took it upon himself to write a combat tactics manual for the new guys. He threw himself into the job, and when done, the treatise found its way to MacDonald's desk. It was an impressive, astute piece of work that clearly outlined the best way to use the P-38 against the lighter, more nimble Japanese fighters. MacDonald was so impressed, he sent it up to V Fighter Command, where it was reproduced and distributed throughout New Guinea and Australia.

It was a small win for Tommy in an otherwise dismal year. As operations officer, he drafted the flight schedules that were then tweaked and approved by the squadron commander. He tried to make sure the missions were flown equally and the men received days off. But sooner or later, most everyone would get cheesed off at their name on the duty roster. McGuire made a point of flying as often as he could, usually taking the longest and most uncomfortable missions in part because he did not want to be accused of cherry-picking milk runs. Also, while a dark horse in the ace race, he still wanted his shot at the title.

The Japanese refused to cooperate with that. The group was seeing less and less of the enemy as spring began. The air battles over Wewak, Rabaul, and Hollandia took a steady toll on the 5th, no doubt, but they were far more devastating to the Japanese. Now their air units in New Guinea were on their last legs, making fewer appearances. Tommy McGuire simply ran out of opportunities. No matter how much he flew—and sometimes he flew sixty hours a month or more—he rarely saw an enemy aircraft.

At times, his frustration boiled over. He'd actually flown on the April 3, 1944, mission to Hollandia where Bong scored his twenty-fifth kill. He never engaged the enemy that day. He was up again on April 12, on the same raid as Bong, and missed that fight as well. Being in the air while Bong was racking his score and he didn't even have a chance to shoot at anything was bad enough. But the favored treatment Bong and Lynch and Kearby had all appeared to receive from the high command outraged him. After Bong broke Rickenbacker's record, he vented to some of the other pilots in the 431st. To Tommy, the race was rigged.

Perhaps Tommy's outburst was fueled by his physical health. He flew two more missions after the twelfth with a persistent headache and aching lower back. He grew sensitive to light, and a rash broke out across the trunk of his body. By the fifteenth, he was too sick to fly. A raging fever set in. Pain-racked and sometimes delirious, the medical staff diagnosed him with typhus. He missed the rest of the month, including the mission on April 16, which would forever be known as "Black Thursday." Bad weather set in over Allied bases that day, after a maximum-effort strike was launched against Hollandia. Forty-six planes went down, most out of fuel when their crews couldn't find a friendly field in the torrential rain. The 475th lost six pilots that day, two of whom were from McGuire's squadron. It is quite possible that a bone-breakingly painful bacterial infection saved McGuire's life.

He recovered surprisingly quickly, just in time to move with the rest of the 475th and 49th Fighter Groups up to Hollandia, which MacArthur's 41st Infantry Division captured on April 21. The invasion there totally redefined the war in New Guinea while supercharging the drive on the Philippines. It was a huge leap west along the New Guinea coast, striking deep into the Japanese rear areas with such surprise that most of the enemy force at Hollandia fled into the jungle as the American troops came ashore.

There were five airfields around Hollandia, which the 41st Division quickly captured. Engineers set to work bulldozing hundreds of wrecked Japanese aircraft out of the way so the fields could be put back into operational service. MacArthur wanted to end the New Guinea campaign as soon as possible. Another great leap westward was in store, but to pull it off, he needed his best '38 squadrons as far forward as possible.

The Knights and the rest of the 49th Fighter Group made the jump to Hollandia in early May. MacDonald led the 475th in at about the same time. The two rival groups were colocated for the first time here in this former Japanese base.

They found the place a horror show. Some of the Forty-Niners discovered a brothel where Southeast Asian "comfort women" were raped daily by Japanese troops. The brothel was a bacchanal of misery. Broken condoms, blood and gore, filth. The place was burned to the ground. But what happened to the comfort women? Most were found beyond a garbage dump, butchered and stacked in a Dantean display of depravity.

In 1942, a group of American female nurses had elected to stay behind on Corregidor Island in Manila Bay after the rest of the Allied army on Luzon surrendered at Bataan. Most of those nurses ended up at Santo Tomas Internment Camp, but some simply vanished. At Hollandia, the Americans discovered what happened to at least two of them. They'd been forced into sexual slavery by Japanese officers, who took the women with them to whatever duty station they were assigned. These American female officers became their playthings. For two years, their lives were a nightmare of rape and abuse. They were forcibly addicted to narcotics, which made them more pliant. Nineteen of those women were taken to Hollandia. Two were found alive near the brothel. Al Blum, a photoreconnaissance Lightning pilot, wrote of them in his diary, noting they were "half crazy from drugs and dope." And, no doubt, trauma.

Near one of the airfields, Americans discovered the Japanese had massacred a group of Korean construction workers. Their bodies were dumped into trenches not far from where the orgy of violence against the comfort women took place. When the Americans found them, their corpses were bloated from the tropical heat, covered in flies and other insects. The stench was indescribable. The pilots who went to look at the sight were sickened and shocked. Their war was largely antiseptic and removed from the killing. At Hollandia, they were surrounded by the worst sights and smells imaginable.

While the pilots moved into tents amid the wreckage and horrors, Allied intelligence teams searched the Japanese planes and the dead for any bits of information. They discovered the landings there destroyed the last remaining Japanese fighter units in the area. The 68th, 78th, and 33rd Sentais were among the outfits totally destroyed, their surviving pilots and ground crew put to flight to face starvation—and cannibalism—in the jungle. The destruction of Japanese airpower in the Southwest Pacific was nearly complete.

The intel teams also discovered the body of a Japanese major. When his swollen corpse was searched, a photograph was found that would soon become one of the iconic images of the war. It depicted a group of Japanese soldiers and aviators watching as an officer raised his Samurai sword to decapitate a bound, blindfolded Australian commando named Leonard Siffleet. It was one of the only depictions ever found of the fate accorded to thousands of Allied servicemen who fell into Japanese hands during the Pacific War. The photo was published in *Life* magazine and in newspapers around the world as evidence of the savagery that defined the Japanese conduct of the war.

For the pilots at Hollandia, these discoveries stripped away whatever shreds of mercy remained toward the Japanese. As one pilot in the 49th Fighter Group later recalled, "There was about as much humanity in a bunch of Japanese as a swarm of fire ants." Hollandia reminded the men why they were fighting. With grim determination, they carried the war to the enemy with even more resolve.

In early May, MacDonald went to see McGuire. The 431st's commander was set to rotate home on leave after more than a year of service in theater. Though the pilots in the squadron still took issue with McGuire's personality on the ground, everyone respected him as an administrator and combat pilot. He may have been obsessed with his personal score, but he never let that obsession trump his real purpose in New Guinea: fighting as part of a team as he helped to run it.

MacDonald didn't like McGuire much personally either. The two could not have been more different characters. Yet, when it came time to select a new squadron leader, he decided McGuire was up to the task. He'd seen enough of McGuire to know the young pilot possessed one of the sharpest minds he'd encountered. Tommy was always two steps ahead of everyone else's thinking process. He sometimes finished people's thoughts because he grew impatient waiting for them to catch up to him. In the air, this translated to an aviator who could think ahead of his aircraft, and think ahead of the fight as it unfolded. He could anticipate where others could only react. He multitasked in such moments, leading and fighting while staying aware of the swirling chaos around him. It made him a tactical genius, something reflected in the manual he'd submitted to MacDonald earlier in the spring. Those things counted a lot more than McGuire's obnoxious personality on the ground. Command was not based on a popularity contest but on who could best do the job of taking it to the enemy and keeping his guys alive. More than one 431st pilot said, "In the air, I would have followed McGuire anywhere. On the ground, I couldn't get away from him fast enough."

On May 3, MacDonald made it official and gave the 431st to the former castaway from the Flying Knights. He was promoted to major shortly after that. Twenty-three years old now, he was a field grade with his own squadron. He set about running it with ruthless efficiency and a rigid devotion to regulations. He was hard on the men, pushing them as intensely as he pushed himself. In fact, some in the squadron later recalled his asshole quotient increased after he took command, making him less popular than ever.

It didn't matter. He worked furiously to help the green replacement pilots get up to speed. He personally flew with many of them to assess their skills. If he didn't like what he saw, he told them. This was a butcher's war, and there was no place for weakness in McGuire's squadron. As McGuire got the feel for his new leadership role, MacDonald was there to mentor him, offer counsel, and guide him along. Though they mixed like oil and water, MacDonald knew Tom was a pure tiger in the air.

McGuire never fit in as a peer and was always most comfortable when in a position of superiority to those around him. It was part of the fuel that drove him to be the best at whatever he was doing—be it playing clarinet or shooting down Japanese. Now, as the senior officer in the 431st, he didn't have to. He was the man who rode herd on the rest of the team, who used the natural barrier of rank to keep distance between himself and the other pilots. It was as much a defense against rejection as it was military propriety. It was also his way of insulating himself from the grief when somebody didn't return. For a man with such an extraordinarily prickly personality, he remained deeply emotional. The responsibility for their well-being weighed heavily on him. At times as operations officer, when pilots failed to return, he took it personally, as if he had sent them to their deaths by selecting them for the day's flight roster. The squadron's first sergeant talked to him about it, seeing at times it was eating away at McGuire. When he pointed out that somebody would be filling in those duty rosters whether he did it or not, McGuire nodded and agreed. Then he added, "But it doesn't make it any easier."

The rank and position of authority gave him the distance he needed to keep functioning. He'd never be one of the guys—he was always the kid looking in at the warmth of friendship and bonds with a mix of puzzled resentment and envy. Now, he didn't even need to try. His place was at the top.

As he led the 431st, he wanted two things out of the experience. Most importantly, he wanted the squadron to continue to build on its success. Personally, he thirsted to beat Bong's record. He had arrived in theater in 1943, when Dick was already a triple ace. He'd had a rocky journey since then, but he made the most of every opportunity. He knew he was the better leader, better administrator, and better combat pilot. He wanted the world to know it. Those things may have been true, but Bong was the better hero for home front consumption. Kenney knew it. Whitehead knew it. Tommy McGuire, the kid from the broken home who never found a way to connect, did not.

Two days after leading the 431st to Hollandia, McGuire's squadron escorted a B-24 raid against Biak Island. Biak was a volcanic spit of land jutting out of Cenderawasih Bay on the western end of New Guinea. The Japanese had built an airfield complex there, and MacArthur planned to seize it as the last major jump in the New Guinea campaign. Take Biak, and Kenney's pilots could support the Navy's Central Pacific drive with long-range bombing strikes against Japanese bases in the Palau Islands. More important, Biak would give Kenney a springboard to the southern Philippines. But first, it had to be captured, a task that fell to the 41st Infantry Division.

The Japanese defended Biak with over twelve thousand men and dozens of Zero fighters the Imperial Navy redeployed to the theater after the post-Hollandia collapse of the Japanese Army Air Force. The Army's units were shredded at Wewak and dying on the vine, or scattered and disorganized on primitive strips in westernmost New Guinea. They would offer only feeble resistance in the final months of the campaign.

As McGuire led the 431st to Biak at high altitude, the squadron encountered four Japanese fighters. The ace led his men down in a slashing attack, taking deflection shots at one Oscar before climbing away and returning for another run. Five months he'd been waiting for this opportunity, and he was not going to blow it. As he reentered the fight, he got behind one of the Japanese fighters and closed the range. Minimal deflection, perfect setup. He pulled the trigger on his control yoke and felt the vibration of his cannon and four machine guns. The Japanese fighter burst into flames, spewing oil, which splattered onto McGuire's windscreen and obscured his view. The fighter fell into the sea, witnessed by other men in the fight.

The Florida Yankee was back.

Two days later, during another escort mission, this time to a Japanese base at Manokwari, McGuire's men tangled with four Japanese interceptors they identified as Nakajima Ki-44 Shokis. This was a late-generation radial engine Army Air Force fighter designed as a fast-climbing bomber destroyer. Till then, the Japanese had deployed them only in the Dutch East Indies and the China-Burma-India theater. They were faster than even the latest Ki-43 models and could dive almost as quickly as the P-38.

Numbers and pilot quality made all the difference that day, though it could have been an ugly disaster since the Ki-44s got the drop on the Americans for a change. Patrolling high above the P-38 top cover, they dove to the attack from McGuire's three o'clock. At eighteen thousand feet, the Americans were used to seeing the Japanese below them, not above. The sudden attack surprised McGuire, and for a moment he didn't react or issue any orders.

But the Japanese had made a fatal mistake. Instead of hitting the 431st first, diving through the squadron and continuing after the bombers, their leader went straight after the B-24s. They blew past the 431st right in front of them, which put their tails to McGuire's men. A split second later, McGuire recovered from his surprise and the squadron skinned tanks and dove after the Japanese.

Tommy caught up to the Japanese, picked out a Ki-44, and hosed it down. His first burst flayed its wings and fuselage, sending up hit sparks across its aluminum skin. A moment later, the aircraft exploded right in front of Tommy. The blast sent the pilot flailing upward—McGuire saw him clearly as he sailed upward over the roiling explosion. As he fell, he deployed a parachute. Tommy had never seen a Japanese pilot hit the silk. The man drifted down into Cenderawasih Bay.

The rest of the Japanese pressed after the bombers. That day, the Flying Knights were flying close cover for the B-24s. They caught the remaining Ki-44s and destroyed three of them. The others fled.

In two days of combat, McGuire ran his score to eighteen kills, which tied him with Jay Robbins as leading active ace in New Guinea. MacArthur's press corps ignored him. The people back home had no idea there was another contender for the crown.

37

The Battlefield Tourist

June 26, 1944
Hollandia, New Guinea

Charles MacDonald floated on his back in the little stream that ran behind the 475th's camp and reveled in the cool water. It wasn't even noon and the temperature hung just below eight-six degrees, with so much humidity that the men sweated through their khakis in a matter of minutes. They all smelled foul—though Tommy McGuire's funk was legendarily awful—and the humidity ensured they all battled heat rashes, jungle rot, crotch rot, and even fungus in their ears. The longer they wore headphones on missions, the more likely they'd return with something sprouting in their earholes.

Showers had yet to be built near enough to the 475th's camp to make it worthwhile to use them, so the men got clean in the stream. Not that this was always such a great idea. Who knew what lay upstream in a place still dotted with the rotting corpses of their enemy?

Mac long since learned to conceal his emotions from his men. He came across as even-keeled. Few ever saw him truly angry. He'd laugh, but not the all-in sort of belly laughing that Wally Jordan could elicit from Gerald Johnson. But if somebody were to look closer, really look into Mac's eyes, they would see what he could not conceal. There was a darkness in him, a profound and soul-weary sadness that his iron self-discipline kept off the rest of his face. Was it being separated from his wife and infant son? The baby had been born after he left for New Guinea, so he'd never seen his boy. Or was it the onus of command? Sending boys barely men to their death day after day took a toll on anyone. Or was there some greater life event that left Mac clouded with that darkness? Nobody knew, and nobody asked. Those who didn't look closely enough or lacked the emotional intelligence to see deeper into their commander chalked it up to aloofness. The professional officer's reserve while surrounded by men just in for the duration. That sadness didn't elude everyone. P. J. Dahl saw it. And when he could, he quietly looked after his commander as he had back in Sydney when the partying and women made Mac so uncomfortable.

He scrubbed himself in the stream's lazy current, an awkward smile on his face. Where Johnson and Bong possessed warm smiles, Mac was cursed with the uncomfortable grin of an introvert. He always looked ill at ease, especially in front of the camera. Still, he was a handsome, trim, and tall man, though his longish hair was prematurely receding. Stress and genes were the curse of many out there in New Guinea.

He finished washing, taking his time to dry off, and put on a freshly laundered set of khakis. In minutes, he was already sweating through the fabric, feeling the funk and film of slime that defined life in the primeval tropics. Boots on now, he traipsed through the half-dried mud back to camp. In New Guinea, it was either pouring rain or had just rained with the spongy ground drying out, or was so dry that sheets of dust blew through the camp, coating everyone. Their sweat was like glue to that powdery dirt. Staying clean was an impossible task, so the interlude between feeling human again and feeling filthy lasted minutes, at most.

He reached the command shack, opened the screen door, and sat down with his deputy group commander, Meryl "Smitty" Smith. Neither was flying this day, though the 432nd Squadron was out escorting the new A-26 Invader strafer bombers the 3rd Attack Group had just received.

The two officers knocked out some admin work, then settled down to wait for the boys to return. Smitty and Mac often played checkers together, and they broke out the board to pass the time. Overhead, the sound of a P-38 filled the air. A lone Lightning usually meant a mechanical abort, so few in the camp paid it any mind that day—at least until it landed.

At the airstrip, the P-38 swung into the pattern and touched down gently, kicking up a swell of dust behind its tricycle landing gear. The ground crews waiting the return of their planes did a double take. The Lightning's nose was decorated with twenty-eight Japanese kill flags. Everyone knew Bong's plane, but they also knew the ace had been gone for more than a month. Was he back?

The Lightning reached one of the 475th Squadron's flight lines, but the ground crew waved him off and wouldn't let him park. The pilot turned the plane and taxied off, finding a spot elsewhere. Curious onlookers watched as a lanky, tall pilot unfolded himself out of the cockpit. No way was his silhouette mistaken for the fireplug of Bong's shape.

Who was this guy?

The pilot shucked off his helmet, revealing a balding head. He was middle-aged, handsome in a low-key way. He looked around at the planes parked nearby, eyes roaming across the nose art of bombers and fighters alike. They were vulgar to him. Appalling, really, especially one nearby craft named *Fertile Myrtle*. He judged the naked woman painted on the nose by the ground crew with the eye of a moralist and the rich Eastern elite's appreciation for art. They were crude and pornographic. He wrote later in his diary how the sight of the aircraft painted like that "nauseated" him.

Not long after landing, he made his way to Charles MacDonald's headquarters shack, where he knocked on the screen door. Mac and Smitty were locked in their game of checkers, hunched over the board, and lost in thought.

Absently, Mac said, "Come on in."

The tall man entered, Mac and Smitty stood up, half listening as he introduced himself and shook their hands. The visitor wore no insignia, just a plain set of khakis. Mac mentally brushed him off as yet another civilian visiting the front without a clue to the nature of combat flying.

Mac and Smitty sat back down and returned to their game of checkers. The new guy looked on, a little nonplussed by their reaction. This was anything but what he expected. After all, he was the most famous American.

"I've come to learn about two-engine fighter operations. I've been sent by General Hutchison," the visitor said.

Mac groaned inside. He'd seen tech reps and civilian know-it-alls blow through New Guinea before. None had asked questions that even hinted at a basic knowledge of combat flying. Since they were sent by generals on high down to them, they were fools who needed to be suffered. Nobody wanted to talk to them.

The game resumed. Smitty, content with letting his commander handle this stupid intrusion, stayed quiet. The newcomer looked on. Mac gave him side-eye, assessing his rank-less uniform. No wings. Not of the brotherhood.

At length, Mac finally asked, "What did you say your name was, and what phases of our operations are you interested in?"

The visitor said, "Lindbergh. I'm very much interested in comparing range, firepower, and your airplane's general characteristics with those of single-engine fighters."

Mac made a move on the checkers board, then considered this response as he waited for Smitty's turn. These were all things that would be really tough to explain to a non-aviator. Flying was the only way to show him.

"Are you a pilot?" Mac asked.

"Yes."

This surprised the quiet CO. He looked up and studied the visitor more closely. Blue eyes, tan face, full lips. "Wait. Not *the* Charles Lindbergh?" he said at length.

"That's my name."

Mac must have nearly fallen out of his chair.

What the hell is Lucky Lindy doing in my shack, and why didn't anyone from higher up tell me to expect him?

Smitty's eyes rose from the checkers board, and he gaped. They went from mild annoyance at the intrusion to starstruck. Lindy was nearly every pilot's childhood hero, the first man to fly solo across the Atlantic. His airplane, the *Spirit of St. Louis*, was a symbol of their generation.

A few minutes worth of conversation confirmed his bona fides as one of the brotherhood. Lindbergh had been an Army Air Service fighter pilot long before he was made famous by the Atlantic flight, the kidnapping and murder of his infant son, and the highly controversial German-leaning, anti-Semitic speeches he gave as part of the prewar Isolationist movement that opposed giving aid to England. It was the latter that prompted President Roosevelt to block Lindy's return to the Army Air Force. He'd resigned his commission as a lieutenant colonel in the reserves back in 1939. As retribution for opposing the president's Lend-Lease program, he would not be allowed to wear the uniform again.

Lindbergh found other ways to serve. He helped set up bomber factories at places like Willow Run. He performed high-altitude experiments in P-47s. Currently, he served as a tech rep for United Aircraft Corporation, working to make sure the F4U Corsairs were optimally employed in the Pacific. He'd quietly departed the States for the Solomon Islands earlier in the spring, flying ground-attack missions with several Marine units. If the president didn't want him in the Army Air Force, fine. He'd found another way to serve his country and get into combat.

That said, he didn't have any business being in New Guinea. He'd leveraged his fame to get the Navy to issue him orders to report to General Whitehead. Once in Australia, he talked his way into New Guinea, where Wurtsmith gave him an hour's worth of flight training in a P-38 at Nadzab. His excuse coming forward like this was that he wanted to study twin-engine fighter operations, but the fact was, the company he worked for had no such fighter type in production or in the development pipeline.

He was freelancing, pure and simple. There were no Japanese fighters left around the Solomon Islands, a fact that disappointed him. Though he'd been an aeronautical engineer for years, under his double-breasted suit beat a fighter pilot's heart. More than anything, he didn't want to watch the war from the sidelines without getting a shot at air-to-air combat. It didn't matter to him that he was a civilian; pure and simple—he came to New Guinea to shoot down Japanese planes.

Mac had no idea how Lindbergh had talked his way into the theater. Instead of going to General Kenney's HQ, he leveraged his prewar friendship with Whitehead and went to see him to get the green light. Whitehead turned out not to be expecting him, and was away from his HQ anyway, but Lindy still was able to get the support of Wurtsmith and Hutchison to reach Mac's little command shack at Hollandia. Had Mac known this was how his visitor had played the game, he may not have said what came next.

"If you really want to know what we can do, the best way to find out is to fly with us on some missions."

Lindy grinned and replied, "That's just what I want to do."

Mac asked him, "We've arranged for a four-plane anti-boredom flight for tomorrow to Jefman and Samate. Can you go?"

"Yes, indeed."

As the squadrons returned from their assigned missions that afternoon, the pilots drifted into the shack as word spread Lucky Lindy was in their midst. Tommy McGuire, who'd hero-worshipped Lindbergh ever since he was a young boy, rushed to meet him as well. An impromptu bull session began as the pilots warmed to Lindbergh's presence. He was of them, an older-generation fighter pilot, to be sure, but he'd flown the modern planes and spoke the language. They spoke candidly of the war as night fell, discussing everything from technical aspects of the P-38 to the fights they'd had with the Japanese.

The men told Lindy they would get him kitted out. He would need a pistol, jungle survival gear, and other equipment. McGuire added, "It helps to take along a few chocolate bars. This target is six hundred miles away and it is a mighty long trip going and coming."

Lindbergh listened intently, then excused himself to go back to General Hutchison's headquarters, where he was supposed to bunk down. As soon as he left, Smitty looked at Mac and exclaimed, "My God, he shouldn't go on a combat mission! When did he fly the Atlantic? Must have been 1927 and he was about twenty-five then. That would make him at least forty-two years old now, and that's a lot too old for this kind of stuff."

Mac, who like the other pilots was probably more than a little starstruck, replied, "Well, he doesn't look that old."

Then he turned to McGuire and asked, "Tom, will you fly on his wing so in case anything turns up you can take care of him?"

The idea of riding herd on his childhood hero tickled Tommy, who answered, "Sure thing. I'd like to see how the old boy does."

After dinner, Smitty and Mac drove up to Hutchison's headquarters shack to talk the mission over. They suggested to Lindy that he stay with the 475th that night since the mission would require a predawn launch. Lindbergh agreed and headed back with them. They settled in at the group's headquarters shack, chatting amiably about Lindy's role with United Aircraft Corporation and his time working on the F4U Corsair program. Many of the group's pilots arrived to join in the skull session, letting their guard down as Lindbergh spoke their language. They thought Lindbergh was in their corner, one of them. He wasn't. He listened to their tales and was shocked at the way they conducted the war out here in New Guinea. His was a civilian's vision of a clean and honorable war, where the enemy needed to be killed, but their essential humanity must always be respected.

When the pilots talked about the way the Japanese shot American crews who had taken to their parachutes, some of the 475th's pilots said they felt no qualms about doing it to the Japanese in return. "The Japs started it. If they want to play that way, we can too," one of the pilots told Lindy.

The conversation lasted well past midnight. At one point, Lindbergh asked about the three silk Japanese battle flags that hung in the shack. They were war trophies, taken from the bodies of dead Japanese soldiers. Lindbergh didn't like that. He liked it even less when the men explained the going rates for such booty. A Samurai sword could fetch upward of seven hundred dollars, while the battle flags went for only about thirty.

That chatter soon drifted into a discussion of prisoners of war. Lindbergh was shocked to hear how often American soldiers refused to take prisoners, shooting them instead. The pilots shared gossip that widespread massacres took place in other areas of New Guinea. The pilots talked of some of the Japanese atrocities that prompted such retaliation, which Lindbergh saw only as a weak justification for murder.

The next morning, Mac gave a final briefing to the flight. They'd go patrol from Mawi Bay to the Japanese airstrips around Jefman Island. With luck, they'd perhaps catch a few Japanese planes in the air. Lindbergh was eager and didn't tell the Angels that Whitehead's

HQ wanted him to stay away from any aerial encounter with the enemy.

They took off and sped west, climbing with the rising sun on their shoulders. Mac kept a close eye on Lindy, who flew rock-solid formation with the rest of the guys. They found no Japanese planes, just a lot of accurate antiaircraft fire. On the way home, they barge hunted and shot up several vessels.

That night, after the mission, the men sat around with Lindy again, who made no pretense at what he wanted. "I'd certainly like to see some Jap planes in the air, but you fellows seem to have knocked the Jap Air Force out of the sky."

McGuire started laughing. Opportunity was what all true fighter pilots wanted. It was another data point to the pilots that Lindy was one of them. "Stick with us and you'll wear diamonds. We have slow periods, but we keep moving up into them, and we should start striking Ceram and Halmahera pretty soon. We're sure to run into Zeroes there."

Lindbergh didn't fly the next day. Instead, he grabbed his .45 and wandered off into the jungle to explore. None of the 475th pilots wanted to join him—they'd run into too many Japanese stragglers to consider that safe. They warned him, but he ignored their advice and headed off to explore.

That night, talk turned to the war and its conduct again. Lindbergh's sense of moral propriety was again shaken by what he heard. He confided in his diary, "I am shocked at the attitude of our American troops. They have no respect for death, the courage of an enemy soldier, or many of the ordinary decencies of life."

As he was getting ready for bed, one of the pilots chose that moment to show him his personal stash of captured booty. When the group had first reached Hollandia, three Japanese stragglers crept into their camp area one night. Accounts differ as to what happened, but according to Lindbergh, the pilots used their sidearms to kill them. They searched the bodies and found a silk Japanese flag, currency, some letters and postcards. They also found some personal photographs. As Lindy looked them over, he was struck by how young the Japanese soldiers in them were. The officer showing him this stuff thought he'd be impressed. Lindbergh may have shown appreciation, but his internal monologue was far different. "I don't blame them for what they did. What I do blame them for is the attitude with which they kill and their complete lack of respect for the dignity of death."

In a war where the enemy routinely killed, tortured, and sometimes ritually ate Allied prisoners and New Guinea villagers, Lindbergh's sense of Stateside propriety underscored the realities of extended combat experience. Those who survived the daily trauma of this vicious jungle fight became desensitized to the fighting. How could there be respect for the dead enemy when Aussies and Americans alike found their people bound, gagged with their own genitals, eyes cut out, and skinned alive? Combat dehumanized everyone. Lindbergh was a visitor. He judged the men through a lens that in a pristine world of Geneva Conventions and honorable treatment was perhaps appropriate. The war in New Guinea was one without mercy, and the truth was, Lindy's view of conflict probably was out of place in every theater, with every nation. This was a national war for survival, and war made men's hearts ugly. Instead of understanding, he was repelled and judged his nation's warriors very badly. Yet he gave no hint of that at the time, as he chatted amicably with the 475th's members. In truth, he was milking his fame to get the opportunities he wanted in the air.

On July 3, Lindy flew with Mac again on a squadron-level patrol. They found no Japanese planes and took to strafing luggers and barges again—the same sort of thing that got Lynch killed and Bong badly shot up. During the strafing runs, several of the pilots reported critical fuel states and headed for home. Lindy's wingman also ran low on fuel. He pulled up over the strafing patterns and orbited, waiting for the rest of the planes to finish as he tried to maximize his fuel economy. When Lindbergh realized he was gone, he radioed him and asked how much gas he had left.

"About a hundred and seventy-five gallons."

Lindbergh did the math. He had plenty left to get home safely, if he managed it well. He told the pilot to set his engine RPMs to sixteen hundred, set his mixture to "auto lean," and open his manifold pressure. The young aviator did as Lindy suggested and made it home with seventy gallons to spare. When the group checked on Lindy's tanks, they found he had 260 still in his tanks.

That night, Lindbergh talked of his fuel-management strategies to the other pilots. At first, Mac thought the idea was crazy. Leaning out the fuel mixture while keeping the RPMs low and the throttles advanced seemed like a perfect way to foul spark plugs and damage the engine's valves. Isn't this how so many Stateside accidents were caused?

Two days later, MacDonald went to see Lindbergh's plane. The group's mechanics had stripped the engines to see how much damage his fuel strategy inflicted. To everyone's astonishment, the plugs were clean and the valves remained in perfect condition.

That sold MacDonald completely. He became an evangelist of Lindy's technique, realizing that it could extend their range so significantly that it could have strategic implications on the drive to the Philippines.[1]

---

1. Somehow, in most postwar accounts of this bizarre episode, Lindy's presence in New Guinea was totally mischaracterized as his effort to help extend the range of the V Fighter Command squadrons. That was never even on Lindy's radar when he first got into theater, but when the opportunity came up to show the pilots how to better manage their fuel, it became his excuse to get back to the front lines once he was pulled out and sent to Australia the first time. That nuance has been missed over the years, and as a result, Lindbergh's trip to New Guinea has been cast as an altruistic effort to help Kenney's men better fight the Japanese.

Before Lindbergh could fly another mission, word reached Kenney and MacArthur in Australia that Lindbergh had sneaked into combat in New Guinea. Reports drifted into their HQs that he was out hunting with the 475th. Kenney ordered this stopped at once. Colonel Morrissey, the deputy commander of V Fighter Command, flew at once from Nadzab to Hollandia to talk the situation over with General Hutchison. Then he called over to the 475th and told Lindbergh to cease flying combat missions immediately.

He flew back to Nadzab, where a few days later Lindbergh received a message from MacArthur ordering him to his headquarters in Australia. When he got to Brisbane, Kenney met him and was in a mood. He was blunt with Lindy and made no bones about the Navy's order sending him to report to Whitehead's HQ. It was pure subterfuge, and Kenney knew it. He told Lindy that nobody at his headquarters or MacArthur's even knew he was there until reports filtered back that he was flying combat missions with the 475th.

There was an aspect to international law that Lindbergh, the moral purist on such things, had not considered. As a civilian flying combat, he had no legal status as a combatant. The closest comparison would have been if he'd picked up a rifle in the Philippines and fought as a guerrilla. The Japanese handled such situations with particular brutality. Kenney made it clear: Lindbergh would be beheaded if he fell into enemy hands, a victim of the dehumanizing barbarity he'd recoiled at since he arrived in theater.

Lindbergh sweet-talked Kenney, telling him he'd not meant to cause anyone any trouble. He thought his paperwork was in order. The contrition cooled Kenney down, who then relented and said he could go back to New Guinea, provided he didn't fly any more combat missions. Lindy had no desire to go up there just to sit around and told the general as much. Kenney always had a weak spot for those who wanted to get into the fight. He sympathized because he was one of them. But he knew his place and his value to the enemy if he went down and was captured, so aside from very rare occasions, Kenney kept himself to where he belonged—running MacArthur's air war. Yet, he still had moments where all he wanted was to strap on a leather helmet and go after the enemy, as he had in his youth.

So he put in a good word to MacArthur's chief of staff, Gen. Richard Sutherland, and arranged a meeting. Lindbergh played his trump card with the general, telling him he could extend the range of the P-38s in New Guinea to almost two thousand miles. He saw no reason why the P-38s couldn't operate 750 miles from base, fight at full power, then return home with fuel to spare.

Sutherland immediately saw the potential in this, and he took Lindbergh to meet MacArthur. As Lindbergh laid out what he could do, offering to return to New Guinea to show all the Lightning squadrons this technique, MacArthur grew excited: "It would be a gift from heaven if that could be done."

Lindy got his ticket back to combat. In later years, accounts of Lindbergh's time in New Guinea focus on the value his fuel-economy techniques provided to Kenney's Air Force. They often assume that's why he went to the SWPA in the first place. In reality, it was pure chance that he discovered the 475th didn't use the P-38 to the edge of its endurance out of fear of damaging engines, which were in short supply. He returned to New Guinea to teach the other squadrons his technique, as he promised MacArthur. He flew some milk runs with the outfits, who were very conservative with their distinguished guest. But what he really wanted was a chance to get a kill. On July 20, 1944, with Colonel Morrissey as his shadow, Lindy returned to the 475th Fighter Group.

The outfit had just made the jump to Owi Island, next to Biak. The 41st Infantry Division had gone ashore there at the end of May, hoping to capture the airfield complex in a matter of days. Instead, a long and bloody fight ensued in the volcanic ridges overlooking the strip. The GIs faced fierce resistance from the Japanese, who dug out natural volcanic caves and honeycombed the hills with underground passages and concealed fighting positions. The 41st took shocking casualties in frontal assaults against these positions. When another division arrived to help turn the tide, they suffered tremendously as well. The men went without food and water resupply, and some were trapped and surrounded by Japanese troops, who infiltrated around them through the catacombs below. It was one of the most savage, close-quarters battles fought in the Southwest Pacific, rivaled perhaps only by Iwo Jima. In the end, of the twelve thousand Americans thrown into the fight, almost five hundred were killed in action, another twenty-four hundred were wounded, and thirty-five hundred more went down with scrub typhus.

But the airfields were cleared. Even as the fighting still raged in the hills around Mokmer Airdrome, both the 49th and the 475th moved up to use Biak as a forward base against the last Japanese outposts before the southern Philippines.

Lindbergh wanted to see the enemy up close. At Biak, he got the chance. He convinced McGuire, MacDonald, Smitty, and Maj. Claude Stubbs, the group's supply officer, to investigate the Japanese positions in the cliffs above their airstrip. The pilots were not in favor of this, but Lindbergh had a hold on them. If he was up for it, they'd go too.

They drove a jeep to the base of a steep hillside, dismounted, and began walking. Japanese corpses littered the area. Blown apart by artillery, or ripped asunder by bullets, they lay sprawled in death poses, covered in flies and maggots. The smell was indescribable. In places, Lindbergh could see where GIs had pulled gold teeth from the corpses.

They crested a hill and made their way to a network of caves. As they walked, they came across a bomb crater filled with perhaps a half dozen Japanese dead. American troops had dumped their garbage on top of the corpses. Lindbergh stood at the crater's lip, looking down at the dead men covered in trash, and felt a profound sense of moral outrage. Later, he wrote in his diary, "I've never felt more ashamed of my people."

They continued on, passing open graves where American troops had dumped Japanese bodies. Finally, they reached the entrance to the cave Lindbergh wanted to explore. At the mouth, they found a shattered artillery piece concealed by logs. A headless Japanese soldier had been lashed to a pole, decapitated by his own people when he tried to surrender. Lindbergh made no mention in his diary of that spectacle.

They crept inside the cave. More bodies. These men had died by American flamethrower attack, their corpses black and charred. Mac and the other men of the 475th wanted no part of this exploration. They'd seen enough of death and horrors; to be a tourist in such a hellish place made zero sense to them. None of them had even brought flashlights on this escapade, thinking it ludicrous to go inside.

Lindbergh was not to be dissuaded. As they stood in the cave, a spearpoint of light illuminating them from its entrance, the aviator produced a flashlight. He'd planned to go investigate deep into the system all along. Now he explained how he wanted to see the way the Japanese connected the tunnels with aboveground firing positions.

They pressed into the system, stepping over bleached bones, body fragments and broken equipment. Scattered rations, shoes, rifles, and ammunition lay everywhere. The threat of booby traps was on everyone's mind. Still, Lindbergh persisted. Finally, MacDonald had had enough. He turned and left the cave. McGuire went with him, but Lindbergh discovered another tunnel, which he set off to explore with Smitty in tow.

Inside it, they found a makeshift hospital. A Japanese soldier, dead on a stretcher, attracted Lindbergh's notice. He recorded the rumors surrounding this area in his diary that night, "This is the cave where the Japs reportedly tried to surrender and were told by our troops to 'get the hell back in and fight it out.'"

It almost seemed that Lindbergh had picked this cave and took this journey to gather evidence of war crimes against American soldiers, with the men of the 475th his unwitting escorts. He had little interest in Japanese atrocities or their conduct, but he heaped scorn and moral outrage on his fellow Americans. Again and again, he wrote how he was "nauseated" by their behavior.

By the time he was finished with his exploration, night had fallen. The men drove back to the airfield, only to nearly be shot by the sentries defending it, who later told them there were still Japanese troops in those caves. Mac, the reek of rotting flesh thick on him, smiled bitterly. "They're all dead. Believe me."

After passing the checkpoint, the men headed for the nearest stream to scrub off the stench of the dead.

38

The Killing Tourist

July 1944
Biak, New Guinea .

Once Tommy McGuire got over being starstruck at the arrival of his childhood idol, his innate need to needle people and prove his dominance percolated to the surface. The other guys in the 475th had seen this from Tommy before; it was one of the reasons why he remained generally unpopular. Tommy's needling was made especially sharp by the fact that he had a brilliant mind and keen grasp of a person's psychological vulnerabilities, and he knew just where to stick the knife. With Lindbergh, he detected a quiet sense of superiority that some of the other pilots missed. He behaved like a member of the Eastern elite, and the comments he'd made in the late-night bull sessions convinced McGuire he needed to be knocked down a notch.

He began ordering Lindbergh around like a servant, asking him to fetch various items. Lindbergh did it, perhaps not wanting to stir up any further feathers. Already, Kenney and MacArthur were having second thoughts about allowing him to go back up to New Guinea. When he was slated to fly an escort mission to the Halmaheras on the twenty-fifth, the high command balked and forbade it. Then the mission was scrubbed by weather. Lindbergh knew his status was very tenuous. The technique he was supposed to be teaching wasn't anything new: it was laid out in the P-38 tech manuals. As one pilot later said, "Lindbergh didn't teach us anything a half-page memo couldn't do." It was just an excuse to get into combat.

So he suffered McGuire's harassment and needled him back. Tommy was extremely superstitious about his five-hundred-hour cap. It was a filthy, crushed mess by July 1944, but he still wore it all the time. His ground crew knew to always have it waiting for him when he landed after a mission. One morning, Tommy ordered Lindbergh to fetch it for him. Lindy went off, found one far larger than Tommy's, and delivered it in silence. Tommy put it on and looked ridiculous. Volley returned.

The next day, Lindy dared McGuire to go back up into the Japanese defenses overlooking Mokmer. They pushed on farther this time, beyond what Lindy thought were American lines until they found themselves in no-man's land, armed only with their pistols. They found another cave, its entrance studded with machine gun nests. The ground was covered with debris. They stepped inside, going about a hundred feet into the system, noting the many galleries and passages leading off in different directions. At length, as the sun began to set, they came to their senses and withdrew from the area.

Lindbergh flew the escort mission to Halmahera the next morning, the 5th Air Force's P-38s covering almost four dozen B-25s as they hit various targets. Lindy was well protected by the 475th and two of the leading aces in theater. McGuire scored his twenty-first kill that day, though Lindbergh saw no enemy aircraft. MacDonald now had eleven. The rank and file in the 475th were filled with outstanding pilots, aces, and aces-to-be. If a civilian had to be flying in combat, the 475th was the safest place for him.

The next morning, Lindbergh flew again with the 475th on a fighter sweep to the outlying islands of the Dutch East Indies. The last Japanese barrier between MacArthur and the southern Philippines stretched from Ambon Island north to Halmahera. Perhaps 150 Japanese fighters defended the area, but they were scattered, disorganized, poorly supplied, and totally outmatched by the ascendant 5th Air Force. Essentially, the P-38s were mopping up the last resistance on the edges of New Guinea, even as their infantry counterparts did the same in the jungles and caves below.

MacDonald led two flights in search of Japanese fighters that day. Danny Miller flew on his wing; Lindbergh led the second element with Ed "Fishkiller" Miller covering his six. The formation climbed to eighteen thousand feet, heading west as aircraft of the 9th Fighter Squadron, now equipped with P-38s again, made their way through the heavy overcast as well, bent on escorting a B-24 strike to Ambon Island. Wally Jordan led the Knights that day. Weather reconnaissance aircraft reported broken clouds over Ambon, so MacDonald decided to press on, even as the weather worsened along the way.

They reached Ceram Island in the clear, but stretches of overcast obscured vast sections of the view below them. No enemy planes in sight, though they increased speed to 250 miles an hour just in case there were interceptors lingering in the bulging clouds above them.

They followed Ceram's south shore to a Japanese airstrip at Amahai, hoping to find some prey. The runway was bare. They were too high to see if there were any planes hiding in the revetments dotting the area around the field, so they continued on, patrolling past three more Japanese strips with the same result.

At last, MacDonald decided to call it a day. He led the two flights north and began to circle back for home.

Suddenly, the radio filled with excited chatter. Wally Jordan and the Knights stumbled across a pair of fixed-geared monoplanes they misidentified as Aichi D3A Val dive-bombers. In fact, they were Imperial Army Ki-51 Sonia light reconnaissance bombers that had taken off earlier on a search mission for two missing aircraft. Leading the pair was the commander of the 73rd Independent Chutai, Capt. Saburo Shimada. Seven P-38s dove on the two hapless Japanese. The plane flown by Shimada evaded every pass the Americans made. The excitement over the radio turned to frustration.

MacDonald led the 475th toward the fight, even as the Ki-51 continued to dodge and juke the 9th's Lightnings.

"Can't somebody shoot him down?" a frustrated Knight called.

"Goddamn! I'm out of ammunition."

"The son of a bitch is making monkeys out of us!"

Mac called to the Knights and asked them their position. They didn't answer, either too busy or uninterested in having the 475th horn in on their potential kills. Mac deduced they were probably back over Ceram, near Amahai Drome. He went off to get the 475th into the fight.

Mac and the other seven P-38s from the 475th reached Elpaputih Bay near Amahai just in time to see a pair of Flying Knights make another run at the Ki-51s. Jimmie Haislip, a 9th Squadron pilot, nailed one as it ran for the nearby overcast. The other, Shimada's plane, broke hard for the airstrip. The sky over the nearby airstrip blossomed with antiaircraft bursts as Shimada's fellow warriors did their best to help him.

The senior Japanese pilot threw the Ki-51 all over the sky, using its incredible agility and slow max speed to simply outfly the P-38 pilots as they made their trademark, 350-mile-an-hour slashing attacks. He finally ducked into a cloud, evading the last of the 9th Squadron attackers. Out of ammo, the Knights broke off the engagement and climbed for home.

MacDonald dove on Shimada's Ki-51. The Japanese saw him coming and rolled into an incredibly tight left turn just as he got into firing range. Mac banked hard and took a split-second, high-deflection shot at Ki-51, knocking pieces off it. Then he went zooming past, racing for altitude to get into position for another pass.

Danny Miller, sticking three hundred yards behind Mac's tail, couldn't get his nose on the Sonia. Shimada dashed out of the way, and Miller pulled up after Mac after a short burst to get some gun camera film of the aircraft. That left Lindbergh and Fishkiller Miller closing on the Japanese plane.

Shimada suddenly went on the attack, holding his tight left turn until his nose was pointed straight at Lindy's Lightning. The Ki-51 carried two 12.7mm machine guns in its cowling, pitiful firepower compared to the P-38s. Still, the Japanese held his course, guns blazing. Lindbergh opened fire. His 20mm tore pieces off the Sonia. It kept coming. Nose to nose now, they hurtled at each other, eating up the distance in seconds. The Lone Eagle held the trigger down, spraying the Sonia with bullets and shells. Still Shimada held course, even as his engine took hits and began to burn.

It looked to Mac and the other experienced pilots that Shimada intended to ram Lindy. Before they could call out a warning, Lindbergh realized it, too. They were too close. He yanked back on the control yoke. His Lightning leapt skyward. Shimada anticipated and pulled up, too, nose ablaze, Sonia trailing a long column of smoke.

Saburo Shimada missed killing America's most famous hero by ten feet, maybe less. Lindbergh climbed out of the way as Shimada's Sonia stalled and went into a spin. He and his rear gunner rode the plane all the way into the bay below. Neither man survived.

A civilian pilot had just killed two uniformed members of a military service engaged in active, legal combat operations against the United States. For a man who seemed obsessed with the illegal and immoral conduct of his fellow soldiers and aviators, Lindbergh had just entered a legal gray area himself. He didn't give it any thought. More than anything, he wanted a chance to do it again.

Back at Biak, the pilots gathered to talk through what had happened. "The son of a bitch tried to ram me!" Lindbergh exclaimed. The pilots had never heard him swear before.

Miller told him that he saw his cannon shells hit the leading edge of one wing. As they talked it over, Lindbergh concluded he likely killed the pilot during the head-on pass.

That night, the men sat together talking over the day's events. One of the group's characters, Capt. Robert "Pappy" Cline, busted out a ukulele and began singing. Others joined in. Soon, even Lindbergh was singing:

Take me off the alert
I don't want to get hurt
Oh my, I'm too young to die,
I just want to go home.

Lindbergh didn't really want to go home, however. He wanted more kills and talked a lot about getting another crack at Japanese planes. MacDonald figured the chances of another fight to the west were pretty slim. One evening at the end of July, he was sitting in the group headquarters shack, losing a game of checkers to Lindbergh. The phone rang. Danny Miller, the 475th's operations officer, reported in that the mission for the following morning would be an escort mission to Amboina. Medium bombers. If the weather was bad, they would go after Ceram instead.

"Okay, Danny, drop on over," Mac told him before hanging up.

Before he returned to the checkers game, Mac's eye caught the map adorning one wall of the shack. He looked it over, his mind racing. Six hundred miles north of Biak stretched the Palau Islands. These were in Japanese hands and reportedly heavily defended by fighters and bombers. He'd looked the area over many times over the past month, wanting to send fighters sweeps over Koror or Peleliu. But they were so far away, the '38s would have too thin a margin to get home safely.

Except now they could fly almost a thousand miles each way, thanks to Lindbergh's teachings. Mac looked over at Lindy and mentioned that they could get over there with the new techniques.

"We could go to Palau and stay at least an hour."

Lindbergh brightened. "I'd certainly like to go if you can arrange it!"

Meryl Smith was doing chin-ups on a rafter beam, eavesdropping on the conversation. He cut in, "You might as well forget Palau. We've got a mission for tomorrow, remember?"

They talked over the merits of the target for tomorrow. Smith figured there'd be a good chance they'd get intercepted, but Mac disagreed. If they wanted air-to-air action, they'd have to go someplace else.

The next morning, as dawn broke over Biak, the 475th's duty pilots lounged at the alert shack, waiting for the weather birds to report in over Ambon. Some dozed in chairs, others played checkers or cracked jokes in low voices. The phone buzzed. Mac snatched it up and listened. Weather delay. He passed the news to the pilots.

The delay ratcheted the tension up. The men hated this state of stasis, waiting as the minutes dragged by, never knowing if they'd go or stay. For some, they wondered if these would be among their final hours of life.

Lindbergh acted nervous. He made quick, jerky movements that caught Mac's attention. The guy was always full of energy, but was there something more to this? The wait was probably getting to him, too.

An hour later, the phone buzzed, jarring a few of the pilots out of fitful sleep. Mac answered. Put it down and told his men the weather didn't clear. The mission was scrubbed. He dismissed them, and they headed back to the group's encampment. All except Smitty, Danny Miller, and Lindy.

"Well, what are we going to do?" asked Mac. "Do you want to go to Palau?"

He'd said it half jokingly, but the other three pilots wanted to do it. Mac talked it through. The weather would be bad for at least part of the flight. There were 154 fighters on multiple airfields in the island group. It could get really dicey. That said, Mac occasionally stole a page from his old group commander, Neel Kearby. He later wrote, "Throughout the New Guinea campaign, it had been a favorite pastime for some of us to take a four-ship flight and make a surprise attack on an unsuspecting Jap stronghold."

As long as they didn't get greedy, kept their altitude and speed up, they stood a good chance of doing some damage if the Japanese were flying. They still wanted to do it.

At 0927, they lifted off from Mokmer Drome, turned north, and began a slow climb to eight thousand feet. An hour later, they hit a solid wall of storm clouds. Mac turned left and looked for an opening as rain poured down below the clouds in shimmering sheets. The clouds themselves were laden, dark, and ominous. He considered scrubbing the mission.

A thinning in the cloud layer changed his mind. The flight tightened up. Danny flew practically on his wingtip, Lindy right behind, with Smitty pulling tail-end Charlie. Together, they plunged into the overcast. In seconds, they were consumed by milky darkness, their planes lashed with rain. They could barely make out each other's wings, but they pushed on. Two minutes later, they emerged in a long valley flanked by cumulous clouds that towered thousands of feet above them.

They flew on, weaving in and out of the weather until they finally broke through it. Ahead and below, all they saw were cotton-ball clouds and the brilliant blue of the vast Pacific.

At noon, they sighted the Palau Islands, thanks to Mac's exceptionally accurate dead reckoning. They climbed to fifteen thousand feet, passing over Peleliu as they made their way from airfield to airfield, hoping to catch some unsuspecting Japanese plane down low. But each airfield appeared empty.

Mac looked down at small boats running between the islands, then glanced east to see a wall of overcast just offshore. He began to have second thoughts about the whole endeavor.

What the hell am I doing here?

The question repeated in his brain like a soundtrack. No P-38s had been to Palau. Only heavy bombers and the Navy had visited the area, so the Japanese shouldn't be expecting them, he reasoned.

But his mind would not quiet. He had good reasons to second-guess the mission. He'd not gotten approval from V Fighter Command. He had Lindbergh with him. They could run into numbers they couldn't handle. Bad weather on the return flight could scatter them. The risks were extraordinary. They were out on a very thin limb.

Yet, the scene below seemed serene. They patrolled for twenty minutes, circling around the islands without seeing anything hostile. What felt incredibly risky grew boring. The whole thing looked like a wash instead of a bad call.

Mac did something uncharacteristic of him. He pushed his luck and decided to give the Japanese a wake-up call. He led the flight down in one of Neel Kearby's classic spiraling shallow dives, building speed up without frosting over the windscreens. At eight thousand feet, the four Lightnings roared over Koror Town, the largest settlement in the Palau group. Three flak bursts blossomed around them.

The wake-up call was thus delivered. Yet nobody came up to play. Mac felt a wave of disappointment. This seemed like it would be fertile hunting ground. Instead, it was just another dry hole. They'd had months of those since Hollandia fell and Wewak was left to die on the vine.

They dove for the deck, gaining speed as they raced over Babelthuap, the biggest of Palau's islands. The airfield looked empty, so Mac took the flight down the east coast to hunt for shipping. Off to their left, a long swatch of overcast darkened the area. The men kept their eyes on it as they dropped to fifty feet, lest they get bounced by some cagey Zeroes hiding up there.

They raced over a lagoon and mast-hopped over a long sailing yacht. Lindy saw its shocked crew staring up at their Lightnings as he blew over it. Then a decent target materialized. A small coastal convoy materialized ahead of them, chugging north as they sped south. The lead vessel, a lugger of perhaps four hundred tons, drew the entire flight's fire. They shattered its bridge and set it afire.

On to the next one. Several thousand yards south, Mac could see another cargo carrier. He lined up on it, but noticed movement in the air at the southern edge of the convoy. Several thousand yards away, a pair of Japanese floatplanes cruised over the vessels, probably providing anti-submarine warfare support. MacDonald thought they looked like Rufes, the same float-equipped type of Zero that Gerald Johnson encountered over Kiska two years before.

Smitty saw them too and called, "Bandits! Two o'clock high!"

Mac replied, "Should be easy, but heads up."

The floatplanes split up, one headed out to sea, diving for the water, while the other turned toward land with Mac chasing him.

In the third position, trailing the lead element by several hundred yards, Lindbergh apparently didn't hear the radio chatter. He saw MacDonald and Danny Miller drop their external tanks. They splashed into the sea ahead of him even as both P-38s ahead of him suddenly banked right and began to climb.

That's when he saw one of the floatplanes. MacDonald was charging after it as Lindy punched his tanks, switched to auto rich, increased the engine RPM to twenty-six hundred and gave the Allisons forty-five inches of manifold. The P-38 surged forward.

The Japanese pilot saw them coming and poured the coals on, trying to get to a nearby cloud before the Lightnings closed to firing range. He almost made it. MacDonald caught up to him quickly and pinned his gun sight pipper on the Rufe. The cannon and fifties made short work of the Japanese plane. The wing tanks exploded, sending sheets of flame back over the tail. The aircraft dropped into the sea just short of the beach.

At that instant, Lindbergh spotted the other Rufe, fleeing along the water. He radioed MacDonald that he was going after it. Mac told him he and Danny would come around and cover them. Lindy assumed Smith was still behind him, protecting his tail. The truth was, he'd lost sight of his wingman after they strafed the lugger.

Lindy dipped his nose and gave chase to his quarry, eager for another kill. He closed rapidly. The Rufe was almost 150 miles an hour slower than a speeding P-38. It stood little chance. The aircraft filled his gun sight. He held his fire, figuring another few seconds and he'd have a perfect shot.

Movement to his left distracted him. He pulled his eye from the gun sight in time to see the dark shape of a fighter spearing downward. It looked like it was on course to intercept him before he could reach shooting position.

Instinctively, Lindbergh abandoned his run, pulled hard into the incoming fighter in a steep, High-G turn. He snapped out a desperation burst with cannon and machine guns, but the deflection was too high and he missed.

With shock, he realized it was Smitty. How had he gotten over there? He'd assumed the group XO was still behind him. Instead, he'd gone left after the second Rufe the same instant Mac went right to initiate the attack on the first one. Lindy was several seconds behind the fight, his situational awareness bad, causing him to make dangerous mistakes.

Smitty blew past Lindbergh's plane, boring in on the Rufe. He hit with his first shots. The Japanese plane smacked into the water, kicking up a spray of white froth before rebounding into the air. Smith hit it again and it exploded, pieces plunging straight into the waves.

Lindbergh was now behind Smith, following his lead, totally unaware that a Zero had just begun diving on him. Where it came from was anyone's guess. Mac saw it first as he came around to cover the other element after scoring his kill.

He keyed his radio and called a warning.

Lindbergh didn't hear it.

Mac sped to the rescue; Danny tacked onto his tail with a veteran's skill. The Zero wasn't closing nearly as fast on Lindbergh as Mac was on it. The Japanese pilot saw him coming and realized he wouldn't be able to shoot before he came under fire. Discretion was the better part of valor for him, and he pulled his Zero into a near-vertical climb and zoomed into the clouds hovering off the eastern coastline.

Mac and Danny breathed a huge sigh of relief. Another couple of seconds and Lindbergh would have been easy meat.

He ordered the flight to assemble and began a shallow climbing turn so Smitty and Lindbergh could join up. Meanwhile, the three veterans kept a careful eye on the cloud cover, lest the Zero bounce them again.

Right then, a dive-bomber lumbered into view, heading back toward the airfield at Babelthuap after another anti-sub patrol. Mac could see it would pass over the convoy in a matter of seconds. He checked the sky. No Zero. He wanted that dive-bomber. He called to Smith and Lindbergh, telling them to stay high, just under the overcast and cover him and Danny. They sped after the dive-bomber. Mac caught it right in the middle of the convoy, its crew probably tired and totally unaware of the danger. It cost them dearly. Mac turned their aircraft into a wreath of flames. It smacked into the sea, a tail of fire describing its final plunge.

They'd been over Palau for thirty minutes, and the dogfight had consumed considerable fuel. They needed to head home, but as Mac assessed the tactical situation, he decided a straight southern run out of the area was too risky. The sky was clear in that direction. They were down low with at least one Zero in the area. He wanted the protection of the overcast to the east. He led the flight out to sea, intending to put the islands over the horizon before rolling onto a southern course.

The fight had spread them out. Lindbergh and Smith were trailing about a mile behind Mac and Miller, with Smitty off to the Lone Eagle's left in the tail-end Charlie slot again.

"Zero! Six o'clock! Diving on us!" Lindbergh called over the radio. He saw the fighter in the rearview mirror mounted atop the canopy, and it was dropping fast on Smith. The P-38 didn't have the speed to run away, so he shoved the throttles forward and tried to climb into the overcast.

He wasn't going to make it. The Zero pilot had turned the tables on the Americans, using their own slashing tactics against them. Lindbergh broke hard left to try to get a deflection shot on the Zero even as Mac and Danny turned right to circle back and help.

The Zero pilot saw Lindbergh's move and realized the American turned too soon. It was a critical tactical error. He broke off his attack on Smith, who vanished into the clouds a second later.

Now it was Lindy facing the cagey Japanese aviator. The Zero, still above, still diving, twisted to get behind the Lone Eagle.

"Lindy, break right! Break right!" Mac called. He wanted Lindbergh to come straight at his element so he could scrape the Zero off with a head-on pass. Lindy made a split-second decision. He couldn't turn any tighter or climb into the Zero's attack to at least get his guns on him. His premature move ensured the Zero was still too high. If he tried, he'd stall the Lightning. All he could do was follow Mac's order. He rolled right and dove to the whitecaps, pushing the throttles wide. The engines roared as he increased their RPMs over thirty-five hundred. He was at war emergency power, but his right turn put his tail square in the Japanese pilot's sights.

The Zero ate up the gap. He had Lindbergh cold, and the old airman knew it. A fleeting thought of his children and Anne, his wife, filled his mind. His last chance was the armor plate behind his seat. He slumped behind it and prayed Mac would get to him in time.

The Japanese pilot opened fire. Tracers whipped past Lindbergh's fleeing Lightning. The Lone Eagle didn't see them, but Danny and Mac did. They were finishing their 180, circling right of the two planes as Mac finally gained a shot. It was a terrible one—a full 90-degree deflection. He pulled the gun sight pipper across the Zero, overstressing his P-38. The wing spars groaned. The aircraft buffeted. He wasn't quite there. The nose seemed to take forever to pull through. At last, he took the shot.

Lindbergh, still hunkered behind the armor plate, eyes locked ahead, felt a moment of pure clarity. The vividness of the scene struck him, and everything seemed to happen in slow motion. His senses were never more alive than at this moment of near certain death.

Mac's stream of tracers arrowed out and slashed the sky around the Zero. The pilot saw the danger. Danny opened up a second later. The Zero took hits, but the pilot pressed his attack.

Suddenly, Smitty's Lightning flashed out of the clouds, shooting as he dove on the Zero. The Mitsubishi belched smoke and rolled into a dive turn toward Palau.

Fuel critical now, the Americans let him go. Shakily, Mac called to Lindbergh, "Did you catch any of that stuff?"

He held his breath waiting for an answer.

"Can't see any holes," came the reply. "My instruments all read okay."

They turned south and ran straight into another Japanese plane. This one, at their ten o'clock high, crossed right over them as they fled on the deck. They were relieved it did not attack. Their fuel state was critical, even with Lindbergh's technique.

They returned safely to Mokmer Drome just after 1600. They'd been flying and fighting for six hours. Exhausted, sore from sitting on their chute packs and life rafts for so long, they limped off to get some food while MacDonald reported the flight up to V Fighter Command. It didn't take long for it to generate a firestorm. Colonel Morrissey called Mac and told him that Wurtsmith wanted to see him in person the next morning at headquarters.

The following day, the young general unloaded on Mac-Donald. Nobody had approved a mission over Palau. When 5th Air Force got word of the mission, a political dustup ensued. Bomber command had been asking for P-38 escort to Palau for weeks, only to be told the Lightnings didn't have the legs to get there. Now Mac-Donald had made a liar out of his commanding officer.

This may have blown over, but the real reason for the storm was Lindbergh. Taking Lindbergh six hours through a storm front to a Japanese base defended by thirty times their number was an unacceptable risk to a command already jittery over the Lone Eagle's presence in combat. It almost got him killed, which would have demolished countless careers. Surely the press back home would have called for Kenney's head. Whitehead and Wurtsmith, Hutchison, and even Morrissey could very well have been relieved and destroyed by such a mess as well. General Arnold would have been swift with his wrath—that much was for sure—especially after what happened to Kearby and Lynch.

For all Lindy's skills as an aviator, he didn't measure up as a fighter pilot that day. His situational awareness was lacking. He made mistakes. He missed radio calls, and very nearly shot down his own wingman. Despite the three kills they'd scored, Wurtsmith and the 5th Air Force considered the entire escapade a terrible error in judgment by a senior fighter leader, who'd only been promoted to full colonel two months before.

Wurtsmith sent Mac back to the 475th, and for a day it looked like he would suffer no consequences beyond the reprimand he received at HQ. Lindbergh felt genuinely guilty for the mess, writing in his diary that he was just as responsible for the mission as MacDonald was. He probably felt that way because he'd made it clear he wanted a real fight and a chance to get more planes to his credit. The entire mission was set up to give Lindy that opportunity. He decided that if MacDonald suffered any consequences, he'd go to bat for him, probably intending to use his prestige and friendship with Whitehead to smooth things over.

Morrissey called the 475th HQ on August 3 to tell MacDonald he'd been grounded for sixty days. Though he wasn't quite due to go on leave, rather than have him sit in place doing nothing, V Fighter Command decided to send him home. Mac was far too good a combat leader and fighter pilot to destroy over this. At the time, he was the best group commander in theater. Yet, something had to be done. Later, the whole thing was characterized by Kenney and others as a tongue-in-cheek sort of punishment. MacDonald was happy to go home and see his son for the first time. The truth was, the Palau flight stained his career permanently. Whether Lindbergh tried to help MacDonald or not is unknown, but if he did try, it didn't help. Mac would never be promoted again. He packed up, said goodbye to his men, and headed for home.

Lindy stayed. After Mac left, Lindbergh moved out of his tent and bunked with McGuire over in the 431st's area. He and McGuire had developed a mutual respect. Neither gave any quarter when it came to practical jokes, but they respected the fact that each gave as good as he got. Besides, Tommy continued to let him fly combat missions because nobody issued an order stopping them. For the next several days, Lindy led White Flight in the 431st on several long-range escort missions, including one where the Japanese intercepted the raid. Several P-38s were lost, and Lindbergh experienced close calls on a number of occasions.

Finally, Kenney personally flew to Biak and ordered Lindbergh out of combat on August 13. Lindbergh protested repeatedly, and kept protesting as he was sent back down from Biak to Nadzab and finally to Australia. Kenney met with him in Brisbane and tried to reason with him, explaining the kind of chaos and harm that would be done to the country and to careers should he be captured by the Japanese and publicly executed. Lindbergh would have none of it. He wanted to fly combat so badly that though he was supposed to head for home, he flew to Guadalcanal and caught a ride up to the Marines fighting in the Central Pacific. He ended up flying ground-attack missions in Corsairs with them until mid September. At least there he was a legitimate representative of his corporation.

Before he left Australia, Kenney and MacArthur implored Lindbergh to not reveal the extent of his combat missions in New Guinea. Both were afraid of the political fallout. Despite the fact that President Roosevelt detested him, Lindbergh remained a hero to countless Americans. His loss would have been a bitter blow to morale. If Washington had learned that he was freelancing with two of the leading pilots in the ace race, it would have caused both generals considerable trouble.

Lindbergh honored their request. He returned to the States satisfied that he'd done his share of fighting. He'd flown fifty missions with the Marines and the 5th Air Force, changed the way the P-38 was employed in the Southwest Pacific—and damaged a good officer's career.

The rest of the summer passed with the ace race in stasis. The last Japanese were swept from New Guinea's skies. Encounters became exceptionally rare, even as the P-38s ranged farther and farther from their bases. McGuire's score was stuck at twenty-one, seven back from Bong. Jay Robbins was his only real challenger for leading active ace in the theater after Mac left. On August 17, 1944, Jay shot down a Ki-43 over the Dutch East Indies. That tied him with McGuire.

The Japanese were caught in a hammer-and-anvil war against Kenney's Air Force and the Navy's carrier task groups running wild in the Central Pacific. In eight months of fighting, the Japanese lost thousands of aircraft and aircrew. They lacked the industrial base for their production to make up the losses, and the training schools could not keep pace with the human cost of the Pacific War, either. The Japanese were simply bleeding out. Now they husbanded their last reserves to make one final stand in the Philippines. They would meet the Americans with the full force of the Imperial Navy, more than half a million combat troops and fifteen hundred aircraft.

MacArthur was coming—of that they had no doubt.

39

Return to the St. Francis

End of August 1944
Union Square, San Francisco, California

Maj. Richard Bong stood in Union Square, no longer anonymous, no longer the Midwest farm boy. The regal edifice of the St. Francis rose before him as it had when he first arrived in San Francisco two years ago. Back then, his wallet held the last nineteen dollars to his name. This summer, when he flew back to Poplar at the end of July for his parents' twenty-fifth wedding anniversary, he paid off their mortgage on the farm—two grand—as his gift to them. Even the majestic view of St. Francis felt par for the course now, after staying at the Plaza and the finest hotels in D.C., Chicago, and Los Angeles.

The styles hadn't changed much. As he watched people coming and going through the square, he saw perhaps more men wearing cuffed pants. It was one of many little signs that signaled the home front was getting restless, and the sacrifices made for victory would not be tolerated forever. He'd seen those little signs all over the country that summer when he gave speeches on his bond tour.

People needed to be reminded that for all the dear-won Allied victories, the Germans and Japanese still had plenty of fight. It would take the country's full measure to get tanks to Berlin and Tokyo. He understood his role in that. He was a symbol whose words, however awkwardly delivered, carried heft to his audiences.

He headed for the St. Francis. The Mural Room, once long out of his price range, awaited. He was so famous now that he used a pseudonym when he checked into a new hotel, hoping that would throw the media off. It didn't really work. His baby face and boyish grin were known from coast to coast. Crowds mobbed him for autographs wherever he went. He couldn't eat dinner in a Hollywood club without being pulled onstage and kissed by a starlet.

On Mother's Day in Chicago, he did a radio show with his mom. Robert Johnson's and Don Gentile's moms were also guests. It was a trifecta of the best combat aviators and their mothers saluting the familial bonds that would sweep America to final victory. Dick sounded stilted as he read his lines. He was no actor, but most saw that as part of his charm.

He walked into the St. Francis, people bustling this way and that. Most men wore the uniform now. The hotel became the hub of last hurrahs after Pearl Harbor, and as the ranks swelled with draftees, so did the men bound for combat wanting a last memory of home in this amazing place. Those who couldn't afford a room came to simply ride the elevators to take in the view of the city.

He didn't really want to return to combat. This summer had been the happiest of his life. At least the parts at home were. He carried the memories without nostalgia—he was too much of an internalizing Midwestern Swede for such sentimentality. But they were beautiful memories nonetheless.

He took the elevator ride to his room, the sweeping vista of the city romantic and breathtaking. He wished Marge were there to share it with him. He'd last seen her at the train station in Superior, her blue eyes wet with tears as she waved her goodbye. He stood on the step of the Pullman car, drinking in his last look at her. Then he turned and went off to find his berth. It was a Hollywood goodbye at a time when he was an A-list guest on the Hollywood party scene.

The elevator stopped, and he found his room. To hell with convention, he should have brought Marge. They could have shared their final moments before he returned to battle here. That would not have been proper, though, and surely there would have been a scandal over it back home. So they had to make do with their train platform moment.

He'd decided that summer his reticence to get married in wartime could be worked around. On the same day Gerald married Barbara in June, Dick parked the family car and reached across Marge's lap to open the glove compartment. It was locked, and he fumbled with it, trying to get the fussy thing open. When at last he did, he produced a pink velvet ring box and handed it to his girl. Marge opened it to see a diamond shining up at her. He said a few words, spoken from the heart. There were tearful affirmations. Dick lifted her hand and gently slid the ring on her finger.

They were engaged now, and the wedding would happen after he returned from combat. He was still determined not to make Marge a wartime widow if he should fall in battle.

He knew there would be more battles in his future, though earlier in the summer, when Arnold ordered him to the Pentagon, he didn't appear eager to go back to the SWPA. During that trip, he ran into Don Gentile and Robert Johnson. Don was affable, quick to tell him how much trouble Dick had been giving him in the race. He and Johnson, though, talked about going back. The Jug ace felt he'd done his part and wanted to stay home. Dick told him the same thing. He'd be home selling war bonds too. "It's a helluva war," he said to Johnson.

Perhaps he'd told Johnson that because he'd just been to see Tom Lynch's family. He flew to Pennsylvania without warning, hoping to elude the press that hounded his every move. He sat in Tom's childhood home, recounting their friendship to his family. Gradually, he circled closer to the final flight. He explained what happened as gently as he could, the pain of the moment stamped on everyone's faces. When he finished, Tom's mom asked, "Is there any hope my son survived?" She was still clinging to the War Department's words that he was missing in action. A slender lifeline, those words. It stalled the finality of loss, pushed the grieving down the road. Dick knew this and did not wish to see them suffer. They needed to know the truth. Tom could not have survived that explosion and fall.

He shook his head and replied, "No. There is no chance he could have survived."

It was the last thing they wanted to hear. But it was the truth.

Away from combat, leaving that meeting, who would want to return to such trauma? No, he was done with it, just as he had told Robert Johnson.

While in D.C., Arnold offered him a regular commission. It was a chance to stay in after the war, be a part of shaping the peacetime Air Force. Bong made no commitment. He still clung to a vision of a small-town life in Poplar. Maybe that wouldn't be enough after all he'd experienced, but for now that was his plan.

In the end, he didn't stay home, though he was sorely tempted to do so after a visit to Lockheed's factory in Burbank, California, gave him a glimpse of the future of fighter aviation. There, at what later became known as the "Skunk Works," Lockheed's best minds were working to perfect a jet fighter capable of speeds only discussed in comic books. It was strictly Buck Rogers stuff. Dick wanted to be a part of it as a test pilot, at least for the duration of the war.

Instead of asking for a slot in the jet fighter test program, Dick went to a new AAF gunnery training school. At first, he struggled. Deflection shots were the bane of his combat flying, and in Texas that weakness was revealed again. But then, it all clicked. He started nailing targets from almost any angle. The training was so good that many times he said that if he'd had it before going to New Guinea, his score would be double.

Perhaps part of him wanted to test these new skills. Perhaps he was defined by his ace of aces status and did not want to surrender it to Tommy McGuire or any other contender. It was who he was. If somebody beat him, what would define him then?

He was going back into combat. He couldn't explain it. To most civilians, it didn't make any sense at all. He'd done his part. He had the pick of any job in the Air Corps. But the truth was, being out of combat made him miss it. It was what he knew, where he was at his best.

It was where he belonged, even if he remained an outsider to those who flew beside him. He hadn't finished his second tour anyway; it had lasted only three months instead of the usual year or more. Returning, he reasoned, was the right thing to do.

His stay in San Francisco was a short one. Hamilton Field soon called him. A seat opened on a flight west. He packed his things and headed back out across the Pacific.

Only a few days after Bong's flight left, Maj. Gerald Johnson checked into the St. Francis with his wife, Barbara. They were tanned and radiant, happily learning how to be husband and wife as they adventured around the country together. The press largely ignored them, which suited Gerald fine. He coveted his privacy and wanted every nonworking moment to be focused on Barbara. They'd gotten to know each other as never before while driving from Oregon to Kansas and back. For a glorious few weeks, they lived together at Leavenworth, Barbara getting a glimpse of what life would be like for an Air Corps wife.

Gerald showed her the St. Francis, as Dick had wanted to do with Marge. That night, they dined in the Mural Room with Air Corps friends, the table filled with laughter and happiness. The hotel photographer snapped their pictures to memorialize the moment. Barbara looked stunning and at ease in the opulence. Until this summer, she'd never even been out of Oregon. She was a tomboy who climbed mountains, learned to ski when city kids were learning to ride bikes. As a nurse trainee at OHSU, she'd seen the harshest side of the war. The wounded convalescing, the psychiatric casualties. The infirm needing care in their final hours. It took a rugged heart to see those days through.

In San Francisco, on her major's arm, a feminine side awoke in her. She loved the whirlwind of the St. Francis. They drank and celebrated their marriage and new life together. They rekindled friendships and made new ones in that short stay. The tomboy became a laughing, happy partner to her mate. The old adage that anyone can make colonel, but it takes a great wife to make general? Barbara was exactly who Gerald needed to reach for that star someday.

One morning, Barbara awoke feeling dizzy and sick. At first, she just assumed it was payback for having too much fun the night before and tried to ignore it. She got up, went into the bathroom, and fainted. Gerald rushed to her side, scooped her up, and laid her on their bed. A quick call to the front desk, and the hotel doctor rushed to their room. He examined her carefully before giving his diagnosis.

Gerald hovered nearby as the doc observed her. "My dear," he finally said. "You're pregnant. You've got morning sickness."

The news hit Gerald like a thunderclap. He'd become a husband. Now he would be a father. The two goals of his young life—he'd achieved them despite the chaos and upheaval the war had thrown in his path.

He doted on Barbara for the rest of their stay at the St. Francis. If she needed something, he dashed to retrieve it so she didn't have to get up. He brought her food, rubbed her feet. Loved her with an open heart.

Internally, he was torn. This summer had been a dream, the happiest of his life, just like Bong's. Yet, a small part of him felt guilty. He knew the men he'd left behind were locked in the violence and horrors he'd seen in New Guinea. Being home, enjoying what he called "dual sack time" like a peacetime newlywed, made him feel like those men who had stayed behind and avoided overseas duty. He was no shirker. He knew that, but he could not shake the feeling. His place, at least as long as the shooting continued, would be out with the men doing the fighting. Anywhere else and he would feel a sense of shame.

I will never be satisfied unless I am back overseas with the real soldiers.

The bond he'd known in combat had come to define Gerald just as Dick's ace of aces status defined him. It was the bedrock of his character now, and even the realization of his closest-kept prewar dreams would have to take a backseat to it. He needed to see this through. Then his heart wouldn't be torn, and he could return to Barbara with no regrets.

A few days later, Gerald kissed his love goodbye one more time. She wept in his arms, unashamed of her display. He held her tight to his uniform tunic. He would return when the war was won. He promised. They parted, Gerald feeling more torn than ever, Barbara feeling utterly alone. That afternoon, she boarded a train home as Gerald's C-54 crossed over the Golden Gate, flying west into the setting sun to the place where aces were made.

40

Reunion

October 8, 1944
Biak Island, New Guinea

Gerald Johnson looked over his two old comrades. Bong looked healthy again. The last time he'd seen him, Dick was emaciated, hurting, and combat fatigued. The summer back home had done him good. Tommy McGuire, on the other hand, looked terrible. He'd gone on leave to Sydney after Lindbergh left the 475th, but by this point he'd accumulated so many combat hours that what he really needed was a long rest Stateside. He returned to Biak in time to see his squadron pack up into a cargo ship in preparation for the next great leap forward. He flew little in September, which helped a bit, yet Biak was anything but restful. In fact, it was rugged and disease ridden. Fresh water was in short supply, as was decent food. The Japanese continued to resist in pockets around the island, and occasional night air raids on Mokmer ensured sleep was a rare commodity. Toward the end of the month, malaria caught up with Tommy. For days he endured chills, 105-degree fevers, vomiting, and diarrhea. Most of the men already suffered from dysentery, and the malaria going around piled on the misery. When the fever broke and his delirium ended, McGuire looked wrung out and skeletal.

Still, he was game to fly, especially now that the band was back together. Bong's reappearance in theater pushed him out of bed and to the flight line. He was six back from Dick's score. A couple of fights and he knew he'd be able to pull even.

Though they were rivals, Bong and McGuire treated each other cordially and never lost sight that they were on the same side. Gerald was something else to the other two, almost like a neutral party. He was Bong's former squadron leader, Tommy's old friend. After all that had happened over the past year since they'd last been together, the truth was they were happy to see each other. The faces in their old units had changed considerably. Most of the pilots of 1943 were long gone—dead, missing, or back home. The few remaining old hands looked as worn out as Tommy. All, except perhaps Wally Jordan, who still commanded the Flying Knights and somehow retained his irascible energy.

McGuire still commanded the 431st Squadron. Johnson returned to the 49th Fighter Group as its deputy commander. George Walker, the CO, was in poor health. He was a capable administrator and ran the group well, but he was in no shape to lead from the tip of the spear on anything but the most important missions. Johnson would be expected to fill that role.

Bong arrived in theater in mid-September, initially assigned to 5th Air Force HQ. Two days before this reunion at Biak, General Whitehead sent him back to V Fighter Command's operations section. His role in theater and how much combat flying he would be allowed remained an open question.

Though they all had different roles and units, circumstance threw the three aces back together again at Biak. They took advantage of it and flew a combat patrol together that morning, swinging around Biak and south, down to Owi, and back. It was the first of many times they found a way to do this. Later, these missions would be dubbed "Fat Cat Flights" by other fighter pilots in the area.

The short flight whetted their appetites once again. Gerald returned disappointed that they hadn't encountered any raiding

Japanese. But this wasn't 1943. The few Japanese bombers remaining in New Guinea flew only at night.

As Gerald settled back in, he saw troubling signs everywhere. The 49th had been in continuous action for two years, and while the pilots rotated home, the ground crews did not. These men were burned and leathery from working under the tropical sun for months on end. They'd endured every imaginable disease, accepting that diarrhea was simply a part of life in New Guinea. They sweated and worked without enough tools, spare parts, or even basic facilities. Hangars simply did not exist in theater. They were as exhausted as Tommy, yet the invasion of the Philippines lay just over the horizon.

It was the same way in many of the old-line 5th Air Force units. The New Guinea campaign ground the Japanese Army Air Force to dust, but the cost to the Americans also had been heavy. For a time at the end of the summer, almost half the 345th Bomb Group's aircrew were deemed non–combat operational and taken off flight duties. Morale dipped throughout the command as the months dragged on with no hope of relief.

Fortunately, the 5th was reinforced by the 13th Air Force, which included several P-38 squadrons and heavy bomber groups equipped with B-24 Liberators. Kenney oversaw both now as the commander of the Far East Air Force (FEAF).

Kenney wanted to use FEAF's heavy bombers to strike a decisive strategic blow against the Japanese before the invasion of the Philippines. The best targets in range were the former Dutch oil refineries at Balikpapan. The best fuel oil in the Japanese empire was produced there, and Kenney wanted to destroy those refineries in hope of choking off that supply right at a critical juncture in the war. Trouble was, the area was heavily defended by crack interceptor units, and every unescorted B-24 raid to the area had suffered heavy losses.

Thanks to the capture of Morotai, Lindbergh's fuel technique, and the arrival of a small number of three-hundred-gallon drop tanks, both P-47s and P-38s could just reach Balikpapan and get home, provided they did not stay over the target more than fifteen or twenty minutes.

On October 10, over a hundred B-24s, escorted by Lightnings of the 475th and 49th Fighter Groups, struck the refineries. The Japanese threw dozens of interceptors at the attacking bombers. The P-38 pilots found themselves overwhelmed with targets. Four B-24s went down over the target area. The Lightnings claimed six fighters in return.

Dick and Gerald had both been slated to fly that mission, but a tooth infection knocked the Oregonian off the flight roster. Bong flew as an element leader in the 9th Fighter Squadron instead, as the group commander, George Walker, led the mission. In the crazy melee over Balikpapan, Bong shot down two fighters in quick succession, running his total to thirty.

The news set McGuire off. Bong had been back for only a matter of days, and already he'd pulled even farther ahead. This after a summer of dry holes. McGuire resolved not to be left out, even if his unit wasn't assigned to these missions. He went to see Gerald and asked him if he could fly on his wing for the next raid. Johnson happily agreed.

On October 14, Dick was back at V Fighter Command headquarters on Owi Island when the Flying Knights lifted off from Mokmer Drome. They refueled at Morotai, then linked up with the bombers bound for Balikpapan again. This time, Wally Jordan led the squadron. George Walker, Gerald, and Tommy flew together with the rest of the Knights. It was like old times.

Twenty miles out of the target area, more than fifty Japanese interceptors bounced the Americans from above and behind. The two aces were part of the last and highest flight, which gave them a grandstand view as dozens of Ki-44s and Ki-43s slashed down through the escorts to tear after the bombers. Simultaneously, some stayed high over the Americans, dropping phosphorus bombs into the B-24 formations.

Johnson pivoted his flight around and climbed for a group of Japanese diving on them. The 9th had just received the newest P-38 variant, the L model, which incorporated hydraulic boost controls. This made the Lightning considerably easier to maneuver, and the increased performance probably surprised the Japanese.

Gerald and Tommy shot their way through a flight of Hayabusas. When they broke clear out the other side, they turned back to see several planes diving on the B-24s. He went after the closest one as it arrowed for a bomber box. The B-24 gunners laced the sky with tracers, but the two Lightning pilots ignored the danger and chased the Hayabusa right through one of the B-24 formations before Gerald finally ran the Japanese plane down and opened fire. His bullets smacked into the Ki-43, riddling the wings and fuselage. The Japanese suddenly kicked his rudder and slewed sideways. His speed bled off and Gerald overshot him. Before the cagey Oscar pilot could exploit the advantage and rake Gerald's '38, McGuire finished him off with a perfectly aimed burst. The Ki-43 erupted in flames and dropped out of the sky.

Just as McGuire scored the kill, another Hayabusa zoomed past Gerald's P-38. It had just finished a diving pass on the bombers, and the pilot probably didn't see the Lightning. Johnson banked hard and tucked the yoke into his stomach, turning directly behind the diving fighter. He put the gun sight pipper right on the plane's cowling and pulled the trigger. The cone of firepower pouring from the Lightning's nose shredded the fuselage. Cannon shells exploded through the cowling, destroying the engine and setting it afire. Smoke billowed back right into Gerald's canopy. He was so close he could smell the burning oil in his cockpit. A second later, the Oscar exploded.

No time to waste. The fight spilled all around them as the Japanese kept after the bombers. Huge mushroom-shaped plumes of smoke erupted around the B-24s as the strange new Japanese aerial phosphorus bombs detonated. Gerald and Tommy glanced around, searching for the closest target. A Ki-44, running flat-out, whipped by only a few hundred feet below them. McGuire followed as Gerald gave chase, climbing right up the Ki-44's tail. He held his fire until he was so close he couldn't possibly miss. No deflection. Less than a football field away. Johnson triggered his guns. Pieces flew off the Ki-44. It slowed. Johnson feared he would overshoot again. He laid on the trigger, hosing the interceptor with his cannon and fifties. The aircraft couldn't take the fusillade. One minute it was there. The next, it was nothing but a massive fireball that filled the sight from Gerald's windscreen.

He was too close to avoid it. His P-38 plunged into the roiling flames as chunks of metal pinged off his wings and fuselage. He felt the heat on his face as the cockpit filled with smoke. A second later, he broke through the other side, scorched and dinged up, but otherwise unharmed.

McGuire called out another Ki-44 and rolled after it. Johnson covered his six. Tommy closed and blew it out of the sky, only to have two more bounce them from above and behind. One went after Tommy, the other after Gerald. The P-38s had been maneuvering. They were slower and lower than the diving Ki-44s. Both men knew they were in trouble. They couldn't turn and clear each other's tails—there was no time and to bleed speed in a bank would simply play to the Ki-44's agility. They had only one play: dive clear of the attack. Both pilots opened their throttles and pushed the yokes to the instrument panels. The Lightnings fell out of the sky.

They pulled away from the enemies behind them, but lost each other in the process. McGuire went after another Ki-44, which he chased to three thousand feet before shooting it down. At the same time, Johnson climbed back into the fight, taking high-deflection snap shots at Japanese fighters speeding around him. Finally, low on fuel, he turned for home, linking up with McGuire on the way.

Back at Biak, the aces celebrated their victories. McGuire thought he got four, but one went unwitnessed. Johnson scored two, and Wally Jordan got one plus a probable. The Eskimos, as Gerald Johnson, Tommy McGuire, and Richard Bong had long ago been dubbed, had not flown together in over a year, but they were back with a vengeance. Happily, they gathered beside Gerald's P-38 and handed a camera to another pilot. The three men took turns throwing their arms around each other and holding up fingers for the number of kills they'd scored.

The celebrating lasted only until McGuire ran into Charles Mac-Donald, who had just returned from his sixty-day grounding and home leave. When Mac discovered Tommy had been freelancing with another squadron, he put the hammer down and told him never to do that again. He'd learned his lesson from the Lindbergh debacle.

The Balikpapan attacks inflicted heavy damage on the refineries, which the Japanese adeptly repaired. The raids failed to deliver a fatal blow to Japan's oil supplies as Kenney had hoped. It didn't matter. By the fall of 1944, the U.S. Navy's submarine force had ravaged Japan's tanker fleet. No matter how much oil Balikpapan refined, the Japanese simply did not have any way to get it north to the Home Islands anymore. Japan's war machine was already starved of oil, the nation existing on its dwindling reserves. Though the end was in sight—there was no way the Empire could survive the American onslaught—the Japanese intended to fight to the bitter end.

For at least three aces, this may have been welcome news. For in Japan's stubborn refusal to see the writing on the wall, they would have plenty of opportunities to score. The race would soon reach a new fever pitch.

41

"Whatever I Am, I Belong to You."

October 27, 1944
Tacloban Airfield, Leyte, Philippines

Gerald Johnson cut his switches and glanced out of his P-38's cockpit to watch his props swing to a stop. Mud caked his engine nacelles and smeared the wings in slimy streaks. His windscreen was spackled with the stuff. It had indeed been a dicey landing.

He popped the hatch and unstrapped himself, stretching his legs for the first time in hours as P-38s taxied past him to park on the edge of the runway. He glanced around. No dispersal areas. Some super-genius built this strip along a narrow peninsula, half of which was a swamp, so there was no room for revetments and a proper parking area.

Wrecked Navy planes lay scattered at both ends of the strip, bulldozed out of the way by the engineers frantically working to make the field usable. So far, they'd been able to lay about two thousand feet of pierced steel planking, laid over crushed coral. The other half of the strip was nothing but mud.

Gerald got out on the wing just as his crew chief, Jack Hedgepeth, climbed up to greet him. They'd been together since those first days at Dobodura, and they greeted each other warmly. As they stood on the wing together, GIs and Filipino guerrillas began streaming toward their aircraft. Filthy uniforms, faces streaked with grime, boots soiled with mud, they were a motley-looking bunch. In their midst was the legendary Pappy Gunn, who'd broken off oversee-ing the construction of a coconut-log control tower to greet the first Army Air Force fighters to the Philippines.

"How's it going, Jack?" Gerald asked his old friend.

"Got ashore yesterday, sir. Navy's had a hard way. Six alerts last night. We pretty much live in slit trenches."

"Not much sleep?"

"Not here, sir," Jack said, shaking his head.

Down the runway, the other 49th Fighter Group pilots climbed out of their cockpits. The group's ground crew rushed to refuel the birds and check over the six that ran off the runway. George Walker, Wally Jordan, and Dick Bong emerged from their birds and climbed down into the mud. They were quickly mobbed by enthu-siastic GIs.

A jeep appeared, racing up the side of the runway, men giving way to it when they saw the stars glittering from it. Sitting beside the driver was Gen. Douglas MacArthur. Behind him, Kenney looked on at his men.

These were his boys: the 49th Fighter Group, the legendary 7th, 8th, and 9th Squadrons. They were the elite, and right now he needed his best pilots protecting this spit of land from enemy air attack.

The original Philippines plan envisioned a careful jump to South-ern Mindanao, well covered by the fighter units based at Morotai and Biak. But after the Japanese defensive plan for the Philippines fell into the hands of a guerrilla cell on Cebu, MacArthur chose to be more aggressive in hopes of shortening the war. Instead of Min-danao, his troops invaded Leyte in the middle of the archipelago. The Navy covered the landings, as the island lay beyond P-38 range. Now, after a week of furious air-sea battles that saw the first use of kamikaze aircraft, the Navy couldn't remain on station defending the Leyte beachhead indefinitely.

George Walker and Gerald handpicked these first pilots onto the half-built strip at Tacloban. Other fields were being prepared elsewhere, but they were nowhere near ready. Tacloban was it, a tiny toehold surrounded by Japanese-held islands and two hundred enemy airfields. Their task: defend the airfield and the cargo ships offloading supplies, and help the troops fighting their way inland whenever possible.

The pilots met in a cluster beside their P-38s, surrounded by rings of guerrillas, engineers, and curious riflemen hoping to catch a glimpse of the great ace of aces, Dick Bong. A few handed him short snorters. He signed them and handed them back as the ground crews explained the situation.

MacArthur's jeep squeaked to a stop. The two generals dismounted and walked over to greet the Forty-Niners. Wally Jordan looked up to see them coming and nodded at Gerald. He turned and saw the brass smiling happily, making their way through the crowd to shake their hands.

Kenney saw Bong and made a beeline for him. He wanted Dick to stay safe, teach the boys the new gunnery techniques he'd learned, and keep his combat flying to a minimum. Now, he was at ground zero of a first-class chaotic mess. Fifty P-38s against hundreds of Japanese aircraft. It was going to be a bar brawl in the days ahead. Kenney knew a lot of the pilots standing around him would probably die.

Bong saw the look on Kenney's face and disarmed him. "Generals Whitehead and Wurtsmith gave me permission to come on up with the 49th, sir."

Colonel Morrissey walked up beside Bong. He'd flown in from Morotai with the outfit and intended to fight, staff responsibilities be damned. This was a crisis, and the best pilots were needed above Leyte.

Kenney nodded at Dick and asked, "Did they tell you if you can fly combat while you're up here?"

Bong said shyly, "No." Then added, "Can I?"

Even MacArthur laughed at that. It was the sort of élan the emergency required. Bong would have no issues getting in the air at Tacloban.

Tommy McGuire should have been with them that morning. He'd somehow talked Charles MacDonald into letting him go up with the 49th, but en route to Tacloban, he suffered engine failure, which forced him to limp back to Morotai. Even without McGuire, the pilots at Tacloban included some of the best in theater: Johnson, Bong, 7th Fighter Squadron ace Robert DeHaven, and four-kill Oregonian Blev Lewelling. Each man was experienced, capable, and totally reliable. All had flown with George Walker and Gerald since at least early 1944. Morrissey was one of the last of the original Darwin crew. If they were going to be outnumbered by the Japanese, at least the Americans would have the first team in the cockpits.

The 475th was due in next. Mac's ground crews were en route to Leyte in LSTs (large landing vessels), the pilots and planes waiting for the *go* order. At the moment, though, there was no place to put them. Engineers working on the strips elsewhere on Leyte around Dulag were running into serious problems, and Tacloban simply couldn't fit any more planes on it until the second runway was built. That second strip would have to be used as a parking area, at least for the time being.

George Walker and Johnson met with Kenney for several minutes as the ground crews finished refueling their birds. Their general, who had waded ashore with MacArthur a week before, during the first day of the invasion, gave them a quick brief on the situation. The Japanese threw everything they had left against the Leyte invasion force. Battleships, aircraft carriers, kamikazes. The landings triggered the largest naval battle in history. The mopping up was still going on, and while the Japanese fleet was devastated, their air units still had plenty of fight left.

Kenney told them to get into the air and stay there. The Japanese would come to them.

By four that afternoon, the birds were ready to go. The ground crews had taken extra time to scrub the mud off their P-38s. Their guns were loaded with every round that would fit in the ammo bays. Armorers slung five-hundred-pound bombs under the wings. Walker, Johnson, Bong, Morrissey, and seven other pilots took off from the primitive strip, climbed out over Tacloban, and went off in search of trouble. They strafed and bombed Japanese holdouts around Dulag, hoping that would help give the engineers a chance to get the new airfields untracked there. After their runs, they returned to Tacloban, breaking into flights to cover as much airspace as possible. If the past week were any indication, the Japanese would run a few low-level strafing raids against the field just before sunset.

It began to rain over the strip. Sheets of it came down on the men laboring to get it fully operational, adding to their misery. Under the weather, four Japanese Hayabusa skittered along the wave tops, roared over the strip, tracers roping out from their cowlings. Men dove into soggy slit trenches, hid behind jeeps, or fought back with antiaircraft machine guns. The four sped down the length of the field and ran out over the bay.

Walker, Bong, Johnson, and Morrissey caught them as they tried to make their escape. Diving down from fourteen thousand feet, Bong got the first shot at them. As usual, he made his run from dead astern, waiting until he was so close he couldn't miss. This time, he opened fire, knocked pieces off the fleeing Oscar, then overshot him. The new P-38Ls were thirty miles an hour faster than the older versions. They also could dive faster and steeper than the Lightnings of 1943. The old hands were yet to get a handle on the additional performance.

No matter, Johnson pounced on the Ki-43 and blew it out of the air, pulling up after Bong to protect the ace of aces' tail. Behind them, Morrissey and Walker went through the formation, knocking down a second Oscar.

Two left. It was Bong's turn. He rolled back into a gun run, Johnson still on his six. Bong shot the third Ki-43 down just as Gerald caught sight of a D3A Val dive-bomber hugging the waves and trying to escape to the north after an attack on the shipping in the bay. He broke hard and gave chase. Morrissey saw it too after zoom-climbing back up to eight thousand feet. The two veterans had the Val cold. Gerald sped right up behind it, peppering its wings and fuselage with well-aimed shots. Crippled, it headed for the water. Morrissey suddenly slashed past Gerald, guns spewing sheets of flame. His burst killed the tail gunner and added to the plane's damage. Johnson kept firing. The Val smacked into the water and skidded to a stop, slowly sinking. The pilot struggled to get out.

Johnson saw he was still alive. The pilots had been briefed on how brutal the Japanese were to the Filipino population. Guerrilla reports were filled with horror stories—murder games, mass executions, torture, deliberate starvation. Downed Japanese aircrew were a threat to the local civilian population, and this Val now sinking in Carigara Bay on Leyte's northern coast was close enough to shore for the pilot to survive.

Johnson climbed and circled, looking down at the Japanese pilot. Two years ago, the boy he was would never have even considered this. Now, after two years of trauma, loss, and the brutal murder of his own friends, the Oregonian showed no mercy. A single strafing pass was all it would take. He hesitated for a moment, considering the power at his fingertips, aware in some vague recess of his mind that he might years hence look back at this like it was a story divided into two parts—everything that came before this necessary action and everything that he would do thereafter. Mercy was an indulgence. Mercy only ensured other people would get killed.

He left the pilot floating dead beside his sinking Val, a halo of blood blooming in the water around him.

The aces returned to Tacloban, landing south to north so they could touch down in the mud and roll onto the pierced steel planking. All eleven birds returned safely A quick debrief as the sun went down revealed the Forty-Niners shot down six Japanese planes that day. Three of the four Ki-43s went down to Johnson, Bong, and Morrissey. Three more dive-bombers rounded out the scoring. If this was any indication, opportunity was not going to be an issue at Leyte.

It had been an exhausting day, one that started with a four-hour flight from Morotai, some 650 miles away. A sketchy airfield and stressful landings followed by a combat mission in a target-rich environment. The pilots were ready for food and rest. But there was no food, and there was no place to rest. In a torrential rainstorm, they drove jeeps to their encampment near Tacloban City, some four miles from the airstrip. There, they found unassembled tents waiting for them. With minimal lights, they slipped and struggled in the watery mud while setting up the tents. By the time they were finished, the men were soaked. Without a fresh change of clothes, they slogged off to find food—K rations only—then returned to collapse in their cots, still covered in muck.

They fell into the sleep of the dead. Seemingly minutes later, the sound of gunfire jerked them awake. A Japanese night intruder buzzed overhead, dropping bombs as the base's flak crews hammered away at it. As the bombs fell closer, they dove out of their tents into the nearest slit trenches and foxholes, covering themselves with ponchos as they shivered in the mud.

All night long, the "Washing Machine Charlies" roamed over the strip, denying the men sleep and keeping them in their slit trenches.

When dawn broke and the pilots assembled to prepare for the day's flying, every Forty-Niner looked haggard and worn. The rain refused to let up. Rivers of mud streamed through the camp, and not a man could brag of dry feet. Still, they piled into jeeps and drove to the strip, where Walker gathered them in an alert tent.

Kenney sent word that the Japanese were landing reinforcements on the other side of Leyte, at a small harbor in Ormoc Bay. He needed his strafers to take them out, but they were far out of range, in New Guinea, languishing out of the fight. The Navy managed to launch a small strike that hit the docks but did little damage. It would fall to the Lightning pilots to do the damage.

They waited for the order to go, listening as the rain pounded the roof of their tent. They shivered as they chatted. Around noon, the rain eased up enough to allow some flying. Walker tasked the Knights with hitting Ormoc. Tacloban still needed to be defended, so he held back enough planes to patrol over the field. Bong, Morrissey, Johnson, and Walker would be the alert flight.

The men slogged out to their aircraft, and the mission began. The '38s all got off without incident, a minor miracle as they kicked up fans of mud and water during their takeoff runs. It reminded Gerald of Adak and his first combat tour. The men dive-bombed supplies in Ormoc, then ran into Japanese fighters. Ray Swift, who'd often flown wing on Gerald after Stanley Johnson was killed, shot down an Oscar. He would not have missed this fight for the world, though by rights he should have been evacuated to a Stateside hospital months ago. He'd fractured his skull in an accident back in New Guinea, but he'd refused treatment so he could keep flying. Now, suffering from blinding headaches and nausea, he was barely combat capable. Yet he still had enough fight left in him to destroy a Japanese fighter. It was that sort of dedication that made Gerald so devoted to his men and the cause. It also filled him with utter contempt for those he considered hiding from combat in cushy Stateside posts.

As the Knights set a course for home, radar picked up an incoming raid. The alert pilots rushed to their planes. Gerald slipped into number eighty-three, Jack on the wing helping him strap into it. A moment later, they taxied to the edge of the runway and launched.

Bong got into the air first, Johnson following with Morrissey and Walker behind. They caught a Ki-43 on the deck, hoping to sneak over the field for a hit-and-run strafing attack. The pilot turned out to be an old hand. He dodged every attack as he edged west. But numbers and the superiority of the American pilots eventually caught up with the Japanese airman. Bong ran him down, losing sight of Gerald in the process, and shot him up and sent him into a shallow dive, trailing smoke and fire. Johnson went after him as the rest of the flight formed up to continue their patrol.

They linked up at a preassigned rally point, Gerald still missing. They couldn't raise him on the radio. They continued the patrol as a threesome, worried about what had happened to their hot-blooded Oregonian.

Another intruder crossed their path over Masbate Island's south coast. Bong chandelled up after him and gave chase. The Japanese pilot carried a bomb under the centerline. He tried to jettison it, but something went wrong with the shackles. The bomb tore off, skidded back along the fuselage, and caught on the tail, tearing it completely off. The Hayabusa tumbled and slammed into the water.

It was the second kill of the day for Bong. Johnson was still nowhere in sight, and attempts to reach him over the radio failed. The men grew concerned. Bong checked his watch. They'd been airborne for under an hour. He and his colleagues had plenty of fuel left to continue their patrol.

They climbed back up to ten thousand feet and pointed their noses toward a Japanese airstrip on Masbate. It didn't take long for them to spot more enemy fighters. This time, almost twenty Ki-43s stacked from three to seven thousand feet appeared under their right wings.

It was a perfect setup—the Americans held the high ground. All they needed to do was swing in behind them and execute a slashing run through their formation. But Morrissey didn't want to attack without help. He turned back toward Tacloban, hoping to get into radio range and call in the incoming Japanese strike. Hopefully, more Lightnings could be scrambled and the entire raid broken up or shot down.

Meanwhile, Bong and Walker stalked the formation, getting above and behind it to keep tabs on where it was going. Suddenly, one of the trailing Ki-43s began to rock its wings wildly. It was a sure sign these planes didn't have radios, as that was the traditional flying signal for enemy aircraft. The Hayabusa pilots, wakened to the danger, jettisoned their fuel tanks and bombs, even as Bong and Walker lit into the trailing fighters. Bong hit two of them, then got hit himself as he tried to dive clear of the fight. The left engine's radiator began trailing coolant. The Allison started to overheat. Bong, still in a dive with Japanese fighters in hot pursuit, feathered the engine and pushed the nose down a bit farther. Walker stayed with him, fighters on his own tail.

Eventually, the diving speed of the P-38 paid dividends. Both men drew far ahead and the Japanese abandoned their chase. They returned ninety minutes after they'd left, Bong with two confirmed and two probables. About forty-five minutes later, Johnson set down at Tacloban, his P-38 unharmed. Where he'd been and what he'd been doing has been lost to history. When he learned of the fight he missed, he was sorely disappointed.

Another night came, and raiders struck the strip throughout it. Once again, the pilots dashed from their tents to the slit trenches to spend hours in mud-filled holes. The next morning, they looked like the walking dead.

At the strip, the engineers worked from 0800 to midnight trying to improve the runway. They'd been able to add several hundred more feet of Marston matting, but the constant rain turned the rest of the field into such a mess that operation accidents were getting out of hand. There were now more pilots than available P-38s, and Walker kept calling for reinforcements. The problem was, the more planes on this narrow strip, the more vulnerable everyone was. Until they got a handle on the marauding Japanese attacks and the runways were elongated, Tacloban would remain the most dangerous place in the Pacific.

As the pilots reached the alert tent to go over the day's missions, the ground crews worked furiously to prep the available Lightnings. Spare parts had yet to reach the strip, and one of the landing ship tanks filled with the group's gear was either damaged en route or sunk. The stuff never showed up. Some of the P-38s didn't have complete oxygen systems now as a result, which limited their patrols to twelve thousand feet or less.

Jack Hedgepeth sat in Johnson's cockpit, scrubbing the windscreen. He was meticulous with the way he cared for number eighty-three, and he'd long since learned that any stray speck on the canopy could be misidentified by an anxious pilot as an enemy plane. As he cleaned it, the air raid alarm sounded. Men bolted from under the other P-38s aligned along the runway, heading for slit trenches. Engineers bailed off their dozers. Work came to a halt. Jack stayed in the cockpit, looking around for the threat. When he didn't see anything, he figured it was another false alarm. There'd been almost as many of those as actual attacks since he came ashore on the twenty-sixth.

He went back to cleaning the windscreen. A single Hayabusa sped in from the bay mere feet off the ground. The pilot found a prime target—a full line of unrevetted P-38s just waiting to be strafed. He triggered his two heavy machine guns, and bullets ripped across the flight line. In seconds, the attack was over. The Oscar pilot, still clipping the trees, sped north unhindered by flak or interception.

The ground crew found Jack writhing in Gerald's cockpit. A stitch of bullets cut across the Lightning's wing and through the canopy he was cleaning. One leg was shattered. Blood was splattered all over the cockpit. His horrified comrades pulled him clear and lowered him down to a waiting jeep.

He went into shock, and a short time later he bled out.

The news devastated Gerald. Jack was a month away from his twenty-fourth birthday, almost exactly his same age. They'd known each other since Gerald first arrived at Dobodura what seemed like a lifetime ago.

His aircraft was scratched from the day's missions as a result of the damage and the state of the cockpit. The rest of the Forty-Niners got airborne as soon as they could, if only to keep the Lightnings from being destroyed on the ground.

The attacks didn't stop. Sometimes the men received a few minutes warning, often none at all. The Japanese Hayabusa pilots became masters of these hit-and-run strafing raids. On the thirtieth, they brought a new and devastating weapon with them.

It was morning again, and Tacloban hummed with determined activity. Pappy Gunn raced to and fro in a jeep, supervising the progress the engineers were making. Kenney was on the scene too, wanting to see his pilots and assess the situation. He knew he needed to bring more fighters in—heck, not even the entire 49th was up here yet, just the thirty-five men Walker and Johnson handpicked. There still wasn't anywhere to put more fighters, though somehow the operational losses would need to be made up.

A single Hayabusa swept across Tacloban, bullets tearing up everything in its path. Kenney dove for cover as men scrambled to the nearest slit trench. The Ki-43 dropped two light phosphorus bombs halfway down the runway. One exploded right behind Pappy Gunn's jeep, blowing him over the hood. Gerald and the other Forty-Niners stood up as the Hayabusa zoomed clear of the field, running for home. They saw Pappy try to stand, take a few steps, then collapse. Men sprinted to the great aviator's aid, and he was lifted onto a stretcher and carried off to the nearest aid station, critically wounded by shrapnel in his arm. He would survive, but his recovery would be a slow and torturous one, and he never fully regained the use of his arm.

That night, a typhoon struck Leyte. Massive swells rolled across the bay, churned higher by the gale-force winds that ripped down tents and blew equipment all over the field. The waves lashed Tacloban peninsula, swamping the one road from the field to the pilots' living area. Slit trenches filled with water and collapsed. The surviving tents were simply canvas stretched above a half foot of liquefied mud. Trench foot, dysentery, malaria—they would be hallmarks of life at Tacloban for months to come.

The exhaustion that came from such harsh natural conditions and constant barrages took its toll. When dawn broke after yet another sleepless night, jumpy antiaircraft gunners accidentally shot down a Forty-Niner trying to come in to land. He was killed instantly in the crash. Later that day, the Knights' commander, Maj. Bob McComsey, was critically wounded during another air attack on Tacloban. Medics quickly rushed him to an aid station and later evacuated him home. George Walker tapped Wally Jordan to return to the 9th and guide it through its most difficult crisis.

Morale sank to new lows. Beyond the mortal danger, the filth, poor rations, and bouts of severe diarrhea were wearing on the men. This was the first time since Guadalcanal that the Americans didn't have complete air superiority over a beachhead. It was also the last time in history that happened, though that would be of little comfort to the men lucky enough to survive Tacloban's many traumas.

The 49th needed help. They were down to only a handful of operational P-38s. Part of the group's 8th Squadron flew in to plus up the beleaguered defenders, along with P-38s of the 35th and 41st

Squadrons. Help was coming, but there still wasn't enough room to park the aircraft. The half-completed second runway was turned into a makeshift parking area, but that didn't make the birds any less vulnerable.

The following day, fourteen more from the 7th and 8th reached the strip. With them was Tommy McGuire, who'd somehow talked MacDonald into letting him go forward into the fight while the rest of the 475th waited for their airfields around Dulag to be finished by the engineers. The 49th needed replacement aircraft desperately, so the 431st Squadron delivered seventeen P-38s. McGuire led the formation into Tacloban, but as they arrived over the field, the ground controller warned them off, as radar detected an inbound Japanese attack. Though they'd flown over three hours up from Morotai, McGuire's pilots still retained plenty of fuel. They began patrolling the area. A Ki-44 appeared behind the 431st. The Japanese pilot saw the odds and he ran for some nearby clouds. Tommy turned around and pursued him with his flight, catching the Shoki in a dive. McGuire raked him with a long burst at three hundred yards, but even after a cannon shell exploded through the canopy, the Ki-44 would not go down. He bored in for the kill. At a hundred feet dead astern, he fired again. Two more bursts until at fifty feet, his cannon blew the tail off the Japanese interceptor. McGuire landed at Tacloban with the rest of his squadron, exultant over his twenty-fifth kill—until the Forty-Niners told him Bong now had thirty-three.

All day long, the Lightning pilots patrolled and intercepted incoming Japanese raids. The Forty-Niners battled everything from Val dive-bombers to Zeroes and Dinah reconnaissance bombers. Hayabusas and even ancient Nakajima B5N Kate torpedo bombers, leftovers from Japan's halcyon days of 1941, filled the air around Tacloban. Altogether, the Americans claimed twenty-five planes that day over Leyte.

November 2, 1944, passed in a nightmarish blur. Pilots from five different squadrons jammed onto one usable runway to take off and land while the Japanese continued their hit-and-run raids. Part of the 475th Fighter Group arrived to add to the confusion, temporarily staying at Tacloban before moving on to the Dulag area's soggy airfields. A Japanese resupply convoy steamed into Ormoc Bay, covered by almost a hundred Japanese fighters. Fights raged over the convoy and spilled all over Leyte as the Japanese launched multiple raids against Tacloban and the shipping nearby. The chaotic day grew even crazier when two patrolling Knights were bounced by Japanese fighters. One pilot was shot down, though he survived the crash. The other, Lt. Bill Huisman limped back to Tacloban on one engine. Badly damaged, possibly wounded, he arrived over the field just as Dick Bong and a flight of Forty-Niners prepared to take off. They sat at one end of the runway, one behind the other, as Huisman attempted to land on the other end, coming at them.

As he was just about to touch down, a 35th Fighter Squadron P-38 appeared behind him. The pilot never saw Huisman's plane. He landed on top of the crippled P-38, severing it in half. Huisman's plane exploded, debris fanning in all directions as the fuselage and part of the wing careened down the runway.

Gerald was standing with several other pilots outside the alert tent when the collision took place. The 35th Squadron's P-38 cartwheeled right over their heads, raining debris. They dove for safety as the aircraft blew up beside them. Two ground crewmen rushed to the wreckage and somehow pulled the pilot clear, but it was too late. He was killed instantly in the crash.

At the other end of the runway, Leslie Nelson, a longtime Flying Knight veteran, watched as the remains of Huisman's P-38 skidded to a stop only a few hundred feet in front of them. He and Huisman had been close friends. Now he saw his brother Knight frantically trying to get out of the cockpit, the wreckage wreathed in fire. The crash must have saturated him with aviation gas, for the moment he got the canopy hatch open, he ignited. Writhing in agony, he fell out of the cockpit and stumbled aimlessly, his entire body afire.

Johnson's mechanic, Doug Harcleroad, charged across the runway and tackled Huisman with one other man, smothering the flames with his own body. Huisman lay on the ground, his seizing body blackened horribly.

At that moment, Bong saw the runway directly in front of him was clear. He opened the throttles and roared past the dying man, his prop wash blasting all three with rocks and debris. Watching the scene, Nelson felt sick. He refused to follow his flight leader into the air until Harcleroad and the other enlisted man carried Huisman clear of the runway. Then he climbed up and joined Bong over the runway.

In strict military terms, Bong had every reason to get airborne as quickly as he could. The Lightnings were sitting ducks on the ground and every minute they were not in the air made them a strafer's target. Yet for Nelson and the others who witnessed the moment, Bong's decision to take off needlessly added to a dying brother's agony. Most never spoke of it out of respect for Dick, but the scene haunted them the rest of their lives.

Huisman was in critical condition. He was evacuated to a ship just offshore, but he didn't survive the night. He was buried at sea the next morning.

The days passed in a kaleidoscope of wrenching moments and furious combats over Tacloban and Ormoc Bay, where the Japanese kept running resupply convoys down to their troops defending northern Leyte. The weather grew worse. The other fields around Dulag were near busts. They couldn't be drained properly, and the runways flooded every time a monsoon swept over the island. Still, Kenney pushed the 475th forward, and for the next week, its planes and pilots streamed into Leyte. They dispersed to the fields around

Dulag, but operated mainly from Tacloban due to the condition of the strips. Because of that, Johnson, Bong, Morrissey, Walker, and McGuire flew frequently together. Most of McGuire's 431st Squadron wouldn't arrive until November 9, which allowed him to keep flying with his old Forty-Niner brothers. They lived in squalor and endured the nightly attacks even as their own scores rose. They had their moments of success and moments of heartbreak.

On November 3, Bong, Johnson, and McGuire flew with the rest of the Flying Knights over to Ormoc, looking for trouble. Word was another convoy had landed supplies. They saw no ships, but they did discover a ten-mile-long vehicle convoy stretching out of Ormoc, heading toward Carigara Bay.

The squadron rolled in on the column with a vengeance. They caught a line of trucks trapped on the road by swamps on either side. Unable to escape, they were sitting ducks. The Knights raked them mercilessly even as soldiers bailed out of the rigs and tried to find cover. Tommy made a pass, and saw his cannon shells hit a couple of vehicles. They blew up, throwing bodies high in the air.

The Knights came back around, this time flying right on the trees as they strafed. Desperate Japanese fired rifles and light machine guns at them, using wrecked trucks and caissons as firing positions. Hundreds of men lay dead and splayed around the scene. The Knights came back for a third pass, but this time the Japanese got lucky. Small-arms fire crippled Lt. Bob Hamburger's P-38. It caught fire. He rolled off his run, climbed to altitude, and bailed out. Fortunately, he was rescued by Filipino guerrillas.

That third pass was enough, the airmen decided. Most of the men were nearly out of ammunition, so they called it a day and reformed above the burning column. They'd destroyed thirty trucks and two light tanks. Later intelligence reports credited the Flying Knights with killing or wounding twenty-four hundred men, almost an entire infantry regiment.

Before the P-38s could clear the area, two Hayabusas suddenly sped through their formation, spewing tracers. Bob Bates was hit in the surprise attack. As the Knights scattered to evade the Ki-43s, they heard him call, "I'm on fire! I'm on fire!" His burning P-38 arrowed into the jungle below. The rest of the squadron ran for home and landed back at Tacloban, two P-38s and their pilots a heavy price to pay for the day's fighting.

When they landed, Tommy McGuire was more sore than usual. After a few hours in a P-38, the guys would get "pilot's ass"—a result of never being able to find a spot where the life raft's air valve didn't stick the pilots in the rear. Sometimes, after ultra-long-range missions, the men would be so sore they'd have to be helped out of the cockpit.

This felt different to Tommy. When he started to stand up and get out of the cockpit, he realized he had been sitting in a pool of blood. During one his strafing runs, a rifle-caliber bullet punctured the side of the cockpit and grazed both his buttocks cheeks. The wound was superficial, but still very painful. He hobbled around for days, limping and ignoring the pain. He told no one of his wound, fearing he'd be pulled off flight status at a time when the hunting was so good. He had twenty-five kills, now ten back from Bong. This was his chance to catch up. So he continued to fly, sitting on his bullet-wounded behind, gutting through the pain. Only a few people ever found out about it, and he never received a Purple Heart for this wound.

The next morning, the Japanese hit Tacloban with nearly forty planes. Racing over the strip on the deck as the first rays of dawn stretched over the horizon, the enemy planes carpeted the field with white phosphorus and shrapnel bombs. In one pass lasting only a couple of minutes, they killed or wounded thirty-four men, destroyed two P-38s, and damaged thirty-nine other aircraft.

The persistent dawn and dusk strikes forced the ground crews to change the way they prepped their planes for missions. The mechanics began preflighting the P-38s at 0300 to avoid being caught on the flight line by surprise strafers. They'd stop work at sunset to await the evening raid, then get back to work in the darkness, using minimal light as they labored over the birds.

And so it went, flying and fighting through endless nights filled with tracers and searchlights, the sound of enemy engines overhead and the misery of the slit trenches. They slept little. Ate less. More men, more pilots came in, but the trickle of reinforcements could not keep pace with the losses. At times, the 475th could field less than twenty of their assigned seventy-five P-38s. In the first two weeks at Tacloban, the men endured sixty-nine red alert warnings and thirty-six attacks carried out by nearly two hundred Japanese planes. After the monsoons washed the road out, the men used DUKW amphibious trucks to cross the bay from their living area to the runway. Even this became an ordeal, as marauding Oscars would often make strafing runs at them.

When they weren't attacking the airstrip, the Japanese went after the ships unloading around it. They set cargo ships afire and strafed barges and landing craft running between the vessels and the beach. During nearly every raid, the P-38 pilots did their best to intercept and inflict damage on the Japanese, but no matter how many aircraft they shot down, the enemy returned the next day. Scores mounted. The pilots who managed to survive continued to wear themselves out.

In early November, the first reporters who reached Leyte began covering the air action and the aces. When the 49th Fighter Group scored its five hundredth kill, the unit's identity was revealed to the public back home. Headlines and stories filled the papers on the exploits of the 49th, focusing on its great aces, including Bong and often Tommy McGuire. The press was finally starting to take

notice of Tommy, though only in the context of his position behind
Bong. Reporters often thought he was part of the 49th since he was
frequently flying with Johnson and Bong. After the truck convoy
mission, an AP war correspondent named Richard Bergholz found
McGuire on the runway at Tacloban and interviewed him on the
spot. Tommy loved to talk and made an excellent interview subject
as a result. He also knew the exact right things to say to the media.
Yet Bong remained the darling of the press and of the public affairs
wonks at headquarters.

On November 10, 1944, a Japanese strike tore up a thousand
feet's worth of pierced steel planking at Tacloban. The strip was now
almost four thousand feet long, thanks to the tireless efforts of the
engineers, so the P-38 pilots could still use it with caution. That was
a good thing, too, as Charles MacDonald discovered his squadrons
dispersed around Dulag could barely operate in the bad weather.
The hardstands and taxiways the engineers built around the strips
there filled with water, and the P-38s mired in the flooding couldn't
get off the ground. Mac told his squadron leaders to do their best to
get the planes off those strips and back to Tacloban.

Meanwhile, everyone who could fly did. That morning, McGuire
flew a borrowed P-38 on a mission over Ormoc Bay, where he got
in a fight with a Ki-43 Hayabusa. After his stint as the squadron
armament and engineering officer, Tommy was very particular about
his guns and would often personally boresight them. With a loaner
Lightning, he didn't want to take any chances with long-range or
high-deflection shots. He got behind the Oscar, closed to can't-
miss, point-blank range, and blew it up with a long trigger pull. The
Oscar's fireball threw debris all over the sky, and Tommy was too
close to do anything but fly through the flaming pieces. A chunk of
Hayabusa smashed through his canopy hatch and struck him in the
head. The blow knocked him unconscious for a few seconds. When
he awoke, blood covered his head and face.

He returned to Tacloban, landed safely, and sat in the cockpit as his crew chief, Sgt. Frank Kish, climbed onto the wing. Seeing the hole in the canopy hatch and the plexiglass splattered with blood, Kish exclaimed, "Christ! Are you all right, Major?"

McGuire was dazed but not seriously hurt. In fact, he was feeling better than he had in a long time. He'd just tied Eddie Rickenbacker's World War I record. He'd idolized Captain Eddie as a kid. He wanted to savor the moment. He tried to make a joke of his wound, telling Kish he'd almost brought the Oscar home with him. Kish suggested he go see a doctor. He knew that McGuire simply had bound his earlier wound with tape. This one looked more serious. McGuire blew him off, telling him, "Let's keep this quiet, too. I don't want to lay around while the hunting is so good."

That afternoon, Bong shot down another plane. Every time McGuire thought he'd closed the gap between them, the Wisconsinite would match him, kill for kill. It was maddening, and McGuire started to fixate on the race.

The truth was, McGuire was anything but healthy after twenty-two months of near-continuous combat flying. Of all the aces, he was the only one who did not go home on leave. MacDonald told him to expect leave at the end of the year, but he'd heard that before. Since the summer, his letters home to Marilynn were peppered with references to possible leave. He desperately needed it, his body covered in jungle sores and rashes. The medics gave him creams that tinted his skin purple but offered little relief. He was gaunt, emaciated from months of bad food, jungle living, and bouts with typhus and malaria, along with the constant stress of combat flying. His body was shot through from the constant adrenaline rushes. His cheeks grew sunken. He walked with a limp, and he smelled terrible from the mix of ointments, sweat, and oozing rashes. He kept going on sheer force of will, displaying great personal courage on the ground at times to motivate his men.

After all the strafing runs the Japanese executed on the P-38s, the ground crews grew understandably reluctant to be out under the birds, working on them during alerts. Since they were usually under an alert, morale began to slide. McGuire made a point of going out to the flight line with the men each morning. As they worked, he watched the sky, his Colt .45 in hand and ready to fire a warning shot should a Japanese marauder appear above the trees. That he risked himself by standing out in the open like that engendered enormous loyalty among his squadron's mechanics and crew chiefs. No officer needed to do that, let alone their squadron leader.

The next day, November 11, Bong stole a march on McGuire. Gerald, Dick, and Morrissey were flying back from an escort mission when they stumbled on a flight of U.S. Navy torpedo bombers. Somehow, the TBM Avengers lost their own fighter cover while attacking yet another Japanese resupply convoy in Ormoc Bay. As they lumbered along, seven Japanese Zeroes tried to jump them.

The Lightnings dove to the rescue. Bong made quick work of two Zeroes. Gerald got two more. Morrissey damaged a fifth. The other two broke and ran. The torpedo bomber pilots returned to their carriers to report how they were saved. Somehow, the Navy got word to Tacloban that they'd like to host the pilots who protected their aircrew. For one glorious night, Gerald and Dick took a small boat out into the bay and messed with the Navy aboard a destroyer. They felt like riflemen pulled from muddy trenches and drawn into a formal meal. Their khaki uniforms were dirty and threadbare compared to the clean-cut sailors and officers they met. They looked more like pirates, less like a freshly minted lieutenant colonel and America's ace of aces.

Seven of their friends were dead. More than forty P-38s had been lost since the twenty-seventh, nine in air-to-air combat. They were bone weary and stared at the white tablecloth in the officers' wardroom as if it were a vestige from a past life. At dinner, they feasted on china plates with actual silverware. They'd spent weeks eating off mess tins or straight out of ration cans.

For a brief moment, they felt human again.

All too soon, it was back to the muddy hellhole of Tacloban, where showers had yet to be built and the men bathed out of their GI standard-issue helmets. Gerald returned to his tent and wrote a note to Barbara. What started as an elliptical reference to the fighting he'd been doing turned, the longer he held the pen, into a passionate love letter.

> *Your letters are priceless, and your spirit and humor give me new energy and stronger faith. I belong only to you, Darling, beyond all eternity—and you know how long that is.*
>
> > *Whatever I am, I Belong to You,*
> > *Just a Fighter Pilot in Love,*
> > *Gerald*

He folded the letter and slid it into an envelope, even as a Japanese night raider rumbled overhead to deny all a chance to sleep. Cursing, the men of the 49th slipped out of their cots and trudged to the sludge-filled slit trenches, the vision of that spotless tablecloth still on Gerald's mind.

42

Lost Perspective

November 1944
Leyte, Philippines

The day after Bong and Gerald saved the Navy torpedo bombers, McGuire led his squadron into a fight over Cebu, where the Angels encountered a new type of Japanese Navy interceptor. The Mitsubishi J2M Raiden looked like a downsized version of a P-47 Thunderbolt. Fast, well armed with four 20mm cannon, the J2M incorporated self-sealing fuel tanks and armor plating for the pilot, features not present in most Japanese fighters McGuire had encountered.

Code-named "Jack" by Allied intelligence, the Raiden in the hands of a skilled pilot could be a formidable adversary for a P-38 flier. Fortunately for the Americans, there were very few skilled Japanese pilots left. The day before, Charles MacDonald ran into a formation of these new fighters and flamed two of them over Ormoc Bay. Not only did the battle give Mac his sixteenth and seventeenth kills, he also learned a bit about its performance, passing that information along when he landed back at Leyte.

McGuire and his men tore into the Japanese like sharks in a frenzy. They dropped four Raidens in only a few minutes of fighting. While their planes were improved, the average Japanese fighter pilot was not the measure of his American enemy, and that negated the extra performance the Raiden gave them.

McGuire's kills gave him another round of publicity. His P-38 now carried twenty-eight kill flags. Bong's score stood at thirty-six. The rivalry between the two men now became a key angle in the ace race. On his radio program, Walter Winchell spoke of McGuire and his score, to the delight of McGuire's father and wife. For almost a year and a half, Tommy received only occasional letters from home. At mail calls, he more often than not walked away empty-handed. But in late November, he received a steady stream of fan letters from Stateside civilians who heard Winchell's broadcast or read of his exploits in the paper.

On November 15, a photographer snapped one of the iconic photos of the ace race. It showed Dick and Tommy leaning on a P-38's propeller blade, shooting the breeze. Dick appeared a little awkward in the photo, while Tommy managed to look jaunty, relaxed, and haggard at the same time. To a close observer, his gaunt face and sunken cheeks betrayed his underlying combat exhaustion. He was a man who should have been home for a long rest. Nevertheless, dozens of papers back home ran the photo for the next month, extolling the virtues of both men. Dick was called the "trump ace" and McGuire was the contender nipping at his heels.

Despite two wounds and his grim physical state, McGuire flew seventy-one combat hours in November, thirteen of them in B-25s when a P-38 wasn't available. In comparison, Bong flew about thirty hours in thirteen missions through the month. Johnson flew a little over twenty combat hours. Kenney later wrote that Bong practically needed his permission to get in the cockpit at this point. General Arnold was breathing down his neck, not wanting a repeat of what happened to Kearby and Lynch. Still, Bong always found a way into a fight when he wanted to fly. The new surge in press coverage included much positive ink on the 5th and its desperate fight at Leyte. The 49th continued to get ample coverage, and photos of the leading aces standing under P-38s at Tacloban ran in papers throughout the country. Still, the battle between McGuire and Bong lent a new sense of urgency to the reporting and invigorated the coverage of the air war in the Philippines. Kenney knew he should put an end to it, but he didn't. He rolled the dice, praying Dick wouldn't get killed as the young major raced to his personal goal: fifty confirmed. It was not lost on the FEAF commander that fifty had also been Neal Kearby's goal.

On November 28, 1944, men around Tacloban that day watched Bong's P-38 taxi to the end of the runway, turn, and start its takeoff run. Everyone knew the bird: the kill board was the largest in the Pacific and could be seen from a distance. As the Lightning left the ground, one engine exploded. The P-38 rolled over and crashed in flames.

For a few frantic minutes, it was thought Dick Bong was at the controls and the ace of aces was dead. The shock sent shivers through the chain of command. In reality, the 49th Fighter Group's assistant operations officer had borrowed Dick's plane that morning, and he had been killed instantly in the explosion. It took time to sort that out and cool the rumors that another national hero had been killed in the SWPA. In response, Kenney told Bong to back off the combat flying and focus on teaching the pilots the gunnery techniques he'd learned.

Bong packed up his meager kit and said goodbye to the 49th. He went down to Dulag, where the 431st was stationed now that the drainage issues were under control. Initially, he shared a tent with Tommy McGuire, but the two men did not get along at all in that arrangement. Exactly what happened remained between the two of them, but it is likely that McGuire's resentment over Bong's special treatment translated into considerable needling. Bong moved to a different tent only a few nights later.

The idea of the top two American aces sharing living space, an arrangement that however brief had somehow gotten out, drew some of the ace race reporters to Dulag. Lee Van Atta wrote the first major profile of McGuire at the end of November. Like the one he wrote on Bong earlier in the year, though not as long, the profile was Van Atta's attempt to image-shape McGuire and his personality. He described him as a laughing, outgoing jokester who talked freely of the air combat he'd experienced. No mention was made of his Florida roots; instead, Van Atta gave his home state as New Jersey. His mom and his childhood in Sebring were kept out of the public eye. Instead, Van Atta called him "the Joisey Kid," as if he had the stereotypical accent of the area, which he did not.

Of the ace race, Van Atta's article read like a sports reporter's puff piece. He quoted Tommy as saying, "I'd like to make one thing clear at this point—Dick Bong and I are good friends, always have been, always will be. We figured to be too smart to let jealousy get either of us bumped off in grudges matches, or exhibitions of that top ace place."

Then Lee inadvertently let McGuire take a shot at Bong. "I'd like to be it [top ace], sure. Who wouldn't? But all of us are still playing the game as squadrons and flights, and I'll get mine with my squadron or not at all."

It was a subtle McGuire-esque dig at Bong and his lack of leadership responsibility that Lee either missed or figured folks back home would not understand. McGuire emphasized teamwork. He was proud of his squadron and his leadership of it. He repeated that theme in future interviews, as well, knowing it set him apart from Bong. If he couldn't be the ace of aces, he considered himself the best squadron leader of the best fighter squadron in the SWPA. And he was right.

Van Atta's article wrapped up with a total fabrication. To prove just how well Dick and Tommy got along, the last portion of the story details how the two aces worked together over Balikpapan in October. That was actually Gerald Johnson who teamed up with

McGuire and worked closely to flame a number of planes. The Oregonian got airbrushed out of the piece to create the mystique of teamwork between rivals. Lee was always a patriotic and courageous reporter. But with this McGuire profile, he slipped from journalist to publicity hack.

As the race reached a fevered peak, so did the air war over Leyte. On December 7, 1944, the Japanese and Americans both ran convoys into Ormoc Bay. The Japanese were simply trying to supply their troops. The Americans came to cut that supply point off, landing the 77th Infantry Division at Ormoc to seal off the port from the Japanese and to get behind their lines in force.

The Japanese threw every available airplane into the air that day, either to defend their own convoy or to attack the American amphibious force. Around the soggy, wreck-strewn fields at Leyte, the pilots of V Fighter Command rose to fight. The air-sea battle raged from dawn 'til dusk. Before the day was out, Bong, McGuire, Johnson, and MacDonald all flew repeated missions.

Johnson scored first. George Walker had sent him to Nadzab for a rest leave at the end of November. Now he was back, refreshed and full of fight. Ten minutes to ten o'clock found Gerald with a patrol of four P-38s from the 49th, covering the U.S. Navy warships in Ormoc Bay. A formation of Japanese twin-engine bombers appeared below them, covered by a flight of three Ki-43s. Johnson spotted the fighters and attacked them first. His first pass knocked one down. He zoom-climbed, then dropped back on the other two, whose pilots tried to evade his charging P-38. Two quick bursts in one pass and both Ki-43s went down in flames. In forty-five seconds, Gerald flamed three fighters, which plunged into the sea only a few hundred feet apart. "Count 'em! One...two...three!" he exclaimed over the radio, before the rest of the flight went tearing after the Japanese bombers. Together, they shot four of nine down. Gerald returned with four confirmed kills, the three Hayabusas and one bomber, giving him twenty-three kills. He'd surpassed Kearby and Jay Robbins to be the third-ranking ace in the theater.

The fighting continued. McGuire led a two-plane patrol over Ormoc an hour later, shooting down an Oscar. After lunch, MacDonald ran into another formation of Mitsubishi Raidens and came home with two more victories.

Then McGuire and Bong flew together on a midafternoon patrol over Ormoc. McGuire led the flight, and Bong took the second element with Maj. Jack Rittmayer as his wingman. As they reached Ormoc, Bong's sharp eyes made out a Japanese Sally bomber running along some clouds. Without calling it out, he suddenly broke formation, charged after the aircraft, and sent it down in flames.

As he rejoined the formation, a half dozen kamikazes sped toward the U.S. ships McGuire was tasked to protect. Tommy charged after them, chasing them into the curtains of antiaircraft fire the warships threw up at these fanatical attackers. He shot one down, Bong got another, and two others fell to their wingmen. Out of ammunition, they returned to Dulag, where McGuire and his wingman seethed over Bong's behavior.

Bong had violated the most basic and inviolable law of air combat in the SWPA: teamwork. He'd abandoned his formation, failed to communicate, and went off hunting. This was a serious breach, one that in the past got Americans killed. Teamwork, the integrity of the formations, and fighting together had been drilled into every pilot coming into the SWPA since 1943. It was the hallmark of McGuire's tactical manual. A month before, an 8th Fighter Squadron pilot had abandoned his flight to go shoot down two Zeroes, and instead of collecting accolades, his actions were written up and V Fighter Command published a combat evaluation report slamming the pilot's behavior.

Bong's actions that day alienated much of the 431st Fighter Squadron. They considered him selfish, only there to score, and obsessed with staying ahead of McGuire. They had a point. The pressure of the ace race was clearly getting to Bong. Later, the squadron historian took savage shots at Dick, writing into the 431st's official record: "Those pilots not assigned to our squadron . . . seemed more interested in running up their individual scores than in protecting themselves and their flight members and following our standard operating procedures." The other pilot referenced in the unit history was Maj. Jack Rittmayer, who had been flying wing with Bong and McGuire through December, though he was also not a member of the 431st.

McGuire ran a very tight ship in the 431st and didn't think of himself as someone who tolerated pilots breaking any of his tactical rules. One pilot later commented along those lines, that had he gone off hunting like that, he would have been bounced out of the squadron. To Tommy, there was zero margin for error, and the safety of the men always came first.

All this drama was kept out of the public eye. It was soon overwhelmed with a tidal wave of new media coverage of the Wisconsin ace. The next day the press broke the news that Richard Ira Bong, America's ace of aces with thirty-nine kills, not only just surpassed Britain's top ace Johnnie Johnson, but had been awarded the Congressional Medal of Honor as well. Four days later, as rain fell at Tacloban, the men of the 475th and 49th Fighter Groups stood at formation as Gen. Douglas MacArthur gave the award to Dick.

MacArthur was at his rhetorical best as he addressed his weary, wet aviators. "The Congress of the United States has reserved for itself the honor of decorating those amongst all who stand out as the bravest of the brave. It is this high and noble category, Major Bong, that you now enter as I place upon your breast the Medal of Honor. Wear it as the symbol of invincible courage you have displayed in mortal combat. My dear boy, may a merciful God continue to protect you."

Ten days later, Dick Bong flew one final combat mission with the 431st, shooting down a Japanese fighter over Mindoro Island. He'd reached forty, earned the Medal of Honor, and now stood two kills over Britain's Johnnie Johnson. He also outscored the U.S. Navy's ranking ace, David McCampbell, whose kill board included thirty-four Japanese flags. Enough was enough. Kenney grounded him a final time.

Dick would never return to battle, and Kenney was pleased with that, happy his acolyte had survived the ordeal, even as so many of Dick's onetime rivals hadn't. The general had helped mold the hero, creating an American legend whose fame was surpassed by that of only one other aviator—Charles Lindbergh.

The night after Dick scored his final kill, Tommy McGuire went to go see Gerald Johnson. The two old friends sat in Johnson's tent at Tacloban, stewing over how the race had been manipulated by Kenney. Bong's protected status and the way he flew with the 431st left a bad taste in McGuire's mouth. It turned out Johnson felt the same way. Bong had changed since the spring of 1943. Though he had rebuilt his friendship with Bong that fall, Johnson watched in dismay as he increasingly focused on his personal goals. The line between duty and ambition was crossed at the cost of mission and teamwork. To these two outstanding fighter leaders, the press hype hailing him as "trump ace" was hard to take.

No doubt, the media frenzy around Bong was partly to blame for all this. The more the reporters pushed and wrote about the rivalry, the more Bong seemed to feel the pressure. It had led to bad decisions, unwarranted risks in the past by others consumed by the race. Here, after all the flying and fighting, it seemed to have finally gotten to Bong as well.

The two aces chatted long into the night. McGuire chain-smoked, talking in machine gun–like bursts. Johnson was smoother, more relaxed, but still rankled by everything that had happened. They made an odd pair, but they'd known each other for so long that the trauma and hardship at Leyte brought them closer together than ever before. Thomas McGuire, always the outsider who defined himself as better than the next man, headed back to his quarters knowing that with Gerald, he possessed an enduring friendship.

In the days that followed, Bong stayed at Tacloban, waiting for final orders home. Kenney visited McGuire at the 431st and ate with the pilots. Afterward, he returned the favor and invited Tommy to eat with him at FEAF Headquarters, where the cook was the former head chef at the St. Francis Hotel in San Francisco.

Air combat around Leyte dwindled in December from almost daily contact with the enemy to a rare occurrence. With Bong well in the lead with forty kills to his credit, and now headed home, it seemed the race had ended. Tommy was nine back with thirty-one. Johnson had twenty-three, MacDonald twenty-one. It appeared very unlikely that anyone could catch Bong. The Japanese air units in the Philippines had been savaged by the 5th Air Force and the Navy's carrier air groups. The surviving units were starting to pull out to make their final stand over Japan.

On Christmas Day, McGuire led the 431st on a long-range escort mission, covering B-24 Liberator bombers as they bombed the last major Japanese base in the area, at Clark Field, Luzon. Tommy's outfit took point over the bomber boxes, with other P-38 units spread out behind, including Charles MacDonald and the rest of the 475th.

The Japanese struck just shy of the target area. Around thirty interceptors pounced on the 431st from above and behind. They dove through the American formation, shooting up several P-38s. McGuire, totally defensive, broke hard left in an impossibly tight turn to scrape a Zero off the tail-end Charlie in his flight. McGuire scored hits on the Zero, but more came spearing through their formation. Lightnings started to go down in flames. The attack had been a masterstroke, but the Japanese weren't finished. Instead of trying to escape, they used their speed to get above and in front of the 431st before rolling into a slashing, head-on attack. They'd taken a page out of the 5th Air Force's own tactics.

They came back through the 431st, tracers crisscrossing the sky. Lightnings broke and dove for safety. Others pulled around after the fleeing Japanese, who were still full of fight. A wild scrum unfolded over the B-24s that would last almost an hour. Three 431st Squadron P-38s went down in flames. Several others took hits. McGuire shot down three Japanese fighters while rushing to the aid of his men. Then his guns jammed while he maneuvered in a High-G turn. Instead of breaking off and heading for home, McGuire made feinting attacks on Japanese fighters trying to break through to the B-24 formations. More Japanese fighters piled into the fight. As MacDonald and the rest of the 475th reached the area, the furious air battle stretched for miles in all directions. MacDonald destroyed three planes before his guns jammed as well. All three squadrons of the 49th Fighter Group charged into the fray as more Japanese planes dropped aerial phosphorus bombs from far overhead, hoping to at least disrupt the bomber formations. Flights and elements fought micro duels all the way down to seven thousand feet as the two P-38 groups grappled with about sixty interceptors.

An hour later, over forty Japanese planes filled smoking craters beneath the great air battle. Back at Leyte, McGuire was not in a celebrating mood. The Japanese held all the advantages at the start of the fight, and they inflicted a lot of damage on his men. Later, one of the downed pilots returned to the outfit after being rescued by Filipino guerrillas. Two others were killed in action.

They had been killed on Christmas Day. It would be a terrible blow to their families back home, made worse by the pall their losses would put on the holiday season for years after the mission. The media circus that followed the mission didn't touch on those losses. Rather, the reporters learned that MacDonald had scored the 475th

Fighter Group's five hundredth kill. The group was hard on the heels of the Forty-Niners, and the press built up the rivalry between the groups. In the days after the mission, Charles MacDonald received more publicity back home than at any other time of the war as a result of that milestone. He barely talked to the reporters, who were left to write their stories without much input from the hero of the hour.

Meanwhile, Christmas night saw the ground crews pouring over the remaining P-38s, trying to get them ready for the morning's mission, a return to Clark. Come dawn, they could only field ten Lightnings.

McGuire led them into the air, linked up with the rest of the 475th and 49th, and covered another B-24 strike to Luzon. As the Americans approached the target area, antiaircraft bursts filled the sky around them. Suddenly, a flight of Zeroes dove out of some nearby clouds, barreling past the 431st and making for the right side of the bomber formation. McGuire dropped his fuel tanks and led his flight down in hot pursuit. It looked like the lead Zero would reach the bombers before the Lightnings could catch up. In desperation, McGuire snapped out a long-range burst—twelve hundred feet with forty-five degrees of deflection. To the astonishment of the rest of his flight, McGuire's bullets sent impact flares all around the fuselage and cockpit.

It stayed on its attack course, but Tommy had inflicted enough damage to catch up to him. He snaked his P-38 right behind the Zero, closed to less than a hundred feet, and blew it out of the air.

No time for celebrating. McGuire bent around in a tight turn and went after another fighter chasing the bomber stream. He hit it with two high-deflection bursts, and it went down in flames. Ed Weaver, who was flying in McGuire's flight that day, later noted he'd never seen such aerial marksmanship before. Ed had done a tour in North Africa as a P-40 pilot in 1942–43 before coming out to the Pacific for a second combat tour. He'd seen a lot of action, but

McGuire was a force of his own that day. Weaver tried to stay with Tommy as the great ace threw his P-38 into a series of violent maneuvers to get after three more Zeroes cutting past them. McGuire was just too quick, too capable of handling the g load. Weaver blacked out and lost him.

McGuire nailed a third Zero with another high-degree deflection shot, then chased another one down to fifteen hundred feet. Alone and low was no place for the ace to be, but he hit the Zero repeatedly, again with high deflection shots. High above the one-versus-one duel, another 431st Squadron pilot, Lt. Chris Herman, saw McGuire score a killing blow right into the Zero's wing root. A fuel tank exploded, and the enemy plane plummeted to the ground.

Back over Dulag, the 431st's ground echelon watched as McGuire returned and executed four victory rolls before swinging into the pattern and touching down.

Thirty-eight kills. It seemed the race may not have been over after all. One more mission like today's, and he'd be the new ace of aces at last.

43

Getting Three for Mac

December 28, 1944
Tacloban Airfield, Leyte, Philippines

Tommy McGuire set his P-38 down at Tacloban after a thirty-minute flight from Dulag. The roads were still such a mess that it was easier to fly between the bases than to grab a jeep and drive over. He cut the throttles and began to taxi. Tacloban looked very different now, compared to when he first arrived. The second runway was finished. The engineers had drained the swampy ground and built an actual dispersal area with revetments. As he found a place to park, he passed every imaginable type of aircraft, from little L-4 Piper Grasshoppers to strafer-nosed B-25s, P-61 Black Widows, and shiny silver Jugs.

General Kenney wanted to see him. After his two-day, seven-kill streak, this made McGuire nervous. He had good reason to be. When he reached FEAF headquarters, Kenney greeted him with, "You look tired. I'm taking you off flight status."

The general's words hit McGuire like a shot to the heart. He sputtered a protest, "General, I've never felt better in my life. Besides, I'm only two behind—"

Kenney cut him off, "That's just it. You are tired and you won't be rested enough to fly again until I hear that Bong has arrived back in the United States and been greeted as the top-scoring ace of the war."

McGuire listened to the news. He was being grounded so Bong could get more attention, more accolades. It was the icing on the resentment cake that McGuire and Johnson had baked for months. The special treatment never seemed to stop, even after Bong left the theater. To McGuire, knowing his days in combat were numbered, this seemed like an insufferable slight. General Kenney did not want him to beat his fair-haired boy.

Yet, Kenney had a point. He couldn't very well send Bong back as the top ace to face all the cameras and reporters only to have that crown snatched from his head by McGuire.

Then Kenney relented a little. "As soon as I get that news, you can go back to work."

McGuire said nothing for a moment. Kenney added, "If I let you go out today, you are liable to knock off another three Nips and spoil Dick's whole party."

That broke the tension. McGuire laughed and assured Kenney he didn't want to spoil anything for Bong. He agreed to wait and go for the record after the nation properly celebrated Bong's achievement.

Dick arrived back at Tacloban later in the day. He'd been up at Mindoro Island, which MacArthur's troops liberated earlier in the month. The engineers there were building an airfield complex to support the final jump to Luzon and Manila, though the Japanese were doing everything they could to disrupt that.

There, at Tacloban, Bong and McGuire said goodbye to each other. Tommy asked Dick to call his wife when he got to San Francisco and tell her that he wasn't going to be able to get home until February. Dick promised he would. The two rivals had flown together for almost two years, fighting in the same battles, enduring the same hardships. McGuire was sure he was the better fighter pilot, and while he respected Dick, his leadership role in the 431st gave him the sense of superiority he always needed around his peers. Dick was a hired gun; McGuire was a fighter leader.

They were mostly cordial to each other on the ground, and they would never say anything otherwise openly to the press. That would have been a violation of their sense of community as combat fighter pilots. Conflict stayed in that family, and outsiders would only see unity of purpose and teamwork.

But notwithstanding the mutual respect they had for each other, they would never be friends like each was to Gerald Johnson.

It had been a lonely war for Dick. The closest he got to feeling the bond that exists in a fighter unit on this last tour came during the worst days at Leyte, when he and Gerald, Bob DeHaven, and Wally Jordan were all together. After he left the 49th, he never felt that connection again.

As diverse as their personalities were, Dick and Tommy shared a similar loneliness. For different reasons, they were outsiders among their warrior tribe.

Dick left for the States the next day. McGuire returned to Dulag and discovered Kenney had relieved him of command. The 431st Fighter Squadron went to "Pappy" Cline, a fine fighter pilot and officer. Tommy was pulled into the 475th Fighter Group headquarters staff to be MacDonald's deputy operations officer. This was the traditional track for an up-and-coming officer destined for fighter group command. Still, McGuire's identity was inextricably linked with the 431st. It must have hurt to lose it. Even if his new job meant he was going places in the future.

As Bong made his way across the Pacific back to San Francisco, Maj. Thomas McGuire ignored his commanding general's orders and began flying fighter sweeps. He wanted those three kills, and his fixation on them started skewing his decision-making. McGuire had always been a faithful and loyal officer. Ignoring direct orders was way out of his wheelhouse.

Though everyone in the 475th knew he'd been put on the bench, they looked the other way as he climbed into *Pudgy IV* and went

hunting. When his crew chief asked him about this, McGuire figured a little subterfuge would keep him safe. Should he shoot anyone
down, he'd just hold back the news until after Bong was properly
adulated back home.

He was skating on thin ice.

He flew three combat missions on December 30, 31, and January
2. Kenney apparently never found out about them. Bong landed in
San Francisco on New Year's Eve and started the publicity victory
lap expected of America's greatest air hero. According to Kenney's
postwar accounts, he cleared McGuire to fly again on January 6.

That evening, Tommy left group HQ, where he had moved his
quarters, and returned to the 431st Fighter Group. He went to see his
men, and now that they were no longer under his direct command,
some of the barriers went down. For months, he bristled whenever
anyone in the squadron called him "Mac." Tommy was even worse.
He expected to be called "Major" and gave anyone who didn't a ration
of grief.

Not that evening. In a tent full of fighter pilots, the drinks flowed
and the chatter became informal. Douglas Thropp, who joined the
431st in the summer of 1944, heard Tommy was back and slipped into
the tent to say hello. He ended up sitting across from him as the festivities continued. Pappy Cline was nowhere to be seen. Later, it came
out that the new squadron commander wasn't in camp that evening.

The typical banter changed when somebody said, "So, Mac, what
are we going to do to get you three?" There was no love lost for Bong
in the 431st after the past month. Besides, it was natural that the
guys would want one of their own to snag the crown.

A lengthy discussion ensued. Where were the Japanese? They
used to be everywhere from Mindanao in the south, scattered around
the central islands and Luzon. But over the past week, hardly anyone
had seen a plane. January 4 was the last time the squadron scored—a
single Japanese fighter downed north of Manila.

McGuire knew Kenney would not give him many chances. From now on, he would be on a tighter leash. He could be grounded again at any time, either on Kenney's orders or Washington's. He needed to make the most of every mission. So far, the three he'd flown since meeting with Kenney had been dry holes. They needed a sure thing.

Somebody mentioned the Japanese were sending warships down to Mindoro to shell the beachhead there. While this happened in mid-December, there had been nothing like that since. It was pure scuttlebutt, but the idea of going up there to find a Japanese task force took hold. Surely if the Japanese didn't have fighters patrolling above their ships already, the arrival of some American planes would cause them to scramble interceptors?

It made sense to McGuire. He asked for volunteers. Capt. Ed Weaver and Maj. Jack Rittmayer immediately said they were in. Weaver would fly McGuire's wing. Rittmayer would take the second element. They needed a tail-end Charlie.

McGuire glanced over at Thropp and asked, "Didn't I just write you up for one?"

"Yes," Thropp replied.

"You wanna go?"

Thropp didn't hesitate. He'd been an infantry officer before becoming a fighter pilot. He was a warrior to the core. "Hell, yes!"

They talked through the mission, then McGuire stood up. "Okay, everyone. Get some sleep. We're going to start early."

He left the tent to go secure aircraft and make sure they were prepped with drop tanks before first light. When he saw his crew chief, Sergeant Kish, he mentioned that he wouldn't be taking *Pudgy IV* on this flight. The news startled Kish. Had he done something wrong?

McGuire told him he thought his luck had run its course with *Pudgy*. It was time to change things up. He borrowed Fred Champlin's P-38 instead. Kish thought it a bad move. Perhaps McGuire did have a bad feeling about the mission, or perhaps he didn't want anyone to see *Pudgy* taking off from Dulag. He never got permission for the flight from group or from V Fighter Command. This was going to be strictly off the books.

They rose just before dawn, meeting up for chow before heading out to the flight line. Four P-38s awaited, each with a pair of 150-gallon tanks slung under the wings between the fuselage and engine nacelles. They'd need the extra gas to get to Mindoro and back, but the tanks had proven to be a major problem with the new P-38Ls. Not only did they sometimes refuse to come off the shackles, as had been the case for two years, but now their tails often sliced through the dive flaps when released. Other times, they stuck to the fuel standpipe, twisted in the slipstream and tore open the engine nacelles or fuselage. Both the 475th and 49th ran tests on this and discovered 70 percent of the time when the tanks were dropped, they inflicted damage on the P-38s, especially when empty. The ground crews took to smearing castor oil on the standpipes, hoping that would help the tanks slip clear. It offered only marginal improvement.

Still, to get to the enemy, the tanks were a necessary evil.

They took off from Dulag at 0620, McGuire in the lead, with Ed Weaver on his right wing. Rittmayer took up station behind the lead element and offset to the left, with Thropp off his left wing. Rittmayer had just come over from the 13th Air Force. He flew with Tommy because they had known each other in Alaska during the days in the 54th Fighter Group. Weaver knew Tommy as well, though the ace didn't remember it. Back in cadet training, Tommy was an upperclassman who nailed Weaver with several demerits. He ended up on punishment duty, something that Captain Weaver never forgot.

Radio silent, they climbed to ten thousand feet, heading west to cross over northern Negros Island before turning north to Mindoro. The Japanese had several airdromes on Negros that were used as staging bases for missions against Leyte. McGuire intended to check them out first to see if they could find any aircraft.

A half hour after takeoff, they ran into bad weather. A solid wall of overcast stretched above them. Below, they saw scattered clouds. Instead of trying to climb above the scud, Tommy decided to drop down low. He threaded the formation through the scattered clouds. The trail element began to fall behind.

They hit a solid patch of cloud cover and flew into it. Thropp kept his eyes fixed on Rittmayer's P-38, concentrating on keeping formation in the soup. When they cleared the bottom of the cloud, Thropp saw Weaver and McGuire at least a mile or more ahead of them. They were way out of position.

McGuire saw it too and radioed to Rittmayer to catch up.

"I'm having engine trouble," Rittmayer reported.

McGuire came back. "Okay. Thropp," he said. "Take the element and close it up."

Thropp bumped his RPMs up, advanced the throttles, and passed Rittmayer on his right. The major stayed in his position and didn't swing over onto Thropp's left wing, as the number-four man usually would.

Thropp approached McGuire and Weaver. He was still a couple of hundred yards away when Weaver's voice broke the silence.

"Zero! Twelve o'clock low. Coming straight at us."

It wasn't a Zero, but a late-model Hayabusa flown by Sgt. Akira Sugimoto, an extremely experienced, high-time Ki-43 pilot who was returning to Fabrica Airdrome after conducting a search for a reported American naval convoy.

The setup was so close, barely anyone had time to react. Sugimoto started the fight a thousand feet ahead of the lead P-38s, converging at perhaps 520 feet per second. McGuire and Weaver had two seconds to react, nowhere near the time needed to prep a P-38 for combat.

The Ki-43 sped straight underneath the lead P-38s, Sugimoto possibly unaware of their presence. At the same instant they merged, McGuire horsed his P-38 into a tight left turn. Weaver stayed with him. Both pilots did not have time to drop their nearly full external fuel tanks. Now, committed to a turn, they couldn't release them. McGuire just entered a dogfight with almost two thousand pounds of extra weight under his P-38. This radically changed the turn rate, speed, and stall characteristics of their Lightnings.

As they turned, Thropp saw the Japanese fighter. He needed to make a split-second decision. He could turn into the enemy plane and take a head-on shot at it, or he could break left and entice the Japanese to follow him. That would let McGuire turn onto the Japanese plane's tail. And if McGuire missed him, Rittmayer behind Thropp's right wing could cut inside his turn and get a burst in at the Oscar.

Thropp turned left and started to climb. This was McGuire's show, and the whole point was to get him kills. Sugimoto took the bait. He rolled right, stood his Oscar on its wing, and bent around after Thropp. He closed quickly. Thropp saw him right on his six, getting into firing position.

Thropp was running full throttle now, but still had his tanks on. He'd never been in a situation quite like this one. He was about to release them when he heard McGuire order, "Daddy Flight! Keep your tanks!"

Thropp did as he was told, then checked his rearview mirror. The Japanese plane was right behind him, gun muzzles flashing.

Where was McGuire? He should have been able to roll out of his left turn and get right in behind this Oscar. But he and Weaver remained in a tight left bank.

Rittmayer saved Thropp's life, firing as he approached from behind and to the left of Sugimoto's Ki-43. A rain of bullets struck the Japanese fighter. He pulled off Thropp, whipped around as Rittmayer passed him, and went straight for Weaver.

Weaver called, "He's on me now!" Thropp didn't hear him, but saw the Ki-43 heading for the other P-38 element. He turned to try to save Weaver, but lost sight of the Japanese fighter. As he came around, McGuire and Weaver were down below him, off his left wing. He passed over them, looking for the Japanese plane.

McGuire saw Weaver's predicament. The Ki-43 cut inside their turn easily, closing behind the trailing American Lightning. Thropp couldn't help. Rittmayer seemed out of position. They were at two hundred feet, so Weaver couldn't dive away. McGuire was his only chance.

He tucked the yoke in tighter, trying to pull the P-38 around to get a shot on the Oscar. The nose shuddered; suddenly the P-38 snap-rolled. The nose dropped. McGuire ended up inverted for a split second, then his fighter plunged straight into the ground and exploded.

Sugimoto used the moment to break and run. Rittmayer may have gotten a second shot on him in the chaos that followed. He limped out of the fight, his Oscar riddled with holes, and disappeared into the clouds above them. Thropp saw a plane burning on the ground and the Oscar duck into the cloud. Unsure of what just happened, he straightened out just under the base of the scud and punched his tanks. If the Japanese pilot returned, he'd be ready for him.

Sugimoto crash-landed a few miles away. He survived, only to be caught at his crash site by Filipino guerrillas, who executed him on the spot. He was found by Japanese troops with six bullet wounds in his chest.

Just then, a Japanese fighter careened out of the clouds to make a point-blank, overhead pass on Thropp. He looked up and saw the fighter's nose and props seemingly just above his head. It zoomed past him and pounced on Rittmayer. Weaver and Thropp assumed this was the same fighter that they'd been battling. Instead, it was a

Nakajima Ki-84 Hayate, the latest-generation Japanese Army fighter, with capabilities none of these Americans had ever seen. With a top speed of four hundred miles an hour, two cannon, and two heavy machine guns, it could out-turn a P-38, outclimb it, and outrun it down low.

Flown by Sgt. Mizunori Fukuda, another experienced pilot, the new plane was just landing at a nearby airfield when Fukuda saw Sugimoto's desperate fight on the deck. He turned, raised his landing gear, and bolted to the rescue. He dove into the fight, blasting past Thropp and targeting Jack Rittmayer. Weaver fired on him but missed. The Ki-84 pulled into an impossibly tight turn, spun around, and planted itself on Rittmayer's tail. A long burst sent cannon shells straight into his cockpit. He closed to less than ten yards and fired again before passing the crippled P-38. As he did, Fukuda thought he saw Rittmayer through the shattered canopy, wearing a white scarf decorated with purple and red. Jack didn't wear a scarf that day. Fukuda saw bone and blood. The P-38 plunged into the ground and blew up a moment later.

Thropp, confused and momentarily out of the fight, stood his P-38 on edge and turned back into the fight. He saw the second explosion but didn't have any idea what had just happened. He thought the Japanese plane had knocked down Rittmayer in a head-on pass and Jack had damaged the Ki-84 with return fire before dying.

At this point, Fukuda charged after Thropp, closing behind him. Thropp saw him in his rearview mirror and realized he was cold meat. All he could was try to dodge bullets. When he saw Fukuda's gun muzzles wing, he kicked the rudder, skidding left. The burst missed him. Fukuda fired again. Thropp skidded the other way. Two more times he skidded out of Fukuda's web of tracers. He figured he was out of time, and luck. Throttles to the firewall, he arrowed up in a zoom climb and vanished into the clouds.

"McGuire, this is Thropp," he called. "I'm out of the fight. You're alone."

No response. He tried again. Nothing. A moment later, Weaver called and said he was above the overcast. Thropp wanted to join up, but Weaver told him to just head back to Leyte.

Fukuda's Ki-84 was badly damaged in the fight. As both Americans vanished in the clouds, he turned back for his airfield. Only one landing gear came down as he made his approach. He set the Ki-84 on the runway, but when the wing struck the ground, the Hayate cartwheeled across the field. It came to rest upside down. Mechanics pulled Fukuda from the wreckage. His injuries kept him off flight status for two weeks. Later, his crew chief told him his Hayate had taken twenty-three hits.

Weaver would later claim he shot Fukuda off Thropp's tail. Thropp, after corresponding with Fukuda, never believed that.

Flying home, both Americans must have been in shock. Thropp kept thinking, *Two majors. Plus a national hero in McGuire. How are we going to explain this?*

He landed ten minutes ahead of Weaver. MacDonald called for him immediately. As Thropp walked into the headquarters tent, Mac demanded, "What the hell just happened, Thropp?"

He explained everything he saw. He was a second lieutenant, tail-end Charlie, who had to tell his commanding officer the unauthorized flight he'd been on violated every single rule of his leader's own tactics manual. They'd fought down low. They'd not dropped their tanks until disaster already struck, and they tried to turn with the enemy.

It was a complete disaster.

Weaver was pulled in next. Mac was utterly confounded. How could one Japanese plane take on four P-38s and kill two men? When he got done relating his account of the fight, Mac sent him away. He looked around at his staff and said, "Their stories are so different it's like the two men were in different fights."[1]

The debacle only got worse. When Kenney heard the news, he was devastated. He second-guessed himself for not sending McGuire home. He'd more than earned leave, but Kenney had chosen to leave him in theater, knowing he was determined to beat Bong's score. When he relieved him of his squadron command, he unmoored the great ace from the one thing that kept his ambition in check—taking care of his men.

Kenney sat down and wrote a deeply emotional letter to Marilynn:

Dear Mrs. McGuire,

The word that Tommy had been shot down brought me one of the worst of a number of bad moments I have had to face since the war began....

---

1. Tommy had a history of not dropping his tanks if he encountered enemy opposition before reaching the target area. At least one other time, P. J. Dahl recalled that happening. As a squadron leader, McGuire had to balance the intent of the mission with the nature of the threat faced en route. Lose that extra fuel early on, and it could compromise the mission. Other Americans might die downstream, especially if they were on an escort mission. Of course, none of those factors was in play during the final moments of McGuire's life. As a result, there has been considerable criticism aimed at Tommy for not dumping their fuel tanks. Weaver never heard McGuire's radio call to hold on to them. In reality, it didn't matter if Tommy ordered that or not. The engagement started so quickly, nobody had time to properly go through the many steps required to get the tanks off the hardpoints. For one thing, to skin them, the P-38 pilots had to be flying straight and level. Two seconds from first sight of the Ki-43, all four P-38s were maneuvering wildly. It was a terrible situation. If Tommy did issue that order, he did it for one of two reasons: either he wanted the fuel so they could continue their patrol to their briefed destination and figured they would make short work of the Ki-43, or he recognized the danger the Ki-43 presented to any of his men who tried to level out and release the tanks in the middle of that point-blank dogfight and wanted to keep them as safe as possible. Whatever his motive, he took it with him, and speculating on it as many have done over the years serves no purpose.

There were no right words for the loss. He went on to write that "Tommy was one of the most capable fighter pilots I have ever known. I cannot express the depth of my regret."

The letter arrived in San Antonio on January 17, 1945. Marilynn opened it, totally unaware of her husband's death. There had been no telegram from the War Department, no Army Air Force officers at her door. She read Kenney's words and sobbed as she held the letter.

Frank Kish came back from a short leave and was told the news by another ground crewman. He was devastated. The men had waited for him to return, holding his five-hundred-hour cap as they always did. Tommy would climb out of the cockpit, shuck off his helmet, and slap the filthy hat on his head. It was his ritual. Now it was almost a sacred artifact to Kish. He took the cap and promised to get it to Tommy's family one day. It would be his way to honor the pilot he'd so long admired.

At 49th Fighter Group headquarters, Gerald Johnson felt Tommy's loss and felt a sense of profound shock. When he learned more of his friend's final battle, he became reflective and sober. Between what befell Neel Kearby and how Tommy died, the lessons were clear. There was a line between duty and ambition that should never be crossed, and Tommy, who was perhaps most reluctant of all the aces to cross it, blew right through the line on his last mission. Some called it getting "Zero happy." It was a fixation on personal score that afflicted not just those in the ace race, but even some of the youngest pilots now coming in to fill the ranks as the New Guinea veterans went home. It led to ignoring the axioms of survival in air combat and risks too great to justify.

One night, alone in his tent, he wrote his thoughts to Barbara:

McGuire was out the other day and made a fatal mistake, so now he is gone.

I've lost many of my closest friends, and they were the best pilots I've known. Yet each one became too eager to do the fighting and consequently stuck their necks out too far. Be assured, Barbara, I intend to die of old age with great grandchildren well through the tooth cutting age.

I have really slowed down in the flying game, Darling. I intend to be the father of several children, and I am satisfied with my present score.

The race of aces was over.

44

We Shall Always Return to Each Other

February 10, 1945
Superior, Wisconsin

A crowd gathered around the Lutheran church, stomping their feet in the snow or eating box lunches they'd carried with them. Dozens at first. Then hundreds. Newsmen from every wire service and major newspaper mixed through the crowd, while photographers stood off to capture images of the scene. The movie cameras of Pathé, Universal, Paramount, and Movietown stood on tripods, their operators panning across the throngs of people. At one point, with over a thousand people filling the streets around this church, which looked more European fortress than Midwestern house of worship, some of the most eager folks in the crowd tried to rush the giant wooden front doors. But they'd been bolted securely—no entry, no exceptions. The police and fire departments had deployed a maximum effort to try to control the scene, but this was no riot. The mood was curious, celebratory, and eager.

Dick and Marge were to be married here that evening.

Twelve hundred tickets went out for the ceremony. Perhaps three times that many showed up by six when the doors finally opened. Guests flooded inside, filling every inch of the pews and cramming together in the upstairs balconies that ran along the sides of the chapel. In front were the dignitaries—General Arnold's personal representative surrounded by a galaxy of field-grade officers sitting with politicians and local officials. It was the social event of the year in Superior. Later, a wire service called it the number-two wedding of the year, three places ahead of Lauren Bacall and Humphrey Bogart's nuptials.

The press was held at bay, forced to wait outside while the couple exchanged vows before family, friends, and luminaries. Later in the day, they were allowed into the chapel to photograph a re-creation of the ceremony. There were so many photographers and movie camera crews that the Bongs had to repeat their vows again and again as they cycled through to get their images. Marge would later joke that on February 10, 1945, she married Dick four times.

They honeymooned in Southern California, doing radio shows together and rubbing elbows with the likes of Bing Crosby, Angela Lansbury, and Judy Garland. They visited movie studios and sound-stages, where the stars asked Dick for his autograph. He signed short snorters, smiled for cameras, and playfully slipped into the newly-wed life with his beautiful young bride. It was an idyllic return from combat.

Back in the Philippines, MacArthur's troops landed on Luzon. The final hour of liberation was at hand, but the half million Japanese fighting men on the island refused to accept defeat. They fought with savage tenacity. The Filipino people, caught in the middle, died by the tens of thousands. Manila was consumed in house-to-house fighting that saw some of the worst war crimes of World War II perpetrated there by doomed Japanese Marines.

Gerald Johnson took over the 49th Fighter Group. He was promoted to full colonel a few months before his twenty-fifth birthday, making him one of the youngest men to hold that rank in

USAF history. Part of him wanted to stay in the air combat game, and he did fly combat after Tommy's death. Mostly, he led the group on ground-attack missions in support of the GIs struggling to clear the islands. They were thankless, ugly missions, dropping bombs and napalm in precision runs as forward air controllers coached them on targets.

In the weeks after McGuire's death, Kenney grew introspective and began to look ahead at the postwar world. There'd be a huge downsizing of the armed forces, no doubt. But there were young studs, leaders of great strength and courage whom the Air Force would need in the years ahead. They would help shape it and ultimately lead it. Those men could not be lost here in the final hours of the Second World War.

On April 2, 1945, Gerald shot down a Ki-44 during a mission to Hong Kong. The news traveled up the chain of command and reached Kenney's desk. He recognized that fighter pilots—the best ones—will always want to fight. They'll always be aggressive and seek out air combat. But with the war grinding to an inevitable victory against Japan, there were larger things at stake now.

On April 12, Kenney sat down and composed a letter to Whitehead, laying out his thoughts.

Dear Whitey,

You have two lads that I am very anxious to see enjoy long and useful careers in the post-war Air Force. They are Dick Ellis and Jerry Johnson.

...Jerry Johnson has almost quit being a playboy and is now performing a brilliant job commanding the 49th Fighter Group. I do not think there is any necessity of relieving him from the group, but I would like to see it impressed upon him that his group will get more Nips if he teaches the rest of the pilots how to get them instead of trying to catch up with Dick Bong's score himself. Pass the word along to Freddy Smith [new V FC commander] and tell him he is not expected to go out on all the missions.

Regarding the need for allocating human resources to the air war with Japan, Kenney had arrived at the same conclusion, though for different reasons, a few months after Gerald did. The Oregonian had endeavored never to let the ace race overcome his discipline to the laws of air combat that kept P-38 pilots alive, nor did he ever let his score matter more than his responsibilities as an officer and leader. MacDonald was the same way, and never got "Zero happy" either.

Mac, still leading the 475th Fighter Group, finished with twenty-seven, outpacing Gerald for third place in the theater. By then, such things didn't matter anymore. McGuire's death ended the ace race. If Bong's record was to be beaten when Kenney's Air Force joined the battle for Japan's Home Islands, it would be done by a younger generation of fighter pilots.

That summer, Gerald received news from home that Barbara gave birth to a healthy baby boy, whom she named Jerry. Gerald's ground crew repainted his P-38 to celebrate the occasion, complete with a baby painted on the nose in front of stylized red letters reading *Jerry*.

Gerald continued to lead from the front whenever he could get away from headquarters. At times, he slipped into the old adrenaline junkie ways that Kenney had characterized as his "playboy" side. He slow-rolled a B-25 over the 49th Fighter Group's airfield at Lingayen, reportedly with both engines feathered—with a USO troupe aboard that had just performed the musical *Oklahoma* for his fighter group. He nearly ended up in Lingayen Gulf when he couldn't get one of the engines restarted.

Another time, he had the radio removed from his P-38, crammed actor and comedian Joe E. Brown into the space behind his armored seat, and took him on a dive-bombing mission against Japanese troops fighting in northern Luzon. Joe E. Brown had been a solid supporter of the Army Air Force. His son had been a fighter pilot who had been killed in a Stateside accident, so he traveled throughout the world honoring his son's memory with his service to other aviators. He and Gerald grew quite close.

Other times, Gerald would get a wild hair and go beat up MacDonald's airfield. He'd drop down in high-speed zooming passes so low that he once scraped the runway and chopped a quarter inch of propeller blades off. He made it home safely, but such antics were wearing thin after so many needless casualties. He'd grown into a fine leader, but still somewhere inside him burned the boy who always did the wildest tricks on his bike on those steep hills in south Eugene.

He and Mac were pulled out of group command in July 1945 and bumped up to headquarters. Mac went to V Fighter Command, Gerald to the plans section of the 5th Air Force, where he began working on the details of the coming invasion of southern Japan. Though he may not have realized it, he'd flown his last combat mission.

He'd earned every medal an Army Air Force pilot could, shy of the Medal of Honor. He even wore the Soldier's Medal now, after he and Jim Watkins rescued a drowning sailor in Lingayen Gulf. What mattered to him was what he became known for among his fellow pilots, not the medals and the accolades from the press crew following them through their campaigns. In 265 combat missions, twelve hundred hours of battle time, Gerald Johnson had never lost a wingman. That was the achievement he considered the most important of his combat career.

Shortly after Gerald was pulled up to the 5th Air Force, Kenney sent him back on rest leave. It was too far to go to Australia, so the pilots would go back to a camp at Nadzab. Jock Henebry was there, running an in-theater training school for incoming replacement pilots. Johnson flew in and found the place a skeleton of what it once was. Already, some of the taxiways were being slowly reclaimed by the jungle. What was once the most prized piece of real estate in New Guinea was a backwater now, a testament to the victories secured and the pace of the war.

Even if it was a sign of impending victory, the desolation of the camp made Gerald melancholy. It triggered memories of the frantic alerts of 1943, the moments of puckish happiness he derived from buzzing Jock's camp in a P-40 before touching down to visit his bomber pilot friends—Dick Ellis, Jock. Those two were still alive, but so many were dead that their losses weighed heavy on him. Others were home in Stateside hospitals, burned or wounded. Missing limbs. Their lives never to be the same. His was a battle-scarred generation, and his friends were among those who'd suffered the most.

In his own pain, Gerald did not think of how these losses affected the families back in the States. He'd sensed from his home leave that he was different from his old friends and neighbors from Eugene. Some fought the good fight, and he respected that. Others he considered shirkers and bitterly turned on them for not giving the same measure as the men he saw in the foxholes of New Guinea. The social fabric back home was being torn asunder by change and loss. It would be a different world when he returned to Oregon.

If Gerald didn't see this from his place out in the Pacific, the wives did. Marilynn McGuire, Virginia Kearby—their worlds had been destroyed by the ace race. Barbara lived in fear of joining their Gold Star agony every day, through the final hours of the war that defined their generation.

Meanwhile, the country's favorite couple, Marge and Dick Bong, wrapped up their honeymoon and settled down in the Los Angeles area, where the Army Air Force assigned Dick to be a test pilot with Lockheed's P-80 Shooting Star jet program. He joined a cadre of hard chargers that included Chuck Yeager, whose jealousy and arrogance toward Dick manifested itself quickly.

On August 6, 1945, Dick was supposed to play golf with Bing Crosby, but the game got postponed. He wasn't scheduled to fly that day, but since his plans fell through, he went to the Burbank Airport. Marge was home in their little apartment, typing away on a book about her husband. She hadn't told him what she was doing, wanting to surprise him with it when she finished.

As she typed, the radio played, giving her a bit of background noise. Suddenly, a newscaster cut into the broadcast and announced that America's ace of aces, Dick Bong, had been killed in a Burbank plane crash.

Marge began to cry. The crying turned to screaming. In despair, she looked around the empty apartment. She was utterly alone. She flew from the place, ran down the hallway, still screaming, to pound on the door of a friend she'd made in the building.

No answer. She kept pounding, beating the door with her fist, unable to comprehend the magnitude of her loss.

What followed passed in a blur. Army Air Force officers filled her apartment. The press mobbed her, camped out around the apartment, forced their way in. Photographs were snapped. Their flashbulbs capturing her pain. She couldn't think. Couldn't function. What had happened?

The accident report filled a small filing cabinet. Debate still rages over what happened. In a letter years later, Chuck Yeager coldly told the family that Dick just didn't measure up and had got himself killed. Some said the engine suffered mechanical failure. Others, that Dick forgot a step in the engine start-up procedure, being inexperienced with the radical new jet. The debate still rages online in aviation circles.

Ultimately, the cause didn't matter. The results did. As he took off that day, his engine flamed out. He couldn't get it restarted, and he was too low and slow to turn back to land. He steered the doomed plane away from a residential area, pointed it at an empty lot, and tried to bail out at two hundred feet. His chute failed to open.

America's ace of aces was dead.

Back in Wisconsin, his parents were visiting friends in Superior when the news broke over the local radio stations. They learned of their son's death the same terrible way as Marge. No contact team. No media blackouts that defined how the military handled such devastating tragedies in future wars. Just the press leaking the news over the airwaves to a family broken by their words.

Marge lived in a daze for the next forty-eight hours as a mix of grief and outrage swept the nation. Demands for inquiries came from all corners. The *Los Angeles Times* wanted to know why such irreplaceable men like Dick were dying back home after fighting so hard overseas.

All of it was lost on her. People came and went. Officers whispered empty words of solace. She lived in a fog, barely functional. On the eighth, she found herself aboard a C-54 bound for home. Aboard were her husband's remains in a flag-draped coffin. She didn't even know that until they landed in Duluth, though the entire flight she had thought she felt Dick's presence.

When the plane taxied to a stop, she made her way to the exit door and stepped onto the stairwell the ground crew pushed against the fuselage. She looked out on a sea of people—over a thousand—who stood in shocked grief behind the Bong family to pay their respects to Dick and support his kin.

They stood in silent reverence as an Army Air Force team carried his coffin from the aircraft and slid it into a waiting vehicle. He was taken first to a funeral home, then to Concordia Lutheran Church, the same one in Superior where, six months before, he and Marge were married. Even before Dick and Marge's family reached the church, the place was filled with average, working-class Americans who came to pay their final respects. Some went straight from their jobs, still in overalls and farm boots so they could stand with their fallen hero and show his family support. For all the grieving, it was a beautiful display of a community circling the wagons in a crisis.

In the Pacific, the news reached Kenney, Mac, and Gerald at about the same time. The news, coming on the heels of the atomic bombing of Hiroshima, deeply saddened Kenney. It seemed so senseless to die back home after surviving so many battles with the Japanese.

Gerald took it harder than Mac, who didn't know Dick as well. He was one of the last of the old Knights, and now Bong's death left him feeling more isolated and lonely. The melancholy he'd felt back at Nadzab took deeper root within him. He was ready to go home.

Kenney agreed to give them leave. But then, as the Japanese surrendered the following week, going home was put on the back burner. Instead, MacArthur tapped Johnson to be part of the greeting party that formally welcomed the Japanese surrender delegation as it stopped on Ie Shima Island en route to meet with General MacArthur. Johnson stood on the tarmac that day in the middle of the row of American officers waiting for the Japanese as movie cameras rolled. The Japanese, flying in a couple of white Betty bombers hastily painted with green crosses, touched down and taxied to a stop. There, the American hosts led their former enemies to waiting C-54s for the journey to Manila and MacArthur's headquarters.

At the end of the month, Kenney ordered Gerald to lead the first contingent of Americans into Japan proper. He was to establish a forward operating post at Atsugi Air Base outside Tokyo and prepare for the arrival of both MacArthur and the 11th Airborne Division.

His C-54 touched down with fewer than two dozen Americans aboard, unsure how the Japanese would respond to their presence. To his surprise, he found them compliant and respectful. His former enemies had accepted defeat. For a young man who'd given so much of his life for the war effort, there was no better way to end the war than at the van of the occupation force sent into Japan.

Still, it was time to go home. Kenney wanted him to go back, get a good rest leave in Eugene, then be ready to start his Army Air Force education. He'd attended an abbreviated wartime Command and Staff college course. It was time to groom him for a star. Orders were being processed. He'd be going home any day to finally see Barbara and meet his infant son.

In the meantime, he flew throughout Japan, locating Allied prisoner-of-war camps and securing resources to get supplies and transportation to those desperately ill and mistreated men. He saw the devastation of the firebombing raids and wrote to Barbara of them:

I have been to Tokyo…there is block after block of nothing but ashes and skeletons of buildings.

One night after such a flight, he sat down to calculate how many points he'd accumulated. The military created a point system designed to ensure those who spent the most time in combat went home first. Things like medals, wounds, and time in service all contributed to each veteran's score.

Gerald was the second-ranking ace still in theater. He wore the Distinguished Service Cross with oak leaf cluster (meaning he was awarded it a second time), the Silver Star, the Soldier's Medal, the Distinguished Flying Cross with five oak leaf clusters, and the Air Medal with ten. Altogether, his combat career was reflected in twenty-one medals and campaign ribbons. It all added up to 222 points. Most combat vets had between fifty and a hundred; Gerald's score was more than enough to send him to the front of the line for transport home.

On October 1, Gerald popped into the personnel department at 5th Air Force headquarters to see if his orders had been cut. They were being prepared, and he was told he'd have leave the minute he got to San Francisco. He couldn't wait for a reunion with Barbara—perhaps again at the St. Francis.

He wrote to her excitedly to share the news with her. In another letter, he wrote of their pending reunion:

Seems like these growing up years we have spent many miles apart have been very valuable. We know that no matter what the separation is—time or distance or both—we shall always return to each other.

A few days later, just as his orders and slot at a Stateside school were nailed down, Gerald flew a B-25 from Japan to MacArthur's headquarters on a courier run to deliver some top secret documents. In Manila, he picked up two officers who wanted to get a quick look at Japan before going home.

On the way back to Atsugi Air Base, Gerald's B-25 ran into an unreported storm. It grew increasingly worse as they made their way to the coast of Honshu. Sunset came and went as they pressed on through hurricane-force winds and driving rain. Turbulence buffeted the aircraft. Johnson and his copilot Jim Nolan fought to keep the B-25 in the air while trying to navigate to Atsugi in zero visibility. Communications failed. They couldn't talk to Atsugi control directly, but a C-46 airborne that evening relayed messages. Gerald and Jim couldn't find any landmarks in the darkness. They dropped down on the deck hoping to figure out where they were. Sheets of rain lashed the aircraft, streaking the cockpit windows with water and further distorting their minimal view. They nearly ran into a mountainside at one point. Gerald pulled them up and over it at the last possible second, clipping a tree that tore three feet from one wingtip.

The C-46, low on fuel, landed at Atsugi. Gerald lost all communications with the outside world. Finally, with twenty minutes of fuel remaining, he ordered everyone to bail out. He would run the Mitchell over the coastline and make sure the crew would drop right over a beach.

That's when their two passengers announced they had not brought parachutes along.

The crew scoured the bomber. No extra chutes. Six men, four packs. The nightmare couldn't get any worse. The crew suggested drawing straws. Gerald would have none of it. "I'm in command of this aircraft." He told them. He gave his parachute to Lt. Col. Robert Underwood. Jim Nolan gave his chute to their other passenger, Lt. Herbert Schaeffler. Gerald told them he would run along over the beach until they were all out safe, then he and Nolan would come around and put the B-25 down in a belly landing.

The four men jumped into the terrible night. Their chutes opened, and even with the wind, they landed safely, though scattered by a few miles. That night and the next morning, they were picked up by local Japanese authorities.

The B-25 vanished into the storm. Gerald Johnson and Jim Nolan were never seen again.

Epilogue

Unintended Consequences

Col. Charles MacDonald sat at the Johnson family dinner table that December 1945, regaling Gerald's family with stories of their boy. Barbara sat quietly, her eyes hollowed out from grief. Like the Bong family, she'd learned the news of Gerald's disappearance from the radio. He was still listed as missing, but after an exhaustive search, they knew there was no hope. Gerald was gone, and they would never get full closure from his loss.

His friends did everything they could to help, which was why Mac made this trip to Eugene. He filled them in on everything he knew about Gerald—everything he couldn't tell them in his hundreds of letters home, fearing the censors would disallow it.

After dinner, they lingered around the table, H. V. listening intently to Mac's many tales. At one point, Gerald's teenage brother, Art, piped up and asked if it was true that Gerald had often buzzed his airfield. Mac deflected the question and changed the subject. Art felt put off, unsure of what he'd said to engender such a response. At the end of the night, Mac signaled to Art to follow him outside. They walked together along West Broadway, over which Gerald had once done aerobatics on his way to Alaska, and Mac apologized for being curt with him.

"Yes. It's true," he told Art, "Johnny used to buzz my strip. And he did take a quarter inch off his propellers one time. He also dinged his tail on the ground during another low-level pass." He sighed, took a deep breath in, as if remembering a moment he couldn't quite put into words. "I just didn't want your parents to know those things. Those risks."

Risk defined the race of aces in a combat environment where the men already lived on a razor's edge. In the sky over New Guinea, the margin for error was so thin that a tiny oversight, a moment of ambition, a lapse in judgment or priorities got people killed.

The race that had inspired the nation had ended in what seemed like the only way it could—with another tragedy. For some who'd survived it, it had served its purpose, in Kenney's eyes fashioning heroes when the country needed them most. What nobody, not even Kenney, anticipated was the cost. In each family, the loss of their ace inflicted generational wounds that continue to ripple through the years to this very day.

Neel Kearby's family suffered the worst. Virginia remarried soon after Neel died. His body and crash site were discovered shortly after the war, and he was returned home and laid to rest beside her brother in a sprawling cemetery on the outskirts of Dallas. Neel's parents may have outlived the war, but they had lost their family. They never recovered from the loss of their two sons.

Virginia's remarriage was a bad one. She spiraled into alcoholism and suffered domestic abuse. She endured five bad marriages over the ensuing decades. Family lore has it that she shot to death two of her husbands in self-defense. She never recovered from the loss of her hero, and her three boys with Neel all grew up with the same sense of wild adventure and recklessness coded into their dad's DNA.

All three boys died in plane crashes. Aviation virtually wiped out the Kearby family. Virginia died in the mid-1980s, the family broken and scattered through the South. Neel's grandson, Corey, bootstrapped himself back into the prosperous class after a generation of hardship and privation. He carries the family torch these days, proud of his grandfather's service. Though much of Neel's letters and personal effects were lost in the decades of chaotic moves and his survivors' descent into poverty that followed his death, Corey still proudly displays the Medal of Honor citation signed by President Roosevelt and counts it a prized possession. The citation is one tangible thing left to the family that reminds them of the heroism and skill Neel displayed in battle.

Tommy McGuire's widow, Marilynn, remarried very quickly as well. That outraged Tommy's dad, and he slighted her or cut her out of almost every event honoring McGuire's service afterward as a result.

In 1946, before she remarried, Kenney awarded her Tommy's posthumous Medal of Honor at a ceremony that included Charles Lindbergh. He was very protective of Marilynn that night, and shepherded her away from the swell of photographers who crowded the event when it became clear she'd had all she could take. For years, she felt abandoned by the Air Force, mistreated by Tom's dad. She quietly put the past behind her and focused on building a life and family. She was married for thirty-five years before losing her husband in the 1980s. In her final years, historian Charles Martin reached out to her to help memorialize and honor Tommy's life. Reluctant at first, she later came to appreciate the warmth and welcome she received at last from people who valued her husband's sacrifice. It almost made up for the decades of poor treatment that added cruelly to her grief.

Tom Lynch's family never gave up hope that he would come home. Even into her final years, his mother did not fully accept his death. Rose, his wife and college sweetheart, never remarried or had children. Tom was the love of her life, and she died with him in her heart.

Marge Bong went from A-list celebrity and America's favorite girl-next-door to yesterday's news. When the shock of Dick's death wore off, the country's attention turned elsewhere. From not being able to eat at a restaurant without reporters and autograph seekers bombarding them, she slipped into a quiet life. She, too, remarried after the war. It was a bad marriage, and a divorce quickly followed.

Marge was a special woman—intelligent, capable, and very tough. She grew and laid to rest her wartime past and found love again. This time, the marriage endured happily into the 1990s. When her husband died, she returned to Poplar and settled on a piece of land a stone's throw from Dick's childhood home. She remained part of the Bong family and lived a quiet life there, helping to raise funds for Dick's memorial and archives in Superior. She had a unique presence about her even in her final years that could entrance and sometimes intimidate.

Barbara never recovered from Gerald's death. Like most of the other widows, she married right after the war. Dave Curtis, a childhood friend of Gerald's, returned from the Pacific War after flying P-61 night fighters. He wore the uniform. He was a pilot. In a sense, Barbara later admitted, "It was as if Gerald had come home."

Dave didn't have the war record Gerald did, and the jealousy that sparked led to a very rocky marriage. He adopted Jerry, and they had four more children together. Nevertheless, Gerald's presence and death cast a half-century-long shadow across their lives. Ultimately, Dave left Barbara for a woman half his age in the mid-1980s. His parting shot to Barbara? As he left the Hall family home in Eugene, he told her that Gerald died because he was incompetent. It was an unbelievably cruel thing to do to the mother of his children, and reopened wounds that never healed again.

Dave suffered a heart attack and died six months later.

Barbara never stopped loving Gerald. After all that happened, she drew into herself, the grief morphing into something more that redefined her view of reality. Once outgoing and daring, she became a recluse. She shunned the spotlight and often turned away historians who were interested in Gerald. But in her attic, she kept his locker box and all his personal effects that came home. The ruby ring she gave him at OHSU in 1942 never came back. He wore it to his death on the dog tags around his neck. But every letter they'd written to each other from 1941 until October 7 remained carefully tucked away with other treasures, such as scrapbooks filled with movie ticket stubs from their many dates.

Charles MacDonald remained in the Air Force after the war. Kenney pulled him along to his next assignment, standing up Strategic Air Command. After so much success in the Pacific, Kenney flopped at SAC and was replaced by Curtis LeMay. Between that and the mess with Lindbergh in 1944, MacDonald's career stalled. He served with distinction, commanding nuclear-equipped fighter-bomber wings in Europe through the 1950s before becoming the air attaché to Sweden. He ended his career as the deputy commander of the 26th Air Division, which was tasked with defending much of the West Coast from nuclear-armed Soviet bombers.

He retired in 1961, built a yacht, and vanished with his wife for eight years. They sailed around the Caribbean and Central America until her death in 1978. He returned to the United States and lived with his sister in the Deep South. He wrote only one published piece on his time in combat—an article for *Collier's* in 1946 that detailed Lindbergh's stay with the 475th. It was a well-written, honest account of that summer that revealed Mac's deep intellect. It also showed the depths to which Mac and the other pilots thought they bonded with Lindy. It wasn't until decades later that Lindbergh's true sentiments toward the 475th, and the Americans doing the fighting, emerged with the publishing of his wartime diaries. While some in the 475th considered this a betrayal, Mac never publicly fired back at Lindy, and it appears their relationship remained intact until the Lone Eagle's death in the early 1970s.

Though many historians and writers approached Mac over the years, he consented to only very few interviews. His name remained out of the public eye, known only to the World War II veterans he served with and the aviation buffs who studied the aces.

He died in 2003 at age eighty-seven. P. J. Dahl, who'd become one of his few close friends after the war, gathered with Mac's family on the Gulf coast to celebrate his life. Together, they boarded a boat, sailed out into the Gulf of Mexico, and scattered Mac's ashes at sea, saying their goodbyes under a tropical sun.

The race lived on in accounts of the war in the Southwest Pacific, in model aircraft, and video games. The aces' planes became popular subjects for aviation artwork, and today all of their planes have become iconic symbols of the Pacific Air War. There are even models of Sergeant Fukuda's Ki-84 now, and color profiles detailing Sugimoto's Ki-43's camouflage scheme. Dick Bong has lived on in collectible cards, figurines, action figures, and of course, toys and models of *Marge*, his P-38. Even seventy years later, a visit to nearly any hobby shop anywhere in the world will probably uncover one of the great aces' planes.

The warbirds community has honored them as well. For twenty years, a poorly rendered version of Gerald Johnson's P-38 was displayed at the Evergreen Air Museum until being sold to the Collings Foundation in 2017. For years, a Lightning painted as Mac's *Putt Putt Maru* could be seen on the airshow circuit, while several P-38s painted as *Marge* and *Pudgy* were put on static display around the country.

The National Museum of the U.S. Air Force in Dayton, Ohio, includes a P-47 painted as Neel Kearby's *Fiery Ginger IV.* Beside her rests the actual tail section of the original, which an Australian warbird hunter discovered in New Guinea years after the plane had fallen from the sky, and gave to the museum.

Though the flying they loved so much came to consume all the aces but Mac, it was their surviving families who paid the highest price.

Barbara was the last of the widows to pass. She did so in Eugene in 2013, in near-total obscurity. One of her closest friends, Bill Runey, had flown with Gerald in the 49th Fighter Group. She and Bill went to high school together, and in the 1990s grew very connected again. When he learned the news of her death, Bill seemed sad, but also a little relieved. He knew the years of emotional torment that she had endured were finally over. "Well," he remarked, "she's with Gerald at last."

Acknowledgments

This book is the culmination of thirty years of research that dates back to my graduate school experience at the University of Oregon. Wanting to study and write about military history was a distinctly unpopular decision at the U of O, but Professor Glenn May, who became my thesis advisor in 1991, was an enduring source of support and encouragement. What started out as a term paper on Gerald Johnson's neighborhood and how World War II tore its social fabric apart grew into my master's thesis and ultimately into *Jungle Ace*, *Indestructible*, and *Race of Aces*. I will always be grateful for Professor May's guidance in the early years of my career.

Jim Hornfischer and I were kicking around next book ideas one day while I was up in the woods writing at a cabin above Detroit Lake. I talked about the race and the things I'd learned over the years about the aces, and Jim coined the title on the spot. After writing *Jungle Ace* I'd often wanted to go back and write more directly about the race itself, but my career took me in a different path. While in Afghanistan, I put together a bucket list of books I wanted to write if I made it home. *Indestructible* became the first; *Race of Aces* was the second. Neither would have been possible without Jim, his friendship, guidance, and judgment.

Mauro DiPreta saw the potential in *Race* and turned me loose. This book was made possible by his belief in it. Thank you, Mauro, for your friendship and your willingness to mentor me along.

David Lamb carried the ball across the goal line after Mauro moved on to William Morrow. David and I had worked together through much of *Indestructible*, so it was a huge relief to me to be working with a great guy who didn't mind my sending him random photos of Gwen, my dog, chasing turkey vultures and my cat, Sylvie, swimming after ducks. David's unerring editorial sense and the trust we've got in each other have been highlights for me through these past years I've had the privilege to work with the Hachette staff. Thank you, David, for all you've done for me on these two books.

Every book is a collaborative effort, though the credit all too often falls unfairly solely to the author. It is a similar situation with the fighter pilots in *Race* and the ground crews who so tirelessly worked to keep their imperfect aircraft functional. In that spirit, I need to give serious props to the Hachette design and production team. *Race* is a beautiful book because of their dedication to it and belief in its story. I am so grateful to be a part of a team of consummate professionals. The team included *Race*'s production editor, Cisca Schreefel, and copy editor, Justine Gardner, who helped bring to life an exceptionally polished manuscript. Cover designer Amanda Kain captured with power the imagery, the look, and the feel of a combat moment over the Southwest Pacific. *Race*'s publicist Michael Giarratano and marketer Odette Fleming need a big shout-out for helping to get this story the attention it deserves.

A heartfelt thanks to all of you. This team is just amazing, and someday soon I hope to be able to meet all of you in person and personally extend my gratitude once again.

While researching *Race* all over the country, the assistance of several people became an invaluable part of the process. Briana Fiandt went above and beyond for me as I worked with her at the Richard I. Bong Veterans Historical Center in Superior, Wisconsin. Briana introduced me to one of Dick's two remaining sisters, Jerry; showed me the church where Dick and Marge were married (and where his memorial service was held); and guided me through the archival collection at the Veterans Center with unerring accuracy. I've never met an archivist with such detailed knowledge of so many files. After I left Superior, we not only stayed in touch, but Briana's been a lasting friend, sounding board, and coconspirator of sorts as *Race of Aces* took shape. Thank you, Briana, for everything you've done for me. I am truly grateful to have you in my life.

Jack Cook is one of those living encyclopedias of knowledge that every historian must either be or get to know. Jack has devoted his life to studying, preserving, and documenting as much material as possible related to the experiences of American aviators during World War II. In the 1980s and '90s, most of his friends were fighter pilots from the Greatest Generation. He's the only person I know who can look at a photo that shows a bare sliver of an aircraft and know not only what plane it is but the variant as well.

Jack and I met in the late 1990s. He's the older brother I never had. Jack's one of my closest friends, but he is also the most impartial and sometimes brutal reader I've got in my corner. I made a mistake in *Jungle Ace*, calling the propeller spinner the "propeller hub." I still haven't lived that one down. Jack keeps me on the historical straight and narrow, and with *Race of Aces*, he read through it for accuracy and handed me a raft of corrections. Jack, thank you for your attention to detail, but more important, thank you for your loyalty and friendship over these many years, even when I was jerk. Looking forward to the next Ed, Jack, John movie fest. Hopefully, it will have a monster as cool as the one in *The Giant Claw*!

George Culley is a masterful sherpa guide into the AFHRA collection at Maxwell. George, thank you for all your help and support on these past two projects. Both *Indestructible* and *Race* are better works of history, thanks to your help and efforts.

Breanna Lohman provided additional research support, chasing down details on the 348th Fighter Group and Charles MacDonald, and pursuing any evidence of Dick Bong's Golden Gate flight. Thank you for the help and support, Breanna!

Chris Fahey, Planes of Fame's flying historian, fighter pilot, and all-around outstanding guy, reviewed the manuscript for historical and aviation accuracy. Chris also bought me a couple of beers (he wouldn't let me pay) in Portland one night in early 2019 and delivered a stern lecture because I neglected his old unit, the 80th Fighter Squadron. Perhaps someday I'll be able to address that, as the pilots in the Headhunters like Jay Robbins were extraordinary Americans—and outstanding pilots. Chris, thank you for suffering through my many jokes on the warbirds forums. Thank you for going over *Race*—your assistance has been invaluable. Most of all, thank you for your friendship. Beer's on me next time.

My dad, John Bruning Sr., also read portions of the manuscript. He's the only person I've ever met who could—and did—have a two-hour discussion on Japanese aircraft metallurgy with the restoration team down at Planes of Fame. Dad, your thoughts and comments on the first draft were much appreciated. Thank you for reading my words. I'm a writer and historian because of you.

My family here in Oregon—Renee and Ed and Jennifer: Thank you for your enduring support, patience, and exceptional amount of love our little family shares. This book would not have been possible without you.

Taylor Marks, as always, your spirit guides me forward. Taylor was killed in Iraq in 2009, and when I delivered the eulogy at his memorial service, I promised to live for him and honor his sense of adventure by developing one of my own. It is because of that promise that I stopped flying and started exploring our country in an Australian-built Pontiac muscle car. On the open road, I can almost feel Taylor riding shotgun, big grin on his face, mischief in his eyes. It is one of the reasons that drove me to Afghanistan.

It has been ten years. The pain hasn't really ebbed, we just grow around it. You will not be forgotten, my 973rd Brother. You were the bravest of us, and that courage will always be my inspiration.

Bibliography and Source Notes

Secondary Sources

Barr, James A. *Airpower Employment of the Fifth Air Force in the World War II Southwest Pacific Theater.* Damascus, MD: Pennyhill Press, 1997.

Bertrand, Neal. *Dad's War Photos: Adventures in the South Pacific.* Lafayette, LA: Cypress Cove, 2015.

Birdsall, Stephen. *Flying Buccaneers: The Illustrated Story of Kenney's Fifth Air Force.* New York: Doubleday, 1977.

Bong, Carl. *Dear Mom: So We Have a War.* 4th ed. Minneapolis, MN: Burgess, 1991.

Bong, Carl, and Mike O'Connor. *Ace of Aces: The Dick Bong Story.* Mesa, AZ: Champlin Fighter Museum Press, 1985.

Bong Drucker, Marge. *Memories. The Story of Dick and Marge Bong (Major Richard Bong, America's All-Time Fighter Ace): A Love Story.* Studio City, CA: Drucker Publications, 1995.

Boyce, Ben S. *Dear Dad Letters: From New Guinea.* n.p.: Boyce, 1928.

Bruning, John. *Indestructible: One Man's Rescue Mission That Changed the Course of WWII.* New York: Hachette Books, 2016.

——. *Jungle Ace: Col. Gerald R. Johnson, the USAAF's Top Fighter Leader of the Pacific War.* Washington, D.C.: Brassey's, 2001.

Bueschel, Richard M. *Kawasaki Ki-61/Ki-100 in Japanese Army Air Force Service.* New York: Arco, 1971.

————. *Nakajima Ki-43 Hayabusa I-III in Japanese Army Air Force—RTAF—CAF-IPSF Service*. New York: Arco, 1970.

Cannon, M. Hamlin. *Leyte: The Return to the Philippines*. Scotts Valley, CA: CreateSpace, 2015.

Claringbould, Michael J. *Black Sunday: When the U.S. 5th Air Force Lost to New Guinea's Weather*. Self-published, 1995.

————. *Forty of the Fifth: The Life, Times, and Demise of Forty U.S. Fifth Air Force Aircraft*. Aerothentic Publications, 1999.

Cooper, Anthony. *Kokoda Air Strikes: Allied Air Forces in New Guinea 1942*. n.p.: New South, 2014.

Cortesi, Lawrence. *The Battle of the Bismarck Sea*. n.p.: Leisure Books, 1967.

Coyle, Brendan. *War on Our Doorstep: The Unknown Campaign on North America's West Coast*. Victoria, BC: Heritage House, 2010.

Craven, Wesley Frank, and James Lea Cate. *The Army Air Forces in World War II*. Vols. 2, 4. Chicago: University of Chicago Press, 1950.

Curran, Jim, and Terrence Popravak Jr. *Check Six!: A Thunderbolt Pilot's War Across the Pacific*. Havertown, PA: Casemate, 2015.

Cutler, Thomas J. *The Battle of Leyte Gulf: 23–26 October 1944*. New York: HarperCollins, 1994.

Dooley, Ken. *Relentless Pursuit: The Untold Story of the U.S. 5th Air Force's 39th Fighter Squadron*. Newport, RI: PiKen Production, 2015.

Dull, Paul S. *A Battle History of the Imperial Japanese Navy (1941–1945)*. Annapolis, MD: Naval Institute Press, 1978.

Dunn, William J. *Pacific Microphone*. College Station: Texas A&M University Press, 1988.

Eichelberger, Robert L. *Our Jungle Road to Tokyo: The Army's Ground War in the Southwest Pacific During World War II*. Nashville, TN: Battery Press, 1989.

Ferguson, S. W., and William K. Pascalis. *Protect & Avenge. The 49th Fighter Group in World War II*. Atglen, PA: Schiffer Publishing, 1996.

Fifth Air Force Association. *Fifth Air Force.* n.p.: Turner, 1994.

Francillon, Rene J. *American Fighters of World War II,* Vol 1. New York: Doubleday, 1969.

———. *Japanese Aircraft of the Pacific War.* Annapolis, MD: Naval Institute Press, 1979.

Gailey, Harry. *MacArthur Strikes Back: Decision at Buna, New Guinea, 1942–1943.* New York: Presidio Press, 2000.

———. *MacArthur's Victory: The War in New Guinea, 1943–44.* New York: Presidio, 2004.

Gallagher, James P. *Meatballs and Dead Birds: A Photo Gallery of Destroyed Japanese Aircraft in World War II.* Mechanicsburg, PA: Stackpole Books, 2004.

———. *With the Fifth Army Air Force: Photos from the Pacific Theater.* Baltimore, MD: Johns Hopkins University Press, 2001.

Gamble, Bruce. *Fortress Rabaul: The Battle for the Southwest Pacific, January 1942–April 1943.* Minneapolis, MN: Zenith Press, 2010.

———. *Target: Rabaul: The Allied Siege of Japan's Most Infamous Stronghold, March 1943–August 1945.* Minneapolis, MN: Zenith Press, 2013.

Gaudette, Paul, and editors of Koku-Fun. *Kawasaki Ki-61 (Tony).* Paul Gaudette, 1967.

Green, William, and Gordon Swanborough. *Japanese Army Air Force Fighters, Part I.* New York: Arco, 1977.

Griffith, Thomas E., Jr. *MacArthur's Airman: General George C. Kenney and the War in the Southwest Pacific.* Lawrence: University Press of Kansas, 1998.

Gunn, Nathaniel. *Pappy Gunn.* Bloomington, IN: AuthorHouse, 2004.

Hata, Ikuhiko, Yasuho Izawa, and Christopher Shores. *Japanese Army Fighter Aces, 1931–45.* Mechanicsburg, PA: Stackpole Books, 2002.

———. *Japanese Naval Air Force Fighter Units and Their Aces, 1932–1945.* London: Grub Street, 2011.

Haugland, Vern. *The AAF Against Japan*. New York: Harper & Brothers, 1948.

Henebrey, John P. *The Grim Reapers at Work in the Pacific Theater: The Third Attack Group of the U.S. Fifth Air Force*. Missoula, MT: Pictorial Histories, 2002.

Hess, William N. *Pacific Sweep: The 5th and 13th Fighter Commands in World War II*. New York: Doubleday, 1974.

Hickey, Lawrence. *Warpath Across the Pacific*. International Research, 1984.

Hickey, Lawrence, and Jack Fellows. *Stories from the Fifth Air Force*. n.p.: International Historical Research Associates, 2015.

Holmes, Tony, and Chris Davey. *'Twelve to One': V Fighter Command Aces of the Pacific*. Oxford, UK: Osprey, 2004.

Hornfischer, James D. *The Last Stand of the Tin Can Sailors: The Extraordinary World War II Story of the U.S. Navy's Finest Hour*. New York: Bantam, 2005.

Ichimura, Hiroshi. *Ki-43 'Oscar' Aces of World War 2*. Oxford, UK: Osprey, 2009.

James, D. Clayton. *The Years of MacArthur*, Vols. 1, 2. New York: Houghton Mifflin, 1975.

Kenney, George, C. *Dick Bong: America's Ace of Aces*. n.p.: Uncommon Valor Press Edition, 2014.

———— *General Kenney Reports: A Personal History of the Pacific War*. Office of USAF History, 1987.

Kidston, Martin J. *From Poplar to Papua: Montana's 163rd Infantry Regiment in World War II*. Helena, MT: Farcountry Press, 2004.

King, Dan. *The Last Zero Fighter: Firsthand Accounts from WWII Japanese Naval Pilots*. n.p.: Pacific, 2012.

Kirkland, Richard C. *Tales of a War Pilot*. Washington, D.C.: Smithsonian, 1999.

Lee, Walter Allen. *One of the Crew, USS O'Bannon, World War II*. n.p.: Trafford, 2007.

Lewis, Tom, and Michael Claringbould. *The Empire Strikes South: Japan's Air War Against Northern Australia, 1942–45*. n.p.: Avonmore Books, 2017.

Lindbergh, Charles A. *The Wartime Journals of Charles A. Lindbergh*. New York: Harcourt Brace Jovanovich, 1970.

Maloney, Edward T. *Fighter Tactics of the Aces*. n.p.: World War II Publications, 1978.

Martin, Charles A. *The Last Great Ace: The Life of Thomas B. McGuire, Jr*. Fruit Cove, FL: Fruit Cove, 1998.

McAulay, Lex. *The Battle of the Bismarck Sea*. New York: St. Martin's Press, 1991.

———. *Into the Dragon's Jaws: The Fifth Air Force Over Rabaul, 1943*. Mesa, AZ: Champlin Fighter Museum Press, 1987.

———. *MacArthur's Eagles: The U.S. Air War Over New Guinea, 1943–44*. Annapolis, MD: Naval Institute Press, 2005.

McDowell, Ernest R. *49th Fighter Group*. Carrollton, TX: Squadron Signal Publications, 1989.

Miller, John, Jr. *Cartwheel: The Reduction of Rabaul*. Amazon Digital Services, 2013.

Millman, Nicholas. *Ki-44 'Tojo' Aces of World War 2*. Oxford, UK: Osprey, 2011.

———. *Ki-61 and Ki-100 Aces*. Oxford, UK: Osprey, 2015.

Milner, Samuel. *Victory in Papua: The U.S. Army in the War in the Pacific*. Amazon Digital Services, 2013.

Mireles, Anthony J. *Fatal Army Air Force Aviation Accidents in the United States 1941–45*. Vols. 1, 2, 3. Jefferson, NC: McFarland, 2006.

Mitchell, Rick. *Airacobra Advantage: The Flying Cannon*. Missoula, MT: Pictorial Histories, 1992.

Molesworth, Carl. *P-40 Warhawk vs Ki-43 Oscar, China 1943–45*. Oxford, UK: Osprey, 2008.

Morton, Louis. *Strategy and Command in the Pacific: The First Two Years*. Amazon Digital Services, 2013.

Murphy, James T. *Skip Bombing: The True Story of Stealth Bombing Techniques Used in 1942*. Troy, NY: Integrated Book Technology.

Ness, Leland. *Rikugun: Guide to Japanese Ground Forces 1937–45*. Solihull, UK: Helion, 2014.

Nijboer, Donald. *P-38 Lightning vs Ki-61 Tony, New Guinea 1943–44*. Oxford, UK: Osprey, 2010.

Oberding, F. H. *Hamilton Field Diary: The Country Club Airbase*. Bloomington, IN: Xlibris, 2011.

O'Leary, Michael. *USAAF Fighters of World War II in Action*. Vols. 1, 2, 3. n.p.: Historical Times, 1986.

Olynyk, Frank. *Stars & Bars: A Tribute to the American Fighter Ace 1920–1973*. London: Grub Street, 1995.

Perret, Geoffrey. *Old Soldiers Never Die: The Life of Douglas MacArthur*. New York: Adams Media, 1996.

Prefer, Nathan. *MacArthur's New Guinea Campaign*. Conshohocken, PA: Combined Books, 1995.

Rasor, Eugene L. *The Southwest Pacific Campaign, 1941–45: Historiography and Annotated Bibliography*. Westport, CT: Greenwood Press, 1996.

Rees, Laurence. *Horror in the East: Japan and the Atrocities of World War II*. Cambridge, MA: Da Capo, 2001.

Robinson, Pat. *The Fight for New Guinea: The Story of MacArthur's First Offensive*. New York: Random House, 1943.

Rodman, Matthew K. *A War of Their Own: Bombers Over the Southwest Pacific*. Maxwell Air Force Base, AL: Air University Press, 2005.

Rogers, William B. *Outcast Red*. n.p.: Larksdale, 1987.

Ross, John F. *Enduring Courage: Ace Pilot Eddie Rickenbacker and the Dawn of the Age of Speed*. New York: St. Martin's Griffin, 2015.

Rothgeb, Wayne P. *New Guinea Skies: A Fighter Pilot's View of World War II*. Iowa City: Iowa State University Press, 1992.

Ruffato, Luca, and Michael J. Claringbould. *Eagles of the Southern Sky, the Tainan Air Group in WWII, Volume I: New Guinea.* n.p.: Tainan Research, 2012.

Russell, Lord. *The Knights of Bushido: A History of Japanese War Crimes During World War II.* New York: Skyhorse, 2008.

Rust, Kenn C. *Fifth Air Force Story.* Historical Aviation Album, 1973.

Sakai, Saburo, Martin Caidin, and Fred Saito. *Samurai!* New York: Bantam, 1985.

Sakaida, Henry. *Imperial Japanese Navy Aces, 1937–45.* Oxford, UK: Osprey, 1998.

———. *Japanese Army Air Force Aces, 1937–45.* Oxford, UK: Osprey, 1997.

———. *Pacific Air Combat WWII: Voices from the Past.* n.p.: Phalanx, 1993.

———. *Winged Samurai: Saburo Sakai and the Zero Fighter Pilots.* Mesa, AZ: Champlin Fighter Museum Press, 1985.

Salecker, Gene E. *Fortress Against the Sun. The B-17 Flying Fortress in the Pacific.* Boston, MS: Da Capo Press, 2001.

Sims, Edward H. *American Aces in Great Fighter Battles of World War II.* New York: Harper & Brothers, 1958.

Sinton, Russell L. *Menace from Moresby: A Pictorial History of the 5th Air Force in World War II.* Nashville, TN: Battery Press, 1989.

Stanaway, John. *Cobra in the Clouds: Combat History of the 39th Fighter Squadron 1940–1980.* Historical Aviation Album Publication, 1982.

———. *Kearby's Thunderbolts: The 348th Fighter Group in World War II.* Schiffer Military & Aviation History, 1997.

———. *Mustang and Thunderbolt Aces of the Pacific and CBI.* Oxford, UK: Osprey, 1999.

———. *Possum, Clover & Hades: The 475th Fighter Group in World War II.* Schiffer Military & Aviation History, 1993.

Stanaway, John C., and Lawrence J. Hickey. *Attack & Conquer: The 8th Fighter Group in World War II*. Atglen, PA: Schiffer Military and Aviation Press, 1995.

Stenbuck, Jack, ed. *Typewriter Battalion: Dramatic Frontline Dispatches from World War II*. New York: Morrow, 1995.

Stevens, Joe M. *One More Pass Before Seeking Cover: The Military Career of Neel E. Kearby*. Gainsville, TX: Stevens, 1992.

Stille, Mark E. *The Imperial Japanese Navy in the Pacific War*. Oxford, UK: Osprey, 2014.

Stoelb, Richard A. *Time in Hell: The Battle for Buna on the Island of New Guinea*. Sheboygan Falls, WI: Sheboygan County Historical Research Center, 2012.

Straubel, James H. *Air Force Diary: One Hundred and Eleven Stories from the Official Service Journal of the USAAF*. New York: Simon & Schuster, 1947.

Sunderman, James F. *Air Escape and Evasion*. New York: Franklin Watts, 1963.

Taaffe, Stephen R. *MacArthur's Jungle War: The 1944 New Guinea Campaign*. Lawrence: University Press of Kansas, 1998.

Tagaya, Osamu. *Mitsubishi Type 1 Rikko 'Betty' Units of World War 2*. Oxford, UK: Osprey, 2001.

Tanaka, Yuki. *Hidden Horrors: Japanese War Crimes in World War II*. Boulder, CO: Westview Press, 1996.

Thorpe, Don W. *Japanese Army Air Force Camouflage and Markings, World War II*. Fallbrook, CA: Aero, 1968.

Tunny, Noel. *Winning from Down Under*. Moorooka, Queensland: Boolarong Press, 2010.

United States Army Center for Military History. *Papuan Campaign: The Buna-Sanananda Operation 16 November–23 January 1943*. Amazon Digital Services, 2012.

United States Government, Department of Defense, United States Air Force. *Weapon of Denial: Air Power and the Battle for New Guinea.* United States Government, 2014.

Wandrey, Ralph H. *Fighter Pilot.* Carlton, 1979.

Willmott, H. P. *The Battle of Leyte Gulf: The Last Fleet Action.* Bloomington: Indiana University Press, 2005.

Woodward, C. Vann. *The Battle for Leyte Gulf: The Incredible Story of World War II's Largest Naval Battle.* New York: Skyhorse, 2007.

Wright, Thomas W. *To the Far Pacific, 1942–1944.* St. Louis, MO: Thomas W. Wright, 1993.

Wyllie, Arthur. *Army Air Force Victories.* n.p.: Arthur Wyllie, 2004.

Yenne, Bill. *Aces High: The Heroic Saga of the Two Top-Scoring American Aces of World War II.* New York: Dutton Caliber, 2010.

———. *The Imperial Japanese Army: The Invincible Years 1941–42.* Oxford, UK: Osprey, 2014.

Yoshino, Ronald. *Lightning Strikes: The 475th Fighter Group in the Pacific War, 1943–45.* n.p.: Sunflower University Press, 1992.

Websites:

Extensive research was conducted through Fold3.com, Ancestry .com, newspaperarchives.com, and newspapers.com.

Also useful was Pacificwrecks.com, warbirdforum.com (Dan Ford's section), and Henry Sakaida's article on Tom Lynch: http:// ww2awartobewon.com/wwii-articles/was-famous-p-38-ace -tom-lynch-executed/ and https://www.ozatwar.com/.

Another excellent source that documents an astonishing number of the hundred thousand aircraft produced during World War II

here in the United States was http://www.joebaugher.com
/usaf_serials/usafserials.html.

Mike Stowe's incredible site, Accident-Report.com, allowed me to
purchase the crash reports detailing McGuire's forced landing in
the Aleutians as well as his P-38 mishaps in Alaska, California,
and New Guinea.

Primary Source Material

Interviews and Correspondence Conducted by the Author

From 1991 through 2004, I conducted oral histories with about fifteen hundred combat veterans for a variety of projects.

The basis of the firsthand accounts of New Guinea is the
hundreds of hours of interviews I conducted with surviving 49th
Fighter Group veterans from 1992–1999 while I was researching
my master's thesis at the U of O on Gerald Johnson. The interviews
most relevant to *Race of Aces* are listed below.

Others—some I conducted for my own research projects, some
I conducted for Dynamix's unreleased flight simulator, *Aces of the
Pacific II*, and still others for EDI/Timeless Media and the Library
of Congress' Veterans History Project. When Dynamix was closed
down in 2001, and EDI a few years later, I was given the original
Betacam SP and digital HD tapes of those interviews. Along with
all the combat footage acquired by EDI, those interviews currently
sit in 330 boxes stacked and indexed in my office.

The non-video interviews I conducted were all done either in
person or over the phone and recorded on cassette tape. The final
interviews I conducted for *Indestructible* and *Race* were recorded
digitally with professional sound gear.

The interviews from all these collections that I referenced for
Race are also below.

54th Fighter Group Veterans
Frank Beagle
Harry Huffman
Sandy McCorkle

49th Fighter Group Veterans
George Alber
Oliver Atchison
Ken Clark
Robert DeHaven
Carl Estes
James Gallagher
Ed "Bud" Howe
Alfred Jacobs
Wally Jordan
Blev Lewelling
Walter Markey
James Morehead
Leslie Nelson
Bill Pascalis
Bernard Peterson
Bill Runey
Troy Smith
Ralph Wandrey
Bill Williams
Bob Wood
Harley Yates

475th Fighter Group
Perry "P.J." Dahl
Joseph McKeon
Joseph Sperling

V and XIII Bomber Command Veterans
Myron "Buzz" Buswell
Jack DeTour
Don Good
John Henebry
Don Tower

Other
Betty Bennett
Bob Bennett
Barbara Curtis
Dave Curtis
Chris Fahey
Marge Goodman Frazier
Nat Gunn
Verla Huffman
Arthur Johnson
Corey Kearby
Gene McNeese
Gary Morris
John Skillern
Gary Smith

Other Interviews Not Conducted by the Author

I am extremely grateful to the 475th Fighter Group Association, which made an exceptional effort to document the experiences of its members through a series of video interviews conducted during the group's many reunions. The Angels were a tight-knit clan, and their families continue that tradition to this day. A special thanks to Joe Kentz of the 475th Association for providing these interviews on DVD for me.

Water Arbanas
Perry "P.J." Dahl
John Ehlinger
Joseph Forster
Fred Gunn
Anthony Kupniewski
Bud Lampert
Howard Max
Jack Olson
Thomas Oxford
Marvin Rose
Douglas Thropp
Curtis Tinker Jr.

Audio Recordings of Oral Histories Provided by the Bong Memorial and the Air Force Historical Research Agency
Elwood Barden
Marge Bong Drucker
Walter Markey
Marilynn McGuire Stankowski
Tommy McGuire (radio interview, December 1944)

Archival Sources

To prepare for *Race*, I spent 157 days in 2017 driving across the country in my 2006 Pontiac GTO, stopping at museums, archives, and memorials. I spent a week in a tent at Oshkosh during the airshow, photographing the warbirds between a week at the Bong Memorial and a week at the National Personnel Records Center in St. Louis. Along the way, I acquired tens of thousands of pages of documents that I either copied directly with my Canon EOS-1D X DSLR on a

copy stand, had photocopied, or acquired in PDF format. The dig-
itized mass of data came to almost two terabytes, some sixty thousand images and files. Additionally, I acquired sixty PDF files from
the Air Force Historical Research Agency, each totaling about two
thousand pages of microfilmed and scanned documents.

The biggest challenge was not the lack of information, but the
overwhelming abundance of it. Fortunately, much of it was set up
in text-searchable formats. The most essential documents I copied
with the 1DX I pulled into pdf files of their own so that those could
be searched as well. All this allowed for cross-referencing everything from V Air Force mission summaries with squadron reports,
personal encounter reports, personal letters, diaries, flight records,
squadron, group, command dailies, morning reports, and photographs. It was through this data mining that I was able to piece
together such things as Neel Kearby's freelancing and Tom Lynch's
arrival back in theater in November 1943.

United States Air Force Historical Research Agency

Among the most valuable documents acquired at Maxwell AFB
were:

- All surviving V Fighter Command documents, reports, and
  files: This included the daily operation summaries that have
  survived and technical reports on aircraft performance and
  engineering issues, as well as reports filed by Neel Kearby on
  the employment of the P-47 over Wewak and engineering
  plans to extend the P-47's range.
- General Whitehead's letters: Whitehead preserved thousands
  of pieces of correspondence through his career, including the
  steady communication between himself and General Kenney
  during their time together in the SWPA. These proved to be
  absolute gems, and it was in this back-and-forth that the Flying

Circus Squadron was approved by Kenney. This material is a gold mine for 5th Air Force historians.

- General Kenney Collection: The research Kenney conducted for his biography of Bong is included in his collection, as are photos and material related to McGuire's posthumous MOH ceremony.
- Other 5th Air Force records: These include daily combat reports, correspondence, intelligence evaluations, and interception reports (called Red Alert Reports).
- Group and squadron records: These include the unit histories, the morning reports, and often the personal encounter reports from air-to-air engagements.
- Debriefing interviews: In 1942–1943, veterans returning from combat overseas were interviewed by the USAAF, Marines, and Navy in an effort to glean what was working and what was not. Maxwell's holdings include hundreds of these, including several key interviews with returning 5th Air Force veterans. I acquired some of these at the National Archives Branch at Laguna Niguel, California, in 1999. The AFHRA's collection is the most complete I've come across, and includes key information on the state of the men at Port Moresby in 1942 (Marbourg interview), a brief interview with Tom Lynch, and even interviews with members of Bong's first unit, the 14th Fighter Group, after they returned to Hamilton Field from North Africa.
- ATIS reports: These include all translated Japanese documents, diaries, letters, and the like captured in New Guinea and the Philippines, as well as interviews with many captured Japanese aircrew. Those prisoner of war interrogation reports provide valuable insight into the state of mind and condition of the Japanese Army Air Force aviators fighting the men of the 5th Air Force.

- USAF Oral History Program: There were many useful transcripts in this collection, including a ribald and blunt joint interview with Clay Tice and Bob DeHaven. Dick Ellis stated in his interview that in his mind, Gerald Johnson was the best ace and fighter leader he saw in action during the war. Several interviews with General Kenney are also included in the program's collection.

- Fourth Air Force and IV Interceptor Command records: The story of Dick Bong's time in California in *Race* is set against the backdrop of a growing crisis on the West Coast as almost half the P-38s produced that spring of 1942 ended up being destroyed in fatal crashes. These records provided insight into how that happened and how it was ultimately solved, plus how the air intercept system in California worked.

National Archives and Records Administration, College Park, Maryland

Extensive use of the USAF's pre-1954 photo collection found in the Still Pictures Branch at College Park was made to support research and illustration of *Race of Aces*. Additional film footage, newsreels, and original radio news broadcasts were also used that have been preserved at NARA, College Park, including *Report from the Aleutians*.

Also of value were the 5th Air Force and V Fighter Command records that are here. The original mission reports for every squadron and group referenced in *Race* are located here.

National Personnel Records Center, St. Louis

St. Louis is a byzantine and difficult-to-access archive in some ways, but the material here is truly remarkable—and most of it has rarely, if ever, been accessed. Among the most important to *Race* were

- Personnel files for four of the five aces: Of the five, only Bong's was complete. Most everyone else's were either destroyed in a fire in the 1970s, or in MacDonald's case, still sealed. However, the 293 files for Johnson and Kearby were full of surprising information, including the data plates pulled off a P-47 thought to be Kearby's that was found after the war. It turned out to be a different Jug and crash site, which caused considerable confusion for years to come. Based on it, at least one historian tried to prove Kearby's men abandoned him in the fight. In this tale, Kearby limped back toward Gusap in a crippled bird, only to be picked off by a lone Japanese Ki 43. Kearby's plane was rediscovered in the 1990s and pieces were sent to the USAF Museum in Dayton, where they are on display. Johnson's file included a description of all his personal effects, as well as a copy of his Missing Aircrew Report.

- Form Fives: The flight records for all USAAF personnel are here on microfilm. There are some gaps, but surprisingly few, given these documents bounced around from the SWPA to the States, only to sit in storage at March AFB for decades before being microfilmed and ultimately sent on to St. Louis, where they currently reside. The originals were destroyed.
- Unit Morning Reports: These incredible documents hold the administrative keys to many mysteries. Every unit in the Army had to report its strength and any personnel coming or going from its outfit every day during the war. This was crucial to unraveling exactly where Neel Kearby went after he was pulled out of the 348th Fighter Group, as well as documenting Lynch's arrival back in theater and Bong's various assignments within V Fighter Command.

Richard I. Bong Veterans Historical Center

This beautiful museum and archive in Superior, Wisconsin, includes a treasure trove of documents, letters, articles, photographs, and interviews related to Dick Bong's life. His surviving high school notebooks, music books, and grades are even stored in the archive. The collection is managed by one of the best archival historians I've ever encountered, Briana Fiandt. This book would not have been possible without the assistance and access Briana granted me. While I was there, I scanned or copied with my DSLR over nine thousand pages of material and photographs.

Seattle Museum of Flight

When the Seattle Museum of Flight acquired the Champlin Fighter Museum's collection, it inherited all the documents archived there related to the American fighter aces association. This included a wealth of material related to Neel Kearby, his last mission, the conspiracy theories behind it, and other letters and documents concerning Dick Bong and Henry Sakaida's efforts to prove he'd actually scored a forty-first kill during the fighting in New Guinea.

475th Fighter Group Association Archives, Planes of Fame Museum, Chino, California

Over the course of two trips to Chino in February and May 2017, Larry Tovaas and I scanned thousands of pages of material donated to the organization by veterans of the 475th Fighter Group. The wealth of material here was simply overwhelming, and two weeks of work in it behind the tail of the Planes of Fame's P-38 barely scratched the surface. Gems found here included the squadron war diaries, personnel records, photo albums, scrapbooks, letters, unpublished memoirs, and reunion information and memories shared at them. The personal side of the air war came alive in this material and gave me considerable insight into the 475th's daily operational realities and what life was like for its men.

National Archives, San Bruno, California, Branch

When I first started the research for *Race*, I drove the GTO to San Francisco and spent six days at the San Bruno branch of NARA. My intent was to try to discover documentation related to Dick Bong's alleged Golden Gate Bridge flight. I was surprised instead to discover a wealth of incredible information on San Francisco at war. The entire first section of *Race* took shape largely from the material gleaned from San Bruno. While there was little USAAF documentation left here (most of it was transferred elsewhere, and a significant amount got lost over the years), the 11th Naval District's records for 1942 still are kept at San Bruno. In them was considerable insight into how the airspace was divided up around the Bay Area and offshore, disciplinary proceedings, interactions with civilians, and how interceptions were handled.

USAF Museum, Dayton, Ohio

The USAF Museum archives are virtually inaccessible to civilian historians, a source of enduring frustration for all who work to document the service's history. However, on display in the World War II section of the museum are medals and personal items that belonged to Dick Bong, Neel Kearby, and Tommy McGuire. Tommy's five-hundred-hour cap, Dick's clarinet, and Neel Kearby's Medal of Honor can all be seen here.

Warhawk Museum, Nampa, Idaho

This extraordinary private museum includes a wealth of personal recollections, diaries, and unpublished memoirs by aviators and veterans. Most important to *Race* was a copy of Shady Lane's diary and excerpts from letters home during his tenure with the 39th Fighter Squadron.

Additional Primary Source Material

- Gerald Johnson's letters: From 1991 through 2001, I was given access to Gerald Johnson's letters to Barbara and his folks, plus his two surviving diaries, photos, and home movie footage he shot while in training and in the Aleutians. This material provided the basis of my master's thesis at the University of Oregon ("Until Tonight, Goodnight Sweetheart: The Life of Colonel Gerald R. Johnson") and my second book, *Jungle Ace*. I copied many of the letters and took notes on key passages. Johnson and Barbara wrote hundreds of letters to each other from 1941 to 1945, including a final letter Gerald wrote on the B-25 he was lost aboard in 1945. He mailed it during a refueling stop in Northern Luzon.

- Film: When I acquired the EDI/Timeless military collection, it included gun camera footage shot by pilots of the 475th and 348th Fighter Groups in late 1943. These invaluable snippets of air combat provided some of the details that went into the air battles from the fall of 1943 that are described in *Race*. Also included in this collection are raw combat footage of Tacloban and of the bombing raids against Balikpapan, Wewak, and Rabaul.

Index

A6M Zero fighter. *See* Zero fighter
A-20 Havoc bomber, 92, 128, 146, 163,
    318, 348
ace race, 255
    Bloody Tuesday, 270
    Bong, Lynch, and Kearby freelancing,
      316–317(fn)
    Bong tying Rickenbacker's score,
      351–353
    Bong's freedom to choose missions,
      350
    Bong's lack of teamwork, 443–444
    Bong's victory celebration, 453
    clouding Kearby's judgment, 297–300,
      307–308, 321–323, 330
    clouding McGuire's judgment, 452–453
    crediting Bong with kills at
      Hollandia, 348–349
    decline in Japanese air units curtailing
      opportunities, 359–360
    Johnson and MacDonald's officer
      responsibilities in the face of, 467
    Johnson narrowing the gap with
      Bong, 252–253
    Johnson's death, 477
    Kearby sidelining Lynch, 293–294,
      294(fn)
    Kearby's ambition and passion for
      flying, 325–326
    Kearby's disappearance and death,
      327–332
    Kearby's entrance into the race, 213,
      233
    Kearby's exile, 324
    Kearby's freelance missions, 241–242,
      291–292
    Kearby's opportunities, 283–285,
      288–289, 291–292

loss of pilots and opportunities, 336
Lynch and Bong's scores, 319
Lynch's relegation to command,
    293–294
McGuire gaining ground in the
    Philippines, 439, 448–449
McGuire-Bong rivalry, 439–442
McGuire's attempts despite fatigue
    and illness, 408–409
McGuire's command of the 431st as
    an opportunity for success, 364–367
McGuire's removal from combat,
    450–451
McGuire's tie with Rickenbacker's
    record, 435
media coverage of the P-38 pilots,
    123–124, 168–169, 196–197
New Britain campaign, 188
origins of, xxii
postwar accounts and symbols of,
    481–482
results of the Markham Valley
    mission, 181–183
rivals and comrades, 409
standings after the Leyte air war, 446
stasis with the decline in Japanese
    forces, 400
Wewak strafing, 202, 208–211
Wurtsmith's pick of the contenders,
    296
Adachi, Hatazo, 191–192
Adkins, Frank, 90–91
Aichi Type 99 D3A Val. *See* Val bomber
Air Medal, 268, 325, 354, 473
Airacobras. *See* P-39 Airacobra
Aitape air base, 336–338
Aleutian Tigers, 62, 66
Alexishafen, New Guinea, 253, 255, 283